The
POLITICS
of
HEAVEN

ALSO BY EARL SHORRIS

Fiction

Ofay

The Boots of the Virgin

Under the Fifth Sun: A Novel of Pancho Villa

In the Yucatán

Nonfiction

The Death of the Great Spirit: An Elegy for the American Indian

The Oppressed Middle: Scenes from Corporate Life

Jews Without Mercy: A Lament

Power Sits at Another Table: Aphorisms

While Someone Else Is Eating (*editor*)

Latinos: A Biography of the People

A Nation of Salesmen: The Tyranny of the Market
and the Subversion of Culture

New American Blues: A Journey Through Poverty to Democracy

Riches for the Poor: The Clemente Course in the Humanities

In the Language of Kings: An Anthology of Mesoamerican Literature—
Pre-Columbian to the Present

The Life and Times of Mexico

THE
POLITICS
★ OF ★
HEAVEN

America in
Fearful Times

EARL SHORRIS

W. W. NORTON & COMPANY
New York   London

For information about permission to reproduce selections from this book, write to
Permissions, W. W. Norton & Company, Inc., 500 Fifth Avenue, New York, NY 10110

For information about special discounts for bulk purchases, please contact
W. W. Norton Special Sales at specialsales@wwnorton.com or 800-233-4830.

Manufacturing by Courier Westford
Book design by Dana Sloan
Production manager: Julia Druskin

Library of Congress Cataloging-in-Publication Data

Shorris, Earl, 1936–
The politics of heaven : America in fearful times / Earl Shorris. — 1st ed.
p. cm.
Includes index.
ISBN 978-0-393-05963-2 (hardcover)
1. United States—Politics and government—2001–2.
2. Political culture—United States. 3. Fundamentalism—Political
aspects—United States. 4. Christianity and politics—United States.
5. Conservatism—United States. 6. September 11 Terrorist Attacks,
2001—Influence. 7. Fear—Political aspects—United States.
8. Death—Political aspects—United States. 9. Pessimism—Political
aspects—United States. 10. National characteristics, American. I. Title.
E902.S56 2007
973.93—dc22
2007012726

W. W. Norton & Company, Inc.
500 Fifth Avenue, New York, N.Y. 10110
www.wwnorton.com

W. W. Norton & Company Ltd.
Castle House, 75/76 Wells Street, London W1T 3QT

1 2 3 4 5 6 7 8 9 0

To my editors,

Starling Lawrence

and

Tony Shorris

A Short History of Our Founding

In John Donne's time a thoughtful man did his work while contemplating a skull. We can imagine such a man, a seventeenth-century preacher or poet, sitting upright and serious, head covered in the presence of God, a fore-finger touching his cheek as if thought required a pose, and on a desk or table nearby, luminous in the wan and wintry light of England, the finely fitted bones that had once held a soul. Among those who contemplated skulls, Donne was without peer: he contemplated his own.

Born a Catholic in a dangerous time for English Catholics, father of twelve, Donne went over to the Church of England to save his skin and put food on his table. At the insistence of his king he joined the clergy and later became dean of St. Paul's Cathedral. Death soon came to interest him more than life; he preached his last sermon on wombs and worms, grisly death to grisly death, he said. When he came very close to the end of life, according to his biographer Izaak Walton, Donne had himself wrapped in a winding sheet, laid out straight, marked in accurate outline on a piece of board. And then the dean died.

He had courted death, but he did not give in to death's demands as he had to those of his king, James I. "Death, be not proud," he had said, perhaps addressing the skull that sat on his desk, but more likely the bony fort that held his own soul. At the end of the sonnet, in his eloquent, adversarial way, he embraced heaven and took another poke at death:

One short sleep past, we wake eternally
And death shall be no more; Death, thou shalt die.

A plague had begun the seventeenth century. Plague had come again to England as it had in 1348, carried on the bodies of black rats aboard ships sailing west; it had killed millions then, more than a third of all the people of Europe. And a plague would come again, in a different form, in 1945, falling from the sky onto Hiroshima. In the seventeenth century, revolution, thirty years of war, and public madness followed. The Ranters, who imagined themselves filled with God, ran naked and cursing through the English streets; the Diggers plowed up other men's land in the belief that the earth and all the goods upon it were held in common; and the gloriously talented, blind, radical poet John Milton wrote Paradise Lost. *By then people had begun to abandon this country maddened by religion, desperate to find a new life and the freedoms that went with it. They left behind almost everything but their theological disputes. The radical Puritan separatists went to the European Continent. A group of Anglicans arrived in the New World in 1607 and named their town for King James. Another, a band of Calvinists, landed farther north in 1620, and called their colony Plymouth. John Donne observed the course of empire and wrote down his observations in a poem that was less art than simple metaphor. He said that these colonists and pilgrims who went to North America explored the continent as he would explore a naked woman:*

. . . and sailing towards her India, in that way,
Shall at her fair Atlantic navel stay.

So the English settlement of North America began with an imitation of love and two theologies for waging war with death: The Anglicans and the

Puritans, who had no use for each other in England, brought their differences with them. They came to America to practice the politics of heaven. After four hundred years, wombs and worms, grisly death to grisly death, occupy our minds again, Donne's words this time meaning the pregnant mother and the mass grave, terror to terror, the shock of the beginning and the fear of the death of everything.

CONTENTS

The
POLITICS
of
HEAVEN

PROLOGUE

As the Republic became democratized, it became
evangelized.

— GORDON S. WOOD
The Radicalism of the American Revolution

In half a century America has gone from love of God and one's fellow man to fear of God and one's fellow man. A national political
movement came to power in the United States in the 1930s. Its
antecedents went back to the end of the nineteenth century. The movement took its name from a phrase used by Franklin Delano Roosevelt:
the New Deal. But the movement was not limited to the actions of Roosevelt and his political party; it extended far deeper into the ethics, politics, religion, and aesthetics of the country. The New Deal did not end
with the death of FDR; it continued for many years. Today, the New
Deal no longer exists. This book is about the movement that replaced
the New Deal, how one movement segued into another, a movement
even more potent and more encompassing than the New Deal; one that
transcends political parties, religions, and sects. It is the most powerful political movement on earth, yet it has neither a name nor a leader.
The intent of this book is to define the movement, locate its antecedents,
place it in the human—and especially the American—context, estimate
how long it can endure, and perhaps even suggest what could stand in
its place.

3

The movement that now holds sway in America came out of a series of apparently discrete events and ideas. There is a chronology, of course, but the dates are not as important as the influence of each event or idea. Most are public knowledge, available in history books and newspapers. I observed one or two of the grand events and was witness to some that were either private or have not been told by anyone else. I have reported what I saw, along with much history, in the following pages.

This book started out to cover a different, although tangential, subject: the religious right. At one time I had thought, like many other people, that the rise of the religious right was the single most important social and political issue in America, and this book should be devoted to covering the subject. Halfway through the writing the events of the last sixty-five years assumed the coherent form of a national political movement in my mind and from that surprise the current book emerged.

The movement is not a cabal or a secret society. It has no code words or arcana. Every event that contributed to it, every aspect of the movement, has always been in plain sight. As I found out, it is easy for a person to be close to a national political movement and yet be unaware of its development, its scope, or even its existence. Most often it is only historians who look back in time and discover great movements. Historians will have a better grasp of this movement than I can offer here, writing from the middle of it, but we live in quick and perilous times, and it is worth having a first look at the movement that has formed in response to peril. This national movement differs in content and speed, but not in kind, from Jacksonian democracy or the New Deal, and like those movements it is of considerable duration, but not forever.

The events that gave rise to the movement began long ago, before the time when my father removed the picture of FDR that had hung in the front window and rolled it up to bury in a sepulchral closet among broken toys and butterflies etherized and never pinned. . . .

One

CONFLUENCE

We are the old, dishonoured ones,
the broken husks of men.
Even then they cast us off,
the rescue mission left us here
to prop a child's strength upon a stick.
What if the new sap rises in his chest?
He has no soldiery in him,
    no more than we,
and we are aged past ageing,
gloss of the leaf shrivelled,
three legs at a time we falter on.
Old men are children once again,
    a dream that sways and wavers
into the hard light of day.

— AESCHYLUS, *Agamemnon*
Translated by Robert Fagles

Old men should make the best soldiers; they have so little left to lose. Fear is as absurd in them as it is uncommon in the young, who think they are immortal, which makes good soldiers of them too. Philosophy, like fearlessness and foolishness, appears at both stages of life. Wittgenstein was just a kid when he wrote a brilliant review that all but destroyed the work of his old mentor, Bertrand Russell. And that's okay. Philosophy ought to keep moving along. Socrates, on the other hand, did his best work when he was old. As a young man, he put on armor and went to war. Later, with the help of an occasional pitcher of seriously watered wine, he took up moral philosophy. By the time he was condemned to death at the age of seventy, he said death was the slow runner. And best of all, he had a sense of humor about it. As he was leaving his trial on the way to drinking the hemlock, one of his acolytes said to him, "Oh, Socrates, they have condemned you unjustly!" To which the old man replied, "Would you rather they had condemned me justly?"

The old man turned down an offer to escape to an island, where he would be safe in his remaining years. He said he did not want to break the law. He was admirable in his old age, which is how it should be. If old men had the physical qualities needed for war, I think they would make the best men in combat. A life, a career, is a small sacrifice when the slow runner is catching up to you anyway. If a republic were no more than "a man writ large," as Plato said, old age would be a good time for risks.

A republic is neither a man nor a dream of perfection; democracy gets made slowly by many hands, and need not die. This book is my argument against the death of an aged democracy. In it I will offer several ideas ripe for dispute, among them a borrowed theory of history, but nonetheless different from those of Hegel and Marx and the less adventurous people who really do think history is just "one damned thing after another." The theory will also differ from those borrowed from Newton's observation that "every action produces an equal and opposite reaction." This Newtonian version of history may be bad theory, but we like it, you and I, because it gives us the chance to call people we disagree with "reactionaries." Newton's idea is perfect for explaining why rockets fly, but democracy is not so simple and justice is still more complicated.

How reaction theory differs from the German philosopher Hegel's idea that history proceeds from thesis to antithesis to synthesis and so on and on and on to the end of history is not always clear. Maybe reaction theory sees the two sides locked in a struggle to the death. It seems that way sometimes.

A way to write about anything that involves history came right at the beginning of writing or maybe a little earlier. Homer told both sides of the story. Writers of fiction do that; they have a way of pointing less imaginative people in new directions. This book is not a history; it is about the national political movement, what might have led up to those politics and what might come of them. In 2006, the composition of the Congress changed hands. The Democrats won control of both houses, but the real victor was the national political movement. Liberal Republicans lost their seats, making the Republican caucus more thoroughly committed to social and fiscal conservatism. On the other side, Democratic Congressional Campaign Chairman Rahm Emanuel recruited conservative Democrats and former Republicans to run for office. In its post-election story, the *Washington Post* said that the country leaned slightly to the right. It would be more accurate to say the election was a victory across party lines for the national political movement. The movement is very much in power now; it is today's question about the future of the country. Since the world didn't begin this morning, the morning can't be considered without remembering something about last night, last week, last year.

There may be yet another way to look at history, an American way, one that applies to a vast and ageing democracy. The southern writer Eudora Welty offered a theory about her own manner of thinking that also serves as a useful way to look at American history. In a lecture given at Harvard in 1983, Welty read a passage leading up to the last scenes in her novel *The Optimist's Daughter*. The characters are a man and a woman aboard a train as it climbs the approach to a high bridge. They are heading south past Cairo at the southern tip of Illinois. The woman looks down, attracted by the reflection of the sun on the waters below. She sees two rivers becoming one. "This was the confluence of the waters, the Ohio and the Mississippi," Welty wrote.

"Of course the greatest confluence of all is that which makes up the human memory." With that observation and her understanding of the marriage of memory and time, her own life and others, "the living and the dead," she comes to the conclusion of her exploration of "one writer's beginnings." When she spoke her essay, she allowed the word all its music and all its meaning: confluence. Junction, union, flow, assemblage; rivers or people or currents coming together; confluence. Welty called it one of the "chief patterns of human experience." The word she chose for her work also suggests a way to look at America, to understand it as a confluence of the streams of history and the activities of the moment, like a great river on its way to some as-yet-undecided sea.

To look at history using Eudora Welty's concept means that everything is considered, but the historian, like the writer editing herself, chooses what is important and sets aside the rest; everything is not included, history is not the world. Welty was a chronicler of the personal and the political, as the best of writers must be. She said she lived a sheltered life, telling us what we think we know of her seated in the upstairs room where she worked, looking out over the street below. But I think it is not quite so. Like my friend Harper Lee, who is many years her junior, Welty had an interesting mind and a deep understanding of the history and culture of the South. And based on what she said to me, she did not spend her life sitting in her upstairs room, looking out the window.

It may be an old reader's generalization, but I think all writers of important books are historians, and the best of them can be heard speaking in what they write. There is only oral history. When I spoke with Eudora Welty, she was funny and sharp and precisely centered in who she was, where she had been, and what she had seen. In her high, clear voice, which really did resemble a bell sound when she laughed; in the accent of a gentlewoman from Mississippi, she spoke all the meaning and the music of the word. Confluence. It is the peculiarly American way of looking at history.

I do not mean to suggest that the sound of a word should be the sound of history or democracy, but Welty could have chosen many words to represent her idea. She was enough of the poet in what she said and wrote to employ every aspect of a word. Imagine confluences as she spoke of them. The word itself flows like a river, beginning sharply, a young stream in the mountains, then slow across a long plain, like the Missouri, joining the Mississippi, gaining speed for an instant as the silt falls away, finally entering the sea in sibilant waves. And then imagine a river made of many rivers and each river made of many streams, beginning with snowflakes and rain. There are eddies, cross-currents, backwaters, turbulences, but the metaphor works as America has worked, because one action predominates: confluence.

This is a book of confluences, not all of them happy. There are places where it would have been better to divert the flow, to wish a stream of history dry. There are shameful examples: Slavery/racism. Genocide. Hunger. Greed. Lawlessness. And now, as we have seen, there is a terrible arrogance at home and in the world on the political right and a new kind of arrogance about the American middle and lower-middle classes on the left. Fortunately what makes America unique is not the shameful things. There is another side. Here follows an example of what I mean, how one part of the confluence happened. And I won't start at the very beginning, which is probably in Athens or the land of Li Po in the T'ang Dynasty or the Sea of Galilee.

Despite the shameful things, which can never be forgotten, the greater contribution to the confluence is what has often been called the American *idea*, the belief that rights are unalienable and ordinary men have sufficient good sense to govern themselves. But the Constitution didn't apply the ideas about natural rights or good sense to blacks. Slavery, in its various forms (chattel, bondage, and so on), had existed in the world, including the Christian world, for thousands of years when the Constitution was written. Not until the latter part of the seventeenth century had there been a new thought among Christians about the institution of slavery: the Mennonites, an American outgrowth of the Anabaptists, wanted to put an end to it.

While the Constitution did not prohibit slavery, by the winter of 1860 a brilliant lawyer had found a way to put the antislavery movement and the Constitution together, to attempt to argue slavery out of the American political psyche. He did not speak of confluence in his argument. And he was careful in the way he phrased it. Abraham Lincoln told an audience at Cooper Union in New York City, ". . . slavery . . . is an evil not to be extended." He did not speak of abolition, only of not extending the institution.

Lincoln had contested for the Republican nomination with William H. Seward of New York, whom he would later appoint his secretary of state. They made an ideal religious-political team on the question of slavery. Lincoln argued the politics and Seward the religion. Seward had come out of the evangelist-Puritan tradition of the New England Protestants, and like them, he now found slavery antithetical to Christianity. They believed God was on the antislavery side, and they worshiped Him with rifle, pistol, bayonet, and sword. Not long after Lincoln's election, the character of the bloodiest war showed up in "The Battle Hymn of the Republic":

Mine eyes have seen the glory of the coming of the Lord
He is trampling out the vintage where the grapes of wrath are stored....

It was a Christian hymn, but it was not the Episcopal priest Phillips Brooks writing "O Little Town of Bethlehem" a few years after the war. In Julia Ward Howe's hymn there was a different Jesus, and her Christianity had about it something of the Christian crusader of earlier centuries:

I have read a fiery Gospel writ in burnished rows of steel;
"As ye deal with My contemners, so with you My grace shall deal...."

Contemner, no longer a common word, means "one who treats with contempt, despises, disdains" and those burnished rows of steel are lines of cannon. In this stanza the song turns away from the righteous Lord aiding His flock in their righteous battle and becomes a God who will exchange grace for the killing of the one who offends Him. Hatred of the person on the other side of the fray, who was considered as one who despised God, killing of that person with "burnished rows of steel" could earn one a place in heaven. The vicious nature of the American Civil War, like that of every civil war, was characterized more by this line than by the "glory in His bosom that transfigures you and me / As He died to make men holy, let us live ["die" in an earlier version] to make men free." The hatred for the slaveholding South was as great then as the Religious Right's hatred for Bill Clinton, the Soviet Union, liberals, and evolutionists is today. There was nothing of the reasonableness of Lincoln in the hymn: whoever disagreed with the singers and the antislavery, pro-union politics of Howe's hymn despised God and God would punish them for it. Some of the character of the movement that came to power over the years following the end of World War II had existed at the time of the Civil War just as it had at the end of the eleventh century when the first crusaders, not yet supported by the hierarchy of the Roman Church, headed east, raping and pillaging as they went.

In the Cooper Union speech Lincoln claimed the antislavery position for twenty-three of the thirty-nine signers of the Constitution and said he just didn't know about the rest. He wanted desperately to connect the prohibition of slavery in the new western territories to the opinions of the signers. The argument hadn't worked in Louisiana, where Jefferson's pale opposition to slavery carried no weight when Monroe made the deal to purchase the territory in 1803. Lincoln wanted his lawyerly argument to succeed in the new territories. He could not say abolition in public, no matter how he might have wished it. There was an election to win and a union to preserve. He did not intend to be a political suicide. Nonetheless, no abolitionist could help but believe he thought their cause was just. And they voted for him.

The antislavery movement, which had its foundations in Puritanism and evangelism, flowed together with the political and economic issues of the time. The Protestant denominations had been at each other's throats until the early part of the nineteenth century. Then the Irish Catholics arrived, and instead of despising each other, all the Protestants, the English as well as the Scots, found common cause in hating the Irish. At the same time, the industrialization of the North flooded into the confluence of politics and religion, changing allegiances and alliances. The Democrats welcomed the southern Protestants while the Republicans became the party of the evangelical antislavery Protestants in the North. Not reaction, not synthesis, but Welty's idea, Welty's word, confluence.

As more events, more streams of thought, flowed in over the course of the years, the Protestant denominations would multiply in number, the character of bringing people to Christianity through evangelism would change, and the Republican Party, which sent Abraham Lincoln to the White House with 40 percent of the vote, would find its strength in the South. In the course of a century, the evangelicals, those people who had seen their role as bringing the good news of the Redeemer to the world, came to see the "good news" differently. Many of those who had given so many of their sons, so much of their blood, in the great

Civil War, would be reborn as a new kind of Christian, a new kind of Republican, many of them fundamentalist, racist, and all ferocious. They would split from the mainline Protestant denominations; the Southern Baptist Convention would become enormous, with more than 16 million members. The descendants of slaves, in numbers reaching toward 100 percent, would find these Republicans odious.

One of the major factors in determining the character of the confluence that we call America comes of the religious culture of the country. America is not only the most capitalistic of the "first-world" countries; it is also the most religious and historically Protestant. Catholics, Jews, Muslims, Buddhists, and so on have come into the country since the first Protestant immigrants. There are atheists and agnostics and a lot of people who have simply found something else to do on Sunday morning. Yet we Americans are, to use a Sunday morning phrase, "singing off the same songsheet." If that seems a curious thing to say about what is usually described as a pluralistic multiethnic society, bear with me. America is still a Protestant country. It just isn't Protestant the way it used to be.

Early Protestantism and capitalism in Europe takes up a full chapter and more in this book, not because it is a history of Protestantism or capitalism, but because the connection of the two—streams in confluence rather than cause and effect—determined much of the political and social development of those years and all that have followed. In Calvinist Europe, specifically England, politics and religion and economics flowed into the same great river. The relations of the workers to the owners and of both to God were the driving forces of the period. While we do not live in England in the late sixteenth century, the way in which religious, economic, and social ideas supported one another during that time illuminates the last half century in America and perhaps our future and that of the world.

Evangelical Protestants do not have the same social, economic, or political power as they exhibited in the sixteenth century, but they do make up an important part of the social and political context now. I have chosen to focus, perhaps too much, on evangelical Protestant conservatives because they have chosen to make themselves the salient religious-political force in the United States. They are not the only such force—

an evangelical Protestant theocracy is a notion for self-promoters and publicists—but they are representative of one aspect of the times. Their relation to economic and political powers and to cultural life is also interesting, although not necessarily emblematic, and certainly not by itself the sole determinant of the course of history. They are only part of a complex of confluences, and they are neither a crop of dreadful people nor a collection of saints. They are, like all the rest of us, afraid to die and concerned with how to live until then. Nor are all people who practice religion seriously Republicans. An ever-increasing number of Christians now oppose the war in Iraq on moral grounds. To equate religion with the Republican Party is a handy way to deal with contemporary America, but not serious. Religious and political evangelism flow into the American confluence, changing it, moderating the character of it, redirecting it a bit here and there. The danger in a country made of confluences lies in the possibility of one river undifferentiated and at flood.

So far, in America, there have been many ideas, dreams, and prayers, all contributing to the confluence of our history and promise. Evangelicals have not been a single stream, relentless and unchanging. Within the evangelical Protestant world, including the fundamentalists, there was a switch from thinking that good deeds of universal Christianity would bring about the millennium and then the Second Coming (postmillennial) to expecting Armageddon prior to the Second Coming (premillennial). These pre- and postmillennial ideas have been bouncing around in America since long before it became the United States. Historians place the most recent reversal in the early years of the twentieth century. During the First World War the timing of the millennium changed for many people, but it was a toothless revision, mainly theological. The sea change in American thinking happened later, at a specific time, on a specific day—August 6, 1945. End time was born again. The events centered around that day, each of which merits separate consideration, matured slowly in the American mind: the Holocaust, Hiroshima, and the Cold War, which became truly terrifying after the Soviets exploded an atomic bomb on August 29, 1949, in Kazakhstan. The end of the world had moved from religious madness into the realm of possibility. It was no longer the message on a sign carried by a religious fool in a *New Yorker* cartoon. Schoolchildren learned to hide under their desks and perfectly rational people built bomb shelters in their backyards and stocked them with canned goods and water against the day when they would wait out the half-lives of radioactive elements. They did not stop to think that some elements could give off radiation for a thousand years.[1]

The Jews who survived the Holocaust struggled to get to Palestine or New York. The Soviet Union devoured most of Eastern Europe, thinking that was its due for defeating Hitler. Nuclear technology spread. Captured German scientists and engineers taught rocket technology to the contestants in the Cold War. Capitalism roared in the West. Stalin and Mao shook totalitarian fingers at their adversaries, whom they dubbed reactionaries. Then Stalin died and Nikita Khrushchev told the world the true meaning of nuclear war: "The living will envy the dead." The Roman historian Tacitus said, with equal eloquence, about war in his time: "They make a desert and call it peace."[2]

In FDR's last State of the Union message, delivered to the Congress by radio on January 6, 1945, the ailing president promised social justice.[3] He did not expect to live much longer. With the end of the war in sight, he wanted one more term to finish the work he had started in 1933, in

---

[1] Earth supports carbon-based life. The half-life of radioactive carbon is about 5,730 years.

[2] *Agricola*, chap. 31. It is from a speech by the Briton Galgacus.

[3] He renewed his ideas of the 1944 State of the Union and strengthened them. His "Economic Bill of Rights" was

The right to a useful and remunerative job in the industries or shops or farms or mines of the Nation;

The right to earn enough to provide adequate food and clothing and recreation;

The right of every farmer to raise and sell his products at a return which will give him and his family a decent living;

The right of every businessman, large and small, to trade in an atmosphere of freedom from unfair competition and domination by monopolies at home or abroad;

The right to adequate medical care and the opportunity to achieve and enjoy good health;

The right to adequate protection from the economic fears of old age, sickness, accident, and unemployment;

The right to a good education.

All of these rights spell security. And after this war is won we must be prepared to move forward, in the implementation of these rights, to new goals of human happiness and well-being. America's own rightful place in the world depends in large part upon how fully these and similar rights have been carried into practice for our citizens. For unless there is security here at home there cannot be lasting peace in the world.

his first term. He proposed a radical welfare state. Government would guarantee the security of every American. No American would ever again go through life ill fed, ill clothed, and ill housed. It was the New Deal, but it was also the application of Christian principles to economic and social problems, the Social Gospel of Baptist minister Walter Rauschenbusch. Roosevelt had been raised to believe in its value in this life and the next. The Social Gospel also had a powerful advocate in FDR's advisor, friend, and relief administrator Harry Hopkins. And there were more. Many of FDR's "brain trusters" and cabinet members were Social Gospelers. But the Congress would have no part of this radical idea born out of the poverty of immigrants and the working class in the great American cities. The Congress was tired of the Social Gospel and tired of Roosevelt, who died without seeing either the end of the war or the creation of the country of his hopes.

Even so, the thrust of mainline Protestant denominations and then Catholics to applying the gospel to social problems did not die. Through the Truman, Eisenhower, Kennedy, and Johnson presidencies the country moved toward the completion of the New Deal. In 1965, the last major liberal legislation was passed. Civil Rights, Voting Rights, Medicare, and then it stopped. Richard Nixon's idea of a guaranteed income, which had no more purchase with the Congress than Roosevelt's last proposals, put period to the economic change that had begun in 1933. And then the rolling back began. Something went wrong in America. Jimmy Carter, a good and God-fearing evangelical Christian, wrote of the horror of Hiroshima, and a few sentences later defended the use of atomic weapons.[4] During World War II the United States at first avoided the area bombing[5] practiced by the British,

---

[4] *Living Faith* (New York: Times Books, 1996), p. 99. Carter was the first important American statesman to visit Hiroshima after the war. The atomic bombs dropped on Hiroshima and Nagasaki resulted in the deaths of 200,000 people. Combined with the firebombings, which were directed by General Curtis E. LeMay and scheduled by the young UC Berkeley graduate Robert McNamara, close to a million civilians were killed.

[5] The British bombed only at night when their planes were less vulnerable to German fighter planes, but the bombardiers could not target accurately and had to be content with bombing areas instead of individual targets. The area bombings caused little serious damage to German industrial and military targets, but destroyed many civilian homes and killed civilians indiscriminately.

attacking only strategic targets from the air, then the American planes not only began area bombing, but called the raids "terror bombing," intended to demoralize the civilian population of Germany. The fire-bombing of the city of Dresden was the most horrific of the European campaign. The firebombing of Japanese cities was, if anything, more horrible. And then came Hiroshima.

What has gone wrong in America had to do with despair and the fear of death and the way in which Americans loved God and believed God loved America. Jimmy Carter called it "malaise." That word alone could have cost him a second term in the White House, but he knew something, and he dared to say it. All that his statement implied has come to pass, but not for any one reason. It is a gathering of many things, which is what Welty meant when she spoke of confluence. She was part of the New Deal. She told me she had photographed the poor and written about them during the Great Depression. She did not give much credence, almost a quarter of a century ago, to the idea of a new national political movement. She did not predict the flood.

Two

DEATH

The Christian claim of victory over death is to the unconverted villager one of the really puzzling things about the faith. Are the Christians just naive or plain hypocritical?

—CHINUA ACHEBE

Death is the great open secret of our time. It defines our prayers and our politics and what we do when we make love, which some writers call the little death. Death hides in the sweetness of angels. HBO and Showtime broadcast prime-time soap operas about the business side of death. Like paintings of angels, those programs are not about real death, not the death we fear; they avoid the idea of death by seeing through it to family squabbles and embraces and adorable sex on the embalming table. The death that influences politics is different. It is the God-only-knows death, the death that herds us along onto ethical or murderous paths. Religious death.

More than economics or war, more than love or hunger, more than pleasure, more than dreams, more than anything else in life, the way we are introduced to death and the timing of the introduction determines our politics. It seems a bit bizarre to say, but death has many children, politics and religion first among them. They are the chicken and egg of death: they could not exist independent of each other, and which came first, politics or religion, has no meaning. No matter what answer you give, it will be wrong. The question, like all questions relating to death, is a trap. The great Russian émigré novelist Vladimir Nabokov, asked what he thought about life after death, said he was more interested in what happened before he was born—a patently disingenuous answer.

Three centuries after John Donne wrote "Death, thou shalt die," the poet Dylan Thomas said, "Rage, rage against the dying of the light." It was a drunkard's admonition, words for his poor old Dad, and as fraudulent as Nabokov's response. Both men begged the question, which may be why the world is so fond of their words. Or how about Mitch Albom and the people he says you are likely to meet in heaven? His next book should be about the people you are likely to meet in the ethereal bank, where those whom God loves make only deposits, never withdrawals, and grow wealthier in infinite degree. Albom sells Calvinism dumbed down and attired in modern dress. The salable version of death, the one that comes in the not-to-worry package, is good for business, but not for politics. It isn't credible. Religion and politics have in common the need to be credible; they cannot duck the central question.

Socrates to Shakespeare, death's question has always been the same, and always paramount: "To die, to sleep, to sleep perchance to . . ." To what? What is the content of the dream? And the place of dreaming? Shakespeare, ever earthbound, hesitant about other worlds except for the sake of comedy, left the characterization of life after death to prophets and preachers and the business of it to the gods. In the twentieth century Elisabeth Kübler-Ross, who became an expert on death and the gentleness with which it should be attended, finally could not hold on to her comfort in a decent death and took up the study of life after death, which was the first and remains the most profound euphemism.

Death is interesting and thinking about it can actually be amusing. Take Descartes, who based his whole philosophy on doubt. He said that everything is dubitable, to which anyone has the right to reply, "Oh, yeah! What about death?" Well, Descartes found out. And Kübler-Ross? Probably.

If it is possible to put the fear of death aside for a while, thinking about it and the great question both Socrates and Shakespeare said it raises may be the key to understanding politics in our time. What comes of the way we think about death may be arrogance or ethics. Death is the great certainty, the one thing of which we have foreknowledge.[1] The trouble comes not from thinking about death, but in trying to imagine what comes afterward.

There are many comforting possibilities: heaven, reincarnation; even hell is better than nothing. But near-death as an experience is a tent-show fake. Death is strictly a go/no-go situation, like all those little machines on your computer's chip. More like a transistor than a transition, and more important to the way we think and live than any invention, even if, as Freud and countless others said, death led to the invention of God. The ancient philosophers understood that were it not for knowing death will come, we would be like the beasts. Because we are human, we await the end, and to a great extent, because we await the end, we are human. All religions, all societies, must answer the riddle of death and the problem of how to live.

The great argument for the politics of democracy reeked of death. It was delivered by Pericles in 431 B.C.E. in an elegant suburb of Athens. The bones of the Athenian dead who had fallen in the first battles of the Peloponnesian War were laid to rest there in the public sepulcher, and, as was the custom, a citizen was chosen to deliver the funeral oration. The chosen speaker, the Athenian general Pericles, spoke from a raised platform so that the great crowd of friends and relatives and other citizens who had gathered there could hear him well. It was not so much an encomium for the dead that one might hear at a modern funeral as it was a speech about the idea of the city-state for which the men had fought and died. The dead could not be commended to heaven, for the Greeks, like the Hebrews, understood death as the end of life; they had no clear sense of a life after death. The Hebrews believed that those who fell in battle had died in service of their God. The Greeks had many gods, but none worth dying for. And by the time of the Peloponnesian War the tribal loyalties of Athens had weakened, replaced in the political structure of the polis by the *demes* of democracy. As Pericles mounted the platform to speak, he had neither heaven nor family, only an idea—democracy—to marry to death in battle.

In the historian Thucydides' version of the funeral oration, Pericles

---

[1] Prior to the election of George W. Bush and the Republican majority in Congress, taxes were said to be as reliably a part of our future as death.

described political life in the Athenian democracy and the effect it had on the citizens of the city, the living as well as the dead. "Indeed," he said, "if I have dwelt at some length upon the character of our country, it has been to show that our stake in the struggle is not the same as theirs who have no such blessings to lose. . . ." And then he turned to speaking of the dead, and that was when he married death and democracy: ". . . if a test of worth be wanted, it is to be found in their closing scene, and this not only in the cases in which it set the final seal upon their merit, but also in those in which it gave the first intimation of their having any. For there is justice in the claim that steadfastness in his country's battles should be as a cloak to cover a man's other imperfections; since the good action has blotted out the bad, and his merit as a citizen more than outweighed his demerits as an individual. But none of these allowed either wealth with its prospect of future enjoyment to unnerve his spirit, or poverty with its hope of a day of freedom and riches to tempt him to shrink from danger. No. Holding that vengeance upon their enemies was more to be desired than any personal blessings and reckoning this to be the most glorious of hazards, they joyfully determined to accept the risk."

The idea that death in the service of the democracy was more desirable than "personal blessings" elevated democracy to the highest place in one's life. To die for the democracy was not defeat, like ordinary death; it was a citizen's death—a victory. And it was not only Pericles who thought this, and it did not happen only in time of war. When Socrates chose to die rather than violate the law, even knowing that his punishment was unjust, it was also a demonstration of the curious and powerful link of death to democracy.

For a long time after the fall of Athens, the democracy having been defeated by plague and its own imperishable dreams, and the collapse of the Roman Empire, destroyed by ambition, external enemies, and a new religion within, there was not a functional democracy anywhere on earth. Perhaps what held back the creation of another democracy in the West for so many centuries was the nature of death, which had changed in the Christian era with the advent of the hope of heaven and the fear of hell. A politics of heaven evolved as the finality of death faded, but did not entirely replace the politics of democracy, not forever. When democracy reappeared and began to grow strong again, in the English colonies and America, and then in France and England, it was not because religion had disappeared or democracy had been divorced from death. The interrelation of death and democracy remained the public idea although religion dominated private life. In America the patriot Patrick Henry said, "Give me liberty or give me death." And long after the democracy had been established, Abraham Lincoln's Gettysburg Address, with its rhythmic language learned from the King James Bible, still had much in common with Pericles' Funeral Oration. Lincoln resolved "that these dead shall not have died in vain" as he equated "government of the people, by the people, for the people" with the value of life itself. To him, as to Pericles, they were the "honored dead," for they had given their lives to preserve the democracy. The strange marriage of death and happiness had lasted twenty-three hundred years, and it went on.

As the country entered the First World War, President Woodrow Wilson said that to make the world safe for democracy "America is privileged to spend her blood. . . ." Privileged! What an extraordinary word to describe the act of sending young men to die! It seemed more fit to describe martyrdom, a sure ascent to heaven. But there was no promise of heaven. Wilson did not preach religion, and the nation that sent the young men to die was separated from Europe by a great ocean; it was six days at best by ship from shoreline to shoreline. They did not die in defense of honor and family. They died for an idea, which is too difficult to teach to the multitude except by the example of those who "gave the last full measure of devotion."

On December 29, 1940, a little less than a year before the Japanese attack on Pearl Harbor, Franklin Delano Roosevelt sought to bolster the connection of death to democracy. There was no doubt that the country would soon be at war, and many would die; in an address to the nation, he spoke of America as "the great arsenal of democracy." In earlier speeches, in his battle with the Great Depression, he had spoken of the accomplishments of democracy, of his wishes for the citizens of the democracy, but it was not until he could ask, like Pericles and Lincoln, that citizens give the full measure of their devotion to an idea that he could rejuvenate the democracy. Perhaps the idea requires some kind of reification to make it credible and beloved. The neoconservative followers of the writer on philosophical subjects Leo Strauss linked the

preservation of democracy to the waging of war. They could understand
Pericles and Wilson, but the meaning of the death of Socrates and Lincoln's words escaped them. It is not death itself, not war, not carnage,
but the willingness to die for democracy that makes the marriage of death
and happiness. When he spoke at Gettysburg of "the last full measure
of devotion," Lincoln clarified the meaning of the funeral oration Pericles had spoken over the Athenian dead. The relation of death and
democracy was not made of fear or rage or the desire for personal blessings; it was a sign of love as great as the love of life itself.

Death has had many solutions, many heavens, while the problem of
life in large societies has had but one. The solution is a bargain democracy makes with death. Rich and poor alike, as Pericles said, make this
bargain. That it is the pinnacle of the social life of man has always
required the proof of man's ability to love an idea, and no better proof
than the acceptance of death in defense of democracy has yet been
made. Many had died in the war when Pericles spoke, and he was soon
to die of plague. But the idea he praised as politics did not die. It was not
the end of the world.

The world was thought to be forever until the fourteenth century
when many people were sure that an outbreak of plague signaled the
end of the world. The nightmare of the Black Death, as the bubonic
plague was known, never disappeared: six centuries later the Rand
Corporation, in a study commissioned by the Atomic Energy Commission, used plague for the only possible comparison to nuclear war.
Almost as an afterthought, the Rand study made the more apt comparison to biological warfare.[2]

In the seventeenth century the Great Plague came again to London, a punishment for sinful living, said many preachers of the time.
Daniel Defoe, in his *Journal of the Plague Year*, written almost a century later, described how the preachers gathered the Londoners in the

---

[2] A grisly aspect of nuclear war could well be the sudden release of plague-bearing rodents into
a weakened and confused society. Plague is endemic in the western United States and many
other parts of the world, said Otto Friedrich in *The End of the World* (New York: Coward,
McCann & Geohegan, 1982). In the same book Friedrich said that one could not conceive of
the end of the world without religion. Had Friedrich been writing a quarter of a century later,
after the spread of nuclear weapons to unstable countries, he might have had a different view.

churches, "and as they brought the people together with a kind of horror, sent them away in tears, prophesying nothing but evil tidings, terrifying the people with apprehensions of being utterly destroyed, not
guiding them, at least not enough, to cry to heaven for mercy. It was,
indeed, a time of very unhappy breaches among us in matters of religion. Innumerable sects and divisions and separate opinions prevailed
among the people."

Yet the plague, the deaths of many ministers, "reconciled them,"
allowing even the Dissenters (mainly Puritans) to send their preachers
into the other churches. The fear took many paths. Debauchery reigned
in the streets in some quarters, while in the rest of the city "death was
before their eyes, and everybody began to think of their graves, not of
mirths and diversions." In perhaps the most curious paragraphs in the
book, Defoe spoke of a traveler who described the behavior of the
Mahometans in Asia, "presuming upon their professed predestinating
notions, and of every man's end being predetermined and unalterable
beforehand decreed, they would go unconcerned into infected places
and converse with the infected persons, by which means they died at the
rate of ten or fifteen thousand a week. . . ."

Defoe's historical novel invites comparisons to the first decade of the
twenty-first century. Predestination guides the Islamic radicals in one
form and the Jewish and Christian radicals in another. As in the seventeenth century, Muslims behave somewhat differently. Christians and
Jews are willing to kill Muslims and Muslims are willing to kill them.
Predestination plays a role on all sides, but, now as then, belief appears
to lead to different behavior. In the West, needing a convenient explanation for faint-hearted behavior or a less encompassing love of God, we
say that Americans and Muslims—in other times Japanese—don't place
the same value on human life. Or is it only a matter of means, the Muslim radicals armed with little more than the willingness to die and the
Judeo-Christian radicals armed with the most sophisticated weapons
ever invented?

First Corinthians has this to say about death. 15:25: "For he must
reign until he has put all his enemies under his feet." 15:26: "The last
enemy to be destroyed is death." 15:29: "Otherwise, what do people
mean by being baptized on behalf of the dead? If the dead are not raised

at all, why are people baptized on their behalf?" 15:36: "What you sow does not come to life unless it dies."

In the seventeenth century, Puritan children were told at bedtime that sleep was a form of death. Parents recited this rhyme to the children:

> *This day is past; but tell me who can say*
> *That I shall live another day.*

Life was understood as preparation for death.[3] The Puritans lived in a time when death was everywhere around them, always grim, and yet fully understood as a part of life. Thirteen of Reverend Cotton Mather's fifteen children died. The New Englanders feared hell as much as, or even more than, death. They were Calvinists and Calvinism laid on the idea of sin. The great sermons of the time awakened the populace to the horrors of hell that awaited sinners.[4] And in the Calvinist view everyone was a sinner. Only God's grace could save them. But who among them was predestined for grace? It was God's secret. According to Calvin, there was nothing they could do to earn salvation through deeds, no matter how good, how Christian. No human being could affect decisions made by God. Some were the elect of God and others were not. And it was only through faith and faith alone that one could receive God's grace. It was a difficult path to follow; the arguments were complex, and behavior could not be controlled with the promise of heaven or the threat of hell. Rather, one loved God through strict adherence to the precepts stated in the Bible. In New England, public morality was maintained by civic rather than religious authorities. The system worked well enough for most kinds of public behavior, but

---

3 George M. Marsden, *Jonathan Edwards: A Life* (New Haven: Yale University Press, 2003).

4 John Calvin (1509–1564), born in France, went to Geneva, Switzerland, where he worked toward complete rule over the state by his version of the Protestant Reformation. He did more than Martin Luther to end all priestly notions in the Protestant Church, producing a grim view of life and death in which everyone was guilty of total depravity, that is, original sin; that God chooses their fate in this life and the next and nothing can be done by humans to change God's will; Christ did not die for everyone's sins, only for the elect of God; and those on God's list of the elect have grace and cannot be deprived of it. Presbyterians and many Baptists, although not all, still follow Calvinist doctrine.

drunkenness was common, and enforcement by civil authorities, backed by Calvinist churches was severe. When the love of God and civil law failed to maintain proper behavior, people were whipped, placed in the stocks, branded for heresy, and in some few instances burned as witches.

New England churches constantly sought more members, often attempting to win them away from another church of the same denomination. The more their membership grew, the more the churches controlled the politics of the community; they had no rival other than their king. Then Roman Catholicism took the throne under James II in 1668, and the Calvinists feared the Antichrist had reached into their lives. What more ominous sign? Death took on an even more dreadful character and drove the politics of the time in Europe as well as America.[5]

Death defines politics at the extremes. It is the extreme act, the extreme end, and in the realm of religion, as in First Corinthians, the extreme beginning. How people learn about death and the afterlife influences the way they live until they die or are near to dying. Fustel de Coulanges wrote in *The Ancient City*, "Death was the first mystery . . . ; it raised man's thoughts from the human to the divine. It was perhaps while looking upon the dead that man first conceived the idea of the supernatural."[6]

The best poet of death was Dante (with a little help from Virgil), although there have been many. The Greeks were pretty good at it; so were Shakespeare and Emily Dickinson; and there is nothing like the New Testament for the down and up of death. I encountered death's poet many years ago, and in a curious way. A new girl came to our school and her family settled somewhat tenuously in our neighborhood. They unloaded only a little furniture from a rented or borrowed truck, and they did not have a dog. The new girl said she spoke *la lingua Toscana in bocca Romana*. Her name was Ida, her English was not as good as she would have liked, and she preferred to be called Anna. She

---

[5] See chap. 6.

[6] Chap. 2, trans. Willard Small, in 1873 (New York: Doubleday/Anchor Press, 1956).

was very small, and she dressed only in white blouses and black skirts, like a novice intent upon marrying Christ. We were little more than children, she and I. She was fifteen; that summer I turned thirteen. We did not go to her house or mine, we chose to meet in the cornfield that began at the end of the street where I lived.

In the afternoon, unless it rained or had rained and the corn was wet, we went to the field, she holding her book and I holding mine. She led me. Sometimes, if she thought we would not be seen, she took my hand. We cleared a little space among the dead cornstalks, and together, Anna speaking and me listening, we went to Hell.

She read aloud in Italian, and she could make the words sound like singing, for she never broke the rhythm of Dante's terza rima. While she read in the language spoken in Florence in the first days of the fourteenth century, I followed along in English. The poem begins

> Nel mezzo del cammin di nostra vita
> mi retrovai per una selva oscura
> ché la diritta via era smarrita.

> *Midway in our life's journey I went astray*
> *from the straight road and woke to find myself*
> *alone in a dark wood.*[7]

The cornstalks were our version of a dark wood.

As the year darkened toward winter, the wind blew hard in the afternoon and the dry leaves made a frightening noise. Even now I associate death with wind and find cacophony a hellish thing.

My edition of the poem had no footnotes, nothing to help a boy who had never before thought of death or what Hell might hold. I did not know what was meant by the middle of life's journey. It could have been distance or duration.

Night came sooner with each canto. We had thirty-three days in Hell. Anna and I followed The Poet's descent, first through fire and

---

[7] John Ciardi, *Inferno* (New York: Signet, 1951).

finally to the betrayers in the ninth circle, where they existed in the trap of ice. We traveled down past names I did not recognize, through puzzling sins. We read until winter came and cornstalks began to fall of their own accord. I imagined Satan, his three mouths, the beating of his wings freezing the betrayers in icy horror. Then it all came to an end. As if Dante himself had planned it, there was no light left in late afternoon. Her family moved away before the end of winter, and we had not yet gotten to Paradise.

At the end of March when the winds subsided, the field was plowed and planted, and summer came. I tried to read the rest of Dante's *Comedy*—that's what he called it, the divine part was added long after he was dead—on to Purgatory and eventually to Heaven, but I was stuck in Hell. I memorized the nine levels, and all the sins, promising myself to commit every one before I died. There was no Hell, I told myself; it was all music, words, and not even English. That was 1949, the summer when I gave up religion. Even though I knew about the Holocaust and Hiroshima, Dante had convinced me somehow that death had no duration. I saw that it was a comedy. On earth hypocrisy was king; why would it be different in Hell? Or Heaven?

We all learn to deny death in some way, otherwise we could not live, we would be frozen in anticipation, like gamblers waiting on the turn of the wheel. What we cannot deny is the death of externalities, hair and hearing, eyesight, wind, the workings of the gut and the rhythms of the heart. Virility evolves into memory, dreaming, and is at last forgotten. Age and illness serve as death's anterooms. This profound comedy, this melodrama of fear, ends with divine laughter. Dead, we no longer fear death. Dante knew; not for nothing did the old wag call his work comedy. Great poets laugh. Socrates, Shakespeare, and Dante make death into a salon—Homer will serve tea in heaven—and the rest of us tremble.

This trembling tells the practitioners of politics there is no more godly work than defense, no more important domestic questions than health and abortion. And the closer to death people get in war or terror or simply time, the greater the demand on politics. Logically, the political focus would be on those least able to defend themselves—children, but the fear of individual death establishes a desire for preferred provider policies and pills. The logic of death can become the horror of abortion and the terror of AIDS. Homophobia, once the fear of our own desires, has mutated into the fear of death. AIDS is everywhere, a spouse could bring it home, an assignation lasting no more than minutes, perhaps an unclean glass, the toilet seat on the flight to grandma's house, could now carry the deadly virus. Someone must bear the burden of blame; there must always be a fallen angel or the virtue of the good life is diminished.

The fear of the death of everything creates a different logic, an encompassing urgency. What cannot be explained away as the error of conservationists (pollution, global warming), the miscalculation of astronomers (asteroids, comets), or the movies (extraterrestrials, mutant monsters) calls for putting politics in the hands of an omnipotent defender. It could be a prince of war or peace; nothing else matters as long as the defender is omnipotent and on our side.

When weapons have become so powerful that one bomb or a few vials of chemical toxin can kill hundreds of thousands and a puff of bacteria breathed into the air could lead to the deaths of millions, total and constant war in the name of heaven becomes the alternative to the death of everything. In the seventeenth century the Puritans and all the other residents of America, immigrant and indigenous, feared death and made constant war. In the end, it was the use of germ warfare—blankets carrying smallpox—that broke the resistance of the Indians. After a plague of smallpox it required only liquor, Christianity, and every now and then the slaughter of women and children to finish them off.

The colonists so feared smallpox they used live virus to inoculate themselves against it. The method, brought from Africa by slaves, had its own risks. Jonathan Edwards, author of the most famous American sermon, "Sinners in the Hands of an Angry God," received a dose of live smallpox virus taken from the pustule of an infected person in 1758, his first year as president of the College of New Jersey at Princeton, later Princeton University. He was fifty-four years old, extremely tall and thin, almost skeletal, a dour, soft-spoken, scholarly man with a long chin. After the inoculation the pox broke out in his mouth and throat. Fevered, suffering from dehydration, he lasted several weeks before the pox killed him.

The end of everything is an old and not entirely credible story: the flood in the *Epic of Gilgamesh*, Noah, Isaiah, the metaphor of the destruction of the Temple and the terrifying warning issued by Jesus—Watch!—in the Gospel of Mark. The book of Revelation is, if anything, more terrible, but less credible. All stories of the end of the world were just that, stories, until the plague of 1348–1350. No politics could defeat that plague or the seventeenth-century plague that Defoe wrote about. The First World War left millions dead, engendering pessimism in a large number of religious people in the United States and in a psychoanalyst born in Moravia, Sigmund Freud, but for many others the Great War did not reveal the dark side of the character of human beings, nor did it portend the end of the world. But they would have to respond again and again to death on a grand scale later in the twentieth century. At the beginning of the twenty-first century when death visited the United States suddenly and with unnerving origins, Freud's genius had passed into disuse in practice and the religious view of the world had gained enormous popularity as demonstrated by the sale of more than 60 million copies of books by Tim LaHaye. Both LaHaye and Freud made the same estimate of human nature. The trajectories of their influence on the public mind crossed as one rose and the other sank during their encounter with the culture of the 1960s and the political reaction to it. LaHaye based his work on the biblical predictions of end-time. He envisioned the end of the Jews as they were made to declare their love for Christ or be burned up in the fires of hell on earth. He claimed to love Jews and the nation of Israel, but he prayed for their eventual conversion or destruction. Protestantism has always had a penchant for raising questions about the meaning of words. Does the wish for the physical or cultural disappearance of another person fit the definition of love? It might be something else entirely.

Genocide, a form of the end of everything, was an old business by the time the Turks tried to eliminate the Armenians and the Germans tried to eliminate the Jews from the face of the earth. LaHaye was merely a variation on a long line of mass murderers. History and technology gave his nightmare ending a great boost. On August 6, 1945, the possibility of the death of everything became as real as it had been in 1348.

For centuries before 1945 the world had been difficult and dangerous. Life had always been tenuous for individuals, but they assumed
that life on earth would continue indefinitely; a funeral oration like the
one delivered by Pericles made sense. Genetic or social immortality,
perhaps both, were all but assured for most people. Life was worth living. On earth as in heaven. And then the possibility of extinction
became more real than ever before. The capacity to build and deliver
nuclear weapons spread to more and more countries, less and less stable
societies: first the Soviet Union, then the weapon appeared in France,
England, Israel, China. India and Pakistan menaced each other with
rockets tipped with nuclear warheads. The North Koreans built a
bomb. Iran built medium-range missiles and worked feverishly to
make an atomic bomb. Politics, which had not provided an answer to
evil between 1914 and 1945, now failed to halt the proliferation of
nuclear weapons. The end of the world, seen now as death had been
seen by the ancients, drove modern humans, as it had driven our ancestors, to think of the supernatural.[8] It demanded a new theology and no
one understood it better than the Reverend Billy Graham (see chap. 7).
Or young Ludwig Wittgenstein, who said, "Death is not an event in
life. It is not a fact of the world."[9]

The possibility of the end of everything required human beings to
believe in the survival somehow of someone somewhere; genetic and
social immortality had to be salvaged. If not, what was the value of the
works and days of this life? A good time and so long! Ashes to ashes,
dust to dust. As in the past the dead had to become holy, gods to the
ancient Greeks, angels on network television, and all waiting on the
Messiah, Jesus, the Mahdi. Man would be saved by his own invention
in the face of extinction: God. And because He (usually not She) was

---

[8] In a 2004 study by Sheldon Solomon of Skidmore College, the thought of death changed
the presidential preference of the majority of a group of one hundred people tested. When
they thought of television, said Solomon, they preferred Kerry; when they thought of 9/11,
they preferred Bush. The study was widely reported in newspapers of the time. I have not
seen the study, but the number of respondents was relatively small and the bias of the
researcher seems obvious from his report that without thinking of death all the respondents
preferred the Democrat.

[9] *Notebooks 1914–1916*, trans. G. E. M. Anscombe (New York: Harper & Row, 1961), p. 75e.

an okay God, death did not exist for everyone. Which raised other questions: Who would merit being saved? Who was fit to become a god? Whole religions were invented, the dreamless lethargy that comes with the acceptance of death was replaced with a frenzy generated by these questions.

Every religion, every sect, found its own exclusive route to immortality. "Straight is the gate and narrow is the way, which leadeth onto life, and few there be that find it" (Matthew 7:14). The rule, not only in Christianity, but according to every religion, was that everyone would not be admitted to heaven. Some would ruin their chances themselves, others would have to be shouldered aside along the way. Calvin was clearest on the question, but Muslims express it too, and with no less certainty. Exclusivity is the glue that binds people to religion; there must be no other sure path to salvation. Why else choose one religion over another? Social, cultural, even political, attraction may play a role, but in the final analysis, death determines the choice. When heaven becomes less likely, when a theologian and political activist like Gary Cass of the Center for Reclaiming America says that 80 percent of the people on earth will go to hell, the choice of religion begins to seem less than ideal. If only one in five escape the horrors of hell, and who shall burn and who shall sit beside the Lord was determined before a person was born, perhaps religion is not the best answer. At 20 percent there can be no peace in the face of death, even the death of everything. Once people become aware of this, they get itchy about their religion and the senselessness and cruelty of such exclusivity. The loneliness of being outside the circle of believers doesn't frighten them so much anymore, and they choose apostasy over the suffocating character of exclusivity. They may not abandon the idea of a deity, but they look for a more hopeful politics, a different economics, new churches, another heaven.

Meanwhile, death is put off until another day.

Three

DINOSAURS

If a man takes no interest in public affairs, we [the
Athenians] alone do not commend him as quiet but
condemn him as useless. . . .

— PERICLES

I saw a darkness around the president's eyes, a sign that had not
appeared before, even in his most difficult years, when he had been
impeached. It would not have been so noticeable, no more than the
expected sadness that came of the closing down of his years as president,
but this was a festive occasion. I expected the smile that had won over the
world. Yet on that morning in early December 2000, President Clinton
had little laughter; instead he spoke bitterly of the Bush victory. He
accused the Republicans of stealing the election, using Scotch tape to paste
the chads back into ballots in Florida. The conversation was private, no
one had asked him about the Florida election or the legal arguments over
it. When he talked about the Republicans, he did not laugh or bite his
lower lip or say he felt anyone's pain but his own. He was a Democrat, he
began with compromise, and before his terms were over, he gave in to the
Republican right wing on some of the most important policy issues of his
time. He was famous for talking too long. But that morning he was brief
and to the point. He expressed what was to become the tenor of American politics in the beginning of the twenty-first century. The president
was not angry. Anger is an emotion of the moment. Bill Clinton, the affa-
ble man of the center, was bitter, and bitterness has a long half-life.

It was not the first bitter ending to a presidency in recent years. Vietnam had been a time of great division in the country, but it was not like the election of 2000. Democrats had been angry at their own elected president during the Vietnam War. And Republicans did not support him. His successor, Nixon, had left office in disgrace and with few defenders in either party. There was a war between the generations during Vietnam, but there has always been a war between the generations. The young wore outrageous clothes in the sixties, were open about sex, and in the usual way of younger generations, they liked a different kind of music. They built a schism in the country that would not heal for generations. At the time, the break appeared to be cultural, and it was that, but it was also a break between life and death, a misunderstanding of international scope. Changes in culture are always the result of deeper changes, a radicalism about life itself. In the sixties the young were fearful about one kind of death, the middle-aged about another, and the old worried over death as it had always been. There was war, Cold War, and the war against the inevitable.

The most overlooked sign of the sixties was the rise to prominence of performance art, a form without hope of immortality. In one of the longer-lasting performances Linda Montano and Teching Hsieh spent a year tethered to each other by a short rope. Montano also appeared reclining on a wooden chair on a busy street dressed as a chicken with very large wings in a work she titled *Dead Chicken, Live Angel*. A year or so after that performance I spent most of a day talking with Montano in a tiny town in upstate New York, where she lived in a rented bungalow. We had a lunch of tepid American cheese and pinto beans melted over another dead chicken in the local restaurant. Montano made me the gift of a red knit watch cap which she had worn during one of her performances. In a faint striving for the permanence of an earlier world, she had enshrined the moment of the performance by attaching a small white price tag with her name handwritten on one side. Before I left, she drove me to another town to show me the ashram where she worshiped. She said she had the chakras (points of power) tattooed on her back. We talked of many things. She was voluble, intelligent, an artist certainly, but an artist in a dying world.

Performance art probably originated with Allan Kaprow's "Happenings," simple acts done for an audience made up entirely of the participants, in the early 1960s. Or it may have begun with a group in Vienna that considered sexual mutilation and eating their own feces works of art. Critics explained the work to audiences as a response to the commercialization of art and sometimes as a response to violence. The impermanence of performance art did not have a place in the critical vocabulary, yet nothing so limned the pessimism of the time as an art form that had abandoned hope for duration. Performance artists awaited calamity; they were the children of the Cold War, inheritors of the modern plague. They worked in light not only of their own death but the death of audiences now and in the future. They were limited to the moment, at most the day, and now and then they stretched out their art to a year. Montano said she would appear in the display window of the New Museum in lower Manhattan on the first day of every month for years on end. Now and then, performance artists betrayed their craft or pessimistic art by permitting it to be photographed or videotaped, but a photograph of a woman dressed as a chicken-angel sitting on the sidewalk while people passed, going about their ordinary routines, is not the same as being there. Performance artists made their work out of the junk left behind by their parents and the feelings that lasted only for the moment; the length of the performance was always exactly timed—it was now.

Over time the inheritors of what Robert Jay Lifton said was a way of living and thinking without immortality grew old and married into the fear that marks the distinction between humans and all other creatures. The schism between the generations would change over time: the Cold War denuded American feelings about the dangers of socialism and communism, and the sixties gave the naked ones the chance to change sides. The nation, revised in the 1860s and the 1910s, again in the 1930s, was revised yet again in the 1960s. The revisions were always engendered by profound changes in the sense of security. And in every change there was the effect Émile Durkheim called anomie, the normlessness that follows on a sudden rise or fall in one's fortunes. At the end of the nineteenth century when Durkheim wrote his theory of anomie, it was connected to thoughts of the end of life. The theory appeared as an important aspect of his study of suicide.

The schism of the sixties fed on a war led by a succession of American presidents from both major parties. New norms were created as the society was remade, but new norms do not necessarily mean some kind of social consensus. On the contrary, new norms generally produce new antagonisms. Vietnam, like the Korean War, was closer to home than the theory of the Cold War. It was hot. Boys were dying, boys were being drafted, sent across the ocean to a strange place among strange people in the fervent hope that the strange people would not come here.

Who would live and who would die and for what reason, in the name of what state, what god, became the question of the time not only in America, but in Europe and Latin America and in Asia, where it was not a speculative issue, not merely a horrifying anxiety; it was real. Millions of people were being murdered by bombs, hundreds of thousands more killed in combat. The war of the Vietnamese people against their French occupiers had become an American war for reasons that in retrospect seem worse than wrong—incomprehensible.

And in the midst of war, civil rights legislation passed through the Congress. Anger raged during this reconfiguring of American culture, but political dialogue did not disappear. And it was dialogue, in the form of powerful protest meetings, the plaintive lyrics of Bob Dylan, the desperate boogie of Janis Joplin, the roar of the Grateful Dead, the acid echo of the Jefferson Airplane, and oh-so-many marchers marching and writers writing and readers reading. However, it was the talkers talking that forced an end to the war and official racism. Dialogue permitted the flow of the American experiment to go on, gathering in the past as it moved forward. An end to dialogue presages an end to confluence and the shattered future that will follow as civil society fails to function in the screeching silence.

Distant Friends

During the sixties the dialogue became strained. People of two cultures were less and less able to speak to each other in civil fashion. My own understanding of politics in the twenty-first century grows in part out of the political dialogue of the Vietnam War and the legalization of civil rights. In 1970, I worked part-time for Dailey & Associates in San Francisco. Peter H. (Pete) Dailey, who owned the company, was a Republican conservative. Politically we couldn't have been much further apart. He went to Reagan Ranch Breakfasts, I wrote for one radical left magazine and helped to edit another.[1] Yet Pete and I were more than employer and employee—we were friends. We talked about his problems buying the company, and we discussed the future of business in the Pacific. We disagreed about the war, but that was okay with Pete. Many of his key employees opposed the war.

Pete and I had similar careers in a way, but his was at a higher level. He had played football in the Rose Bowl; I had wrestled at the University of Chicago. He had been a Navy officer; I had been an Air Force enlisted man. Pete was to become a confidant and advisor to presidents, U.S. ambassador to Ireland and NATO; to serve on the National Security Council, negotiate nuclear weapons agreements, and act as personal counselor to the head of the CIA. And I . . . Well, forty years have passed, and although we live in different levels of the world, we are still friends.

Pete stayed in California until he moved to Washington and then Ireland; I moved to New York. When he took over the public face of Nixon's November Group, he asked me to join him. I said, "Pete, have you got the wrong guy!"

"I thought you might have changed your mind," he said. "It was worth a try." And we laughed. Sometimes we do not connect for years, but when we meet, we can talk easily, we respect each other, and we understand that having political differences pales before the confluence Welty knew: the greater politics of citizenship. When I asked for help with this book, he did not hesitate.

Not long ago, we talked about power. He said, "When I first went to Washington, what surprised me most is that they're just like us. Until then, I had thought there was something special about the people who run the government."

On the U.S. invasion of Iraq, he was blunt. Dailey knew the Middle

---

[1] The history of *Ramparts* and its role in raising dissent during the Vietnam War is well known.

The other magazine had a short and ungrammatical life. In testimony before Congress, John Dean said that his first assignment from President Nixon was to shut down *Scanlan's* magazine. He did the job well. The magazine never published another issue.

East. He had traveled the CIA stations there for years. He understood the importance of the madrassas and he admired the way Jimmy Carter had handled Arab-Israeli relations. When Defense Secretary Donald Rumsfeld told Dailey about plans to invade Iraq, Pete's response wasn't exactly diplomatic: "Don, that's the craziest fucking thing I ever heard."

I do not know many people who speak so straightforwardly about power and the penchant for its misuse, certainly not people who know what they're talking about. Dailey intuited something about the world of politics and "people just like us" right from the start. When he ran the advertising for the Nixon presidential campaign, it was his first venture into national politics, but he thought through the possible pitfalls and decided to let an outside accounting firm handle the money. He never wanted even a breath of scandal in politics, government, or business, and there never was one. It was a rarity.

Jack McNulty, a Johnson Administration speechwriter, used to tell me, "You think the game is on the level," and then he laughed and had another drink. At first I thought he was laughing at me, at my naïveté, but he was laughing at himself, at his inability to be a true cynic. There are dreadful people in politics—Newt Gingrich, Tom DeLay, Rudy Giuliani, and the president of the United States, among others—in America, but I think there are not many true villains, not many Kissingers or men like Gingrich, who went to the hospital to tell his wife who suffered with cancer that he wanted a divorce. Most of those we find despicable are educated fools, company men, like Paul Wolfowitz and the pompous Richard Perle; a few are mean-spirited and opinionated, like Lynne Cheney; and some are miserable, mean, mistaken, and arrogant, like Cheney's husband Dick.

Pete Dailey is neither a villain nor a fool. After a long career in the public and private sector, he still has the personality most often described as winning. He likes describing himself as an "Irishman"; he has the twinkle of shrewdness in his eyes and the easy laughter associated with those other Irishmen, the Kennedys. Like John Kennedy, he is bigger and more broad-shouldered up close than he appears from a distance. He drives a Jaguar convertible, has a naval officer's measured stride, holds on to his loyalties, sits on the boards of many companies, and has no personal economic anxieties. I am glad for his good fortune, as a friend should be, but there is something gnawing at us. We might be dinosaurs.

If Dailey and I were younger now, we probably would not be acquaintances, let alone friends. American political life exists now in two distinct worlds, separated by style as well as substance. The style has been greatly influenced by the constraints of time and the influence of the computer, which runs on tiny machines that make only positive or negative decisions at astonishing speed. Extreme brevity and the computer helped to push discourse off the stage of history, leaving politics to the bitterness of polemic. As yet there is no way to know how well a democracy can function without civil dialogue or how long it will take for the contemporary world to adjust to the pace and style of the new century. In the past the form of the political process has always been adjusted for technological change. It survived the great shift from print to electronic distribution. Now, however, the political process has been forced to adjust to several major shifts at the same time: The computer delivers a profound change in speed and the speed increases the amount of information available instantaneously. More and more decisions are made by computerized systems instead of human beings acting alone or in concert. The language of interpersonal communication has changed to accommodate the computer as a participant and the Internet as a source of entertainment and interconnection—a new kind of isolation. And the contemporaneous advent of these major changes has caused problems.

Democracy is an old and disorderly way of going about life, best when it moves slowly. Twenty-five hundred years ago a democratically elected leader in Athens made a point about the conduct of politics. He said that action did not suffer from discussion, but problems arose when there was a lack of discussion before taking action. In other words, dialogue is an essential element of governing in a democracy.

Not in America anymore. Dialogue is seen now as an impediment to governing, and unnecessary to politics. Bloggers rant. Incumbents avoid debates. Cable commentators shout. Radio talk-show hosts set traps and lie in wait. Even in presidential debates the candidates are not allowed to speak to each other. They answer questions from a moderator who proudly announces that no one else knows what he or she will ask. The faux debate is a lonely business, and apolitical; not debate, not dialogue, but a duel across a distance.

Slow Cooking

Democracy in America began differently. The dialogue went on for years, beginning long before the Declaration of Independence. Not until July 23, 1787, did the Constitutional Convention convene to begin the task of codifying the results of the dialogue. After a draft document had been completed, Benjamin Franklin closed the Convention with a brief speech: "I agree to this Constitution, with all its Faults, if they are such: because I think a General Government necessary for us. . . ." Then a contest commenced over the adoption of the proposed Constitution. The argument was nasty at times, even ludicrous, but it is best remembered for producing brilliant political dialogue. The American republic was defined, debated, redefined, debated again, until the country finally agreed to a lasting framework. But it did not happen in a hurry; the Congress did not meet for the first time until 1789. Some of the debate was hauled to and from Europe by sailing ship; much of it, painstakingly written by hand, was carried from state to state by men on horseback. Time was on the side of reason; it permitted political dialogue.

The theory behind Franklin's belief in the necessity of a "General Government" carried through to the conversations Dailey and I had in 1970 and still have today, but such conversations are rare now. Conservative professors in New York and Michigan tell me their liberal colleagues will not discuss politics with them. Another man said he often sits alone in the faculty dining room. A man in North Carolina who read a brief essay I wrote critical of Straussians asked, "Aren't you afraid they'll kill you?"[2] Of course they are not going to kill me, but his question, said in front of a group of people at Duke University, hints at the character of the times.

---

[2] Straussians are followers of Leo Strauss, an émigré professor who spent most of his U.S. career at the University of Chicago. He died in 1973, leaving behind books, acolytes, a passion for political philosophy, and a militant intellectualism that would come to affect American government and the world.

By the beginning of the 2004 presidential campaign, the form for doing politics had already undergone several changes since its Athenian and American beginnings. There had already been two technological changes in the twentieth century, both important but not decisive. Before then the technology, if it merits the name, had not changed for centuries. Gathering converts in the New England colonies in the seventeenth century was a way to gain political power, because people then as now voted with their congregation and most often on the advice of their preacher. The gathering in the seventeenth century took place through dialogue, because preaching is always a dialogue about the future carried on between a preacher and a person's past. In the eighteenth century, dialogue about the Constitution was carried on by letter, in print, and from the pulpit. The Civil War followed the same pattern, which continued through World War I: print and the pulpit, augmented by parades and popular songs. During the Great Depression and World War II, radio brought a new aspect to democracy. Franklin Delano Roosevelt could have intimate contact with millions of people across the country at exactly the same instant. For the first time a national political figure entered the homes of the people as they gathered around the radio to hear Roosevelt's "Fireside Chats."

Roosevelt did not win over the entire country, and desperate years of economic depression and world war may have had as much to do with the force of his words as his personality, but FDR—patrician, handicapped, eyeglasses pinched onto his nose, smoking with a cigarette holder, drawling in a high voice born of wealth—was on intimate terms with the American public. His supporters, many of whom were "ill-fed, ill-clothed, and ill-housed," embraced the voice of the father whom they could not see. There was a biblical quality to the experience of an unseen speaker. I was a small child then, and I thought he was holy.

When Kennedy faced Nixon in the first televised debate between presidential candidates, the form of the dialogue underwent another change: Kennedy and Nixon could have been actors in a silent movie. Their facial expressions, gestures, posture, and makeup described them as much as what they said. More. Nixon could not negotiate the change from radio to talking pictures. The shadow of his black beard, the shifting of his eyes under dark and portentous eyebrows, made him look like a crook, a persona he later denied. Kennedy, young, charming, with a mischievous brilliance, played the movie hero to Nixon's villain.

Johnson was a throwback. He had a powerful effect up close, but he could not make love through the eye of the camera; it made him a caricature when he wanted so desperately to be a star. But it was Ronald Reagan who epitomized the period: he *was* a movie star. The elder George Bush (41) had no such qualities, and he could not compete with Bill Clinton, who was, in his own way, as much a star as Kennedy or Reagan. Al Gore made the wrong gestures, took advice from too many directors, remembered his lines too well, too mechanically. Gore suffered the unsolvable dilemma of a transitional man. He lived between the movies (or television) and the computer. He had no time, no place, to call home. An unsuccessful program, he appeared to all the world as a robot manqué.

His opponent, who became the 43rd president, had little to say, and what he did say came in short bursts. His speech approximated the style of e-mail more than what had previously been thought of as political dialogue. Bush 41 is a halting speaker, but Bush 43 seemed to have switched *2 codes u don't get :)*. As with e-mail, he does not waste time correcting errors. When he says "nukuler" he knows that his audience will make the translation. On television his appearance changed frequently. At times he was the rugged, handsome cowboy brush-cutter; at other times his face looked as if it had been squashed to fit the still common 3-to-4 ratio of the television screen. He morphed, like a computer-generated object, but in what little he had to say, he was utterly consistent. He had learned to fly jet fighter aircraft, to speak in crackles of data, to attach himself to the banks of computers, to trust his life to the go/no-go decisions of multiple machines. No man of his years could have been programmed more thoroughly by his time. He is the man celebrated in Malcolm Gladwell's diatribe against the pace of reason, *Blink*.

In 2004 the Democrats fielded an anachronism, a man whose face and speech belonged to the written word of the late nineteenth century. He did not fit into the style of radio, film, or the computer-driven age. Like Bush 43 and his party, John Kerry and his party embraced polemic, but Kerry could not master the polemical style of his time. He talked too much. The polemics of the twenty-first century pass in an instant; they do not have the quality of narrative; the succession of thoughts or events that form a narrative do not fit into the allotted time of twenty-first century polemic. On television, facing his opponent, Bush could not fill his two-minute or ninety-second turns to speak. Even when he was given only thirty seconds, he had trouble filling the time. He had no capacity for narrative; he could not build a logical case; he behaved more like a gun than a person. For most of American political history the old rules of rhetoric set down by Aristotle generally produced a winning candidate. Not so in 2004.

Aristotle named three "speech capacities": logical argument, character, and appeal to the emotions. Logical argument had little place in either campaign, for both men had supported a misanthropic war, and no one could make a logical case for that. Thus it became a contest of character and emotion, or in more pertinent terms, of hope and fear.

Bush's failure to speak at any length, to elaborate on his positions or make subtle distinctions, was more than a personal quirk. Richard Wirthlin, the pollster-strategist behind the Reagan "Revolution," said that the contentious character of twenty-first-century politics is driven by the brevity of television: he gave the twenty-second commercial as an example. It does not permit nuance and is not conducive either to gentle eloquence or the rhythms of the King James Bible that inspired Lincoln.

One or Zero

Then came the computer. As the Industrial Age did not entirely replace agriculture, the computer has not replaced radio and television; it transformed the production and broadcasting of television but not the medium itself. Television, however, belongs to an earlier stage of the current technological era; this is the Age of Information. This generation prefers the computer to the television screen. What we see is no longer how we live. More than television, the computer determines the form of our lives. We trust it far more than what we see. But the ubiquitous machine cannot think.

The most advanced computers calculate at almost the speed of light, and the closer the little machines on the chip, the faster information moves. Resolution of all but the most complex problems takes place instantaneously. The infinitesimal gates of the little machines open and close at speeds only a few people can imagine. Positive or negative. The transistor has no between, no maybe. It cannot shrug or wink. Unlike the human brain, the computer, once programmed, operates on irremediable choices. The tiny machines at the source now of our daily lives cannot take Benjamin Franklin's position at the close of the Constitutional Convention. Franklin, like the rest of the framers of the Constitution, understood democracy through knowing its origins. But democracy grew out of reflection, a thoughtful dialogue between liberty and order in which the people did not choose either extreme. They invented a middle way—self-government. The tiny machines cannot tolerate a middle way, they cannot reflect, they cannot govern themselves.[3]

Computers affect the culture by showing us the powers of speed, simplicity, and certainty. The computer may tell us it does not have enough information or it may become overloaded and shut itself down, but it can't arrive at Franklin's political decision. I once asked the British philosopher A. J. Ayer if he thought machines might eventually be able to think. He harrumphed, as Oxford dons should, and said, "A priori I don't see why not. The trouble is, if you kick them, they don't feel." At the moment, the machines have not climbed the hierarchy of intelligence to wisdom, although they have had a profound effect on the thinking of human beings. Some people enjoy better material lives because of increased productivity based on computing. Others have become dispensable because of the computer; their lives have worsened. In the woeful world of the fallen the computer has been elevated to a place near omnipotence.

We are either grateful to the computer or in awe of it. Then why not emulate it? Why close the conscious or unconscious gates to its lesson? What is the apparent harm?

First, this: the dominant technologies of the twenty-first century contribute to a different kind of politics. The equation is very straight-

---

[3] The positive and negative function of the transistor is utterly unlike the dualism we see in nature. The male-female duality of the more complex forms of life results in union, not choice.

forward: the number of words is determined by the amount of time. Twenty seconds is about forty words. Some of the time in a political commercial has to be given over to the boilerplate: "I'm (name) and I approved this message." Jack Sprat is a more efficient name than Franklin Delano Roosevelt. FDR was an improvement in a broadcast world, W is even better, but not so good as K or A or N, because it takes more time to say W. Even so, W was a candidate reduced to a keystroke, eight bits, no more than that.

Time determines much of present-day politics, but not all. The tiny machine has another quality besides speed and its demand that we adapt to it. And that quality is exactly congruent with one of the most important values held by people in our society. Wirthlin has a theory of values as they relate to politics:[4] changing an adult's underlying values through reason is difficult, if not impossible. He was among those who early on abandoned Aristotle's idea of three modes of persuasion—reason, character, emotion—as the sole requirements of political campaigning. If Wirthlin is correct, politics then becomes a matter of having a candidate say and do things that agree with the values of the voters. And here he and Aristotle are in complete agreement, because Aristotle said that rhetoric is not a way to teach; the audience is not there to learn, but to judge. He said they were not interested in theoretical wisdom from a rhetorician; they wanted practical thinking, something they could get their arms around, worldly stuff. In Wirthlin's terms, they wanted appeals to their core values, but not direct appeals; those would be too bold, off-putting. He described a ladder leading to values, one of which is consistency. Human beings may not always be consistent, but the same question asked innumerable times to

---

[4] Wirthlin does not agree with the use of the word "values" to mean opinions about social issues; he now modifies the word with "core" to refer to those values some sociologists think of as the basis for a society. Not everyone agrees, but the debate over the role of values in creating and maintaining societies is not useful here. That people hold some "core values" and do not easily change them is important to the examination of contemporary politics, as is Wirthlin's view that consistency is one of these values.

Max Weber (1864–1920) is generally credited with first defining the place of values in social science. Weber proposed value-free social science. Other sociologists have argued that values are the very stuff of which society is constructed and sociologists are members of society, therefore cannot be value-free.

the same computer will elicit the same response.[5] Perhaps one of the reasons for the easy acceptance of the computer was its congruence with this widely held value.

Consistency has never been so admired in politics as in this century. It is often now confused with principle; that is, a candidate who expresses a point the electorate finds questionable may turn the dubious view into a principle simply by repeating it. The repetition of the simply stated position soon redounds to the candidate's advantage by implying that he or she is a principled person and consistent. By 2004 the computer's consistency had reinforced the long-held value, making inconsistency a political liability that could not be overcome. Every person I spoke with who voted for George W. Bush in 2004, including many Christian conservatives, named consistency as one of the key reasons for supporting him. It came as a surprise, because I had expected Christian conservatives to talk about social issues. And social issues were certainly important, but this is the go/no-go era. There is no time for the inconsistencies of the examined life[6] or the changes it may bring about.

A person must take a position. And there are only two choices: on or off, war or peace, win or lose, yes or no, good or evil, life or death, 1 or 0. An example of 1-or-0 thinking in politics is the red-blue dichotomy adopted to suit the computerized machinery of television broadcasting. It grew out of the need of the television networks to find a go/no-go description of the way states would vote in the electoral college, but it

---

[5] Eventually the mechanical parts of the computer will break down. An early sign of the breakdown of the machine is vagary beyond statistical variation. A cause of variation in the responses of the computer besides the breakdown of the mechanical parts is the proximity of the tiny machines to each other on the chip; it is not impossible in the more advanced computers for a single errant photon to trigger an improper response.

Information theory, invented by a Bell Laboratories scientist, has to do with correcting the errors caused by this kind of "static." As the amount of information transmitted increases and the number of errors increases, the error-correcting aspect of the system is more and more burdened until it reaches the limit of the amount of information that can be transmitted. Optical fiber, for example, has a lower error rate than copper wire, which is one of the reasons why so much more information can be transmitted using light rather than electrical current.

The amount of information transmitted within the physical limits can also be increased by efficient coding.

[6] "The unexamined life is not a fit life for man." Plato, The Apology.

has come to describe the entire political, social, religious, and economic character of a state. States are either one color or another, like the positive or negative of the little machines. The reality represented by the red-blue dichotomy is not the reality of the electorate, but of the two gates of the transistor. The electoral reality has no red or blue states, only states in which the majority of voters in one election on one day voted Democrat or Republican for one office. The red-blue reality is nonsensical, because it is only one bit (1 or 0) of information.[7] The red-or-blue-state designation can be used only as a blunt weapon in the war we know as polemic.

In 2004 one candidate argued that reason led him to inconsistency, the other claimed consistency as perhaps his single greatest virtue. The one who argued for reason spoke in the complex style of nuanced argument, the other developed his points into bullets, like a computer-driven business presentation. Bulleted points do not allow for nuance, and once they have been programmed in the computer, no conversation between the audience and presenter can change them. They resemble e-mail statements, and like most e-mail, once sent and read, they cannot be recalled.[8]

When candidates must be consistent and there is no time or place for nuance, dialogue has lost its role in politics and polemic holds the stage. Polemic has no historical relation to politics, which comes from the Greek *politikos,* pertaining to citizenship. Polemic signifies the failure of politics; it comes from the Greek word for war. The sharp cut of a polemic could not be better suited to an age of yes or no. The long siege of reasonable dialogue belongs to another era. The reasoning candidate will have to adjust to the tenor of the times. He or she faces a difficult choice: conquer the style of the omnipresent machine through irresistible dialogue or surrender to it and reduce politics to an

---

[7] A bit is the smallest unit of information in a computer. It is a single digit in a binary number. If red is zero, blue is then one. Bits may be part of mechanical, electronic, or optical systems. When one speaks of an errant photon, that is of course an optical system. Mechanical systems break down very easily. Electronic systems (transistors) are more durable, but far slower than optical systems.

[8] Some systems permit an e-mail to be recalled until the intended recipient has "opened" it.

exchange of polemical signals: 1 or 0, on or off, yes or no, war or peace, life or death. And that is only the beginning of the task; the reasoning candidate will have to look beneath the surface of the professed politics of the people and find the necessary substance. Otherwise, he or she may not know what to say.[9]

---

[9] A candidate might also have good ideas and just clearly present them to the voters, but in the age of paid political consultants, polling, and the nearly ubiquitous focus group that seems unlikely. One potential presidential candidate, Senator Barack Obama, Democrat of Illinois, has begun to argue for something other than go/no-go politics.

Four
___

SILENCE

The individual in any given nation has in this war a terrible opportunity to convince himself of what would occasionally strike him in peacetime—that the state has forbidden to the individual the practice of wrongdoing, not because it desired to abolish it, but because it desires to monopolize it, like salt and tobacco. The warring state permits itself every such misdeed, every such act of violence, as would disgrace the individual man. It practices not only the accepted stratagems, but also deliberate lying and deception against the enemy; and this, too, in a measure which appears to surpass the usage of former wars. The state exacts the utmost degree of obedience and sacrifice from its citizens, but at the same time treats them as children by maintaining an excess of secrecy, and a censorship of news and expressions of opinion that renders the spirits of those thus intellectually oppressed defenseless against every unfavorable turn of events and every sinister rumor. It absolves itself from the guarantees and contracts it had formed with other states, and makes unabashed confession of its rapacity and lust for power, which the private individual is then called upon to sanction in the name of patriotism.

—SIGMUND FREUD
"Thoughts for the Times on War and Death" (1915)

*   *   *

Polemic has no better weapon than silence. It came into use shortly after the dawn of human society when silencing political opponents meant forbidding the worship of certain gods. The oldest method for silencing enemies was murder, and it still has a place in the world. The Hutus and Tutsis kill each other, the Sunni and the Shia, the Israelis and the Palestinians, the communists and the capitalists, the Americans and the Taliban, the Americans and the Vietnamese, the Americans and the Salvadorians, the Iraqis and the Iranians, the Iraqis and the Kurds, and it was not so long ago that the Germans were killing the French and the Americans were killing the Germans, the Germans were killing the Jews, the British and the Germans were bombing each other's cities, the North Koreans were killing the South Koreans, and Stalin and Mao and Pol Pot were killing dissenters by the millions. It isn't over yet. At the beginning of the twenty-first century the number of people being slaughtered in the Sudan merited the term genocide and shortly after the U.S. invasion a religious-political civil war began in earnest in Iraq. In the use of killing as a means of silencing enemies, the only progress since the wars of the cave dwellers has been technological; gory murder in hand-to-hand combat has not disappeared, but it has an anachronistic stench in an age of precisely targeted rockets and improvised explosive devices detonated by cell phones.

With the sophistication of human beings came both the rise of religion and the first inklings of politics beyond the family. Rule by the best killer evolved into rule by consensus. At the same time, the next life grew in importance. Gods were needed to explain the destiny of human beings. And the gods were a jealous and hungry lot. "Thou shalt have no other God before me," was standard fare. Early on, the gods developed a taste for human sacrifice. The willingness of believers to give up the blood of loved ones or captives to lift the spirits of the gods marked their devotion in the time of Abraham and his son Isaac and in Mesoamerican civilization, where it culminated in vast numbers of sacrifices made by the Aztecs. The ultimate act of sacrifice remains the story of God willing his "only begotten son" to die on the cross . . . with a little help from Rome, which eventually fell, in no small part due to the spread of the word of the very person it tried to silence.

Contemporary human society has not abandoned the old ways. Nothing has replaced the efficacy of bloody murder in accomplishing religious or political goals. In most of the world religion and politics have remained inextricably bound. The connection is weakest in China, parts of Southeast Asia, Russia, and Western Europe. The Chinese government resists religion most strongly; the Museum of Atheism still stands in Moscow, but the churches and synagogues and mosques have opened again. Efforts by Christians and Muslims to proselytize each other as well as atheists and various kinds of deists go on all over the world, and when promises of paradise don't work, the love of one's fellow man often turns to silencing unbelievers and other dissenters by killing them.

Within putatively democratic societies murder may not be necessary, but silencing an opponent by whatever means can be tantamount to murder. After all, we have no better definition of human society than the exchange of words. To be deprived of the full range of human exchange is to be deprived of the fullness of human life, to be only partly alive, like a dying or damaged person, unmoving, yet still awake. The ancient Athenians silenced their internal enemies with exile, which they considered as good as death. Exile had one major disadvantage; troublemakers had a way of coming back and overthrowing their antagonists. The Romans crucified enemies of the state, which was messy but not noisy. There was no talking. The cross paralyzed the diaphragm; the dying could barely breathe, let alone cry out, and crucifixion, unlike exile, was final, with the one notable exception. English monarchs were almost as thorough. They either locked their enemies into prison cells, hanged them, beheaded them, or reduced them to screaming as they were torn limb from limb. This last, considered an excellent deterrent and a crowd-pleaser, was reserved for males; females were burned at the stake. The last drawing and quartering of an individual in England took place in 1820. The reason for silencing individuals or groups was sedition or fear of sedition, any threat to power, either religious or political, although religion and the state were one and the same throughout most of history, and there are some groups who would like to have it that way again in America.

In the American colonies witches (heretics) were burned at the stake, and not all went quietly to their final silence. It was a fine old Christian custom and popular among indigenous people too. The French Revolution, having observed that prison and exile have their limitations and preferring its meat *saignant*, silenced its enemies with the guillotine. The French Republic now and then erred on the side of impermanence, in one instance sending Captain Dreyfus off to Devil's Island. It left him there to rot, until Émile Zola broke the silence with the famous phrase *J'accuse*.

The brutal public silencing of dissenters prior to the twentieth century served two functions. It got rid of the dissenters, and it served as an object lesson to those who remained. The act became more complex, both more subtle and more terrible, in the twentieth century, and it is still too fresh in our social memory to be spoken of in scornful sentences. The problem of silencing the thousands had become one of dealing with the millions and tens of millions. Rulers, even ruling parties, alone could not effect silence; they needed the complicity of large parts of the citizenry. The tactic of silence became the politics of silence.

In modern totalitarian societies, those that grew out of the corruption of democratic institutions, like the societies described by Hannah Arendt and J. L. Talmon, the pursuit of silence did not stop with the death of the enemy.[1] The Nazis, who had a diabolical understanding of the politics of communication, buried the murdered dead in mass graves so that even their grave markers could not break the silence. It was an integral part of the juggernaut of totalitarianism. No system has ever been as thorough about silencing its victims. To rule is to seek to rule completely as in what Talmon calls "totalitarian democracy," when the majority silences all opposition through fear or murder.

To augment fear, death, disappearance, agreement, unhappiness, or the contemplation of last things may be connected to silence. Silence may be active, as in murder, or passive, as in secrecy; the nature of a silence and the meaning of its use can be found only by examining the context. Contrary to the cliché, silence does not indicate assent. Neither

---

[1] *Origins of Totalitarianism* (New York: Harcourt, 1951), and *The Origins of Totalitarian Democracy* (New York: W. W. Norton, 1951).

does it indicate dissent, unless the person in power demands spoken agreement; for example, "Say that you love me" or "Swear you are loyal to the state." The silences caused by the tyrannical exercise of power— regal, feudal, religious, oligarchic, autocratic, or democratic—come in many forms and have a variety of origins. Silence can be as complex and have as many forms as speech.

A monk who does not speak, yet spends his days writing, is not silent, if by silence we mean no communication, but a person can also speak and not say anything, as in "I have no opinion" or "The question you have raised would be better put to a person in the agency empowered by directive 156A subset 4 paragraph IIIb1 number 15c2 to bring your question to a spokesperson." Both are well-thought-out forms of silence. Maybe, we'll see, perhaps, let's think about it, and the psychoanalyst's famous posture behind the patient's head where neither sound nor ges-ture break the silence are all words, phrases, actions in the lexicon of silence. Physical silence (sound), which the *Oxford English Dictionary* and *Webster's* unabridged define second, after social silence (communica-tion), can never be complete.[2] The universe began with a bang, a noise so loud that physicists can still find traces of it in outer space.

The bang came just as the universe was created. Before that instant there was nothingness, silence of a kind we do not know and cannot imagine. Perhaps it was the same as the nothingness that may await us. We do not know that kind either, but it terrifies us. We desperately want to deny it. In defense against the possibility of a silence after death, both the Judeo-Christian Bible and the Koran proffer a noisy alternative: heaven. Or hell. Anything but unimaginable silence.[3] Sheol, Hades, Tamoanchan. Believers in reincarnation would rather exist as cock-roaches than face the silence. The worst hell for Dante, the ninth circle,

---

[2] In English, social silence appears in the early thirteenth century (1225 *Ancren riwl78* Ine silence & ine hope schal beon ower strencðe—*OED*, 2nd ed.), physical silence in the late fourteenth (1382 Wyclif *Isaiah viii.* 6 The watris of Siloe, that gon with cilence—*OED*, 2nd ed.); physical silence does not occur in the Old or New Testament, except in Revelation 8:1, and the meaning there of half an hour of silence in heaven is unclear.

[3] The idea of death as silence occurs only once in the Old Testament, in Psalm 115:17: "The dead praise not the Lord, neither any that go down into silence." The word comes from the Hebrew *dumah*, which originates in a root verb meaning "dumb," as in mute.

There is no silence in heaven or hell in the Koran.

was not crackling fire but soundless ice; he came as close as a poet dares to the horror of indescribable silence. For all the poetic grandeur of the work, it was also a work of politics, even petty politics, vengeance by art, with no punishment greater than the icy silence at the bottom of Hell. Dante understood the threat: when deathly silence overwhelms the issues of public as well as private life, the politics of heaven take control.

Leaving death and the question of the afterlife aside for the moment, silence among the living, social silence, can be much closer to perfect than physical silence. The leftover noise from the big bang will never, so far as we know, disappear from the universe, but the silence of the mass graves of the unidentifiable ashes of the ovens of Auschwitz could have been complete. If the Third Reich had lasted a thousand years, as Hitler prophesied, the death of millions would have gone unheard for a millennium, perhaps forever. Complete social silence is the ultimate oppression, yet silence need not be complete or permanent to be an effective means of control. It must only be a constantly increasing phenomenon, the promise of utter control, endless silence. From the barbarous simplicity of the mass grave to the falsehood so intricately knit, it cannot be unraveled, silence contravenes freedom.

By its very nature silence defends itself against the noble cacophony of democracy. Those it silences cannot speak against it, and those it disarms through the use of secrecy have nothing to talk about. In a democracy under extreme political, economic, military, or religious pressure, there may be only a brief window for citizens to defend themselves against the tyranny of silence. Leo Strauss said the liberal democracies must be strong to resist collapse, but Strauss also condoned one of the least democratic kinds of silence as a means of strengthening such societies: lying. How Strauss's readers might interpret his defense of lying by the state and whether or not Strauss was a true supporter of democracy will be discussed later. History, meanwhile, makes it clear that ancient Greek writers, among them Plato and Aristotle, were correct in their view that democracy[4] is not an invulnerable form of government.

---

[4] It should be noted that their understanding of democracy was simple rule of the majority, without the complex constitutional safeguards and social welfare policies that make modern democracies less vulnerable.

The first democracy in the Western world, the one that set the pattern of self-government, came about slowly, in stages, and fell painfully over many years. The Athenian democracy could not support its imperialistic aims. Like some giant creature stumbling and rising again, overreaching, attacked by plague, weakened from within, humbled by enemies from without, the magnificent invention finally could not last the night; in death it became a gift to the future.

Germany fell from democracy in a single day. All civil rights were suspended on February 28, 1933, the day after the Reichstag fire.

Lenin suffered a severe stroke in 1923 and died on January 21, 1924. Josef Stalin, who stood guard at Lenin's bier, became the leader of a totalitarian state.

On October 30, 1922, King Victor Emmanuel III of Italy asked a Fascist member of parliament, Benito Mussolini, to form a government to restore order in the country and prevent a Communist takeover.

On August 23, 1973, Chilean President Salvador Allende Gossens, his country suffering an economic and political crisis engineered in large measure by Henry Kissinger and the CIA, gave command of the Army to General Augusto Pinochet.

Democracy—or the imitation of it—in Cuba ended on April 17, 1961, as 1,300 CIA-supported exile troops landed at the Bay of Pigs.

In every instance silence attended the fall of the democracy, marking the moment of the fall and dominating the state afterward. Democracies, as history tells us, go gently and quickly into "that good night." Silence, the unheard speed of a great fall or the unsounded sigh of acquiescence, accompanied all the moments in the descent from democracy. Murder, imprisonment, and exile in great numbers ensued in every case. The silence surrounding the destruction of democratic institutions or the perversion of civil society was not perfect, but the end of democracy and civil society does not require immediate, total silence. Over time, the opposition to silence is itself silenced until it reaches the point where a democratic government becomes a totalitarian society. Talmon was correct: the democratic destruction of democracy, as bizarre as it sounds, is what happens.

The sequence of events that caused a democracy to collapse seems clear enough in retrospect but was difficult to comprehend at the time.

The Communists bore the blame for the Reichstag fire, Pinochet presented Allende with what appeared to be apolitical assistance, Mussolini offered a way out of chaos and Communist domination, and in 1931 the first democratic election in Spain in almost sixty years was expected to produce a peaceful, prosperous, enduring democratic republic. Richard Nixon turned on the Castro he once admired and called him a Communist, driving him into the waiting arms of the Soviet Union. All political activities are contingent, and democracy is a fragile idea in any event, one not always viewed by its constituents as the most effective form of government.

Perhaps historians will look back at the United States and marvel at the way the democracy was able to endure the World Trade Center attacks of 1993 and 2001 and whatever may follow. But September 11, 2001, or August 9, 1945, or October 25, 2001, the day the Congress passed the Patriot Act, or some combination of these, or perhaps some future date, may mark the day or the event that saw the many forces for silence coalesce and bring down the longest-lasting democratic government on earth.

In the United States, efforts at creating silence in one form or another have met with a democratic howling, but often not immediately. And not yet now. There is no strong political movement in opposition to the silence, and the press, long the trusted ally of democracy, now and then squeals but does not roar. The CBS television network collapsed under pressure from the right after its news anchor, Dan Rather, made what may have been a mistake about George W. Bush's military record. *Newsweek* magazine turned tail and ran for the cover of admitting error when it said a copy of the Koran had been flushed down the toilet at the Guantánamo Bay prison camp, but it remains unclear just how the desecration of the Koran was used in the mental torture of prisoners at Guantánamo.

New York Times reporter Judith Miller published erroneous information about the existence of weapons of mass destruction in Iraq that gave credence to the claims of the Bush Administration. One of the stories she published was about Iraq purchasing aluminum tubes for use in making nuclear weapons. Ambassador Joseph C. Wilson wrote an op-ed piece in the *New York Times,* saying that the Bush Administration story about Iraq buying aluminum tubes in Africa to use in centrifuges to make weapons-grade nuclear fuel had been wrong, a hoax. The tubes were not of the quality needed for nuclear centrifuges. Robert Novak, a right-wing newspaper columnist, published a story revealing that Ambassador Wilson's wife, Valerie Plame, was a covert agent of the CIA. Novak's information was correct. Plame resigned from the CIA. But who had leaked the information to Novak? And who had leaked the same information to *Time* magazine reporter Matthew Cooper? Had it been an act of revenge by the White House, a way to get back at Wilson for embarrassing the administration?

Three years later, Richard L. Armitage, who was then deputy secretary of state, admitted that he was Novak's source.

But the story was far more complex. A special prosecutor, who knew the leaker was Armitage, nevertheless charged Miller and Cooper with contempt when they refused to divulge their sources. When Miller and Cooper were facing prison, *Time* magazine editor Norman Pearlstine turned over Cooper's correspondence to the prosecutor. Cooper succumbed to pressure a few days later. His source was I. Lewis Libby, Jr., the vice president's chief of staff. Miller and *Times* publisher Arthur Sulzberger, Jr., agreed that she would not name her source. Miller, who had never published a word about Plame, went to jail.

The effect on the press showed up quickly. Two days after *Time* and Cooper succumbed to pressure, the *Cleveland Plain Dealer,* a Newhouse newspaper, announced that on advice of its lawyers it was not going to publish two stories based on confidential information for fear of suffering the same fate as Miller and the *Times.*

Miller was released from jail after she agreed to testify, saying that Libby had released her from her promise of confidentiality. And there was more: Miller claimed she had a security clearance that did not permit her to reveal certain information, even to her editors, an arrangement that is anathema to the idea of freedom of the press. The press had long been considered a bastion of free speech, and the *Times*, which publishes under the banner "All the News That's Fit to Print," was no longer trustworthy. The paper had fired a young black reporter for fabricating small stories and sent Howell Raines, its executive editor, packing, but the involvement of Bill Keller, the new executive editor, who had killed stories by his own reporters about the Miller case, was more important than the fabrications of a cub reporter. Keller stayed. Miller left the paper. *Times* staffers speculated about the circumstances: Did she jump or was she pushed? The consensus was *pushed*.

Her departure did not alter the fact that her stories had given credence to the Bush Administration's arguments about the urgent need to go to war. One of the country's leading newspapers, which was known to insiders as a pro-war journal up until the time when the war began going badly, had not only been a willing tool of the government, it had been a vigorous participant in what turned out to be one of the most damaging deceptions in American history. The *Times* had published specious arguments by Harvard Professor Michael Ignatieff in favor of war in Iraq and a piece by former leftist Paul Berman about Sayyed Qtub, a radical Muslim writer, which served to stir up anti-Muslim sentiments and support the need for war. Judith Miller had written about the existence of weapons of mass destruction as if it were gospel, and the editors had published her story without the powerful caveats it merited. In the past the *Times* had been accused of publishing handouts from various administrations in Washington, but it did not behave quite so cravenly as the *New York Herald-Tribune* in failing to defend its reporters against Joseph McCarthy and his ilk. The *Times* had simply been faux liberal, never complicit in the silencing of America.

Melor Sturua, a correspondent from the Russian government newspaper *Izvestia*, told me during the Cold War that his newspaper was just like the *New York Times*: it did not have to clear its stories with the government; the editors knew what the government wanted them to say. If it had been overstatement then, his view did not appear to be an overstatement in 2005; the "liberal" press, following the lead of the population, assented to silence. It has not always been so in America. This was a feisty country, one that carried the Bill of Rights as its sword and shield. The democracy was often embattled, but never so timid, never so ineffective, never so willing to accede to the poisonous silence as the United States had been during the run-up to the Iraq War; not even the witch-hunters of the 1950s had reached so deeply into the society.

The American model for silencing came early in the nation's history with the Sedition Act of July 14, 1798:

*Sec. 2. And be it further enacted, That if any person shall write, print,
utter, or publish, or shall cause or procure to be written, printed,
uttered, or published, or shall knowingly and willingly assist or aid in
writing, printing, uttering, or publishing any false, scandalous, and
malicious writing or writings against the government of the United
States, or either house of the Congress of the United States or the President of the United States, with intent to defame the said government,
or either house of the said Congress, or the said President, or to bring
them, or either of them, into contempt or disrepute; or to excite
against them, or either or any of them, the hatred of the good people of
the United States, or to stir up sedition within the United States, or to
excite any unlawful combinations therein, for opposing or resisting
any law of the United States, or any act of the President of the United
States, done in pursuance of any such law or act, or to aid, encourage
or abet any hostile designs of any foreign nation against the United
States, their people or government, then such person, being thereof
convicted before any court of the United States having jurisdiction
thereof, shall be punished by a fine not exceeding two thousand dollars, and by imprisonment not exceeding two years.*

The intent of the act was to aid the Federalists in their struggle with Jefferson's Republicans, but the citizenry frowned on the use of the act.
The Federalists were defeated, and the act was allowed to expire, but it
was not a harbinger of the future of the Patriot Act, which was renewed
in 2006. Nonetheless, the Sedition Act set a precedent: the First
Amendment was not invulnerable.

There was more to come, almost always when the nation was at
war, as now. The difference between all preceding wars and the current
conflict is that the Bush Administration is preparing for a state of perpetual war. At this writing there is no expectation of an end to war in
Iraq, anti-U.S. forces have started to fight again in Afghanistan, and the
administration has not abandoned the possibility of war with North
Korea or Iran. Only days before the 2006 elections, Secretary Rumsfeld
sent a classified memo to the president saying the war in Iraq was going
badly and suggesting a change in strategy.

Precedent for silencing dissent sadly belongs to one of America's great jurists. In *Schenck v. United States*, a socialist who sent circulars to draftees telling them not to report to their induction centers during World War I was convicted of conspiring to violate the Espionage Act of 1917. Upholding the convictions of Charles T. Schenck and Elizabeth Baer, Justice Oliver Wendell Holmes wrote for the majority: "The question in every case is whether the words used are used in such circumstances and are of such a nature as to create a clear and present danger that they will bring about the substantive evils that Congress has a right to prevent. It is a question of proximity and degree. When a nation is at war many things that might be said in time of peace are such a hindrance to its effort that their utterance will not be endured so long as men fight and that no Court could regard them as protected by any constitutional right."

War has often been an excuse for tossing the Constitution aside, but the definition of war has become a question for every person who now opposes any act of the Bush Administration. The Holmes decision is clear. Circumstances determine when the Constitution is in force. The question then and now is, Who decides when silencing opposition to the government is more important than maintaining the rule of law? The old saying about the rule of men and the rule of law may be comforting in the abstract, but in reality the rule of law applies only when people, even great jurists, think it is affordable.

During the Cold War the House Un-American Activities Committee led an effort to silence dissent on the left. Some people, the famed Hollywood Ten among them, went to prison for refusing to identify colleagues who had been members of the Communist Party or other left-wing organizations; others lost their jobs in the movies, television, and the press. Had it not been for the lunacy of Senator Joseph McCarthy and his staff—young Robert F. Kennedy and his supervisor Roy Cohn among them—the effort to silence dissent in the United States probably would have lasted longer and been more successful. McCarthy's behavior so exceeded the bounds of rationality and decorum during congressional hearings on the U.S. Army that special counsel Joseph N. Welch asked, "Have you no sense of decency, sir, at long last?" and the country suddenly recognized McCarthy as a drunk, a liar, and himself an enemy of democracy.

Witch hunts of one kind or another, on religious, racial, or political grounds, have been common throughout American history. The Ku Klux Klan began as a witch-hunting organization, its original purpose to silence blacks by keeping them from voting during Reconstruction. The federal government used troops to suppress the Klan, but as soon as Union troops left the South, the Klan again silenced blacks and their supporters. Blacks did not vote again in the South in large numbers for nearly a century, and the silencing of African Americans by denying them the vote has still not ceased completely. During the "Red Scare" of the early part of the twentieth century, almost anyone could be tainted with suspicion. Jane Addams, Sinclair Lewis, even Will Rogers, were all thought to be Communists by one group or another of "superpatriots."

Eugene V. Debs was convicted in 1918 under the Espionage Act for making a speech defending socialism and imprisoned socialists. Debs was sentenced to ten years in prison, but not effectively silenced. He ran a presidential campaign from his prison cell in 1920, getting close to a million votes, not many fewer than in 1916 when he traveled the country.

In 1920, Nicola Sacco and Bartolomeo Vanzetti, Italian immigrants with anarchist ideas, were convicted, on very weak evidence, of murder. Their real crime was holding unpopular ideas during a time of national paranoia about Communists. They spent seven years in prison awaiting execution. In 1927 the governor of Massachusetts appointed a three-member commission, including the presidents of Harvard and MIT, to investigate the case. Although the commissioners had no credible evidence of the men's guilt, they said the verdict had been just. As people all over the world protested, the two men were silenced by electrocution.

Franklin Delano Roosevelt demonstrated little concern for the civil rights of people of color or unpopular political opinions. Although his wife, Eleanor, worked hard for antilynching legislation and other civil rights issues, he never initiated or openly supported a civil rights bill. On the contrary, he interned Japanese-Americans during World War II in one of the more shameful episodes in American history. And the courts and the country went along with him. His attempts to silence those who disagreed with him, on both the left and the right, although resisted by his attorneys general, often succeeded. He demanded the prosecution of Nazi sympathizer William Dudley Pelley, publisher of *Roll Call*, the *Galilean*, and *Liberation*. Pelley was finally sentenced to fifteen years, and lest the question of silencing was somehow unclear, when Pelley was released on parole after ten years, it was with the proviso that he stay out of politics.[5] Roosevelt insisted on denying mailing privileges to the magazine *Social Justice*, published by right-wing anti-Semite Charles Coughlin, a Roman Catholic priest. He had an even-handed policy toward silence: FDR looked at the Socialist Workers Party journal, the *Militant,* and took away its mailing privileges.[6]

Despite protests around the world and a plea from Pope Pius XII to spare their lives, Julius and Ethel Rosenberg were electrocuted on June 19, 1953, at the height of another Red Scare. They had been convicted of passing atomic secrets to Klaus Fuchs, who sent them on to the Soviet Union. Fuchs was convicted of passing far more sensitive information to the Soviets than the bits supposedly sent to him by the Rosenbergs, but his life was spared by a British court. The Rosenbergs had no such luck; they were tried by a cowardly Jewish judge who feared charges of favoritism and the calumny of anti-Semites if he did not sentence the couple to death. They died in the middle of the Cold War, when the execution of the parents of small children was thought to be an effective means of bolstering efforts to silence dissenters on the left.

During the Civil Rights Movement and the Vietnam War, silencing bloomed again in America. Civil rights marchers were beaten, attacked with vicious dogs, washed down with fire hoses, imprisoned, and murdered. President Kennedy, Dr. Martin Luther King, Robert F. Kennedy, and Lee Harvey Oswald were assassinated. Protesters were shot down on the Kent State campus. Police murdered members of the Black Panther Party. War protesters were arrested. And the police rioted to silence protesters during the 1968 Democratic National Convention.

For all that fear and foreign wars lead the United States in the direc-

---

[5] Information on the Roosevelt-era activities comes from Geoffrey R. Stone, *Perilous Times* (New York: W. W. Norton, 2004). Mr. Stone's excellent book concentrates on First Amendment issues during time of war. The post-9/11 period has so far been a time of constant war, with no end in sight.

[6] Stone reports, in *Perilous Times*, "some thirty publications excluded from mail" by the middle of 1942.

tion of silence, nothing so concentrates the government on silencing its supposed internal or neighborly enemies as an attack on United States territory. Prior to 2001 the last attack on the American mainland came at Columbus, New Mexico, on March 9, 1916, when forces loyal to Pancho Villa killed 19 people; that attack produced an invasion of Mexico. The Japanese attack on Pearl Harbor in 1941 led to America's entrance into a world war and to the detention, without trial, of loyal American citizens of Japanese descent in poorly outfitted prison camps.

After the attack on the World Trade Center in 2001, the federal government reverted to the silencing tactics of the past. Congress quickly passed the Patriot Act, which permits electronic surveillance and secret searches. In some instances a warrant signed by a judge is no longer necessary. Until the act was passed, such searches had been considered violations of rights protected by the Constitution. The full effect of the Patriot Act and other responses to 9/11 has yet to be determined. As General John J. Pershing hunted Pancho Villa, who probably did not take part in the raid on Columbus, and Roosevelt declared war on Japan (and Germany and Italy), Bush went to war in Iraq. The question of civil liberties was raised after 9/11 as it had been during World War I, World War II, the Cold War, and the Vietnam War. Arrests, detentions, violations of rights guaranteed by the Constitution, have become commonplace, and all in an atmosphere of silence. Prisoners at the military prison at Guantánamo Bay, Cuba, are held incommunicado, without the right to trial by civilian or military tribunal. Other prisoners have been held by the CIA in secret locations. Habeas corpus, one of the pillars of American jurisprudence, has been de facto suspended. How Arab-Americans and other Muslims will be treated if there are more attacks will further test the U.S. commitment to the Constitution.

In each instance in the past the silence was broken; the democracy survived the challenge. Current and future assaults may not be so easy to repulse. Technology has yet to be fully understood as it relates to silence. The Internet was thought at one time to be a technological version of the coffeehouses, free press, and large public associations that created the lively public dialogue of the eighteenth century.[7] However,

---

[7] There have been some serious objections to the idea of the Internet as a worldwide commu-

it would be risky to designate the Internet the last best hope for democracy. The problem with the Internet in the United States is not that it is used by so few, but by so many. The Internet carries within it the potential to create a profound silence based on noise. Various government intelligence-gathering organizations have already provided some insight into what may lie ahead. Despite their large staffs and state-of-the-art electronic sorting programs, these federal agencies cannot examine Internet traffic with sufficient dispatch to determine who might pose an imminent threat to the nation. There is just too much of it.

As Internet traffic grows and more people have Web sites and produce blogs (Web logs), the number of people with whom each one communicates will decline inexorably toward zero. Before long, Web sites and blogs may not have any appreciable political effect. Internet magazines have had difficulty sustaining themselves through subscriptions or advertising, and other periodicals more and more use the Internet as a medium for sampling by potential subscribers of either a hard copy or an Internet version of the publication. The Internet holds out great promise as a delivery system but not as an originator of credible content. The bloggers and owners of Web sites, some of whom provide carefully checked news and information content, face the problem of creatures in an overcrowded and increasingly polluted environment. Like the white-noise machine that drowns out other sounds for light sleepers, these vast numbers of individuals and groups all speaking at the same time create silence through noise; in effect, drowning themselves out.[8] Yet the Internet does not have the technological potential to guarantee any single

---

nity on the grounds that minorities, the poor, people in underdeveloped countries, those who speak languages not translated by the computer, and so on would be barred from the dialogue.

[8] An opposing point of view holds that market forces will affect Internet sites as they have affected other forms of media. Some will survive to be viewed by large numbers of people while the rest disappear. The flaw in this argument is that there is no economic incentive to close a blog or a Web site. Doubtless a message in a bottle tossed from the deck of a sinking ship will be found by a stroller on a distant beach, but the message may not be found in time to save the drowning person or the fictional man marooned on an island, and the Internet bears increasing resemblance to the bottle in the ocean. The message may not be found at all. Google turns up more than 25 million different sites for "George W. Bush." If the "W." is removed, the number doubles. By searching just for "Bush," the number nears 100 million. Reading 120 an hour, 24 hours a day, it would take almost a hundred years to read them all. To read all the entries under the word "Iraq" would add another century of reading.

user's privacy. Sophisticated hackers can invade any networked computer, and do it from anywhere in the world undetected, in complete silence. A government can examine networked computers entirely in secret. Dialogue may be fractured into near silence on the Internet, but some of the whispers are still audible to those in power.

Silence is no longer merely potential in America, and it comes in many forms: torture, spying, censorship, and bribery—both overt and subtle—among them. On a single day, September 8, 2006, the *Times*, which had turned hard against the war as the polls showed public opposition to the war, published these stories:

> *A U.S. corporation, Hewlett-Packard, under the leadership of its chair, Patricia C. Dunn, had spied on members of its own board and on the press.*
>
> *Former President William Jefferson Clinton appeared on television, enraged over what he said were errors about his administration and Osama Bin Laden, in an ABC-TV "docudrama" to be broadcast in two parts on September 10 and 11, 2006. Samuel R. Berger, Clinton's national security advisor, former Secretary of State Madeleine K. Albright, and defeated Democratic presidential candidates Kerry and Gore also claimed the program had erred in its fictional portrayal. The Senate Democratic leadership and over 100,000 people, whose signatures were gathered by the Democratic Party, joined in demanding that ABC cancel the program. The censorship of a work of fiction about public figures was accomplished. ABC said it would edit the program to reflect the views of Clinton, Berger, Albright et al. The Democrats were unsatisfied with prior censorship; they continued to insist right up until air time that ABC's Entertainment Division be silenced. The program, as broadcast, contained some material that misrepresented the actions and attitudes of members of the Clinton Administration. The broadcast was of little consequence compared to the effort to silence it.*
>
> *Wal-Mart's business practices and usefulness to the public, especially low-income people, were defended in articles and essays in newspapers and other publications by executives and fellows of the American Heritage Foundation, the Manhattan Institute, the Pacific*

Research Institute, and the American Enterprise Institute. Wal-Mart,
through the Walton Family Foundation, has donated $601,900 to the
four foundations.

And the Bush Administration, which has been attacked for tor-
turing prisoners, sought to push a bill through Congress that would
legalize forms of torture banned in the new Army Field Manual
published only two days earlier.

The democracy here has not collapsed and is nowhere near collapse,
but since George W. Bush took office, joined by a Republican majority
in Congress only seventeen months later, political silence both in kind
and degree has become more prevalent, and increases almost daily in
government and private institutions. To illustrate each of several kinds
of silence I have provided a few examples in the footnotes.[9]

---

[9] Airlines now have secret "watch lists." A man in Washington, D.C., who has the same
name as a person on the watch list has been strip-searched several times as he attempted to
board a flight. The searches and investigations last up to half an hour. The man has tried
repeatedly to have the name removed from the list or find some other way to avoid the
searches and interrogations, to no avail. He does not know what to do, and he is afraid to
complain in a public way for fear of retaliation.

As the response to 9/11 became more pervasive, other aspects of American society were
silenced. For a time in New York City, photographs could no longer be taken on the subway. Civil liberties groups had to put up a fight to get the rule rescinded.

During the 2004 Republican National Convention, New York City barred a protest
meeting from Central Park. Protesters were arrested on the streets and held without being
charged. Similar meetings were barred in cities across the country, from New Mexico to
Illinois to California. A large number of the arrests in New York City turned out to have
been groundless. Videotape recordings showed that no violation of law occurred, yet the
protesters were held in jail for days, often until the convention was over. The city government eventually conceded that it had made "preventive arrests."

At the same convention the Virginia delegation sat near the CNN booth. Some members
of the delegation tried to shout down the CNN broadcasters, chanting, "Watch Fox News!
Watch Fox News!"

Six-year-old children and elderly women in wheelchairs are subjected to body searches
at airports. Complaints by parents or the elderly or women who have been body-searched
by men only result in the complainants being detained, perhaps for a few minutes, perhaps
long enough to miss a flight.

The government established secret "no-fly" lists, different from "watch lists," prohibit-
ing certain persons from boarding airplanes. How the government created the list, why certain people cannot be passengers on airlines, who is on the list, are all secret. The government
announced that passengers would be required to give more information to airlines to avoid
"further scrutiny at airport checkpoints." The additional information includes date of birth.

Silencing others, including the press, is a tried and true method of breaking down a democracy, but keeping silent oneself is equally effective. Since 2001, when George W. Bush took office, secrecy has been used consistently as an instrument of power by the federal government. In its most common form government secrecy is the classified document. Under U.S. law the government may choose to classify—that is, make secret—any document in any government agency.[10]

Airlines already have credit card numbers, identification cards, and, in the case of foreign travel, passports to peruse.

And woe to the person who attempts to pay for a ticket with cash.

Upon entering the country from a trip abroad, U.S. citizens are subject to fingerprinting and eye scans.

The Office of Personnel Management has established a Combined Federal Campaign which insists that all charitable organizations compare their personnel files to government "watch lists." The requirement touches thousands of charities, from the Red Cross to the American Sleep Apnea Association. It has no purpose but to put dissenting as well as terrorist organizations on notice.

[10] According to Sen. Ron Wyden, the federal government headed by George W. Bush classified over 14 million documents in one year.

Executive privilege can be used to keep secret information that should be made public. Vice President Cheney maintains secrecy about his dealings with energy companies despite repeated requests by the press. No one knows what influence his meetings with energy company executives had on national energy policy.

The 9/11 Commission reported that government secrecy was one of the reasons why the United States was unable to defend itself against the attacks even though the hijackers gave themselves away time and again. Members of the same commission, which decided to form a second group, the 9/11 Public Discourse Project, to continue its work by monitoring the response of the Bush Administration to its recommendations, said on August 6, 2005, that the Bush Administration had refused to respond in any way to the requests of the group, still headed by former New Jersey Gov. Thomas H. Kean, a Republican. Kean gave the media copies of letters to the secretary of defense, the secretary of state, and so on.

The Patriot Act gives the government the right to make secret wiretaps and search the homes of citizens in secret; that is, not advising citizens that the search took place.

From 2002 through mid-December 2005 the National Security Agency spied on thousands of Americans, intercepting their international telephone calls and e-mails, in an operation authorized by President Bush. No warrant was ever issued by a U.S. court of law permitting the domestic spy operation.

People may now be held in various forms of detention entirely in secret, with no right to seek release under habeas corpus. Secret military trials may be held. All this according to government rulings.

The Bush Administration has made it a policy to keep records secret from the U.S. Congress. It keeps records from examination by the press or other members of the public through a new category of secrecy it calls "sensitive information," which means it is unclassified but still secret. The Bush Administration refused to make available to the United States Senate materials relevant to the confirmation of John Bolton as U.N. ambassador.

Secrecy not only permits silence to act as a mechanism of control, it cannot be detected and defeated by the citizenry, like a known act. Secrecy thwarts the ability of people and their elected representatives to act intelligently as citizens in a democratic society.[11]

Eventually most secrets become known, but eventually is a long time, and until that time comes, a government may do a great deal of harm. Secrecy defends itself by virtue of being secret. If that sounds tautological, it isn't. Logically no one knows where to look for a secret because it is a secret. Even so, secrets soon lose their value. By the time the press finds out what Vice President Cheney promised the oil industry, his term in office will have ended. Cheney's meetings weren't even kept secret, just the content of them. The Sierra Club sued in Federal Court, asking for release of the names of the oil company executives who advised the vice president on energy policy. The case went through the appeals courts, was turned down by Justice Antonin Scalia at the Supreme Court, and sent

---

[11] The Freedom of Information Act, a law that was presumed to enable citizens to know what their government is doing, is not binding on the government. The Clinton Administration ruled that government agencies had to give out information sought under the act unless they could prove it would do harm to the nation. The Bush Administration turned the rule on its ear. It ordered the Department of Justice to defend government agencies whenever they said information was exempt from release under the law. In other words, the government will defend the same agencies from public scrutiny. The ruling has made it all but impossible to find out what arrangements were made between energy companies and the Department of Energy or the Defense Department and the Halliburton company.

Documents have been classified secret retroactively.

The Reagan Administration's ruling on opening presidential papers on public issues after the president leaves office was reversed by the Bush Administration. Now presidential records will be kept secret, even if they are not related to personal matters and their release would not compromise national security. George Bush has kept his papers as governor secret by locking them away among his father's presidential papers.

The Bush Administration has maintained secret the high-level responsibility for the abuse of prisoners at Abu Ghraib through the early months of 2005. Vice Admiral Albert T. Church III conducted an investigation without interviewing a single person from the Department of Defense and then said he found no one there responsible for the failure to set out proper procedures for the treatment of prisoners.

On February 5, 2005, Defense Secretary Rumsfeld issued a memorandum expanding the "rendition" of prisoners, suggesting they be sent from Guantánamo to Saudi Arabia, Yemen, or Afghanistan, where torture was a common practice that could be done in secret. At some time, perhaps September 2003, the United States began sending prisoners to Uzbekistan, a nation known for torturing prisoners, where boiling limbs or entire persons is not uncommon. Human rights organizations reported several deaths by boiling in Uzbekistan. No press or international relief organization has access to prisoners in Uzbekistan; the silence is complete.

back to the appeals court, which found for the government. The silence surrounding the meetings will remain. No one can know what was said by the oil industry executives because no one knows for certain who they were. What has become known is that a former employee of the American Petroleum Institute, now a White House official, has been changing the language and tone of scientific reports on global warming to water down the seriousness of the issue and make the conclusions comply more closely with oil industry views. This form of lying is fully justified by the Bush Administration's understanding of ethical behavior by government. It was kept secret until the Government Accountability Project, a nonprofit group, found out the details and informed the media of the work of the White House Council on Environmental Quality. What is not known is how the arrangement was made between the White House or Cheney with the oil industry. Every time a piece of a secret comes public, it implies other secrets. And there are few aspects of silence more difficult to combat than secrecy. It is the unseen enemy of democracy.

Similar logic holds true for the silencing of individuals, where secrecy is itself the most powerful weapon for maintaining secrets. Take the case of the file the FBI found on your computer when two agents entered your house while you were at the office. Using the "sneak and peek" provision of the Patriot Act, they were not bound by law to tell you what they found. After they showed it to the security group at the company where you worked in the engineering department, you were fired. The reason given for your termination had nothing to do with your file of quotations from the Koran. Since you have never met anyone who planned to attack the United States, it would not occur to you to think the FBI had searched your computer files.

Silence may be created overtly by closing off avenues of communication or in more subtle ways, one of them being the use of the antonym. When political groups use antonyms instead of nouns and adjectives that pass the test of reason, the dissonance functions as "white noise," obliterating other sounds.[12]

---

[12] Socialist "realism" under Stalin was anything but realistic.

The secretary of defense is still the secretary of war, despite the name change. There is,

Refusal is another form of silence.[13]

---

in fact, a Department of Homeland Security, which ought to be the "department of defense," if war were not named defense.

President Bush calls conquest democratization; "boots on the ground" is his way of saying "freedom."

The announcement of the rise of democracy in Russia under Putin may actually mean the end of democratic institutions.

Jerry Falwell's Liberty University has a religious and political code of limitation and restriction.

Mel Gibson said he produced the movie *The Passion of the Christ* because he loved Jesus. Tim Schultze, a highly educated, deeply religious Calvinist, thought otherwise. He described it as a movie showing the Romans "beating the crap out of Him."

Dr. D. James Kennedy of Coral Ridge Presbyterian Church, in Ft. Lauderdale, teaches his ideas to members of Congress and delivers a lecture on Thomas Jefferson's "opposition" to the separation of church and state.

Fox News claims, with a sneer, that it is "fair and balanced," as it presents overtly biased coverage of politics and other news.

In the Bush Administration, Douglas Feith ran the Defense Department's disinformation section; in other words, he was in charge of antonyms. Abraham Shulsky, also a disciple of philosophy professor Leo Strauss, held the job during the Reagan Administration.

The Bush Administration sends news reports on videotape to television stations, but the news is really propaganda, which is the opposite of news.

[13] Corporations now regularly refuse interviews on questions relating to their misdeeds.

President Bush refused, at first, to be interviewed by the 9/11 Commission, claiming executive privilege. Forced by public opinion to speak to members of the commission, he agreed to do so only if the vice president was at his side during the interview, which was not to be recorded by any means other than the memory of the few members of the commission present in the room.

George W. Bush told author and former assistant to President George H. W. Bush Doug Wead in a surreptitiously recorded conversation that he thought Al Gore had made a mistake when he admitted using marijuana: "I wouldn't answer the marijuana questions."

In Senate confirmation hearings Bush nominees for cabinet posts refused to answer direct questions about memos they had written, positions they had taken. Attorney General Alberto Gonzales, asked about a memo advocating torture that he wrote while serving as counsel to the president, refused to discuss the content of the memo.

Secretary of State Condoleezza Rice refused to discuss a memo she had written asking the Senate to disavow a resolution put forward by Sen. John McCain opposing the use of torture by U.S. intelligence agencies. Secretary Rice, who was national security advisor when she wrote the memo, answered again and again that it had been covered by a previous law. When Sen. Barbara Boxer asked if Secretary Rice thought McCain, who had spent years as a prisoner of war, did not understand torture, Rice simply repeated her one-line statement, saying that torture was covered by another statute.

Sinclair Broadcasting, which by its own account reaches 24 percent of U.S. television viewers, refused to broadcast an ABC *Nightline* program listing the names of fallen Americans in the Iraq War.

At the international level the United States now regularly refuses to participate in courts and agreements, preferring the cold silence of withdrawal to the heat of argument.[14]

Governments impose silence through secrecy and fear, but no government can do so without the complicity of the people. In every instance of the fall of a democracy, the people played a role, sometimes passive, more often urging the government on. One of the salient characteristics of authoritarian and totalitarian societies comes from the willingness, often in a despairing hour, to see others silenced. In these societies people at all economic and social levels choose the state over its inhabitants and elevate one person, one clique, to lead them. They do it because of some presumed benefit to themselves. The benefit may be immediate, a higher standard of living or protection from attack by a real or imagined enemy, or the expected benefit may be in the next world. If so, who will help the people avoid eternal silence? The question is not about tomorrow's dinner or the deterioration of the siding on the north side of the house. To think otherwise, to imagine it is a question of economics, to claim people act contrary to their own interests, to make them

---

[14] Attorney General Gonzales laughed off several requirements of the Geneva Conventions as "quaint."

The United States refused to sign the Kyoto accords on greenhouse gases.

In 2001 the United States effectively withdrew from the International Biological Weapons Convention to which the United States had been a signatory since 1975.

While arguing its case for the invasion of Iraq before the United Nations in 2003, the United States pressured the UN to cover up a large tapestry that reproduced Pablo Picasso's *Guernica*. The work depicted the horror of the attack on the Spanish town of Guernica on April 26, 1937, when Nazi aircraft dropped tons of incendiary bombs in an attempt to destroy the Basque resistance to the fascist rebels during the Spanish Civil War. Secretary of State Colin Powell knew that the U.S. plan to bomb Baghdad could prove as terrible as the bombing of Guernica. The fires in the Basque town lasted for three days; not long compared to the fire bombings of Dresden or Tokyo, but Powell could not be certain that the bombing of Baghdad would not be worse. He silenced Picasso, the attorney for the women and children of Iraq.

In 2005 the U.S. withdrew from the International Court of Justice in the Hague.

The invasion of Iraq constituted a withdrawal from the authority of the United Nations.

The United States withdrew from the permanent International Criminal Court in 2002. Rep. Tom DeLay of Texas said the court, formed with the backing of the Clinton Administration, was "an institution of unchecked power that poses a real threat to our men and women fighting the war against terror."

out to be fools when they understand their eternity is at risk is to mis-
understand the nature of fear and to demean the ability of human beings
to expect their own death.

Anything that nibbles at a person's eternity is intolerable. It must be
silenced. Government of the fearful for the fearful will either create a
silence so profound that only the murmuring of their prayers will be
heard, or it will perish. Many evangelical Christians see a crisis loom-
ing, and not just a crisis exploited in a series of potboilers about "the
rapture." They see very clearly that a political-religious decision is in
the offing in 2008 and heaven itself is theirs, if they win. At the
Reclaiming America for Christ Conference, February 18, 2005, Dr.
Richard Land, moral issues spokesman for the Southern Baptist Convention, said that the next ten to fifteen years will determine whether
America succumbs to a "neo-pagan triumph"[15] or returns to a Judeo-
Christian moral consensus wherein rape and illegitimacy are rare,
marriage and child-rearing are valued, and prisons are turned into
museums.

"Evangelical Christians" is a very broad term, often defined as people who have had a "born-again" experience, make an effort to win over
converts to Christ, and believe in a literal interpretation of the Bible.
Not all evangelical Christians are politically conservative, but the term
has come to be synonymous with "Christian conservative." Fundamentalist Christians are evangelicals, but not all evangelicals are fundamentalist; that is, they are not antimodern in their religious or cultural
beliefs.[16] Evangelicals are an important part of the larger movement,
which accepts silence as the price of winning its desires, from a diminished government to amassing capital to obeying what it believes are the

---

[15] Quoted in the conference press release.

[16] Some people generally characterized as fundamentalist—the Falwell followers, for example—do not accept the label, which was given to them by University of Chicago Divinity
School's Martin E. Marty. Falwell and other "fundamentalists" speak of their admiration for
Marty, but dislike being categorized as fundamentalists along with other antimoderns of the
world's religions. One of the best brief works on Christian fundamentalism is by Nancy T.
Ammerman and appears as a long chapter in Martin E. Marty and R. Scott Appleby's five-
volume *Fundamentalist Project* (Chicago: University of Chicago Press, 1991).

acts required of the faithful. To bring about the kind of America envisioned by President Bush and conservative members of state and federal legislatures, to save themselves as they save America and the world, they have undertaken their own campaign to silence those who imperil their place in eternity.[17]

---

[17] Prevent homosexuals from saying marriage vows.

Change the laws requiring 60 votes for cloture in the U.S. Senate to silence filibusters by the opposition. Senate Majority Leader Bill Frist later said it was only a tactic to force Democrats to negotiate a compromise on what they had previously said were unacceptable ideologies. The Democrats capitulated on three extreme right federal court nominees, but retained the right to filibuster in some situations. The Republicans, of course, retained the right to change their minds and change the rule on cloture to a simple majority. The battle to silence the opposition would arise again if the Republicans recapture the Senate and win the presidency in 2008.

Demand changes in PBS programming that is not in accord with conservative religious and political views. Or stop federal funding of PBS altogether, since it corrupts the morals of the nation, as Rush Limbaugh, an admitted narcotics abuser, advised. Kenneth Y. Tomlinson, chairman of the Public Broadcasting System and a Republican, has been responding to the cries of Christian Conservatives about the "bias" of PBS not so much by including voices from the right as by seeking ways to silence voices from the left. He sponsored a study of liberal views on Bill Moyers's program *NOW*. It was the only program studied. The House of Representatives voted to cut off funding for PBS entirely. After the 2006 election the remaining Republican caucus became much more aligned with the national political movement. Should Republicans retake the House in 2008 they will almost certainly repeat the vote to withdraw funding from PBS.

Cut off federal funding for any group that advocates family planning in the United States or abroad.

Cut off funding to any group or country that advocates the use of condoms as a means of preventing the transmission of HIV or other sexually transmitted diseases.

Punish people who expressed their politics by indicating they voted for a candidate other than the one endorsed by the pastor of the church, as in the case of the Reverend Chan Chandler in Waynesville, N.C., who threw out nine members of his congregation who said they voted for John Kerry. A scandal over Chandler's decision led him to resign as minister of the East Waynesville Baptist Church. The Roman Catholic Church in some areas of the country said it would not give communion to people who had expressed similar views. Chandler told the press the issue for him was abortion. The Catholic Church added same-sex marriage to its list.

Overturn the *Roe v. Wade* decision permitting women to express their choice in the case of unwanted pregnancy, a situation that wider use of condoms, sex education, and other means of birth control might prevent.

Eliminate references to evolution in textbooks.

Stop the entertainment industry (movies, television, music, Internet, etc.) from producing and distributing material religious conservatives deem obscene or otherwise different from their views.

Forbid bilingual education in schools and inhibit the use of foreign languages, particularly Spanish, by using only English in public documents, signage, licensing examinations, and voting materials.

Democracy has many antagonists, none greater than silence. For a democracy to survive it must be raucous and open, free. What this American political movement, which has chosen George Bush and given great power to the religious conservatives, cannot grasp is that democracy must be an endless argument, a filibuster against the permanent hierarchy of authoritarian rule, the talking cure for oppression. But democracy comprises more than mere talking, something beyond noise; the people in a democracy must communicate. The contemporary German philosopher Jürgen Habermas posited five conditions for successful communication. The listener has to agree that (1) the utterance is true; (2) the speaker is sincere or truthful; (3) the utterance responds to the appropriate values; (4) is fitting to the relation between speaker and listener; (5) and is comprehensible.

Habermas is also concerned with what he calls discourse ethics, by which he means an ethics based on people communicating successfully to make decisions that are acceptable to all. The participants may begin with different views, but they cooperate "freely and equally" in a search for truth in which "nothing coerces anyone except the force of the better argument."

In his ethics, communication takes place in what he called the public sphere, an imaginary locale where reasonableness reigns and people gather together to tell the state (government) their needs. This public sphere, the ideal place for the making of public opinion, provides a wall against the enemies of democracy. Everyone has equal access to the public sphere; there is no hierarchy. In the public sphere people can depend on the rule of law; everyone in the public sphere makes a commitment to reason, all the arguments are logical. The question that must be raised in relation to the political movement that has taken hold in America is how it differs from Habermas's ideas. How is discourse in the United States now different from the public discourse he proposes? At first glance, the country since 1965 would appear to be going in the direction suggested by his discourse ethics. The differences come first in the commitment to reason. A large part of America is committed to faith rather than reason, and an even larger part is involved in the contest between faith and reason. An important characteristic of government after 9/11 has been to limit access to argument by capturing control of media or working through local or federal government on such issues as providing only textbooks that do not differ from the views held by those who support the group now in power.

The kind of political dialogue Habermas envisioned has not taken place on a national level in the United States since 2001. A loud polemic replaced it in 2004, and since then one of the most effective polemical weapons of the Bush Administration has been to silence opposition. The administration went so far as to hide the return of dead soldiers from its war in Iraq, as if there were some shame at having died in combat. Surprisingly the public, even the families of the dead, accepted the silencing of the brave. It demonstrated the change that had taken place in the American political character, for in no previous era would such disrespect for the war dead have been tolerated.

In the past the government has attempted to silence its opposition, but never before has religion been joined to politics and war in the effort. Every previous attempt to use silence to control the country soon languished for lack of agreement by the people. There is the beginning of a struggle against silence now. By some measures the 2006 elections represented that struggle. The war dead and the failure in New Orleans have given courage to those who oppose silence. This time their task is more difficult, because the silence does not come from one political party or a petulant president or a drunken senator; the will to silence the opposition comes from the people as well as the government. Expectations have changed since 2001: silencing the opposition will be rewarded not only at the ballot box, but in heaven.

Five

PROTESTANTS

In [Revelation] 17:1 the great whore . . . is all corrupt, apostate religious systems, especially professing Christendom.

— LIBERTY BIBLE COMMENTARY

What we do on earth is a speck in time.

— MARISA MARY RUMMEL
Spring, Tex.

All Americans are Protestants. Catholics, Jews, Mormons, Muslims, Buddhists, Kiowas, Shintoists, Navahos, Sufis, Cherokees, Chickasaws, atheists, deists, agnostics, anarchists, economists, poets, prostitutes, playboys, and policemen are Protestants. They are, all of them together, the American confluence.

Of course, everyone does not agree. In 2004 the National Opinion Research Center (NORC) at the University of Chicago announced with some fanfare that the long dominance of Protestantism in America was about to end. Protestants, the NORC said, would soon cease to be a majority. Perhaps it had already happened. They had interviewed more than 2,000 of the roughly 300 million Americans. And those were the facts! Who could argue? NORC was careful. Its report did not say that America would no longer be a Protestant nation; it said only that the majority of Americans would no longer identify themselves as Protestants. The finding demonstrates the usefulness of an idea that has occu-

pied the minds of Englishmen since the sixteenth century: follow
Plato's advice, define your terms. We will see that, in truth, all Americans are Protestants.

To think otherwise is to miss the point about this country as it exists
now. There are many aspects to be considered, beginning with our history, politics, economics, and ethics. And then there is America's growing inability to distinguish between evangelism and imperialism.
Meanwhile, we see the steady dissolution of the state and its attitude of
responsibility for those least able to fend for themselves under the conditions of laissez-faire economics. The foundation for this society and
for the political movement that now grips it was laid by the first Englishmen to arrive on the shores of the continent. They established many
communities, various churches, denominations that grew, split, grew,
split, and so on, but the commonality of these religious-social-political-
economic communities is as great as their diversity.

When the great waves of immigrants arrived, they shared a common idea of America as a land of opportunity. Catholics and Jews did
not choose to abandon their ancestral homes and cross an ocean to venerate the pope or the Talmud. They could have stayed where they were.
Unlike the Puritans and others who came for political and religious reasons, they were driven by economics. Many of them had suffered religious and political persecution, but they made the trip because there
were no potatoes or too little pasta or there was said to be gold in the
streets in America.

They soon found out they were not going to be Venetian doges or
kings of Israel or the Irish equivalent of British royalty. Where and how
they prayed mattered far less than where and how they worked. They
did not abandon God in any of His forms or put aside their missals and
Bibles and books of common prayer, they took up the hammer and the
hoe. They still venerated the pope and the Talmud, but they venerated
God in a new way, the Protestant way; they learned to treasure time,
which they soon understood as a possession of the Lord, like the earth
and all the things upon it. In that way they were Protestants, even though
the other Protestants despised them for their popery or money-changing.

How America came to be a Protestant nation does not begin at
Jamestown or Plymouth. The confluence of factors governing the eco-

nomic and religious history of America happened in Europe centuries before the first English colonists arrived. Max Weber[1] and later Richard H. Tawney[2] wrote brilliant investigations of the confluence. At the beginning of the twentieth century Weber published a new theory of the origin of capitalism. He described what he saw as the effect of religion on economic organization, giving great attention to Calvinism, the ideas of predestination, election, and the concept of a calling, which was originally a religious principle but changed after the Reformation to mean a person's place in the world, his labor or trade.[3] As good Christians had been obliged to follow a religious calling prior to the Reformation, they were now obliged to devote themselves to worldly work. They could not waste time, for time belonged to God; they had to work hard and efficiently. Moreover, good Christians could not only accumulate capital and use it to increase their wealth; it was their duty. Before the Reformation, according to Weber, the accumulation of wealth, through trade or interest on capital, was considered usury. Weber was simply wrong. Capitalism, which he attributed to Protestantism, was practiced in the Low Countries and parts of Germany in the twelfth century or even earlier. This is not to deny Weber's connection of Protestantism and capitalism, only to put the history in order, which changes the likelihood of Protestantism being the cause of capitalism. In fact, there were rules against making money, but rich Roman Catholics managed to avoid suffering for their sins by using their wealth to buy indulgences from

---

[1] *The Protestant Ethic and the Spirit of Capitalism*, trans. Talcott Parsons (New York: Scribner's, 1930, originally published in German in two sections in 1904–1905).

[2] *Religion and the Rise of Capitalism* (New York: Harcourt, Brace & World, 1926).

[3] "It is an Use of instruction to every Christian soule that desires to walke by faith in his calling. If thou wouldst live a lively life, and have thy soule and body to prosper in thy calling, labour then to get into a good calling, and therein live to the good of others; take up a calling, but that thou hast understanding in, and never take it unless thou mayest have it by lawfull and just meanes, and when thou hast it, serve God in thy calling, and doe it with cheerfulnesse, and faithfulnesse, and an heavenly minde; and in difficulties and dangers, cast thy cares and feares upon God, and see if he will not beare them for thee; and frame thy heart to this heavenly moderation in all successes to sanctifie Gods name; and if the houre and power of darknesse come, that thou beest to resigne up thy calling, let it bee enough that conscience may witnesse to thee, that thou hast not sought thy selfe, nor this world, but hast wrought the Lords workes; thou mayest then have comfort in it, both before God and men." John Cotton, *The Way of Life* (London, 1641).

Pope Julius II and his successor Leo X. Despairing of a Church he deemed corrupt, Martin Luther wrote his ninety-five theses and nailed them to the gates of the church at Wittenberg.

For a merchant, shopkeeper, or landowner who did not buy indulgences, putting his money to use by lending it at interest was a sin. To earn a profit by selling goods at more than cost, was equally sinful. Thomas Aquinas had propounded the theory of the "just price," which comprised the amount of labor and materials in a good or service, and no more. Not just loaning money at interest, but anything over the just price was considered usury. Since commerce required money and no one wanted to put money at risk without some reward, lenders asked for interest. It was a conundrum. Prudence required interest to cover risk, interest involved the use of money over time, but time belonged to God, not to man, hence the lending of capital was sinful—usury, no matter what the rate or purpose.

How to put together God and money required some genius. Weber, the sociologist, believed he had identified the main cause of the rise of capitalism (labor organized for profit) in a society that had been opposed to it as sinful. He saw a vital connection between the sixteenth- and seventeenth-century Protestant revision of the idea of a "calling" and the end of the religious prohibition against earning a bit of interest or otherwise turning a profit. It was a marriage made in heaven. Workers had a moral duty to follow their calling (in other words, to work hard) and the wealthy had the moral duty to use their money. Raw materials gained in value as they were turned into cloth and coats and breeches, chairs and pots and beds and boats, whatever could be made more efficiently by the systematic application of labor.

Capitalism, the economics of the organization of labor and the use of the materials provided by nature, produced desperate working conditions. The capitalist was the financial as well as the moral beneficiary and the laborer earned barely enough to keep him alive as he enjoyed the moral benefits of pursuing his calling. Subsistence wages were paid to the worker who was expected to raise children who would, in turn, produce more wealth for the owner of capital. And it was all for the glory of God. Among the best evidences of the effects of what Weber called the "Protestant ethic" were the British government "blue books" describing labor in the mills. These "blue books" were to become a powerful influence on Karl Marx.

Although well aware of the suffering of workers in the early shops and factories, Weber concentrated on what he called "the spirit" of capitalism. He focused on the Puritans, the second-generation descendants of Luther and Calvin. In the late sixteenth and the early seventeenth centuries, the Puritan rejected the surplices and symbols of the Catholic Church of England and the Church of Rome, putting his faith in the word alone. He was an ascetic, but his asceticism did not prohibit making money, only the enjoyment of it in some sinful fashion. The new attitude toward wealth was exactly opposite the pre-Reformation understanding of poverty as a sign of goodness.

Jesus loved the poor. In neo-Calvinist[4] doctrine poverty had only negative connotations. The poor did not fulfill their obligation to God to work diligently to make use of what had been provided them on earth. St. Paul had said, "He who will not work shall not eat," and the Puritans, like contemporary conservatives, thought people were poor because they were lazy and therefore did not merit help from man or the grace of God. No one could be certain whom God had chosen to receive His grace, although, based solely on their economic state, the poor were most likely not the "elect of God." Weber made a powerful comparison between the New Testament expressions of the renunciation of worldly goods and the Calvinist interpretation of God's will when he wrote "To wish to be poor, it was often said, was the same as wishing to be unhealthy." So different was the Calvinist understanding of God's will from the idea that sent many Roman Catholic priests, monks, and nuns into a life of penury!

The worker had his rules too. And he was to be no merrier than the rich man. Again Weber: "The ascetic importance of a fixed calling provided an ethical justification of the modern specialized division of labor." A hundred and twenty-five years before Weber the concept of the division of labor had been examined in Adam Smith's *Wealth of Nations*. At the beginning of the twentieth century Weber saw

---

[4] Since Calvinism went through many phases, I have used "neo-Calvinism" to identify the later stages.

how Smith's pin factory had come into existence, what forces flowed together to drive men to work at subsistence wages without complaining while others exploited them without thinking it sinful. The laborers on the assembly line in Smith's example of the pin factory each had their places, their callings; each did as commanded by God. If they worked long hours under debilitating conditions, with few pauses except to wolf down a miserable meal or hurriedly use the toilet, they did this mindless work in conformance with the Puritan admonition not to waste God's time, not even in contemplation of Him, except at the proper time, on Sunday. God preferred the active pursuit of one's calling over all other things.

Weber did not say that Protestantism alone could account for the rise of capitalism. He wrote his masterful essay on the single issue of the influence of an interpretation of John Calvin's *Institutes of the Christian Religion* as it applied to the economic conversion of the Western world in the sixteenth and seventeenth centuries. His understanding of the particular phenomenon provided an explanation of many of the psychological changes that accompanied the sudden turn in ethics and economics in the West. Gone, as Marx and Engels noted, were the ancient connections of feudal society, replaced by "cash payment." Yet cash payment alone did not explain the new ethics. Weber made it clear that along with cash God had to intervene. He concentrated on the changed use of religion as justification for economic behavior rather than regulation of it.

Economics

In a foreword to the 1930 Talcott Parsons English translation of Weber's work, Richard H. Tawney, a British economist, Christian socialist, and longtime member of the British Labour Party raised anew some of the criticisms of Weber he had made in *Religion and the Rise of Capitalism*. At first glance, it seemed that Tawney simply took the opposite point of view: economic conditions, nascent capitalism, gave rise to the Protestant Reformation. But to imagine the sociologist and the economist as mere opposites would be both to underestimate Weber's consideration of the influence of ideas outside religion and fail to recognize the breadth of Tawney's work.[5] Granted, he took an economist's look at history, but he grasped the other factors as well. Like Weber, Tawney thought commerce had a direct and important influence on the rise of freedom in the Western world. Weber put religion before commerce and Tawney reversed the two, but neither man separated them from freedom. Tawney looked at medieval society and cited examples of peasant revolts against church and state beginning in the fifteenth century.

It may have been the Age of Faith, but by the fifteenth century the difference between the Church's prohibition of usury and its usurious practices was widely known and resented. Labor was respected, trade was suspect, but the merchant could be excused if his profit was considered his wage. Then he was a worker, like any other. If a man pursued wealth beyond his needs, the Schoolmen of the thirteenth century accused him of avarice and labeled him a sinner. The middleman between the worker and the merchant, however, could not be excused under any condition. He profited by other men's necessity, not by adding the value of his own labor to the goods sold. Tawney joked, "The descendant of the doctrines of Aquinas is the labor theory of value. The last of the Schoolmen is Karl Marx."

Tawney felt a certain nostalgia for the Catholic [or universal] Church of the Middle Ages, which he said "stood for the protection of peaceful labor, for the care of the poor, the unfortunate and the oppressed—for the ideal, at least, of social solidarity against the naked force of violence and oppression." He conceded that the Church had its flaws, but men "had not learned to persuade themselves that greed was enterprise and avarice economy." Only with the "growing complexity of economic civilization" did the Church find itself unable to deal with the moral and economic world as it had in the past.

---

[5] This very brief summary cannot convey the depth of thinking of the two men, nor can it even begin to suggest the richness of their scholarship. Tawney both supported and expanded Weber's work. He never failed to explain that Weber had looked only at the effect of religion on capitalism and not at the economic influences or the history as it developed from the Middle Ages. The universal Church, by which Tawney meant the Roman Catholic Church before the Reformation, was not a major part of Weber's work. Without it, he could not discuss the change in social or ethical views that led to what he called "the spirit of capitalism." Weber, who made his book of two separate essays written for a periodical, had to begin *in medias res*. Tawney was beholden to Weber for the initial sally.

The peasant revolts, and there were many, were but the first inklings of the desire for freedom. Developments moved quickly. In Antwerp, a great center of commerce during the late Renaissance, the leaders of commerce praised the Church for giving them the freedom to do business on the bourse. Luther, a young lawyer who turned to religion when he was struck by lighting and survived, found the Church corrupt, but Luther still maintained the Church's ethical view of commerce. He abhorred it. And Calvin was not significantly different except for his view of small amounts of interest on loans. Tawney said it was 150 years after Luther at Wittenberg that the Protestant Reformation took hold across Europe and on into the New World. Economics drove it, demanding that religion conform to the needs of economy, to accept a new definition of usury, to encourage trade, to see the increase of wealth as doing God's will. The denominations that separated from Rome and then from the symbols of Rome did not, according to Tawney, immediately change their ethical view of the world. Calvin did not reject the Catholic opposition to exploitation.[6] It was rather the remaking of the ancient relation between master and serf into capital and labor that changed the world. Religion had no choice but to follow. The chief country of the Counter-Reformation, Spain, once rich beyond all imagination, the powerhouse of the great European bourse, foundered as the Protestant nations prospered.

Economies on the Continent and the British Isles became more complex and more productive. Trade broadened across Europe, and along with the change in productivity the serf became a freeman in name, if not in reality. He was free to move from place to place, but he labored under terrible conditions for little reward. The newest group of

---

[6] The question of Calvin's acceptance of usury is so often debated, it may be useful to paraphrase it here. He talked about lending money in a letter to his friend Oecolampadius. In it he said that money was truly "barren," but need not be, for it was like a house or a field. The walls and the roof were barren until the house was rented to someone who made use of it. A field was barren until it was sold to someone who made money by farming. In the same way money was barren until it was loaned to someone who used it to make money. What worried Calvin were the circumstances in which money was loaned. He said clearly that no interest should be charged on money loaned to those in urgent need, nor should interest be charged on money loaned to the poor, nor should the amount of interest exceed the legal rate.

capitalists gained ever greater power. Religion had either to go along with the new economy or get out of the way. It chose to bless the idea of capitalism. Calvinism was interpreted to mean the rich are the elect of God. Capital connoted grace. Individualism reigned. Had Calvinism been interpreted otherwise; it could have led, in the sixteenth century, to something more like the Christian Socialist rather than the capitalist model, but the strict Calvinism that had been instituted in Geneva and followed in Scotland did not hold in seventeenth century England or on the Continent.

No one quarreled with the economic growth of the period, the rising average standard of living. Protestantism divided and divided again, like an organic thing growing. The Arminians in Europe rejected Calvinism. The Pietists wanted a simpler, more spiritual religion than Calvinism. The radical Puritans, followers of Calvinist discipline, rebelled against the Church of England. The state church could tolerate the Calvinist presbyters of Scotland, but the Puritans of England, dressed in their dour outfits, made ever greater demands on King James I. The most radical of them decided to separate from the Church of England rather than attempt to reform it from within. Some of the separatists were imprisoned and eventually executed. Others fled to Europe and America, where they became Congregationalists.

The voyage was long and arduous, but the Virginia Company, a group loyal to the English church, had landed at Jamestown in 1607, only to be nearly wiped out by disease and natives several times before being permanently established as a crown colony. In 1620 the Mayflower landed with its shipload of Puritan separatists. The rocky shores and cold winters of New England were not quite so hospitable as Virginia's marshes and woods. Half of the Puritan colony died out soon after the landing, yet the Puritans of New England more than the English church in Virginia defined the American adventure in its early years. And those who landed at Plymouth felt less connected to the state and the state church that had made a misery of their lives than to the lawyer who had made a theocracy of his adopted Swiss city. It was not England but the economic and religious descendants of John Calvin who established a colony at Plymouth.

The Puritans had little concern for the poor, having developed a harsher view of life than that of the universal Church or Luther or Calvin himself. The freedom of religion the Puritans had demanded of the Church of England was in turn demanded of them, and denied by them, pushing another group of separatists out of Massachusetts to found new colonies. Early on, the truly Calvinist rules of the market, essentially no different from those of the universal Church, were strictly obeyed. Any variance was punishable by a fine, imprisonment, and for the worst cases excommunication from the Congregationalist Church. Nonetheless, the pattern of freedom had been set.

The Puritans tried to control New England in much the same way the Calvinists had controlled Geneva, but their control did not last. The shift from the medieval concept of nature as a moral force, limiting human activity, to nature as the repository of human desire changed the worldview of the colonists. Individualists rather than members of the pastoral flock, they believed nature "endowed [them] with certain unalienable rights." These natural rights had never been recognized by the universal Church. Theirs was a new ethics, a new politics. It had begun when Luther took a step away from universal ethical control, grew mightily when Calvin permitted a small amount of interest on loans, breaking the centuries old moral hold of the Roman Catholic Church. But it was finally the economic growth of the late fifteenth and early sixteenth centuries that demanded the new definitions, the new freedom, the new understanding of man's ability to use God's organizing principle: time. Did not all Bibles, all translations say, "In the beginning . . . ?" God had made sequence at the outset of His creation, and now, with Calvin's blessing, man had taken the essential of God's world for his own. When Benjamin Franklin said, "Time is money," he immortalized the most basic concept of the new religion and the new economy.

Time was not only money, it was the way to make money. "A penny saved is a penny earned" made no sense unless the saved penny could be used to make money. Neo-Calvinism, grown from the small seed of the acceptance of the idea of interest on money loaned, had blossomed into a new justification for the economic life of man. Tawney summed it up with devastating accuracy: "After all, it appears, a man can serve two masters, for—so happily is the world disposed—he may be paid by one, while he works for the other. Between the old-fashioned denunciation of uncharitable covetousness and the new-fashioned applause of economic enterprise, a bridge is thrown by the argument which urges that enterprise itself is the discharge of a duty imposed by God."

Thus all Americans are not only Protestants, but the economic and ethical descendants of the Frenchman Jean Chauvin, who became John Calvin of Geneva, Switzerland. Like him, we are critics of everything that is; we reinvent ourselves, our religion, and the world. We are his intellectual followers: prayerful proselytizers, and discontent.

Six

SECTS

There is something treacherous, delusive, and ambiguous
in the temptation of power.

— VACLAV HAVEL

Grover Norquist, who heads Americans for Tax Reform, a central
meeting place for people who represent some aspects of the current political movement in America, lumps all Christians into one
Protestant denomination. Norquist has neither background nor interest in theology; in fact, he knows very little about religion. He is an
operative, and like all operatives he has an aversion to anything that
does not serve the operation. Norquist does not know the political history of his closest aides, nor the history of the United States beyond a
few glib phrases that support his thesis. Theology bores him; he uses
theologians—he has no interest in the details of their beliefs. As an
operative, it would be foolish for him to behave in scholarly ways. Like
the early Puritans, he understands activity as doing God's work, and
saves contemplation for his day of rest, if and when that day comes. It is
no failing on Norquist's part to devote himself to activity; he pursues his
calling, as an operative should.

Norquist the operative, a man who was once a registered lobbyist
for Angola and an economic advisor to Jonas Savimbi's UNITA rebels
and, by the long arm of inference, to the Apartheid government of
South Africa. Norquist married a Muslim Palestinian woman in 2005,

prompting fulminations from Daniel Pipes and others.[1] If, as Pipes and his informants suggest, Norquist is in the process of converting to Islam, it would be amusing, given his connections to the Christian Right and his Puritan compartmentalizing of contemplation, but whatever his interests as an operative or a spouse, theology has not occupied much of Norquist's thinking. He said he did not know the difference between premillennialists and postmillennialists, going so far as to ask me to define the different beliefs about the Second Coming and the ensuing thousand-year reign of Jesus Christ on earth. Norquist dismissed the importance of religious differences: "People tend not to bring that part of it into electoral politics. The guys who are various forms of evangelical tend to vote pro-life issues, care about their guns. They may have all sorts of religious views, but they're all consistent with American constitutionalism, and that's why you get guys like Pat

---

[1] The following is a complete Internet posting by Daniel Pipes, a neoconservative and author of several anti-Muslim books and articles:

Is Grover Norquist an Islamist? Paul Sperry, author of the new book, *Infiltration*, in an interview calls Grover Norquist "an agent of influence for Islamists in Washington." When asked by FrontPageMag.com why a Republican anti-tax lobbyist should so passionately promote Islamist causes, Sperry implied that Norquist has converted to Islam: "He's marrying a Muslim, and when I asked Norquist if he himself has converted to Islam, he brushed the question off as too 'personal.'" As Lawrence Auster comments on this exchange, "Clearly, if Norquist hadn't converted to Islam, or weren't in the process of doing so, he would simply have answered no."

Indeed, Norquist married Samah Alrayyes, a Palestinian Muslim, on April 2, 2005, and Islamic law limits a Muslim woman to marrying a man who is Muslim. This is not an abstract dictum but a very serious imperative, with many "honor" killings having resulted from a woman ignoring her family's wishes.

Alrayyes has radical Islamic credentials of her own; she served as communications director at the Islamic Free Market Institute, the Islamist organization Norquist helped found. Now, she is employed as a public affairs officer at the U.S. Agency for International Development—and so it appears that yet another Islamist finds employment in a branch of the U.S. government.

Norquist has for some years now been promoting Islamist organizations, including even the Council on American-Islamic Relations; for example, he spoke at CAIR's conference, "A Better America in a Better World" on October 5, 2004. Frank Gaffney has researched Norquist's ties to Islamists in his exhaustive, careful, and convincing study, "Agent of Influence," and concludes that Norquist is enabling "a political influence operation to advance the causes of radical Islamists, and targeted most particularly at the Bush Administration."

But if Norquist is indeed a convert to Islam, it could be that he is not just enabling the Islamist causes but is himself an Islamist. (April 14, 2005)

Posted by Daniel Pipes at 10:29 PM | Comments (0)

Robertson and Jerry Falwell and Orthodox Jews all on the same team. They don't think each other's going to heaven, but they're willing to leave each other alone."

Faced with the polling data about the coming end of the Protestant majority in America, he said, "Actually, I think its going the other way. When you look at the institutional Catholic Church, it's becoming more Protestant. The number of nuns and priests and brothers and stuff like that is just collapsing. And a quarter of the Mexican-Americans or Hispanics is Protestant, which is an assimilation rate beyond anything the Europeans ever did. And the Catholic Church itself is halfway to being Protestant. I mean what's a cafeteria Catholic if he isn't really a Protestant? A Catholic who doesn't buy into papal infallibility and the doctrines of the Church is a Catholic? Or just, like, ethnically Catholic?

"If you divide Catholics into those who [do and] don't go to church very often, [those who don't] vote just like everybody else, and the half that go to church once a week vote like the Christian coalition. There was an interesting study done during the 2000 election. The nonactive Catholics, they're just like Presbyterians or something. They don't vote as a block. But active Catholics who go to church every week, they look and sound like the Christian coalition does."

Norquist has enjoyed a long career as an operative; perhaps his view of the homogeneity of Protestantism should be accepted and the whole issue let go at that. At the time of the interview, Republicans held the presidency, majorities in both houses of Congress, the majority of state-level offices throughout the country, and in 2005 had begun the process of changing the federal judicial system to an extension of conservative political activism.[2]

---

[2] It is rare for such majorities to hold during midterm elections, and in the sixth year of a presidency or in time of war, even less common. In the 110th Congress, Democrats had won a 51–49 voting majority in the Senate and held a 31-seat majority in the House of Representatives. When Norquist and I spoke, the Republican Party was likely to lose seats in the coming midterm election, but the Democrats who would replace them would often hold the same views on social issues as the people they replaced. A good example was the Senate election in Pennsylvania. The Democrat, Robert "Bob" Casey, Jr., and the Republican, Rick Santorum, were both pro-life. Casey opposed stem-cell research and favored capital punishment.

The usual pattern held, but the Democratic victory did not come close to that of the "out" party in 1942, when Republicans gained forty-seven seats in the House of Representatives. Even so, New Deal ideas remained dominant for another thirty-eight years until they were eclipsed by the current national political movement.

The strength of Norquist's position was clear. All Americans were Protestants. The weakness in his position was less apparent, but perhaps more interesting. All Americans were Protestants, but what kind of Protestants? The religious controversy had given birth to the word "polemic" in the seventeenth century, and then its antonym, "irenic," which had to do with theological peace and religious unity. Not one quantitative study of Protestant America agreed with Norquist and not one agreed with any other.

The Gallup Poll claims that 42 percent of Americans are "born-again" or "evangelical" Protestants.

If the Pew Survey on Religion and Politics is to be believed, 56 percent of Americans still say they are Protestant, compared to 49 percent in the Gallup Poll.

And if the Gallup Poll is correct, only 7 percent of Protestants are not either "born again" or "evangelical." A disagreement of 7 percent is not insignificant; it represents some 15 million people old enough to make religious choices.

According to Pew only 30 percent of all Americans say they are born again, and 24 percent consider themselves evangelical.

The Barna survey, which has a "Christian" orientation, says only 7 percent of Americans are evangelicals. It has a much more stringent definition than the Gallup questionnaire.[3]

One survey says church attendance among young people is declining, while another says it is increasing.

The only point on which the surveys all agree is that Americans become more religious as they grow older. And logic would tell us that

---

[3] The Gallup Organization offers this view of its numbers on born-again or evangelical Christians: "It's worth pointing out that this estimate of the percentage of the population that is 'born again' is very dependent on how the question is asked. Note that the question wording . . . includes the phrase 'evangelical' Christian, which probably has the impact of enlarging the number of people who respond 'yes.' A more complex question pattern Gallup has used in the past involves three separate questions, asking: a) if the person has had a 'born again' experience '. . . when you committed yourself to Jesus Christ,' b) has the person ever tried to encourage someone to believe in Jesus Christ or to accept him as your savior, and c) does the person believe that the Bible is the actual word of God and is to be taken literally, word for word. The results indicated, in 1995, that just 19% of American adults answered affirmatively to all three questions."

In the Barna Survey the number falls to only 7 percent.

very old people think of little else. Death does focus the mind, but the age at which death enters the consciousness of a person is now too variable for generalization. Terrorism and the recent rise of the fear of nuclear weapons into the forefront of the mind of many Americans changed the age at which the shadow of death comes over one's outlook. As the threat becomes more prominent with the spread of the weapons to more countries hostile to the United States, age will no longer drive belief. The young will be no different from the old in a foreshortened world.

Since no one really knows how many evangelical Protestants there are in America, it is not very useful to know that the Pew survey found evangelical Protestants are now more likely to be Republicans (43 percent) than Democrats (22 percent). The number for Democrats, based on anecdotal evidence, seems a bit high, but then the definitional question arises along with the eternal problem of induction. It may be best to depend more on knowing a lot about a few people than on knowing virtually nothing about a great many. For example, John Phelan is a Democrat, Dean of the Evangelical Covenant Church's North Park Theological Seminary, and the possessor of one of the more interesting minds in the American clergy. But "one swallow does not a summer make," as Aristotle said. Other members of Evangelical Covenant churches I have met are all Republicans. When they refer to Phelan's party politics, they include a sigh of Christian love for the wayward, and then profess their love and admiration for him.

Democrats who deal with religion and politics, Jim Wallis and his *Sojourners* magazine and John Podesta of the Center for American Progress, would suggest that I have been looking in the wrong places. They see Democrats everywhere. They may be correct, but where to look, whom to ask in America, is difficult, because the definition of an evangelical Protestant is hard to pin down. The Barna survey has one definition;[4] Wallis has another; Elizabeth Sifton, the daughter of

---

[4] According to the Barna update of February 10, 2003, born-again Christians are "defined in these surveys as people who said they have made a personal commitment to Jesus Christ that is still important in their life today and who also indicated they believe that when they die they will go to Heaven because they had confessed their sins and had accepted Jesus Christ as their savior."

  "Evangelicals" are a subset of born-again Christians in Barna surveys. In addition to

the theologian Reinhold Niebuhr,[5] has another. And that is just the beginning.

Nonetheless, some quantitative studies of religion in America pass the test of reason. The finding that almost a quarter of all evangelical Protestants are Democrats is not one of them. According to the most stringent definition, a person could rarely be both an evangelical Protestant and a Democrat, unless either the Democrats or the evangelical Protestants changed their views on both abortion and gay marriage. The Barna survey uses nine criteria. To be counted as evangelicals, Democrats would have to be sure, among other things, of the inerrancy of the Bible; believe that Satan exists; that Jesus Christ lived a sinless life on earth; maintain that eternal salvation is possible only through grace, not through works; and see God as the omniscient, omnipotent, perfect God, creator and ruler of the universe. Moreover, they would be evangelizing, which Barna phrases as having "a personal responsibility to share their religious beliefs about Christ with non-Christians." For one person to meet the Barna definition and also be a Democrat is a highly unlikely aberration, and for a fourth of the Barna evangelicals to be Democrats is impossible by definition.

Other findings make more sense. The United States is by any measure the most religious of all the industrialized nations. Even so, fewer people regularly attend religious services each year.

The fastest-growing group in the United States is nonbelievers (atheists, agnostics, humanists, etc.).

Women are more religious than men.

Republicans are more religious than Democrats.

Southerners are more religious than northerners.

---

meeting the born-again criteria, evangelicals also meet seven other conditions. Those include saying the Bible is accurate in all that it teaches; saying their faith is very important in their life today; believing they have a personal responsibility to share their religious beliefs about Christ with non-Christians; believing that Satan exists; believing that eternal salvation is possible only through grace, not works; believing that Jesus Christ lived a sinless life on earth; and describing God as the all-knowing, all-powerful, perfect deity who created the universe and still rules it today. Being classified as an evangelical has no relationship to church attendance or the denominational affiliation of the church they attend.

[5] *The Serenity Prayer* (New York: W. W. Norton, 2003).

Race makes a difference. According to all surveys, blacks are far more religious than whites. Given the history of people of African or partly African descent in America, theodicy, which is the vindication of God's holiness and justice, especially in light of the existence of evil, has a different meaning and use for African Americans than for whites; they have no choice but to think suffering in this world will be rewarded in the next.

The middle and upper classes, in Max Weber's view, have a different theodicy. They don't have to wait for the next life. They understand their good fortune as God's way of dealing with evil in the world: He enriches the good and impoverishes the bad. How the growing number of middle- and upper-middle-class African Americans will deal with the differences between history and the moment will take a generation or two to come clear.

For the general population of American churchgoers, the Barna survey offers a Christian outlook, a very large sample, and some curious and for Christians disconcerting results. They looked at what they considered an ordinary week in 2004 and broke it down to look at the component parts. The Barna results were widely challenged, especially on divorce, but George Barna was quite open about the divorce rate among "born-again Christians"; he said his polling showed it was higher than the average for all Americans. What is most interesting about the survey is the attempt to produce a fully rounded picture of a churchgoing week. What is lacking is a breakdown beyond the denominations. There are more than 1,000 and perhaps as many as 1,500 Protestant sects in the United States. No survey could be expected to sample all of them.[6]

In 2004, during an average week, 43 percent of adult Americans had

---

[6] Howard Dean, chairman of the Democratic National Committee, started off the month of June 2005 by telling the world that all Republicans were the same, all white, all Christian, to which Ken Mehlman, chairman of the Republican National Committee, replied by suggesting what a surprise it would have been to the people who attended his bar mitzvah. Dean's mischaracterization of Republican voters was one of many political errors in Dean's career, but it suggested that Dean, now privy to the DNC's polling information, had accepted the general misconception of Americans as a few huge monolithic groups.

attended a church service other than a wedding or a funeral.[7] By 2005, according to Barna, the number had increased to 45 percent. Other surveys have put the number as low as 20 percent. Barna has been accused

---

[7] Of these, 64% were Protestant,
     27% were Catholic;
By race:
     72% were white,
     14% black,
     11% Hispanic;
By gender:
     57% were female,
     43% male;
By age:
     21% were Busters (Barna's term for people between the ages of 18 and 33),
     45% were Boomers (between the ages of 34 and 52),
     24% were Builders (between the ages of 53 and 71),
     8% were Seniors (age 72 or older);
Another Barna Survey reports that Busters were less likely than people over 55 to attend church. It put church attendance at 51% of those over 55;
By income:
     25% earn $30,000 or less annually,
     36% earn between $30,000 and $60,000 annually,
     22% earn $60,000 or more annually; there is a bigger middle class here than in the rest of the country. The U.S. Census for the same year reported 20% of the country with household income above $86,000 and 40% below $34,000;
By family status:
     63% were married,
     36% were single,
     23% have been divorced sometime in their life,
     40% have children under the age of 18;
     nondenominational Christians have the highest divorce rate at 43%, Baptists come next at 29%, followed by Episcopalians and Pentecostals at 28%, Methodists at 26%, Presbyterians at 23%, Catholics and Lutherans at 21%. The Catholics and Lutherans had a curious companion in the group with the lowest divorce rate: atheists and agnostics;
By political self-definition:
     41% identify themselves as conservative,
     44% identify themselves as moderate,
     8% identify themselves as liberal,
     15% are not registered to vote;
By political party:
     28% are registered Democrats,
     30% are registered Republicans,
     15% are registered Independent;
By religion:
     61% are born-again Christians,
     of these 16% are evangelical Christians.

of having a dim view of Christian life in America by other pollsters, which lends some credence to his numbers.

Who does attend church in any given week and who does not describes a significant part of America. If only 3.5 percent (Barna's figures) of these are liberals, the direction of American politics would be clear, but churchgoers are far less liberal than the rest of the country. Richard Wirthlin's nationwide polling shows a greater balance between conservatives and liberals, with a large and growing group of moderates. The numbers of self-identified groups are important, but they do not determine the outcome of elections at the presidential or congressional level. Ronald Reagan won the presidency with the liberals still a slightly larger group than conservatives. The weight has moved a bit toward the conservative, according to Wirthlin, but there have been no grand shifts in American political views. What appears to have happened is a grand shift in the way people define liberal, conservative, and middle-of-the-road. A better distinction would be those who are part of the national political movement and those who are not. When the *Washington Post* described the country as "leaning slightly to the right"—in other words, toward the movement—it was correct.

Candidates may win by large margins, although certainly not in 2000 or even in 2004 at the presidential level, but that may have to do with the candidate, the issues at the time, the temper and culture of the country at the moment, as we have seen. The character of the argument, the polemical rather than dialogical tone, has some basis in the history of America as a Protestant nation. Protestantism is less settled than older religions, more disputatious; it is the critical religion: rebellious and contentious from birth. There is no universal Protestantism as Roman Catholicism was the universal Church in the Middle Ages. Protestantism is a second-generation religion that has fostered many denominations and sects within its ranks; it has no mechanism, no central authority like a pope, to resist change. Its ethic is modern, unlike that of many other religions, coming as it does out of Calvin's justification of economic activity once considered sinful. No other religion or congeries of religions found under one political-economic banner could have formed the United States, with its passion for God, freedom, critical thinking, and profit, although not always in that order.

This is a Protestant country comprising millions of people—Jews, Catholics, and so on—who would be surprised to find themselves in the category of Protestants. There are disputes within the category as might be expected. Any consideration of religion in America must include Mormons, members of the Church of Jesus Christ of Latter-Day Saints. About half of the 12 million Mormons live in the United States, where the religion developed. Mormons account for 57 percent of the population of Utah.[8] Methodists, the Southern Baptist Convention, Presbyterians, and Catholics do not think of Mormons as Christians, although many Christians welcome them as a late offshoot of Protestantism. Ronald Reagan, raised in the Disciples of Christ Church, had no problem working with Mormons; his pollster and strategist, Wirthlin, is the son of the former head of the Mormon church and Richard Wirthlin later became an elder in the church.

If Plato were to hold a conversation with the world's Protestants, he would begin with his foundational admonition, "Define your terms!" In Protestantism this problem of definitions appeared soon after Martin Luther nailed his 95 Theses to the gates of the Wittenberg Castle Church:

DISPUTATION OF DOCTOR MARTIN LUTHER ON THE POWER
AND EFFICACY OF INDULGENCES
October 31, 1517
Out of love for the truth and the desire to bring it to light, the following propositions will be discussed at Wittenberg, under the presidency of the Reverend Father Martin Luther, Master of Arts and of Sacred Theology, and Lecturer in Ordinary on the same at that place.

Luther, a Catholic priest, did not intend to start a new church, only to reform the Catholic Church, which was gathering the money to build St. Peter's Basilica in Rome by selling indulgences, guarantees that the giver's generosity would be rewarded in the next world. The reformer soon enough found himself in disagreement not only with

---

[8] American Religious Identification Survey (ARIS), conducted by the City University of New York (2000).

Catholics but with other Protestants. At the end of his life he became convinced of the coming end of the world, and blamed all evils on papists, Muslims, Jews, and uncontrollable Protestants.

The "uncontrollable" Protestant groups went their own way based on Second Corinthians 7:1, which advised Christians to separate themselves from unclean things. They took the idea of unclean things to mean a manner of worship different from what they divined as the true and only way to serve the Lord. And that eventually led to the definitional problem. Adam Nicolson gives an example of the concern with definitions during the English reformation in his book about the writing of the King James Bible, *God's Secretaries*.[9] Bishop Lancelot Andrewes is visiting Henry Barrow in Fleet Prison. They begin arguing over the difference between a schism and a sect, an important question for Barrow, who languishes in prison for no other reason than his separatist views. As Nicolson tells it, the bishop and the prisoner call for a dictionary to settle the issue. It is difficult to imagine Barrow demanding the dictionary. He had been locked away in a cell for three years and undoubtedly expected he would either be executed or left to rot in his cell.

For Protestants of all varieties, not merely those we identify as Puritans, *the word* itself had been elevated to holiness; Protestants had no other anchor, no ritual, no symbols, no crucifixes bearing the image of Christ on the cross. They had only *the word*. No scene could reveal more about the difference between Protestantism and Roman Catholicism. Barrow and Andrewes studied "the etymologies [of "schism" and "sect"], but they could come to no shared conclusion," wrote Nicolson. Three years later, Barrow was executed.

The belief that cost Barrow his life at the beginning of the seventeenth century was rooted in Luther's declaration of almost a century earlier. The battle between Puritan separatists and the Church of England turned as much on the wearing of surplices and the sacraments as on the theology itself, although it is certainly the case that the radical separatists among the Puritans believed they followed a far more intellectualized version of religion and therefore a purer religion than did James I and

---

[9] Published as *Power and Glory* in Great Britain (Harper Collins, 2003).

his church and even its gentle disputants, the accepting Puritans. Barrow had his Second Corinthians, and he and all the rest had the postings at Wittenberg to bolster their views. Luther's work began:

1. *Our Lord and Master Jesus Christ, when He said Poenitentiam agite (Repent ye), willed that the whole life of believers should be repentance.*
2. *This word cannot be understood to mean sacramental penance, i.e., confession and satisfaction, which is administered by the priests.*

Definitions had such power during the centuries immediately following the Reformation that the word "religion" was itself a key issue. When used with the definite article in English it meant Reformed or Protestant, while Spanish Catholics, the force behind the Counter Reformation, used *la religión* to mean Catholicism. The struggle could be summed up in the two conflicting usages of the word. Modern theologians of different denominations or sects appear on the surface to be less confrontational, but the bitterness between the Presbyterians who are willing to accept a gay minister and those who are not threatens to produce a major schism (or new sect?) within the denomination.

The Southern Baptist Convention has to work hard to hold together the very Calvinist, somewhat Calvinist, and anti-Calvinist groups. The anti-Calvinists maintain that God did not decide the fate of human beings on a whim. I asked Ed Hindson, whom Dr. Jerry Falwell's associates suggested as the best person to resolve such questions, to offer some contemporary definitions. Dr. Hindson, who is the assistant chancellor and acting head of Liberty University, was coauthor of *The Fundamentalist Phenomenon*,[10] a book that briefly traced the history of Protestantism.[11] By page 2 the book came to "The Problem of Definitions." The authors accepted George Marsden's definition of fundamentalism as a

---

[10] Ed Dobson and Ed Hindson, *The Fundamentalist Phenomenon*, ed. Jerry Falwell (Garden City, N.Y.: Doubleday Galilee, 1981).

[11] The word "fundamentalism" comes from a twelve-volume series of essays published between 1910 and 1915. Publication of the books, *The Fundamentals: A Testimony to the Truth*, was funded by a grant from Lyman Stewart of the Union Oil Company of California.

"twentieth-century movement closely tied to the revivalist tradition of mainstream evangelical Protestantism that militantly opposed modernist theology and the cultural change associated with it."

Hindson went on to say that "evangelical" is the category that encompasses the three main groups:

Evangelicals are all those who believe in the inerrancy of the Bible, the deity of Christ, and the gospel of salvation; they include charismatics (those who are intent upon restoring the spiritual gifts or *charismata,* like Pentecostals,[12] but also Pat Robertson, Oral Roberts, and John Hegge) and fundamentalists (Jerry Falwell). Hindson puts Jehovah's Witnesses outside the evangelical mainstream, largely because they believe Jesus came back to earth in 1914, which other Christians find heretical.

He said the idea of fundamentalists as mere intellectuals, a view often expressed by people with an experiential orientation, was in error: "Fundamentalists also have a religious experience." But fundamentalists do come out of a more "intellectual" tradition than some of the unaffiliated churches, like Abundant Living Faith. Baptists may live what some people view as a dour life, but fundamentalist Jewish sects live not much differently. The question of who is a fundamentalist leads to an issue that concerns Dr. Hindson very much. He admires Martin E. Marty, the University of Chicago theologian, but he does not accept Marty's characterization of fundamentalism as a way of believing that may be found not only among Christians but among Muslims, Jews, Hindus, Buddhists, Sikhs, Confucians, and so on. In Marty's view fundamentalism is a feisty manner of opposing modernism[13] as it may affect any religion in any culture. Applied to any one religion the definition suffices, but Hindson has a point: as an all-inclusive category it does not serve very well.

---

12 Pentecostal, Nazarene, and other charismatics that trace their origins through the holiness movement back to John Wesley, the eighteenth-century English revivalist and founder of Methodism. Pentecostals connected to a major group, Assemblies of God or Foursquare Gospel, and those who appear to have adopted most of the views of Pentecostal religion but remain independent offer scathing comments about one another.

13 My paraphrase of far more complex definitions in the five-volume *Fundamentalism Project*, ed. R. Scott Appleby and Martin E. Marty (University of Chicago Press, 1991).

Definitions, which so concerned the English at the beginning of the seventeenth century, may yet prove to be the most important aspect of the relation of religion to politics in the United States. Mennonites, whose name derives from Menno Simons (1496–1561), are Protestants related to the Amish, who are also descended theologically from Simons. They differed with Catholics and other Protestants on the question of infant baptism, and in the early United States on slavery and war, which they, along with their relatives the Quakers, opposed. The Anabaptists, as they were called somewhat disparagingly, favored the separation of church and state, an idea that had little currency in the English colonies. Which political party appeals now to people who do not accept the idea of infant baptism and also oppose war and favor the separation of church and state becomes a matter of determining who is a Protestant among Protestants.

Nor will the word "evangelical" suffice to distinguish Democrats from Republicans. Baptist may describe a Republican's religion today, especially in the South, but in the 1930s Baptists had a profound influence on the formation of the New Deal. And definitions become an even murkier problem when the conversation moves from theologians to members of various congregations, from a political party to a national movement. Differences among the leadership of the church groups (a phrase used here to avoid the denomination-sect confusion) do not necessarily appear among the members of the congregations. Most lay people have only the vaguest understanding of the doctrinal questions that separate one church from the next. Without knowing much of anything about religion, tens of millions of Americans are eager to talk about it. They drift from one church to another, liberal to conservative, exegetical to experiential, for reasons other than theology, and few if any would be so willing as poor Barrow to suffer and die for theological reasons. Instead, they find themselves comfortable within the general direction of a national movement that does not have one leader, but many; not one center, but many. "In my father's house are many mansions" (John 14:2).

The ease of shifting from one church to another and with it the possibility of a diverse and inclusive movement in a Protestant nation comes of the very nature of Protestantism. The sects and denominations lack any sense of organization, any common view of how a person should live and what will happen to that person after death. In 1979, Jerry Falwell tried to overcome the question by creating Moral Majority, which is often described as a "fundamentalist" Christian organization, almost the exact opposite of Falwell's idea. Falwell's ambition was to lead a national movement. He wanted it to include fundamentalists and also all other evangelical Christians, Catholics, Jews, and so on. Falwell himself came out of a mixed religious and irreligious background. His grandfather had been an atheist, his father an agnostic, and the Protestant members of his family belonged to several denominations. It was all but inevitable that Falwell would see that the strength of any national movement that was both conservative and religious had to come out of union rather than competition among the denominations and sects.

The key problem for him and others, like Rev. D. James Kennedy of Coral Ridge Presbyterian Church in Fort Lauderdale, Florida, was the separation of church and state. Without overcoming the separation, there could be a national political movement, but the movement would only include religion, it would not be the way to a "Godly" nation. The movement could not be subsumed under even the broadest view of religion. Falwell and his friends struggled against an old American solution to the problem of government and religion. By the time of the writing of the Constitution, the tension among the denominations was great enough that the founders had to choose between the separation of church and state or no state at all. Efforts by members of one church to proselytize members of another, disputes within the denominations, the splintering of the denominations into sects, guaranteed American pluralism, made the history into innumerable confluences instead of the one great religious-political-social river imagined by the Puritans. To be an American was to be a Protestant in the sense of ever increasing diversity serving as the unending commonality of social, economic, political, and intellectual practices. Falwell knew enough about American history and politics to understand that the religious beliefs he espoused could not affect the direction of the country unless some unifying and enduring idea could be found. What he had to do was wean the United States away from its multifaceted Protestant character, find the one idea that would unite all the separate churches, make one extended family out of millions of women and men whose only commonality was their difference one from the other. God had not been a sufficient unifier since Wittenberg. Falwell chose the word "moral," which is so variously defined that almost anyone could subscribe to it.

He took his word and set out to create a faction that would last until the millennium. It held together through eight years of Reagan, and was not disbanded until 1989, when Falwell said the work of the organization had been done and he could spend more time with his Liberty University. Pat Robertson started his Christian Coalition the same year. After the 2004 national elections, Falwell started a new organization, the Moral Majority Coalition. He allied it with other well-known Christian conservatives, including James Dobson of Focus on the Family. The founding of the new organization came at a difficult time for Falwell. He had severe health problems. His many projects had cost too much money. And after making a foolish statement about homosexuals and abortionists causing the catastrophe of 9/11, it became difficult for Falwell to raise money. He could not carry on alone. He turned projects over to his sons and his old friends and companions in the complex of Falwell organizations. Falwell had been closer to a throne of Protestant leadership than any person in recent years, with the possible exception of the Reverend Billy Graham. But he was weary: the "majority" eased into a "coalition." The change of names indicated a new recognition of the lack of any hope of a center. The organization no longer had a "pope" in Falwell, but was a coalition run by "presbyters." With or without him there was still a national movement that was both Protestant in the American sense of diversity and yet unified, bound not by God or Jesus, but as we shall see, by the tides of loneliness and death.

Seven

APOCALYPSE

Will there still be a world when I'm seventy?
—MICHAEL, AGE NINE, 2006

On December 2, 1942, under the old West Stands of Stagg Field at the University of Chicago at a little after three o'clock in the afternoon, the pile of uranium-235 inside a structure built of graphite blocks went "critical." It began producing neutrons as fast as they were absorbed by the surrounding material. Enrico Fermi, Leo Szilard, and their colleagues had produced the first sustained man-made nuclear chain reaction. The world would never be the same.

Eight years later, as a student at the university, I visited my math professor in the office he shared with Fermi. All the walls were covered with blackboards and all the blackboards were filled with mathematics beyond my imagination. In those years we climbed the stairs to a lab in the old West Stands for physics class, thinking not about Avogadro and Huygens, but about the men who had done the famous work in the great room below and how they must have felt, what they must have thought when the pile went critical. Were they afraid? Szilard or Fermi? Did they know what they had loosed upon the world? By the time the Manhattan Project produced the great explosion in the desert of New Mexico, the director of the project knew the answer. J. Robert Oppenheimer said a line from the Bhagavad Gita, "I am become death, the destroyer of worlds." In November 1950, while I labored over the physical proofs of common things and the grass on Stagg Field turned to brown, the United States exploded the first thermonuclear weapon at Eniwetok Atoll.

The Blackness of a Thousand Suns

In 1852, William Thomson, Baron Kelvin, a Scottish physicist, proposed a rational scientific theory of the end of the world. Entropy, from the Greek for "transformation," describes the inevitable equalizing of heat throughout the universe until it nears absolute zero, when entropy stops in the icy end of all movement. Thomson wrote: ". . . within a finite period to come, the earth must . . . be unfit for the habitation of man. . . ." The baron was a man of enormous hubris. He disputed Darwin, arguing that there simply hadn't been enough time for evolution to have taken place. He said airplanes would never fly. But Thomson made clear and useful the Second Law of Thermodynamics, the conservation of energy. He also gave a name to the end of the world through entropy: Heat Death. Unlike frauds and fools, Baron Kelvin did not predict the day, month, and year on which the Heat Death would occur. Entropy is a slow business; sure, but slow.

By 2000 it was becoming increasingly clear that Thomson's mid-nineteenth-century prediction did not take into account man's own ability to make the planet uninhabitable. Human beings were burning up the earth, creating a molecular smoke that retained a daily more destructive heat; they were poisoning the ground and water on which many species lived, cutting down the fecund and refreshing forests, spreading disease at an unstoppable rate. Over it all there loomed the energy of the atom threatening a different kind of Heat Death, this one a hell of nuclear fires. At the current burn rate the reign of carbon-based life on the planet will not last long enough to test Baron Kelvin's theory.

Thomson's science did little to disturb the way the British and others conceived of the world. Soon enough, intellectuals were chuckling over Lord Keynes's brilliant riposte to the idea of economics in "the long run." Keynes wrote, "In the long run we are all dead. Economists set themselves too easy, too useless a task if in tempestuous seasons they can only tell us that when the storm is long past the ocean is flat again." There is no common ground among economists, scientists, and theologians about the end. Scientists do not concede a return to the status quo ante: Thomson saw the earth cooling enough for human life and then becoming too cold for humans to survive. Theologians do not concede that we will all be dead "in the long run" (they see the long run as eternity in heaven, purgatory, or hell). The difference may be no more than a matter of definition. Scientists, economists, and theologians all have different definitions of both death and the long run. Most agree, however, that the world as we know it is neither safe nor durable, meaning that something outside the world must be found as a substitute for our present earthly life. The scientists look to distant planets, solar systems, galaxies, even alternative universes. It is a difficult task they set for themselves: one generation passing on the search to the next. Theologians for the most part look to predictions of an afterlife that were first offered between 2,000 and 6,000 years ago.

> *Now I lay me down to sleep,*
> *I pray the Lord my soul to keep.*
> *If I should die before I wake,*
> *I pray the Lord my soul to take.*

> —CHILD'S BEDTIME PRAYER, EIGHTEENTH CENTURY

The initial fears of the end of the world were no different from the fear of sleeping that stays with us from the beginning of consciousness until the end, the final sleep from which we do not awaken, the endless night, which is for us the end of the world. So it is with the sunrise, the analogue of waking. There was a time when human beings could not be sure the sun would rise. Even now we wonder. "If I should die before I wake. . . ." In the earliest societies people gave the sun primary place. If it did not rise one morning there would be perpetual darkness, they knew—the end of the world. The ancient Aztecs described the history of creations by the names of the suns. Ours is the fifth and final sun; its calendrical name is 4 *ollin*, 4 movement. It will end in earthquake and fire. The Aztecs waited. They sacrificed human beings to be certain the sun would rise again the next day, they staved off the end of the world with hearts and blood, with magic. They had many gods, a grand pantheon, but they were not fools; they placed their bets on the sun. The sacrifice of a human was a curious kind of utilitarianism: the death of one for the good of the many.

In addition to the Aztec Tonatiuh, there was Aten, the sun god of the Egyptians, and even the Sun King of the French. In the Book of Genesis: "And God said, 'Let there be light': and there was light.

"And God saw the light, that it was good. . . ."

Sun.

In the ancient world nothing terrified people more than a full solar eclipse. "And the sun stood still," we read in Joshua. Revelation contains numerous references to the sun and to suns. It is a late work. The sun has become a metaphor; the end of the world is a dreaming. We know now that the end, if it comes quickly, will be caused by nuclear weapons, each one exploding "with the light of a thousand suns." At Hiroshima the horror was the heat, the nuclear burning, but there was something else, not light but darkness, nowhere better told than in the now classic novel about Hiroshima by Masuji Ibuse, *Black Rain,* in which the narrator, recalling his diary of the day of the bombing, writes of the cloud he sees after the flash:

> *Although the cloud seemed at first glance to be motionless, it was by no means so. The head of the mushroom would billow out first to the east, then to the west, then out to the east again; each time, some part or other of its body would emit a fierce light, in ever-changing shades of red, purple, lapis lazuli, or green. And all the time it went on boiling out unceasingly from within. Its stalk, like a twisted veil of fine cloth, went on swelling busily too. The cloud loomed over the city as though waiting to pounce, and my whole body seemed to shrink from it. I wondered if my legs were not going to give out on me.*
>
> *"That over there, underneath the cloud—it looks like a shower, doesn't it?" said a polite, woman's voice. . . .*

I screwed up my eyes and gazed into the sky, but the impression was less of a shower than of a dense mass of small particles. I wondered if it could be a whirlwind. It was like nothing that I had ever seen before. I wondered, my flesh shrinking at the idea, what would happen if it came in this direction and we were rained on by those particles.

He had seen the black rain, the mix of mud and ash that rose into the sky, darkened the world, and fell to earth again to poison and burn. A few pages later, the narrator rubs what he thinks is some dirt off his face, and it comes away like pieces of parchment. It is his skin. He looks around to see the others who are still living, walking naked in the street, the clothing burned off their bodies. He sees puffed-up faces, hair falling out, hideous burns, bodies covered entirely with blood, large pieces of skin hanging like wet newspapers. He sees dead gardens, burned trees; bridges, houses, large buildings gone, disappeared; and then comes the terrible thirst that drives the victims to drinking radioactive water. Yet Ibuse is not writing of the end of the world. In the last pages of the novel the narrator sees water weed growing in a pond and he hopes he will see a rainbow prophesying the cure of atomic sickness in a loved one. The optimism of the water weed and its purple blossom fades away in the last line—he writes of the hope for the curative rainbow, "He knew all the while it could never come true."

The world has not yet ended; Ibuse is neither optimistic nor pessimistic about the future. More than thirty years after the event the author could not say with any confidence that the black rain would not fall again. He wrote during the Cold War, when the world considered MAD (mutual assured destruction) the best route to safety. Ibuse's novel came out twenty years after Karl Jaspers, a psychiatrist and philosopher, published *The Atom Bomb and the Future of Man*,[1] a book that remains one of the most thoughtful considerations of the problem, and it was prescient. Considering atomic weapons in the context of the larger question of the role of reason in historical analysis, Jaspers quotes Max Weber: " 'You can't reason with warriors for faith.' In other words,

---

[1] Chicago: University of Chicago Press, 1961.

politics has a fundamentally different import when there is no place for reason." He worries over democracy: "The trouble is that democracy, which is to make the people rational, presupposes a rational people."

In the final chapter of the book Jaspers, unable to arrive at a psychiatric or philosophical solution, accepts the nightmarish logic of his time. He sees no technological "escape routes." He cannot imagine a cure for radioactive sickness. He turns to "a balance of terror." Since the weapons will never disappear, he proposes more weapons, not fewer: "the less the terror, the more the danger of war." Writing almost half a century ago, before George W. Bush refused to consider the existence of global warming despite the scientific evidence, before the other dangers recognized by most reasonable people in the twenty-first century, Jaspers wrote, "Mankind will not commit suicide."

Had he ended on that confident note about man, the book would have been a paean to rationality, but Jaspers could not find the solace he sought for himself and his readers in human rationality. Like the fearful in our time, he looked for some reason for living that was beyond life itself, some immortality beyond works and generations. Without a sense of eternity, Jaspers said, there was no reason not to commit suicide. There had to be a reason for living, and it could not be other than eternity. He quoted Jesus: "Behold, the kingdom of God is within you." We are left with the implication that without a belief in eternity humankind will commit suicide. Facing the question of the end of the world, the psychiatrist-philosopher—mentor to Hannah Arendt, author of books on Kant, Jesus, Buddha, and Socrates, as well as psychiatry—concluded that we must go outside the world to save it.

Jaspers lived through the worst, most murderous years of the twentieth century, the worst decades for the sheer numbers of people murdered and killed in wars in the history of the world. The trajectory of history told him of yet worse to come. For the first time, technology had provided the Frankenstein species with the ability to end the world, not with a whimper as T. S. Eliot had so glibly said, but with a bang no longer beyond imagining. Jaspers had begun his book by saying that political thinking had no place in the realm of extremes, and he ended it with an appeal to eternity to save the world. In the mouths of evangelists it became the American argument.

Unthinkable

Shortly after dawn on October 14, 1962, Major Richard Heyser climbed into the cockpit of his plane at Edwards Air Force Base near Los Angeles and took off on a long semicircular flight plan that would bring him to the Caribbean in the early morning hours. At 7:31 A.M., flying at 72,000 feet, he headed due north on a course that would take his U-2 spy plane 60 miles west of Havana. He began his pass over the island at exactly 7:37. The 300-pound camera aboard the soaring aircraft began clicking off film. It would expose more than a thousand frames in the time it took the U-2 to cross the narrow western part of the island. Heyser was prepared to take evasive action if he saw the white contrail of a Russian SAM-2 surface-to-air missile rising from the island at 2,000 miles an hour aimed by ground crews at his unarmed plane, but the Cuban radar had either failed to find him or had located him too late for missiles to be launched. A few minutes later Heyser landed at McCoy Air Force Base in central Florida, and the film was taken out of the camera and flown to the CIA's photo interpretation center, where it was developed and interpreted.

The prints and interpretations were delivered to McGeorge Bundy, President Kennedy's national security advisor. Early on the morning of the sixteenth Bundy brought the photographs to the president, who was still wearing his pajamas as he looked at the disturbing prints. On an island only 90 miles off the coast of Florida, the Russians were installing missiles capable of carrying nuclear warheads. Then began a contest of nerve between Kennedy and Soviet Premier Nikita Khrushchev. Aerial reconnaissance photographs showed Soviet ships carrying offensive missiles and nuclear warheads in the Atlantic Ocean presumably headed for Cuba. American missiles in Turkey, Strategic Air Command B-52 bombers carrying nuclear weapons, submarines armed with missiles tipped with nuclear warheads, and intercontinental ballistic missiles were aimed at preselected Soviet military and civilian targets. Aircraft were moved into position to destroy the Soviet ships in the western Atlantic. Other planes targeted sites in Cuba. They would take out the SAM-2 sites first. Preparations were made to defend West Berlin against attack by Soviet bloc forces.

Kennedy established a blockade line around Cuba and warned

Khrushchev to turn the Cuba-bound ships around before they crossed the blockade line. And the world waited. For the first time since the bomb burst over Hiroshima, it was possible that the world would suffer a nuclear holocaust. Only seventeen years after the first use of an atomic weapon, many people believed the end of civilization was only days, perhaps hours, away: the blast damage, the panic among those still living, and the vast cloud of radiation released into the atmosphere by the discharge of the complete Soviet and American nuclear arsenals would almost certainly make large parts of the planet uninhabitable.

The standoff went on for days. Neither side blinked. On October 22 at 7 P.M. President Kennedy went on national television to make America and the world aware of the missiles in Cuba and the establishment of a naval blockade around the island. The next day U.S. Ambassador to the United Nations Adlai E. Stevenson displayed copies of the U-2 photographs to the Security Council. The day after that the Soviet freighters came to a stop at the U.S. blockade line. On October 25 the Soviet freighters turned around and headed home. Fidel Castro had urged Khrushchev to order a first strike with nuclear weapons if the United States invaded Cuba. The cornerstone of the movement had been laid: nuclear war was no longer unthinkable.

The Loophole

In 1957 while Karl Jaspers was writing his book, a group of Protestant ministers in New York City appealed to the young evangelist, Billy Graham to come to the city to help them in their work. Graham came. The advertising agency Bozell, Jacobs publicized the visit for him:

> *You're born.*
> *You suffer.*
> *You die.*
>
> *Fortunately, there's a loophole.*
> — BILLY GRAHAM CRUSADE IN CENTRAL PARK

In 2005 the city refused to allow Graham to conduct his "crusade" in Central Park. His staff moved it to the borough of Queens, a subway ride from the center of the city, but a borough filled with African Americans and immigrants, many of whom were likely to attend the revival meetings. Similar communities in the Bronx, Brooklyn, and Manhattan would have to ride the subway system for as long as two hours to hear Graham in person, but the tiny evangelical community of New York City in 1957 had grown to more than a million by 2005. He would have no shortage of congregants.

The loophole Graham promised differed very little from the eternity of Karl Jaspers. Rather than tracing a long and sometimes arcane route through philosophy and psychiatry, Graham began with Jesus. The crowds at his revival meeting of 1957 grew out of the realization that the apocalypse was no longer merely a metaphor; the end of the world was more likely after 1945 than it had been at any time since the Black Death of the fourteenth century killed a third of the population of Europe. If, as has often been said, there are no atheists in foxholes, there were also no atheists in bomb shelters during the Cold War. Recognizing the opportunity early in his career, Graham did what Jaspers could not, he connected great numbers of people, millions, with the concept of eternity. He was a revivalist walking in the footsteps of George Whitefield, Peter Cartwright, and Charles Grandison Finney, three careers that shed some light on the politics of heaven in the twenty-first century.

Cartwright received his "exhorter's license" from the Methodist Church in 1802. He was sixteen years old, with little formal education, but how he could preach! He traveled the middle of the country—Indiana, Illinois, Ohio, and south to Kentucky and Tennessee, drawing huge crowds everywhere. Cartwright did not separate his revivalist spirit from politics, which led to a second career. He was elected to the Illinois statehouse twice, and aspired to more influential posts, but when he ran for the U.S. Congress from his Illinois district in 1846, the revivalist lost to a man who never claimed membership in any church, Abraham Lincoln.

Finney also had a second career, as president of Oberlin College in Ohio. He left behind several influential books, including *Lectures on Revivals of Religion*, according to which Graham's crusade in New York should not have been successful. Finney wrote in his concluding point in Lecture IX : "It is easy to see why revivals do not prevail in a great city. How can they? Just look at God's witnesses, and see what they are testifying to.

"They seem to be agreed together to tempt the Spirit of the Lord, and to lie to the Holy Ghost! They make their vows to God, to consecrate themselves wholly to Him, then they go bowing down at the shrine of fashion—and next they wonder why there are no revivals!" He went on to say of the city folk: "They declare by their conduct that there is no truth in the Gospel. Heaven might weep and hell rejoice to see this. Oh, how guilty!"

Finney concluded his lecture with the same point about Christians not being truly born again or filled with the Holy Spirit that Billy Graham made 180 years later: "They testify by their lives, that if they make it a profession and live a moral life, that is religion enough. Oh what a doctrine of devils is that! It is enough to ruin the whole human race!"

Finney's *Lectures* gave his readers a manual on every aspect of a revival meeting, from how to organize it to what to say and how to make it emotional rather than purely intellectual. Jonathan Edwards said his sermons flatly, but Finney, who was interested in singing and law as well as preaching, shouted, cajoled, whispered, and sang. He put on a show for Jesus. He had a heavenly message, and an earthly promise to bolster it: if all Christians could be trusted, did business on principle, voted only for honest men of good morals, they would "run away with the business of the city" and, applying the same behavior to politics, "sway the destinies of nations." Conservatives now praise Finney for his support of business and his Wilsonian ideas for changing the world. Liberals point to Charles Finney the abolitionist and defender of the equality of women.

Only at the end of his series of lectures did Finney deal with the revivalist's frustration. He described what was then and continues to be the geography of left and right in America. The great urban centers belong to the left and the rest of the country, from the suburbs to the farms, Finney's conquerable world, belongs to the right. The Civil War, which brought a temporary halt to revivalism's great sixty-year run in the nineteenth century, was in one respect a war of the urban North against the rural South. The North had its share of farms and the South its Atlanta and New Orleans, but the ethos of one was urban and the other rural.

Finney had shaken the hands of the small businessmen and "dirt farmers." He grasped what Gordon Wood said was the radicalism of the American Revolution,[2] the shift away from the power of the holders of vast farms and forests to the owners of tiny shops and stores and service businesses. He had read the boomtown advertisements touting imaginary places of opportunity out West, always farther west. He knew the heart and soul of the country as it had been defined economically and politically by Calvinism, slavery, Watt's improvement to the steam engine, Whitney's cotton gin, and the daring embrace of the Holy Spirit as the core of religion by John Wesley, the eighteenth-century founder of Methodism. Finney's preaching loosened the strictures of Calvinist predestination. He told his audiences that their obedience to the teachings of the Gospel would lead them to salvation; everyone could be saved, if only they came to Jesus. He moved the center of man's destiny from the inexorable decision of God to the inconstant soul of man. It accorded perfectly with the American's new sense of himself as free and capable of determining his own future.

Strict Calvinism, especially the doctrine of predestination, was not palatable in nineteenth-century America. Finney's refusal to accept predestination made him, according to many of his critics, a theological Arminian;[3] even so, his influence, like that of Whitefield, is found in all contemporary revivals. Finney codified the practice of revivalism in 1835, and there have been only technological (mainly by Dwight L.

---

[2] *The Radicalism of the American Revolution* (New York: Knopf, 1992).

[3] The following, from the Thomas Jackson 1872 edition of the complete works, is the Arminian John Wesley's description of the difference between Calvinists and Arminians:

"The errors charged upon these (usually termed *Arminians*) by their opponents, are five: (1.) That they deny original sin; (2.) That they deny justification by faith; (3.) That they deny absolute predestination; (4.) That they deny the grace of God to be irresistible; and, (5.) That they affirm, a believer may fall from grace.

"With regard to the two first of these charges, they plead, Not Guilty. They are entirely false. No man that ever lived, not John Calvin himself, ever asserted either original sin, or justification by faith, in more strong, more clear and express terms, than [Jacobes] Arminius has done."

The five points of Calvinism (the acronym is TULIP) are: total depravity, unconditional election, limited atonement, irresistible grace, and perseverance of the saints.

Moody) changes since. Although Finney was a Yankee abolitionist, he is a heroic figure in the eyes of Protestants across the political spectrum: Jerry Falwell and Billy Graham, as well as the liberal Pastor Jim Wallis. Finney came to preaching out of a religious experience. He said the Holy Spirit passed through his body: "I could feel the impression, like a wave of electricity, going through and through me. Indeed it seemed to come in waves of liquid love, for I could not express it in any other way." And it happened at an opportune time.

At the beginning the nineteenth century all the necessary pieces were in place for an industrial revolution and the making of the country that Finney knew and that today remains essentially unchanged in its religious and political geography. The great waves of immigration of the nineteenth and twentieth centuries only confirmed Finney's insight about the political geography of America. The Catholics and Jews settled in the urban centers of the North, while the South, rural and embittered by the Civil War, took on its enduring political and religious character. In the 1950s, the new highway system made it possible for city dwellers who identified more with Finney's audience than with the urbane world to abandon the cities for the suburbs and then the exurbs; like farmers in the seventeenth and eighteenth centuries, they did business in the city but did not live, pray, or raise children there.

How was it then that in sixteen weeks in 1957 in New York City, the largest urban center in America and one of the most cosmopolitan cities on earth, more than 2 million people attended Graham's Crusade, and in 1991, at least 250,000 people went to a revival in Central Park to hear him? George Whitefield had famously drawn 20,000 of the 700,000 residents of London to a revival in the eighteenth century; Billy Graham pulled a slightly higher percentage. The North Carolina farm boy was famous by then. He had made his mark preaching in a tent in Los Angeles in 1949. William Randolph Hearst noticed him, liked his politics and his preaching, and directed Hearst newspapers around the country to make a national figure of the tall young man with the long, sharply chiseled face, backwoods sincerity in his voice, and fire in his words. Graham could preach, but he was no saint. He was always a man of the time, one who took the American pulse before he spoke. He was a red-baiter, a supporter of Senator Joseph McCarthy; later he agreed with Richard Nixon's anti-Semitism, and he preached the apocalypse long before Tim LaHaye made his fortune with the end-time series. But Graham discovered something about the American psyche—perhaps consciously, perhaps it had welled up out of his deeply held feelings: the fear of death had been transformed by the bombing of Hiroshima. His ability to connect emotionally to the new fear of collective death made him famous, which is not to say that he did not believe what he preached, only that he had found his message and his voice.

A year after his 1957 triumph in New York City, Graham preached a defining sermon in Charlotte, North Carolina. The *Charlotte Observer*, taken with the national success of a native son, proudly transcribed his sermons every evening and reproduced them in full in the newspaper the next day. On October 11, 1958, according to the newspaper account, he preached on the end of the world. What he said, in his mix of love and hellfire, epitomizes the mix of Christianity, eschatology,[4] and politics that gave birth to the religious right in America. By 2005 the movement was full-grown, and Graham claimed he had never been political, except for one meeting with Richard Nixon. These excerpts from the sermon in Charlotte might lead one to think otherwise:

> *All of this scientific advance and scientific achievement of the past few years has brought about a discussion all over the world in intellectual circles about the possibility of the end of the world as we know it. Almost all agree everywhere about the possibility of the end of the world. Some of the titles of the current best-sellers recently listed in* The New York Times *book review section I am going to read to you. Here they are: NO PLACE TO HIDE; MUST WE HIDE?; THERE WILL BE NO TIME; MANUAL FOR SURVIVAL; FEAR, WAR, AND THE BOMB; MUST DESTRUCTION BE OUR DESTINY?; AFTER DOOM—WHAT? . . . since 1945 a five-foot shelf of books have been written about the physical destruction of the world.*
>
> *Our philosophers today—many of them—are admitting the*

---

[4] Theology having to do with death and judgment, from the Greek for "last," *eskhatos*.

possibility. Bertrand N. Russell recently said he would not give a fifty-fifty chance that one person would be alive on this planet forty years from today. Our political leaders are talking about the end of the world. An American senator said, "A war of annihilation seems to be inevitable." Former President Truman said, "Fantastic new weapons are available which could destroy civilization." Sir Winston Churchill said some time ago as he threw up his hands in despair, "Our problems are beyond us."

Science is predicting it. A German scientist some time ago said, "It is now possible to depopulate the entire earth." Rear Admiral Ellis(?),[5] our wartime chief of naval intelligence, said some time ago in an article entitled "Wartime Weapons, More Deadly Than One Atom"—I am going to read it to you, here is what he said, "There are today in the arsenal of several of the great powers, other absolute weapons besides the atomic bomb, physical and psychological weapons more devastating than the atom. They are capable of exterminating the last vestige of human, animal, and vegetable life from the face of the earth. This is not a prediction of horrors to come," said the admiral. "These weapons exist now. They are being manufactured right now while you are reading these words. They are not an American monopoly. Several nations are known to have them, and to be making them, and to be proving them. Furthermore, unlike the atomic bomb, they are of such a nature that smaller nations with limited industrial facilities are in a position to develop them." In other words, our leading scientists are saying today that there are weapons now in existence that could be unleashed to bring about the destruction and the end of the world system as we know it tonight.

Contemporary theology also teaches the return of Christ, or it teaches the end of the world. There is a return of the study of eschatology today.

Ladies and gentlemen, on the dark horizon of the present moment I see no other hope. There is really no other possibility I see

---

[5] He probably meant Rear Admiral Ellis M. Zacharias, who was deputy chief of Naval Intelligence during World War II. The question mark in parentheses appeared in the newspaper report of the sermon.

at the moment for solving the problems of the world than the coming again of Jesus Christ. The world is in darkness, and the darkness is growing blacker—frustration, confusion, the world on the horns of a dilemma.

The communist is offering the world a hope. The communist says there is something wrong with the world. The communist says, "We are going to rebuild the world. We are going to bring the kingdom in without God." But Jesus says the kingdom will never come until the Prince of Peace has His rightful place as King of kings and Lord of lords in the hearts of men. Communism will never bring it. The United Nations will never bring it. It will come only at the climactic point in history when Christ Himself shall take over and take control. Then shall the kingdom of God come.

Yes, the Bible teaches that there is coming a climactic point in history. The end of the world system as we know it is definitely on the horizon. How long will it be? I do not know. When it will be I do not pretend to know. It may be a thousand years; it may be two thousand years. I do not know. I only know that this book is filled with predictions of the end of the world. (Apparently holds up a Bible) This book is filled with hope that Christ will come back again. Jesus said, "As it was in the days of [Noah],⁶ so shall it [also be] in the days [of the coming] of the Son of man" [Luke 17:26]. We are told in Scripture that the world was destroyed before, and that conditions prevailing at that time were to prevail again toward the climactic point in history. In other words, history will repeat itself.

In 2005, in Queens, Graham preached for three nights; on the third night he returned to the theme of the end of the world. He saw signs, he said, murders of children; the end was coming near. In interviews before the crusade he spoke of his own death, his expectation of heaven. Although he had not preached about poverty during most of his career, as he neared the end of his life, he said poverty was the problem that bothered him most. There was a loophole, as the advertisement said,

---

6 The newspaper printed material in brackets where it was unsure the transcription was perfect. There is no record of disagreement with the transcription.

and Graham was apparently looking for it. Like Pat Robertson of the *700 Club* and other evangelicals, he spoke proudly of the millions his organization had raised for victims of the tsunami in Southeast Asia, then as if he had heard the hubris in his voice, he said what a small amount it was, a mere pittance. He told interviewer Larry King, a Jew, how much he regretted his anti-Semitic remarks, how he had never believed what he said about Jews.[7] He distanced himself from his son, who attacked both Muslims and Jews, saying neither group would get to heaven. "God loves you," Graham said again and again, denying everything about predestination, sending Calvin to the trash heap.

If Graham did not lead the entire evangelical movement, he epitomized it. His turn away from anti-Semitism was echoed in the evangelical profession of love for Israel. Graham, the young preacher who appeared like a whirlwind out of World War II, carried the two terrible human burdens that came out of the war: the existence of the bomb, and the Holocaust. The Hebrew word for the Nazi attempt to destroy the Jews *shoah* (catastrophe) had a more apt synonym in English: holocaust. It was an old word, made of the Greek words for "whole" and "fire." "Holocaust" meant the consumption of the whole in fire. It had been limited to animal sacrifice until an English writer used the word in 1942 about Nazi ambitions for the Jews. The holocaust was as real as the atom bomb. Together they gave the credence of history to end-time thinking. What could happen had already happened. There were no limits.

Death and the Crusader

In Europe the reality of the Holocaust (after the end of the war it became a proper noun) produced an antireligious, if not atheistic majority. Albert Camus made the reason clear enough in his essay, "The Unbeliever and the Christians."[8] He spoke of the forces of terror and the forces of dialogue. Children were murdered by Nazi soldiers

---

[7] King did not raise the logical question: was Graham lying then or now?

[8] *Resistance, Rebellion, and Death* (New York: Knopf, 1961).

only seconds after they were born to women in concentration camps. There was no possibility that the newborns had sinned. If God was both omniscient and omnipotent, then He knew of the murder of innocents and permitted it. God failed even to meet the rules of morality we demand of humans, the Europeans said, and chose not to believe in such a God. They denied the concept of original sin. Barring the Calvinist idea of total depravity based on the sin committed in Eden, theodicy was no longer possible. Europe had witnessed massive failures of religion for many centuries: Christians had been killing each other with savage regularity since long before the Reformation tore apart what had been the universal church of Rome. There were rumors that the Roman Catholic Church had been complicit in the Holocaust.

At the center of Camus's response to the Holocaust, history showed the problem of limits had no solution. In 1949, the same year that Billy Graham came to prominence in Los Angeles, Samuel Beckett, in Paris, offered his response to the world revealed by the Second World War in *The Unnameable*: ". . . you must go on, I can't go on, I'll go on." Americans did not suffer Beckett's conflict between existence and oblivion. There had been an attack on the U.S. fleet at Pearl Harbor, many Americans had died fighting in Europe and Asia, but a foreign war had not come home. The United States emerged from the war as the most religious developed country on earth. The existentialist's response to dread did not cross the Atlantic.

Graham preached the American response. Instead of a universe in which no possible system of thought, no order except that of the physical universe existed, Graham found order and reason in the Bible. He chose a path exactly opposite that of the Europeans. In response to the American idea of collective death, a holocaust made of Hiroshimas without end, he held out no more hope for the world than the Europeans, perhaps less. He expected the apocalypse, he had no doubt about it, but there was a loophole. It was called heaven. And there was only one way to find it: Americans had to come to Jesus.

He called the meetings "crusades." The choice of such a bellicose term was not without meaning. He could have said "revivals." Eisenhower had used the word "crusade" to describe the allied war effort in Europe, an effort that eventually included what the military called "terror bombing" of civilians. The First Crusade, at the close of the eleventh century, did not begin as a holy war; it was political, with the church in a supporting role. The Church of Rome first promised eternal life to a crusader who died in battle, then remitted the sins of the surviving crusaders as well as the fallen. The enemy was Islam. By definition a holy war, a crusade cannot exist without an object, some evil, an enemy, which raises the question of the identity of the villain in Graham's crusade. Whom did Jesus say to kill? Should Jesus, because he spoke of a metaphorical war between two kings in Luke 14:31, be thought of as a crusader? And if so, was Jesus a vengeful leader of killers, one who fomented the slaughter of innocents, which has always been a part of holy war? Why attach the word to the work of "the Prince of Peace"?

Clearly, there had been a change in theology after World War II, a change even more dramatic than the revision of his views of human beings that came to Sigmund Freud during World War I. Freud saw a vicious streak in the character of human beings that led them first to religion and then to terrible wars, mass killings, like those occurring on the fields of France and Belgium. Graham saw something else: "the imminence of the eschaton." The end of human history, the eschaton, was no longer a metaphor predicted by John in Revelation. The final book of the New Testament, rejected by many Catholics as inauthentic prophecy, became the centerpiece of theology, Hell had not lost its horror, "the worm"[9] had not disappeared from the afterlife, but the punishment of individuals had become the punishment of the world. Graham had chosen the word "crusade" carefully; history does not record a crusade of one—it is a mass movement: the world's response to the punishment of the world.

Graham was not alone in his view of the role of nuclear weapons. On July 3, 2005, Dr. Ed Hindson, the theologian who heads Jerry Falwell's Liberty University, preached on television and the Internet on nuclear war. When he and I talked in April of that year, Hindson was polite, well-spoken, but somewhat different from the man I saw on

---

[9] Mark 9:46, "Where their worm dieth not, and the fire is not quenched."

television, especially on the subject of nuclear war and the eschaton. He said: "We do not like to think about nuclear war. No right-thinking person wants the world to end in a nuclear explosion. I don't believe the end is right around the corner." Yet, there was the issue of imminence. "Cooler heads prevailed in the Cold War," he said. "With Moslem extremists . . . if they had a nuclear weapon they would probably use it." When he preached on television, Hindson, a tight-faced man who looks younger than his sixty years, held a Bible in one hand and offered a sermon both exegetical and hortatory. He spoke of nuclear war, the horrors of it, the lasting effects on the land, and then he said that it had been predicted in Revelation. He preached on the beasts shooting fire from both ends, comparing them to modern weapons, giving John the power of technological prophecy. Hindson spoke of the thunders God told John not to reveal because human beings could not bear to hear of them. And then Hindson, who often traveled with Tim LaHaye and preached with him, said, "Jesus is coming soon." For those who rejected God, he said, there was only "eternal doom." Like many evangelicals, Hindson vacillates on the timing of the end of the world. They are all certain it will start in the Middle East, which is not a bad bet, given the history of moral errors and military miscalculations and the current failures of the Bush Administration in the area. A few weeks into the Israeli-Hezbollah war in Lebanon, some evangelical groups began praying for the return of Jesus and the beginning of his thousand-year reign on earth.

Dr. Ronald Godwin, president of Jerry Falwell Ministries, added his argument to Hindson's for the coming apocalypse. He said of nuclear weapons, "Pandora's Box had been opened." Godwin's idea reflected the most sophisticated and terrible understanding of what had happened under the West Stands of Stagg Field when the physicists and mathematicians there effected the first nuclear chain reaction: The only way to end the threat of nuclear weapons is to destroy the world and all memory of the science and technology of the weapons. The idea of a perfectly ironical act of survival exists not only in theory, but is found in nature. According to Claude Lévi-Strauss, a maggot found in South America kills the animal it wants to eat by injecting a poison into the flesh. As it eats the flesh, the maggot consumes its own poison and dies. Godwin implied that this was happening with the pollution of the earth, air, and water.

Emended Men

The transformation of the evangelical movement in America came slowly. The social idea that had inspired the New Deal lost its hold on America before the end of the Second World War. The evangelical movement, especially the Baptist church, had largely withdrawn from worldly concerns. In his autobiography Jerry Falwell spoke of the turn away from the Social Gospel and its worldly works. Good works could not win God's grace. Faith and only faith could lead to salvation. Evangelical Christian concern on an institutional scale for the suffering of the poor was virtually nonexistent. This failing had two causes. One was theological, but the more powerful cause was their own poverty. The South had not yet completely recovered from the Civil War. Falwell's family were mountain people. He came out of a family history of atheism, alcoholism, and fratricide. As a young man, he chose to be saved. He had three talents: He could preach on almost any text, organization came to him as if by magic, and he loved publicity, which he equated with serving the Lord by spreading the Good News. It was not long before his Thomas Road Baptist Church grew to more than 10,000 members. He preached on television. The big man with the soft face and the steely certainty about both the end of the world and the salvation of those who came to Jesus was irresistible. He preached through the decade of the sixties and into the seventies without ever considering politics except to believe in the separation of church and state defined in the Constitution and the debates leading up to it. He told a convention of clergymen that their work was to "attend to the spiritual needs of the people."

At the end of the Second World War, Jerry Falwell was a young teenager. His family did not greet the surrender of Japan with concern for those who had been incinerated at Hiroshima or Nagasaki; they had a problem much closer to home. They came to the realization that Falwell's father was an alcoholic. Like the Falwell family, other evangelicals struggled against their own suffering; they did not devote much time, if any, to the suffering of unbelievers and enemies of their country. They saw American life in simple terms: harsh, hungry, racist, and religious. Women bore children, worked in the house and in the fields or the store, prayed, and served men. That was the way God wanted it. Falwell was no rebel. His television program, which appeared on over five hundred stations, more than any other program in America at the time, was called *The Old Time Gospel Hour.*

In light of the evidence of history, however, the old theology no longer served. Billy Graham grasped the problem sooner than Falwell, who did not deal head-on with nuclear war until 1983 when the Old Time Gospel House published and distributed a small book: *Nuclear War and the Second Coming of Jesus Christ.* The old evangelism of the Social Gospel had been discarded and replaced in much of the country by fundamentalism, a sect proudly proclaiming itself reactionary and in fierce conflict with postwar cultural freedoms. Fundamentalism spread, but it could not comfort everyone in a world in which man had declared perpetual war on himself and the earth that sustained him. Incomprehensible people came home from the war.

Many of those who had seen Auschwitz or Hiroshima or Dresden before they were sanitized lost their anger. They did not become meek, they turned into searchers, looking for something they did not know they had lost. I saw this conundrum in a man I knew well. He had been the second person to walk into a "liberated" Nazi death camp. His load had been heavy—he carried the radio equipment used by the officer who walked several steps ahead of him. He did not recall more than that, not the inextinguishable odor of the ovens, not the pitiable sounds of those few left alive inside the camp. He did not undergo a metamorphosis, he became an emended man. The experience came to him like an editor's blue pencil marking out a sentence in the genetic makeup of his mind. He was not a phlegmatic man, not stolid, he could be animated at times, but the experience had left him incomplete, unable to take a political position, unwilling to challenge authority, able to smile but not to laugh. He did not remove his suit coat on the hottest days; he wore it like armor. He took his meals alone or not at all. He was the father of a beautiful child who bore no resemblance to him. It was not so with the camp survivors or combat veterans, not from that war or the next or the one after that; they prayed and raged and protested like other men. Those who had seen a holocaust in Europe or Asia were the only ones who were emended in this way. They grew old, they wrote books against nuclear war. No one listened to them.

It soon became clear that to have known the Holocaust, with its implied limitlessness, produced different kinds of people, who had different needs from God. Those who survived the Holocaust could become terrorists in Palestine or suicides, like Primo Levi, or tragic survivors with their memoirs tattooed on their forearms, witnesses in an insentient middle-class world. Those who knew the Holocaust in Europe or Asia through close observation sought forgiveness. Only God's grace could relieve them of the sin of having lived in the world during that time. Original sin was no burden at all compared to what they had known. They had killed or permitted killing in great numbers. Their experience denied comparison. With the exception of biblical floods and plagues, nothing without limits had been known before. They had no kin in the historical world. They bore a double burden; it was as if they had succumbed to Satan by tasting the fruit of the atom and then, like Romans, nailed Jesus to the cross of war. The light of these few was dimmed, if not extinguished. One such man said he wanted to leap from an airplane into the hideous apartheid of South Africa.

"And kill the whites?" someone asked.

"No. And die."

Did he expect heaven or hell? No one asked. Perhaps he wanted nothing more than dreamless sleep.

Of the others, the almost uncountable majority of humankind, nothing similar can be said. They have not experienced with their own senses the results of man without limits. They have only history. In his brief essay "On the Concept of History," the last work published during his lifetime, Walter Benjamin, the historian and literary critic, already under pressure from the Nazis, wrote eighteen brief theses. The last of these gains more importance in light of what would soon happen to the author, who left unfinished a brilliant and original examination of history in a book-length meditation on the arcades of Paris. He was traveling with a small group across the Pyrenees from France to Spain in an

effort to escape the Nazis. The group was detained at the Spanish border and told they would be kept there for the night and turned over to
the Gestapo in the morning. During the night Benjamin committed
suicide. The next morning, the guards, perhaps chastened by the suicide of Benjamin, allowed the others to pass. Benjamin had written in
the last paragraph of the essay on history: "We know that the Jews were
prohibited from investigating the future. The Torah (Pentateuch) and
the prayers instruct them in remembrance, however. This stripped the
future of its magic, to which all those succumb who turn to the sooth-
sayers for enlightenment. This does not imply, however, that for the
Jews the future turned into homogeneous, empty time. For every second of time was the strait gate through which Messiah might enter."

Like Graham, Falwell, LaHaye, and millions of others, Benjamin
saw the darkness coming, and he knew that in their fear of darkness
falling over the world men could do no more than muse upon the messianic moment. Benjamin had seen the beginning of the apocalypse; in
the German response to his attacks on fascism, he saw Armageddon.
We do not know if, in the last second of his life, the Messiah entered,
and it was paradise.

Billy Graham notes certain signs now that signal the end of the
world. He spoke of the revelation inherent in a single act: the murder of
a child. For Falwell it was the *Roe v. Wade* decision. He wrote that he
could not bear what he believed was the slaughter of innocents. Unlike
the Europeans who learned of the killing of newborns, he turned to God.

Benjamin lived and died at the beginning of the Holocaust, before
Hiroshima, before the reconsideration of the theological problem,
before theologians had to decide how to respond to the reality of collective death. He was either the last man of the old theology, a suicide of
one, or the first person to grasp the new. What did Benjamin, the
soothsayer of reason, the man who could read the history of a nation in
a potter's stall, foresee? Could he have had foreknowledge of the effect
of his death on the lives of his companions? Did he understand them as
a tiny collective of life? A miniature? Had "If I should die before I
wake . . ." become "If we should die before we wake . . ."?

Given the quality of his mind, Benjamin's suicide cannot be devoid
of meaning beyond his immediate situation. One more uncertainty

attends his death. Some speculators on the events of the night in question claim Benjamin carried the last part of the manuscript of his unfinished masterwork, *The Arcades Project,* in the knapsack he left behind there in the Pyrenees. If so, did he expect his work to be salvaged by his companions who were saved by his suicide (after all, Benjamin was the famous person in the group, the antifascist the Nazis were hunting)? Had he made a writer's bargain with posterity: my life for my work? Or did the contents of the knapsack confirm his despair of the world? A third possibility exists, and it is the essence of the new theology: the end is near, the Gestapo is coming, surrender to faith; but also act, in the event there has been some error and grace depends on deeds. Deny death, but lawyer judgment. Only one certain thing now sustains theology: Billy Graham's promise of the heavenly destiny of those who accept Christ: "There is a loophole."

How different is Benjamin's one second—when the Messiah may enter—from the premillennial ideas of contemporary evangelicals? Millennialism, known in earlier times as chiliasm (the Greek for thousand was replaced by the Latin), held no interest for Luther or Calvin. The idea, which the early Christians took from the Jews, faded after less than five hundred years and was not much considered again until the sixteenth century, an epoch so enamored of the macabre that Aldous Huxley said of it in 1935, "A good death-appeal was as sure a key to popularity as a good sex-appeal in the present time." The embrace of the macabre as well as the new concern with the millennium was most likely inspired by memory of the Black Death, but millenarian thinking did not gain an important place in Christian theology for another three hundred years. Today, Christians along with Jews await the Messiah. But no one is quite certain now of what will precede His coming. By the time Benjamin wrote his essay on history, he knew what the Nazis intended for him and for the antifascist world. They were pushing down through France toward the Spanish border, leaving Benjamin with what he thought was certain and horrible death, his own personal experience of Armageddon. Like Jaspers, like Graham, like Falwell, he looked beyond this world for a solution to catastrophe. He acted. To save himself? To save the others? The manner of his death posed the unspoken theological question that would come to haunt American evangelicals after the Holocaust and Hiroshima. In a dangerous world, must one act? Is faith alone also a form of suicide?

Perfect Friendship

Among the most serious questions separating Protestants one from another are the conflicts between faith and action, worship and service; past, present, and future. No single question dominates Protestant thinking more than the millennium. And it is not only those who call themselves Protestants, but all Christians, all Jews, Muslims, agnostics and atheists, everyone. The millennium is the human hope or nightmare, it can be secular or religious; in either form it hounds the Western world, and every day, with every killing in Iraq, Spain, England, Bali, Sarajevo, or Darfur, it becomes more pressing. On July 13, 2005, the secretary of homeland security announced a reorganization of the agency, with far greater concentration on detection of nuclear weapons. As Michael Chertoff spoke, the nuclear terror that had reigned for decades during the Cold War arose from the grave of the subconscious. A Chinese Army major general, Zhu Chenghu, speaking in perfect English only three days after Chertoff's announcement, said that American military intervention in a war between China and Taiwan would result in a Chinese "first-strike" nuclear attack on the U.S. mainland. And to drive his point home, he described the destruction of thousands of American cities.

How will it all end? Will it be "heat death" from the gain or loss of heat? Sooner or later? Will the Messiah reign on earth before or after Armageddon? Has the period known as pretribulation begun? The questions surrounding the expectation have no earthly answers. The problem with believing is always the same: What to believe? Whom to believe? Religion is inherently unstable, because it relies on surmise and dreaming; nothing out of this world can be known, much less proved. Everything must be done in the here and now. "Strait is the gate . . ." was the rule, and it is now the loophole. Rick Warren, the pastor of a huge unaffiliated church in Los Angeles and author of best-selling books, warned his readers with a Hollywood metaphor, "Life on earth is just the dress rehearsal for the real production." And then he wrote that earthly existence offered many choices, while eternity offers only two: heaven and hell. Warren does not describe either of the choices, although one can be sure that heaven is a very good place to spend eternity. How good? one might ask. "Frankly," Warren wrote, "the capacity of our brains cannot handle the wonder and greatness of heaven. It would be like trying to describe the Internet to an ant."

Rick Warren is a serious fellow in a Hawaiian shirt. He does collective therapy in a metaphysical way in a time of collective death. Few men preach the gospel of the new theology better than Warren: Faith and action, follow me! "Live each day as if it were the last day of your life," he wrote, contrasting the idea with the old saw "This is the first day of the rest of your life." He sells death. He would never use the phrase, but the "imminence of the eschaton" is his message. And then he tells his audience what to do about it. Near the end of his book, Warren sums up all the reasons for choosing to follow "God's purpose." He sets aside the preacher's Hawaiian shirt for a moment, dons the philosopher's robe, and then, in one memorable sentence, promises the millennium *and* defines the loophole: "One day history will come to a close, but eternity will go on forever."

There is a gathering of preachers like Warren in America now. Following Falwell's stroke of genius, which was to include all like-minded religious conservatives under the banner of morality, it has changed from a congregation or a conference into a faction. Therein lies the question about the future of the United States. The republic has at its very foundation several ideas: natural rights, property rights, and community. Jefferson, who was familiar with Aristotle's works on politics, ethics, and rhetoric, wrote a declaration motivated surely by Francis Hutcheson's idea that "the greatest good is the happiness of others" and Locke's idea of the ownership of property by attaching one's labor to it. He embraced the concept of natural rights and of community. While natural rights were God-given, according to Locke, and thus "unalienable," community was entirely secular. Jefferson and the authors of the Constitution shied away from the danger of the state embracing religion. They described a community that contained all religions and even all rejections of religion, which is where they deviated from Locke's idea of religious toleration, which draws the line at atheism. A completely tolerant state, utterly divorced from religion, the founders believed, would be both strong and enduring.

Aristotle provided the best definition of community and the best warning of the chief danger to a community. His idea was of a community made of friends and a place where friendship could thrive. He did not say how many friends. The number was small, yet "Friendship," he wrote, "seems to hold states together." And he gave clear advice on the subject: "Expel faction as the worst enemy. . . ." Aristotle gave most of Book VIII of the *Nicomachean Ethics* over to discussing friendship, dividing it into three distinct kinds: friendship for the sake of having good company, the friendship of utility, and finally what is to him the most important aspect, which he calls "perfect friendship." It "is the friendship of men who are good and alike in virtue; for these wish well alike to each other *qua* good, and they are good in themselves."

If Aristotle is correct about the state being made of friends who wish each other well and are "good in themselves," and such a state has no enemy worse than faction, the United States now faces a serious problem: there is another definition of community now in America and it has many adherents. For evangelical Protestants, community on earth came at first through the conversion (saving) of individuals. It is the duty of evangelicals to bring others to Jesus; in the strictest conception of an evangelical, a person must try to convert at least one other person every year. That does not make bad people of evangelicals. Evangelism could also come under the definition of friendship. What greater act of friendship than to save another person's life for all eternity! What better way to be good in oneself than to share the *evangel*, the Good News? The new theology, however, can no longer be content with saving individuals. "Save one and you save the world" will not do. "Save the world" has itself become the question. The new theology has moved from friendship to faction, from the one-at-a-time to the collective. To accomplish its goals, which the new theology sees as moral, a return to the life it holds to be virtuous, it seeks to create the kind of state in which it believes a community of the good can exist.

The question of faction and its dangers was discussed early on in the debates on the Constitution as they appeared in the newspapers of the time. James Madison, writing as Publius, in *The Federalist*, No. 10, made his concern clear: "By a faction I understand a number of citizens, whether amounting to a majority or minority of the whole, who are united and actuated by some common impulse of passion, or of interest, adverse to the rights of other citizens, or to the permanent and aggregate interests of the community." He saw the main cause of faction as the unequal distribution of property, and the solution to the problem in a republic as opposed to a pure democracy. "A Republic," he wrote, "by which I mean a Government in which the scheme of representation takes place, opens a different prospect, and promises the cure for which we are seeking." He went on to say, "The two great points of difference between a Democracy and a Republic are, first, the delegation of the Government in the latter, to a small number of citizens elected by the rest: secondly, the greater number of citizens, and the greater sphere of country, over which the latter may be extended." He discussed the number of representatives, which he thought should be great enough to avoid cabals and small enough to avoid "the confusion of a multitude." If they were chosen by a larger rather than a smaller number of citizens, he thought it would be "more difficult for unworthy candidates to practise with success the vicious arts, by which elections are too often carried. . . ."

In *The Federalist*, No. 14, he spoke of union as "the proper antidote for the diseases of faction, which have proved fatal to other popular governments, and of which alarming symptoms have been betrayed by our own." In Madison's view a large society was less likely to have a single faction so great it could overturn laws. Even so, what worried him and the other founders was that faction is simple, and the antidote, a republican form of government, is complex. The Republic of the United States required the people to agree to a constitution mandating indirect democracy through elected representatives and a balance of executive, legislative, and judicial powers. The constitutional safeguards against faction worked quite well for more than seventy years, until the Civil War. The Constitution was defended, the Union was saved, but the fact of the Civil War cannot be dismissed. The Constitution promulgated by the founders was an imperfect defense for the "diseases of faction."

This is not to suggest that the imaginary "blue" states will soon go to war against the imaginary "red" states. But the danger of faction driven by religion can be seen in the debates over slavery leading up to the Civil War. E. Brooks Holifield, in his comprehensive work on Christian thought from Puritanism through the Civil War, *Theology in America*,[10] wrote: "Political economists and politicians debated about slavery in their own language of constitutionalism and power, but the theologians spoke in the language that made sense to the largest number of Americans." An agreement over interpretation of the Bible on the question of slavery might not have stopped the pro- and antislavery factions from going to war, but there is little doubt that religious backing for the two positions spurred the disputants on to secession and slaughter. Now, after a period in which religion functioned in the sphere of worship and conscience, there is a return to the kinds of arguments and the religious vehemence that characterized the polemic about slavery before the Civil War. Underlying this change is the idea of collective death, a mix of the Old Testament story of Sodom and Gomorrah and the New Testament promise of eternal life, which, Rick Warren tells us, "goes on forever."

Among millions of Americans the expectation of the end of everything is overt. They are waiting. For others, like Jon and Kelly Peterson, the possibility exists, but she believes she is going to die in her bed when she is a hundred years old and then see "the pearly gates." The Petersons are both thirty-two years old, have lived in the El Paso, Texas, area all their lives, belong to a nondenominational church and are the children and grandchildren of people who expected the world to end during their lifetimes. The survival of the world through two generations of family chiliasts leaves them believing in end-time, but with a wink. They attend church regularly, have dinner several times a year at the pastor's home, but they have never heard of John Calvin, are vague about Martin Luther, think they know who John Wesley was, are not quite sure what is meant by the word "millennium" or when the "rapture" is going to occur, and if it will affect them. They speak in tongues and tithe, welcoming the Holy Spirit into themselves and taking care of "the loophole." They do not trust government, which they think is

---

[10] New Haven: Yale University Press, 2003.

hopelessly corrupt. The only government functions they find use defense and police work. In that sense they have abandoned the community at the city, state, and national levels. They consider them-selves patriots, but people with their views who live in a very large country are not patriots in the fullest sense. They are secessionists in all but police and defense matters.

Their view harkens back to John Locke's *Second Treatise on Civil Government* in which he said that in a commonwealth citizens would have to give up certain rights in return for the protections the Petersons expect of government. Like most conservatives, the Petersons are not anxious to give up what they consider their rights. The Petersons are not racist or classist; they are glad to belong to a church that has a very diverse membership. It pleases them when the poor who once came to their church for free food and clothing are sufficiently well off to be able to offer food and clothing to others. The Petersons are likable, in many ways admirable people, but they are not members of the national com-munity.[11] They are not patriots by that definition, yet they support the war in Iraq and they speak of knowing the grief of the parents of the American dead. They voted for George W. Bush at every opportunity, they believe he defeated John Kerry in the debates as well as in the elec-tion. Like many others who voted for Bush, it was his "constancy" and his stance on social issues that they admired. That, among other things, brings Bush supporters into the fold of those who hold Christian moral-ity as one of their most treasured values.

In the realm of virtues, few achieve the importance of constancy. Jane Austen said it was the virtue without which no other virtue could exist.

---

[11] This is not intended as a "communitarian" argument, whatever is meant by communi-tarian other than Bill Clinton's attachment to a "third way," which was neither liberal nor conservative. For Clinton it meant opportunism. There are so many other definitions that each one must use the name of its primary exponent to be understood at all—i.e., Amitai Etzioni's communitarianism, Alasdair MacIntyre's communitarianism, Robert Bellah's communitiarianism, Michael Walzer's communitarianism, etc.; unless one prefers "civil society," a term first used by G. F. Hegel. In the most basic terms a civil society is one in which people depend on each other while maintaining their individual personal and prop-erty rights. Hegel can be understood to mean what we think of as "business" or it could mean culture and politics. It is generally defined as anything that exists between the family and the state, which leaves a lot of room for civil society.

For all those who have read Austen or otherwise know her view of constancy, George Bush is a man of great virtue or, more accurately in this context, of possible virtue, while John Kerry, whose inconstancy was the salient of his character, was therefore incapable of virtue. Constancy is a far more modern idea of the *sine qua non* of virtue than anything Plato or Aristotle or Jefferson would have fixed on. It fits with an age of information technology, the speed of the computer and the constancy of the little machines inside it. Although the machines are a direct product of Enlightenment thinking, which is rejected by many evangelicals, especially the fundamentalists, there is apparently no prohibition of working with these products of the Enlightenment. George W. Bush flew jet airplanes; one of the leaders of Focus on the Family, Dr. Del Tackett, spent twenty years in the Air Force and then served as director of technical planning for the National Security Council during the senior Bush's administration. The constancy that was key to Jane Austen's idea of virtue and admired by the Petersons and millions of other Americans should have inhibited what Madison called "the disease of faction," but it did not. The members of the national political movement did not remain constant in their love of liberty and their fellow human beings; they drifted away from those principles and attached themselves to people and ideas "adverse to the permanent and aggregate interests of the community." They became a faction, having adopted a new set of principles: their own physical, economic, political, and racial security. They are now constant in regard to those principles, but it should be recalled that constancy is not, in itself, a virtue; it is only the possibility of virtue.

The Petersons follow the pattern of the new theology in that they see their actions as well as their faith leading them to the "pearly gates"; it is the action of their community, in contrast to a self-serving government that enables them to count on going to heaven. They are unusual in their lack of interest in Revelation (they read it, but said they could not understand it) and end-time. They have in a very real way left both the communities of heaven and earth. They have a business relationship with God and no business with the government. They live in an island of worship and action separate from all other religious sects. They do business and practice antipolitics. For the Petersons and millions like them the separation of church and state is more profound than ever before in America. They are part of a growing force that sees two distinct states, each with its own set of rules, its own definition of morality, and they wish nothing more fervently than the triumph of God's state as they understand it and claim the rewards of membership in it.

Families like the Petersons think they are the product of a state that failed them, although it is difficult to understand how it has failed. They live well. He has businesses in two locations supplying parts for mobile homes. Mrs. Peterson stays at home with their two children. They have enough to tithe and to give more for special projects. But they attribute none of their good fortune to the society in which they live. It is all God's doing. "God is good," they say again and again in the course of a long conversation: God is on their side and the government is "out for itself." They oppose any religion that speaks of an angry or vindictive God. All good things come from God, all bad things from Satan. The separation of God from government is explicit; the connection of Satan to government is only implied.

Imperfect Friendship

It is unfair to burden two people as nice as the Petersons with the breakdown of the sense of community in America. Some writers—Alan Wolfe, Robert Bellah, and others—see the country still bound by traditions into a national community. In 1985, Bellah called these traditions "habits of the heart,"[12] a phrase borrowed from Aristotle, but these habits no longer guide many Americans. The end of the world is not a habit of the heart, and the aim of conservatives like Grover Norquist to destroy the government by starving it of taxes is not the kind of habit that Aristotle advised us to adopt in the *Nicomachean Ethics*. After 1945, Americans began to seek out different habits. Fifteen years later a madness took over the country, and it was not very different from the two competing kinds of madness Defoe described in his *Journal of the Plague Year*. The wildness of the sixties accompanied the dour, selfish behavior of many evangelicals, especially fundamentalists. On the one hand, the

---

[12] Robert N. Bellah et al., *Habits of the Heart* (Berkeley: University of California Press, 1958).

Sexual Freedom League flourished in San Francisco and homosexuality broke free of its shackles on both coasts. On the other hand, Baptists, Pentecostals, Nazarenes, Jehovah's Witnesses, and others insisted there be no dancing, no drinking, no smoking, no revealing clothes, no lipstick, no rouge. Fundamentalist Jews went along with everything but the prohibition of dancing, and added their own rule that married women must shave their heads. The country split over religion and an insane war in Vietnam. And within the divisions there were further divisions, and within those divisions yet more divisions took place.

A new hypocrisy, a variation on the kind of hypocrisy attributed to Calvinism by R. H. Tawney, appeared in the sanctimonious house of American evangelicals as nationally known preachers sank into a morass of sexual and financial misconduct.[13] And the hypocrisy has only grown worse with time. Churchgoing evangelicals get divorced at a rate higher than the national average. The Christian Right broadcaster Dr. James Dobson of Focus on the Family, a psychologist by training, advises people who listen to him on the radio to solve their marital problems by becoming churchgoing evangelicals. Mark Pestana, a professor of philosophy at Grand Valley State University, a conservative who emulated the Scottish philosopher Alasdair MacIntyre's journey from communism to Catholicism and conservatism, is outraged by the hypocrisy: "Guys will do one-night stands and then say they are pro-life."[14] For Pestana the only place where MacIntyre's "community" can survive is in home schooling. He says he is interested in MacIntyre because of the Scotsman's idea of the failure of the Enlightenment and because MacIntyre thinks

---

[13] Jim and Tammy Faye Bakker and Jimmy Swaggart, the televangelists, were the most famous of these. The Bakkers became so rich at one time in their career that they built and owned a Christian amusement park. Jim Bakker went to jail; Swaggart delivered a weeping apology on television for having sex with a prostitute. The Bakkers' television program, the *700 Club*, was taken over by Pat Robertson. Jerry Falwell, a fundamentalist Baptist, made an attempt either to save or take over the Bakker PTL (Praise the Lord) Ministry and broadcasting organization. He became chair of the PTL board of directors, and as his first move fired the entire staff of the organization. Falwell called Bakker a liar, an embezzler, and "the greatest scab and cancer on the face of Christianity in 2000 years of church history." Jim Bakker later called him "totalitarian." Falwell would not permit Bakker's Pentecostal followers, who talked in tongues, to enroll at his fundamentalist Liberty University.

[14] More about MacIntyre in the next chapter. He is concerned largely with moral theory, and owes much to Aristotle.

community can exist only in small jurisdictions. It is an old and oft-said (Aristotle, Rousseau, Montesquieu) idea and not very useful in the twenty-first century, when political jurisdictions comprise hundreds of millions, even billions of people. To achieve the multitude of communities suggested by MacIntyre and admired by Pestana in contemporary circumstances would mean the wreck of the state, chaos; yet it is a hope, and increasingly often a goal, of the national political movement.

The movement can create the most profound form of friendship, the making of a community of people whom God loves, a low-tax congeries of home-schooled communities in opposition to the larger community of government, a separation of church and state so profound it forces the movement and the state into a struggle that cannot end until one side or the other capitulates and the direction of the country is settled, either in a return to the ideals that gave birth to the New Deal and the Great Society or to a weakened state at the mercy of its religious and philosophical leaders. A major stage of the capitulation may already have been completed. President Clinton invented a euphemism for it: he said his policies were "the third way."

The new politics, which depends in large part upon the new theology, grows out of the belief in Armageddon, either soon or not quite so soon, a collective death by suicide bomber, poison, bioterrorism, or nuclear holocaust, this last being the most feared. At first it seems unreasonable to think of the creation of a religious antistate when the kind of death that drives it is itself a collective, a community of the dead. And it is correct to speak of a community of the dead; that is, many dead at the same time. A community of the dead, however, cannot claim friendship between even two of the dead, let alone among all the dead. No death can be communal, the uniqueness of death cannot be compromised. Each person owns one death, and it cannot be divorced from that person, no matter how he or she wills it. In place of the traditions that held Americans together in a Lockean embrace, the belief in Armageddon in which nothing is shared but the vague sense of doom and the wish to avoid the moment of death separates an ever growing number of conservative evangelicals one from the other and the whole of them from what was formerly a government by consent. The Bible, read now by Catholics as well as Protestants, has little power to unite, as the princes of the Roman Catholic Church long knew; they interpreted the Bible for their flock. Just as every person who dies dies differently, every person who reads the Bible reads it differently.[15] To create a theocratic community requires conformity to one interpretation of both the history and the destiny of a nation, an iron-clad tradition. The authors of the U.S. Constitution took pains to reject the possibility of theology challenging the authority of the state. The document could not forestall a civil war defined by regionalism in the nineteenth century, and it may not be strong enough to fend off the challenge of the deadly combination of religious and secular pessimism in the twenty-first century. The traditions that bound America into one nation could not have been religious; the only possibility was politics.

The Speech

While the country still trembled over the Cuban Missile Crisis and mourned the assassination of its young president, an event occurred that signaled the beginning of a new political ideology: in the San Francisco Cow Palace during the 1964 Republican National Convention, the crowd shouted down New York Governor Nelson Rockefeller and gave the nomination to an ultraconservative former Air Force general from Arizona, Barry Goldwater. Most of the people in the hall were too far from the podium to see anything more than the figure of a man in a dark suit; they had to imagine the black-rimmed eyeglasses, the hard-edged pioneer face looking straight into the glare of the fiery lights. He had a dry voice, but he was certain about what he said. He was a cowboy retailer in the Cow Palace, and he spoke of "freedom under a government limited by the laws of nature and nature's God."

Rockefeller had said the Goldwater conservatives were "radical, sinister, extremist." He accused them of "intimidation." All this before Goldwater's speech accepting the nomination, when he said, "extremism in the defense of liberty is no vice . . . ," and he had to thank the audience five times to quiet them so they could hear him say, ". . . moderation in the pursuit of justice is no virtue."

---

[15] Deconstructionists would no doubt have a comment to offer here.

Later that year a washed-up movie actor who traveled around the country making speeches for the General Electric Company made a television appeal for Goldwater. Actors had no place in politics then, George Murphy and Shirley Temple were just California comedies. Before Reagan the last actor to have any real political influence was John Wilkes Booth. Ronald Reagan was a simple man, gracious, good-humored, uneducated, a liberal unionist who accepted the ideas taught to him by his second wife, Nancy, and became a conservative. People who knew him well said his main problem was that he liked everybody. He was one of the most ill-read men ever to hold the highest office in America; his kitchen cabinet in California affirmed to me that he never read books, only reports; his real frame of reference was the movies. And even there he had but little ability. Reagan had two great gifts. As people who held key positions in his political campaigns said, he was lucky. And he had the gift of rhetoric. Perhaps he had learned some of the skills during his acting career, but Reagan seemed to have been born with the ability to use the three qualities Aristotle said were necessary for rhetoric to succeed. His talent was astonishing. Every speech was made of simple (1) logic, a strong appeal to the (2) emotions of the audience, and a demonstration of the speaker's good (3) character. It was as if he had been tutored in rhetoric by Aristotle. Peter Hannaford, who wrote many articles and speeches for him, said Reagan could not write an article or an essay himself, but he could write or rewrite a speech to turn it into rhetoric that moved a nation.[16]

On October 27, 1964, the actor Ronald Reagan delivered a nationally televised campaign speech for Barry Goldwater. When the speech was over, the man who had appeared on television and at Rotary and Elks and Moose club meetings across the country to tout the virtues of General Electric had moved from show business and public relations to politics. It would be sixteen years before the national political move-

---

[16] Although we are as far apart in our political beliefs as two men could be, Peter and I have been friends since the early 1960s. The high point of his career as a speechwriter came when Nancy Reagan asked him to come back from a business trip to the Far East to write an acceptance speech for her husband to deliver at the 1980 Republican National Convention. Hannaford spent weeks on the speech, which Reagan rewrote in his own idiom before delivering it at the convention.

ment coalesced around him, but he had intuited something about the feelings welling up in the American people.

Reagan began the televised speech by telling his audience that no one had written the speech for him, these were his own words and his own ideas. He said he had been a Democrat for most of his life, but now followed "another course." And then he laid down the principles of a new Republican Party; he started what would become known as the Reagan Revolution and continues in 2007 as the stated policy of the right wing of the Republican Party and the mantra of an American political movement:

Lower taxes.
Privatize Social Security.
Strengthen defense.
Reduce the size of the federal government.
Let government be controlled at the local level.
Reduce the national debt.
Reduce government regulation.
End welfare as we know it.
Do not trade freedom for the soup kitchen (creeping socialism).
Base government on "what we know in our hearts is morally right."
Spread freedom throughout the world, even at the risk of war.
The United States is "the last best hope on earth."

And he ended with a slight paraphrase of Franklin Delano Roosevelt's famous line: "We have a rendezvous with destiny."

Goldwater suffered a massive defeat, in some part due to the single airing of a commercial made by the advertising firm Doyle Dane Bernbach for the Johnson for President campaign. It showed a little girl pulling the petals off a daisy as the announcer counted down to a nuclear explosion. Goldwater probably would not have been elected in any event—the movement had not gathered enough adherents, but a sense of his recklessness and the fear of nuclear war finished him. It had been only two years since Kennedy and Khrushchev took the use of nuclear weapons out of the realm of nightmare and moved it forever into the real world.

Eight

PHILOSOPHERS

Calvin and Luther could not abide the tone in which
the humanist Erasmus spoke of holy things. Erasmus!
His whole being seems to radiate the play-spirit.

— JOHAN HUIZINGA

My opinion is that the most important part of a man's
education is to discuss poetry intelligently.

— PROTAGORAS

Government is the problem, not the solution.

— RONALD REAGAN

Laughter

There has been precious little holy laughter since Dante. The Holy
Spirit does not fill the faithful with jokes. Hasidic Jews who once danced
with joy while swinging chickens around their heads have become as
dour as Calvinists. Baptists won't dance; don't ask them. Liberal pastor
Jim Wallis has a salesman's smile, but there are no "funnies" or jokes in
his *Sojourner* magazine. Pope Benedict XVI learned his lighthearted
ways during his early paramilitary training. And there is much rocking,
but no rolling with laughter, in a madrassa. In the massive study of fundamentalism edited by Martin E. Marty and R. Scott Appleby, there is

no mention of laughter.[1] Religion is an inherently serious, if not unhappy, business. Since death is the mother of faith and laughter is the only acceptable apology for life, the two have little common ground. Erasmus and Dante wrote most of the jokes, and Dante was more bitter than funny, Erasmus more filled with joy than giggles. Augustine used to have wild times when he was a young Manichean, and then he found religion and that was the end of the hot times on those North African nights. Wit has often been applied to religion, but religion has less to do with wit than with martyrdom, and there are no funny martyrs.

Among philosophers the closest thing to laughter belongs to the Dalai Lama, if he is indeed a philosopher and if those expressions of mirth are really laughter and not simply amusement. The world is, after all, a ludicrous place, funnier than the best pratfalls invented by Cervantes and as mean as anything the Spaniard drew from his own life of captivity and suffering. The best Socrates could do was a witty line or two in the face of death. In the great conservative fashion, Aristotle never laughed, unless the lost book of *Poetics*, the one about melodrama or comedy, really existed, and in it Aristotle got other men's jokes and told a few knee-slappers of his own. About Kant, Heidegger, and Hobbes, there is no sense even inquiring. Schopenhauer famously saw no reason in this world for laughter, and pessimist that he was, he advised his readers to become artists, thinking perhaps they would enjoy the penury, pain, and rejection associated with the calling. Machiavelli did not advise the Prince to hire a jester! And Nietzsche's metaphor for man, "a rope stretched across an abyss" may be the setting for a fall, but not a pratfall. Judging by his writings, Marx was a sweet and somewhat dreamy young fellow, deeply in love with Jenny von Westphalen, when he wrote *The German Ideology*, but he was nasty when he turned on his friends, and in the years of penury, when he was forced to pawn his clothes and send his children to stand in front of the house and beg, he wrote great books but never implied the "withering

---

[1] *The Fundamentalism Project*, 5 vols. (Chicago: University of Chicago Press, 1991–1995). I have read only two of the five volumes and several articles in the remaining three, but there was no hint in anything I read of laughter in any of the forms of fundamentalism.

away of the state" would be an occasion for joyous laughter. Imagine Ludwig Wittgenstein: "I had it all wrong the first time, ha ha ha!" Not likely. There is a philosophy of laughter, but there is no rib-tickling philosophy. To make the gods laugh, they say, tell them your plans, but those guffawing gods are not in the least like the nonanthropomorphic God of the Hebrews, Christians, Muslims, and so on. The old gods had human foibles, but they could laugh; they were interesting gods, if a bit capricious, the kind of gods you would like to invite to dinner. The Judeo-Christian God would definitely not be a good dinner guest. As imagined by His worshipers, God has a foul temper and no sense of humor. A God who sends his only son to suffer and die on a cross or one who tells his first follower on earth to sacrifice his only child is not a funny guy or gal.

Philosophy should have been a response to man's idea of a sour deity, and perhaps it was. It began when the Greeks, who liked their gods to be a little like their next-door neighbors, brought the big questions down to earth, but philosophy never caught on to the idea that the world might be funny. Classic authors laugh, Shakespeare laughs, even literary critics occasionally laugh, but philosophers stop laughing the moment they take up the quill of immortality. Logical positivists laugh, but only because they do not think the idea of God is verifiable, which leaves them as earthbound as oaks. Deconstructionists may or may not laugh; depending upon how you or I understand what they are doing, maybe it's all a joke. Moral philosophers, those who do not think anything is worthy of consideration unless it is either eternal or incomprehensible or both, never crack a smile. They devote themselves these days to the grim task of bringing back old virtues or equally ancient political philosophy. All other profound questions are lately returned to heaven, where the Greeks found them.

There is a theory that all philosophy since Plato is nothing but commentary on Plato. Students who read that rubbish in Alfred North Whitehead's take on philosophy can be lost for a lifetime. It happened to Allan Bloom, the author of *The Closing of the American Mind*, which was really about the closing of Allan Bloom's mind. Men like Bloom would never have admitted it, but the liveliest people in Plato's time were the Sophists. Protagoras, who was the most interesting of them, loved the arts, especially poetry, which Plato thought was a thoroughly corrupting pursuit. Plato leveled the following accusation against Protagoras. "Do I understand you . . . and is your meaning that you teach the art of politics, and that you promise to make men good citizens?" Protagoras replies: "That . . . is exactly the profession which I make."[2] Bernard Knox, who has a marvelous, easy way of talking about the classics, said the Sophists taught the humanities as a foundation for democracy.[3] Nothing could have irritated Plato more. He despised democracy, in no small part because of the conviction and death of his mentor, Socrates. Worse than that for Plato, the Sophists had a playful view of life.

Imagine Plato, who wanted his guardians to keep people in line and in their place in his Republic, which bears an unhappy resemblance to a totalitarian state, encountering the Sophists as described by Johan Huizinga:

> The sophist's performance is called epideixis—an exhibition. He has . . . a regular repertoire and charges a fee for his disquisitions. Some of his pieces have a fixed price like the fifty-drachma lectures of Prodicus. Gorgias made so much money out of his art that he was able to dedicate a statue of himself to the god at Delphi, made of solid gold. The itinerant sophist like Protagoras booked fabulous successes. It was an event when a famous sophist visited a town. He was gaped at like a miraculous being, likened to the heroes of athletics; in short, the profession of sophist was on a par with sport. The spectators laughed and applauded at every well-aimed crack. It was pure play, catching your opponent in a net of argument or giving him a knock-

---

2 Benjamin Jowett translation.

3 See *The Oldest Dead White European Males* (New York: W. W. Norton, 1993), one of those glorious little books (144 pp.) that anyone who cares about democracy should have a look at. It contains his Jefferson Lecture in the Humanities for the National Endowment for the Humanities. The NEH at the time was chaired by Lynne Cheney. Always modest, ever gracious, Cheney used the NEH magazine, *Humanities*, to attack Knox's Jefferson Lecture: she didn't think he knew much about the Greeks. Garry Wills came to the defense of Knox in a nicely said appreciation of him in the *New York Review of Books*, May 13, 1993.

out blow. It was a point of honor to put nothing but twisters, to which every answer must be wrong.[4]

Laughter and democracy enjoy an intricate and mutually support-ive relation. The wedding took place early in the history of democracy in the West, and whenever the lovers have been separated, even briefly, the result has been disastrous. Plato did his best. He has become an untouchable oracle again in some quarters, and the Sophists, his great enemies, have become the villains of philosophy. In our time all the fun has gone out of philosophy. Spectators at philosophy matches no longer laugh. There are, in fact, no philosophy matches in our time. A few decades ago, two Harvard philosophers, the liberal John Rawls and the conservative Robert Nozick, would have made an interesting pairing, but a great encounter, the modern version of a match between Plato and Protagoras, never took place. Plato had seen to that; he fixed the match not only in Athens, but for all time. He wrote the Sophists as he wanted the Sophists to be, the world took fiction for fact, and stopped laughing. Plato left behind two ways to interpret the methods of the Sophists. Fol-low him and Sophists are people who know how to make the worse appear to be the better. Follow the Sophists and they are people who know how to make the weaker case appear to be the stronger.[5] They were the defense counsel for art and democracy. They never stood a chance against Plato.

All this talk about the Greeks may seem far removed from the pol-itics of heaven in the twenty-first century, but there is a connection. Without the lost second volume of Aristotle's *Poetics* to guide us, we lack good evidence about the history of laughter in Athens; we know, however, that once the city set out on the second stage of the Pelopon-nesian War in 431 B.C.E., the laughter was over. The imperialistic aims of the city-state under Pericles had begun to change the character of the

---

[4] *Homo Ludens: A Study of the Play Element in Culture*, written in 1938, published in Switzerland in 1944, then by Roy Publishers in 1950 and Beacon Press, Boston, in 1955.

[5] The weaker case is not always the worse. Plato would argue that the Sophists know how to make a murderer appear to be a victim. The Sophists would say they know how to defend an innocent person when an eyewitness claims to have seen the person commit a murder.

Athenians. Then came the plague, the terrible defeat at Syracuse, and a new worldview. The democracy that fell into the hands of tyrants was restored, but comedy had been replaced by devastating satire. Aristophanes offered his audience a defecating bird as a sop to slapstick in one play, but one toilet joke does not obscure the bitterness of satire in that play, nor could an imagined pratfall lighten the mean-spirited character of any other. In a wounded society there is no laughter, only unhappy philosophers and bitter satirists. A Danish newspaper offered an example of this when it published cartoons offensive to Muslims. Muslims responded with the kind of lunacy that could have produced bitter laughter in a grim world had either the cartoons or the act of publishing them been the least bit funny. Whether democracy was dying in the ancient city-state of Athens more than two thousand years ago or captives were suffering decapitation on one side and humiliation on the other now in the aftermath of a dead dictatorship in Iraq, there is very little cause for comfortable laughter. Happiness comes with hope in this world, bitterness accompanies the last dreams.

The America of burlesque, slapstick, Chaplin, Laurel and Hardy, the Marx Brothers, on through Milton Berle, Sid Caesar, Ed Wynn, and Jackie Gleason, the country of love and laughter, started to turn sour during the Cuban Missile Crisis, and went from sour to bitter during the Vietnam War. Imperialism affected the United States as it had Athens. Mort Sahl and Lenny Bruce and Paul Krassner were no match for Aristophanes in eloquence, but they excelled the master in bitterness. Literature sank into nastiness: Bruce Jay Friedman and Philip Roth set the early pace. Ken Kesey took advantage of people in a world that took advantage of him. To those of us who knew him, he was all the characters in *One Flew Over the Cuckoo's Nest*, including Big Nurse. Saul Bellow passed from the robustness of Augie March to the dour conservatism of Mr. Sammler and then became the promoter of democracy's deceitful opponent, fattening Allan Bloom—Ravelstein for the kill.[6] Dick Gregory was angry and good, Bill Cosby was a throwback, but it was Richard Pryor who set the style and tone for the popular entertainment

---

6 On September 4, 2005, the *New York Times Book Review* published an attempt by a journalist with opportunistic politics, Jim Sleeper, to resurrect the reputation of Bloom.

that followed. He had lived part of his childhood in a brothel, and he never stopped understanding the world from that vantage. He was the sweetest, most unhappy case, a satirist whose life itself could be viewed as a satire on American views of race, sex, drugs, and marriage. Without him, there could have been no rage and certainly no wit in hip-hop; people would have been satisfied to keep singing the blues. Had Pryor not pioneered the use of his own painful situations to satirize American life, Showtime could not have produced *Weeds*, its sentimental satire about a soccer mom who supports herself by selling marijuana. The history of the country can be read in this descent into satire. As America ate the rest of the world out of house and home, killing as it went, its artists, like those of Athens, preferred irony to reality, thought satire was the only rationality, and spoke only sarcasm and obscenity.

These popular philosophers turned life into bitter smiles. Comedy clubs proliferated, but the comics produced dyspeptic grimaces in their audiences. Larry David traveled from droll to dreadful; Jon Stewart made a career of smirking; Bill Maher strutted and slashed as he whined. Lewis Black based his career on pure misanthropy. George Carlin is the perfect antithesis of Will Rogers: he never met a man (or woman) he liked. Chris Rock traveled from sweet anger to vulgar misogyny. Dennis Miller announced his television show with the promise that he would not attack President Bush; he claimed the events of 9/11 had changed him. It was a desperately antinomian act: a foul-mouthed comedian in search of an audience among the "moral majority." Miller had done the most inventive thing of all; he had surpassed even Aristophanes and the Roman poet Martial in bitterness: he had satirized himself.

Miller could not find an audience. True laughter depends on optimism; it flourishes when Buster Keaton falls on his face or Charlie Chaplin cooks a shoe as human society takes a detour on its way to perfection. Many Americans now see themselves again through the work of Jonathan Edwards, walking on a thin crust above the fires of hell; the house of the Lord is an unsmiling place, a waiting room in which it is all too easy to keep one's feet warm. They do not think it is a time for laughter. Yet, curiously enough, the megachurches advertise themselves as places for people who wish to put some laughter back into their lives.

But it is not true laughter they embrace, for laughter, like art, is outside the mainstream. Every guffaw is a revolutionary act. Not the cruel laughter of Aristophanes, but the soul of Shakespeare at play. Mark Twain. Laughter is the enemy of pessimism; hilarity may be the most effective way to change the direction of American politics. If we are to survive as a society, we have to agree once again that the greatest philosophers are Charlie Chaplin and Harpo Marx. We shall have to take them at their word.

Picking Chickens

Evidence of the effect of philosophers on the ways of the world is not as easy to find as signs of the work of economists, but the effects may be deeper and longer-lasting. Theologians, of course, have greater effect, because theology deals more directly with death. The three disciplines fall into a neat order of importance: theology, philosophy, and economics. For people who reject the idea of eternal life, philosophy, especially ethics, becomes more important than theology; economics as a discipline has a long life given over mainly to confounding the economists. In modern society the disciplines are like the threads that make up the warp and woof of a square of cloth. When the degree of difficulty is just right, the task of separating these threads can have a calming effect on the one who does the work, enabling the person to use his or her powers of reason.[7] It was known in the days before the invention of psychotropic medicines, when mental patients were housed in vast institutions, as "picking chickens." Agitated patients were given small squares of tightly woven cloth and asked to pick apart the constituent threads. The work was intense, absorbing, and depending on the intricacy of the weave, it returned the person to the state Aristotle famously described as "the natural desire to know."

It should be possible, on the picking-chickens theory, to sort out the threads of theology, philosophy, and economics, to locate the work of specific advocates of religious or philosophical or economic thinkers, as long

---

[7] The workhouse in *Oliver Twist* had a different end in mind for the boys who pulled apart the strands of rope to be reused by the British Navy.

as what they said was not completely irrational. To test the theory I looked for evidence of the work of two important contemporary philosophers—one devoted to Plato, the other to Aristotle; one who died in 1973 and the other who still writes and teaches at a midwestern university. For the piece of cloth as it were, I chose a single column by David Brooks in the *New York Times* published one Sunday in 2005. The choice was very nearly random. Intrigued by the headline, I read the Brooks column on the day before I began writing this page. In the column, which incorporates the work of the two philosophers, without mentioning them, Brooks affords us a glimpse of the influence of these men on ethics and political philosophy. He declared, with no apparent satirical intent, "America is becoming more virtuous."[8] Had he been a late-night television comic, the statement would have been worthy of Aristophanes. Had he included an obscenity or two or three, as in "Shit, man, fucking America is becoming a more virtuous motherfucking country," the statement could have been made by Dennis Miller. But Brooks is not a satirist. The column suggests that he may be foolish, or a liar, or simply in need of competent researchers and an alert editor. It is difficult to conceive of his work published on that Sunday as the end product of two brilliant minds—the philosophers Leo Strauss and Alasdair MacIntyre. Yet there it was; the threads separated out with relative ease.

Setting aside for the moment the unholy fudging of statistics by Brooks, the definition of a virtuous country in his column is an extremely serious indictment of the moral stance of the current national political movement in America, for Brooks represents the movement at its best. Brooks lies by omission several times in a way best characterized as silly, but more often in a way that harms the country. On the silly side he tells his readers that the consumption of hard liquor has declined in America; an indication, according to Brooks, of virtue triumphant. The hard-liquor statistic was correct, but the consumption of wine and beer rose at an astonishing rate as liquor consumption fell.[9]

---

[8] August 7, 2005.

[9] Lest the wine statistic appear an unfair attack on Mr. Brooks, it came from an article in the *Washington Times*, a newspaper more devoted to the politics favored by Brooks than to accuracy; however, there it was on September 8, 2004, from the UPI wire.

People did not stop consuming alcohol, they simply changed the way they consume it.

Some of the virtues he touts are bizarre. "Teenagers are losing their virginity later in life," he says, which means Brooks is either lying or has accepted Bill Clinton's claim that he "never did have sex with that woman." Brooks may be right about virgo intacto, but the *New York Times*[10] reported years earlier that fellatio has often replaced intercourse among the young. Perhaps Brooks means to curry favor with *Times* readers by implying that fellatio is virtuous. Which leads to another of the Brooks statistics: he touts a decline in teen pregnancy as a sign of virtue, without noting, as his own paper reported, that fellatio is a fool-proof method of birth control. Teenage girls also retain their virginity out of fear of AIDS and other sexually transmitted diseases. Pregnancy among teenagers did decline in 2005, but remained the highest in any industrialized nation. Births out of wedlock rose to 37 percent in 2005, the highest percentage ever. The divorce statistics are no less suspect: "There's even evidence that divorce rates are declining" is all he says. No source, no data.[11] Brooks apparently neglected to consult his fellow conservatives before writing the column. Conservative Christians are quick to point out that the divorce rate among them is higher than the national average because, they say, Christians marry and others just live together. In sin.

Lying—and deception is a form of lying—is not generally considered virtuous, so it is fair to say Mr. Brooks is not himself contributing

---

[10] Tamar Lewin on April 5, 1997: "In part because of the fear of AIDS, and in part because of a basic shift in sexual practices, those who study adolescent sexuality say, oral sex has become a commonplace initiation into sexual activity, widely perceived by many young people as less intimate, and less risky, than intercourse. Many girls also see it as a means of avoiding pregnancy and of preserving their virginity."

[11] In the *New York Times*, April 19, 2005, the following sentence appeared: "In 2003, for example, the most recent year for which data is available, there were 7.5 marriages per 1,000 people and 3.8 divorces, according to the National Center for Health Statistics." The *Times* story said that the figures were misleading; the divorce rate was not 50 percent as some people had claimed. Perhaps, but when there are about half as many divorces as marriages, and there is some number of people who live together without getting married, a lot of people are getting divorced. Whatever the actual percentages, to claim a decline in the divorce rate as proof of increasing morality in America is a specious argument. It starts from the assumption that divorce is not a virtuous act, which may not be true in all cases.

to virtue in America. But he does not deal with honesty as a virtue. Not even the blatant lies of the president of the United States and his staff appear to interest Brooks, nor does it seem to concern him that the former exterminator, Tom DeLay, who led the right wing in Congress, is a tainted man. Or that the virtuous government Brooks posits would soon have more troubles because of corrupt acts. At this writing, the Securities and Exchange Commission is investigating the Senate majority leader for violating a blind trust agreement. And I. Lewis Libby, Jr., the vice president's chief of staff has been indicted on five counts, including perjury and obstruction of justice.[12] Brooks makes no mention of WorldCom or Enron or the incessant cheating by financial firms as large as Merrill Lynch and Citicorp, because large corporations are allies of writers who promote the national political movement. Brooks sets aside the character flaws of the political right and corporations by saying he believes virtue is coming from the bottom up. The very bottom, of course, is prison, and the fact that America has more than 2 million people in jails and prisons does not enter the Brooks accounting of virtue. Beyond that, the unfairness of keeping people in prison for years, even decades for nonviolent crimes, mainly drug possession, is not a sign of virtue in the judicial or penal system.

Worse perhaps than prison, as if one social failure must be compared to another, is child poverty. In the eighth paragraph of the column, Brooks wrote that poverty is down among children, "even allowing for an uptick during the last recession." The UNICEF study "Child Poverty in Rich Countries 2005" put the United States and Mexico at the bottom of the list. The child poverty rate in the United States, according to UNICEF, is more than nine times that of Denmark. To say that this puts the richest country in the history of the world within "the

---

[12] Jack Abramoff had not yet entered into a plea bargain that would lead to the shaming of a considerable number of Republicans in the Congress, and a few Democrats. Practically everyone in government, from George W. Bush to Hillary Clinton had accepted campaign funds from Abramoff.

Shortly before the 2006 election U.S. Representative Mark Foley of Florida did inestimable damage to the Republican Party when it became public knowledge that he had made sexual overtures to adolescent congressional pages.

recognized moral laws or standards of right conduct" (as in the *OED* definition of virtue) is an affront to the intelligence of every reader.

The Brooks column followed the pattern of lying by omission favored by conservatives in the Bush Administration and the Congress as the number of Americans killed in Iraq passed 3,000 and there was talk in Washington of the need for a military draft to replace the drawdown of reservists and members of the National Guard who had served in the invasion and occupation. Democrat Charles Rangel of New York said he would introduce a bill in 2007 authorizing a draft. Brooks had talked about the number of murders falling, but did not mention the number of Americans who had been murdered in Iraq or the count of those who survived their wounds but were left blinded, deafened, or dismembered. There was, of course, no mention of the innocent Iraqi dead—more than 3,000 were murderd almost every month in 2006. The disaster in New Orleans after Hurricane Katrina showed the Bush Administration lying flat out about not having been warned of the probable collapse of the levees and the death and damage that would be caused by the ensuing flood.

Unspoken in the Brooks column, but carefully implied, the credit for virtue in America belongs not merely to the Christian right, but to the broader coalition, the one that includes Jews and Catholics, the national political movement. To be sure no one could miss the implication, Brooks carefully credited neighborhood and community groups, nongovernmental organizations, for bringing virtue to the villainous. Brooks is not a philosopher. The national political movement prefers theology to philosophy. Both speak of virtue, but theology more often speaks of good and evil now. Virtue is a philosopher's tool; Plato's cardinal virtues of prudence, fortitude, temperance, and justice are still widely discussed among students of philosophy, and virtue ethics has become an important topic in the academy, but the cardinal virtues seldom make the papers. The theological virtues of faith, hope, and charity have not been entirely left out, but they have an antiquated air about them, like something dusty and diaphanous found in a trunk in the attic of an old house. Or a grandmother's given name. Conservatives have built their case on seeking God's grace, not on human virtue. They leave the cardinal virtues to the liberals, as Brooks did in his column

(Plato was talking about *sophrosyne*, not teetotaling, when he spoke of temperance). According to Brooks, virtue has to do with genitals and alcohol and divorce and one kind of killing. He could not be expected to mention the cardinal virtue that conservatives like least: justice, especially in the form of social justice. Nor did he measure the fount from which all other virtues flow, if we are to believe Jane Austen: constancy. Perhaps he felt no need to give constancy a pat on the back. It already has a place of honor in the movement's thinking and political methodology, having carried George W. Bush to his second term in 2004.

How the ideas of contemporary political and moral philosophers make their way into the behavior of the nation is not always apparent. It may be that a philosopher's rise to prominence is just an echo of public sentiment, an academic exercise in mimicry. Or a philosopher's work may influence the course of history. However it happens, the path of philosophy never goes in a straight line. It usually takes years, if not decades, before a philosopher's ideas appear in the Sunday papers or pop out of a politician's grab bag. If philosophy were history, it would be different. It could be late getting to work, and no one would notice, but philosophers are not content to muck around in the past. It's the future they're after.

The influence of contemporary liberal-left philosophers appears to have been far less than that of conservative-reactionary thinkers, but given the time it takes for ideas to work through a vast and complex society, the right may already be in philosophical decline.[13] Jürgen Habermas and the idea of the public sphere, John Rawls and his liberal notion of justice as fairness, Ronald Dworkin's philosophy of law and his reworking of Rawls's just-distribution theory may all be rising. Marx, Marcuse, and Mao may be waiting in the isolation of academe for their resurrection. Embattled Darwin could emerge again as reason's darling. Tomorrow they may influence major social and political decisions, but not today. Their work did not provide a framework for argu-

---

[13] The terms "left, right, liberal, conservative, reactionary, Democrat, Republican," and all their variations and combinations are ill-defined today and will be ill-defined in a slightly different way tomorrow, but they will have to make do. The alternative to imprecision is silence, and silence in politics is a form of oppression.

ment against the invasion of Iraq, nor did it keep a Democratic president from signing the Welfare Reform Act. It has not deterred the Bush Administration from putting into effect many of the policies first outlined in Reagan's speech for Goldwater more than forty years ago, and the gap between rich and poor in America, which rose rapidly under the Clinton Administration, has continued to rise.

The ideas of the conservative philosophers appear frequently on radio and television and in magazines, newspapers, and political speeches, although often in simplistic or perverted form. No Democrat with media access equal to Brooks or the Fox Network or Rush Limbaugh carries on the ideas of Habermas or Rawls or Dworkin. The best the liberal-left can do in broadcast media is Al Franken. The most widely read liberal-left print outlets are the *The Nation* and *Harper's*.[14] *The Nation* has long been a staunch supporter of redistributive economic policies; *Harper's* has somewhat more mainstream economic views but takes equally strong political positions. Only Paul Krugman has access nearly equal to the conservatives via the *New York Times*, and he is an economist-polemicist, just as Brooks and Limbaugh and the Fox Network are opinionist-polemicists; if Democrats with real or potential power seek his advice or approbation, they do it quietly.

Brooks is not the only conservative to have written about virtue. William J. Bennett wrote a best-seller on the subject. He called it *The Book of Virtues*, and the psychologist Robert Coles and *Time* and *Newsweek* thought the book ought to be some sort of bible for child-rearing. PBS turned it into a cartoon series for children. From his post atop the pinnacle of virtue Bennett lectured Republicans and hectored Democrats. He had a list of vices as long as his list of virtues. The book had faded from public view when it was revealed that Bennett was an obsessive gambler who had lost all the profits from his works on virtue playing slot machines. Then, in late September of 2005, Bennett, a former secretary of education, was doing his thinking on the radio. He told his audience: "I do know that it's true that if you wanted to reduce crime, you could, if that were your sole purpose, you could abort every

---

[14] The combined circulation of the two magazines is about 500,000. *The Nation* is a for-profit operation. *Harper's* is a nonprofit.

black baby in this country, and your crime rate would go down." When asked about his statement, Bennett said, "I was pointing out that abortion should not be opposed for economic reasons. . . ." And later, he told Fox News that he thought aborting all black babies was "morally reprehensible." Bennett's racism was so profound he did not realize that attributing crime in America to blacks was also morally reprehensible. Neither Ronald Dworkin nor Alasdair MacIntyre, both of whom have written books with the word "virtue" in the title, have been accused of deceit, certainly not of the monumental deceit of the gambling racist of the right.[15]

Fools and polemicists aside, the work of two recent conservative philosophers can be discerned now in public policy, which is not to say that Hobbes, Burke, Spencer, Comte, Oakeshott, and the economists Smith, von Mises, and Hayek are no longer part of the conservative arsenal. The more current ideas, however, come from the German émigré political philosopher Leo Strauss and the Scottish-born former leftist Alasdair MacIntyre. They are the philosophical fathers of the national political movement, great-great-grandchildren of Plato and Aristotle. Strauss died eight years before MacIntyre published his major work, *After Virtue*,[16] often credited with reviving interest in moral philosophy and virtue ethics.[17]

Strauss was more interested in what he preferred to describe as political philosophy and the interplay of this philosophy with geopolitics. He was stern, brilliant, arrogant, and yet much of his work can be read as a reaction to fear, and not of the most admirable kind. Less is public in the life of MacIntyre, who is more original than Strauss in his thinking. MacIntyre is a modest man, always interested in the comments of his critics, always trying to make difficult concepts available to

---

[15] *Sovereign Virtue* (Cambridge: Harvard University Press, 2000). Early on in the book Dworkin develops the concept of equal resources as a response to the requirement that a government have equal concern for all its citizens. In a key sentence he wrote: ". . . if we accept equality of resources as the best conception of distributional equality, liberty becomes an aspect of equality rather than, as it is often thought to be, an independent political ideal potentially in conflict with it."

[16] South Bend, Ind.: University of Notre Dame Press, 1981.

[17] Virtue ethics has its roots in Books II–V of Aristotle's *Nicomachean Ethics*.

his readers. Both men could be described as reactionaries; both appear in their work to be driven by ghosts of intellectual disillusion; both wrote out of a pessimistic view of the world, although MacIntyre said he did not want his work to be understood in that light. If the word neoconservative were applied to philosophers, it would apply to Strauss and many of his political progeny, some of whom rose to high positions in government and caused untold suffering at home and grave danger both at home and abroad. The curious thing about Strauss and MacIntyre is that their work and the work of philosophers whom they find interesting or admirable either came out of the Greeks or the wish to return to them. In this way, Homer, the pre-Socratic philosophers, Plato, Aeschylus, Sophocles, Aristotle—all play important roles in the way we live now.[18] Moses, Jesus, Mohammed, Luther, and Calvin occupy the foreground, but the Greeks are ever there at the foundation of thinking, participants in the dance of faith and reason. There are many intermediaries, but there is no one on earth whom they do not touch. Strauss and MacIntyre, the modern philosophers of conservatism, pay homage to tradition, and tradition, as they read it, informs their acolytes.

Virtue

MacIntyre's work, although of increasing influence in the academic world, is not yet as widely known as the little shelf of books written by Leo Strauss. There is no MacIntyre.net, and no MacIntyrians have attempted to take over the Department of Defense or any other government agency. His major work, *After Virtue*, is very dark. At the end of it he concedes that it may appear to be a descent into darkness and tries to rectify the problem with a blunt denial of "social pessimism." He offers the denial almost sheepishly in a touching sentence fragment, reminiscent of Prufrock, at the end of the next-to-last paragraph of the

---

[18] The omission of Socrates was not an oversight. He does not get much play these days. Professors find lecturing much less taxing than the method employed by Socrates. There was a discomfiting egalitarian strain in his life and work, but it could be his tendency to go barefoot, drink too much watered wine, or ogle pretty boys that has done him in. His opposition to writing down his thoughts may irritate publishers.

book: "Not at all." MacIntyre, the Scotsman, and Leo Strauss, the German, are both beloved by conservatives, but MacIntyre is described by Kelvin Knight, his editor and interpreter (if that is what friends do), as a revolutionary rather than a conservative. MacIntyre is read by liberals too. Morris Berman, a liberal social critic, takes his own view of America having entered a new "dark ages" straight out of MacIntyre.

One way to approach MacIntyre's work is to look at a piece written for a wide audience rather than for professional philosophers. It will show why his readers and critics have so much difficulty deciding if he is a conservative or a liberal. Before the 2004 election he wrote a brief article, more like an op-ed piece than an essay, that shows two of the many sides of Alasdair MacIntyre and reveals in a few paragraphs the essential contradictions in his thinking.[19] He stated his position at the end of the first paragraph of the piece: ". . . the only vote worth casting in November is a vote that no one will be able to cast, a vote against a system that presents one with a choice between Bush's conservatism and Kerry's liberalism. . . ." These are, he said, "two politically intolerable alternatives." As MacIntyre fleshes out his argument for abstaining in 2004, it reveals the two not-quite-parallel paths he has followed over a long career (he was born in 1929). Raised in Gaelic and European traditions, educated in Greek and Latin, once a member of the Communist Party, then a socialist, he now follows Roman Catholicism with the same devotion he once gave to those other, more worldly routes to paradise. He is "pro-life," which, he said, excludes the possibility of voting for Kerry. He tells his readers to practice a politics that does "whatever is most effective in reducing the number of abortions." MacIntyre does not, like many Roman Catholics, go his own way on social issues. His *After Virtue*,[20] ends with a search for community in America, in both the Aristotelian sense of a community based on friendship and the Catholic idea of two communities: one on earth and the other in heaven, making him the perfect hero of the new national political movement: a conservative communitarian who denies he is a communitarian, the intellectual version of Bush's "compassionate con-

---

[19] The article is available from the *Notre Dame Center for Ethics and Culture*.

[20] Second edition, 1984.

servative." The heavenly community, MacIntyre says, is represented on earth by the Roman Catholic Church.

If he had been content with a pro-life stance as the basis for his politics of abstention, he would have seemed an obedient simpleton, but his argument, even in the brief paper against voting, is indicative of a mind in terrible conflict. He cannot vote for Bush either, because "the basic economic injustice of our society is that the costs of economic growth are generally borne by those least able to afford them and that the majority of the benefits of economic growth go to those who need them least."

The conflict concerning virtue in MacIntyre's work and that of many communitarians is a modern version of the conflict in ancient Athens. We can see the conflict more clearly at that great distance than in the "third way" of Bill Clinton. In Homeric Greece the primary virtues were courage and the fulfillment of one's role in the community. Later, in the Athenian polis, Plato defined a different set of virtues— prudence, fortitude, temperance, and justice. However, in that same Athens conflicts arose between being a good citizen and a good person. The good citizen was presumed to be virtuous, because it was assumed that Athens was the best state, the best way to live. But a problem developed in Athens: the good citizen and the good person were not always one and the same.

In *Antigone*, Sophocles portrayed the conflict between the two roles—person and citizen. Antigone had to choose between loyalty to family and loyalty to state. The conflict is tragic, because it cannot be resolved. She had to choose, and there was no right choice. She could only choose her own death. Death was a defeat, and for her brother to die without burial, for Antigone to see him left on the field of battle to be devoured by dogs, was the worst defeat of all. The death of the hero is one of the rare moments when MacIntyre considers death and the community. He does not deal with the Christian idea of death, except for that one astounding statement: "the Roman Catholic Church is God's community on earth." For the rest he concerns himself with the almost unbearable conflict of our time: the person or the state, the one or the many. He returns to the ancient arguments about how one should live, how character is formed, why we do what we do, what we mean by virtue and why we seek it.

MacIntyre founds his argument about virtue on having a *telos*, an end or final cause as described by Aristotle, ("Happiness, then," said Aristotle, "is something final and self-sufficient, and is the end of action.") I do not think the end MacIntyre seeks has changed much over his long career, from Communist to Roman Catholic, only the means for getting there. To decide that he has finally become a conservative, however, is to take the conservatives' view of his work. He can also be understood as a radical critic of the contemporary world, a revolutionary. But it would be a mistake to think of his ideas as revolutionary in the usual sense. MacIntyre is much more a revolutionary in the manner of the Catholic saints, particularly St. Benedict of Nursia (480–543), the founder of Western monasticism, who revolted against the world and worldly things. In an earlier time it might have been said of MacIntyre that he is in revolt against wickedness. He speaks of the world being in the hands of the barbarians, of a new Dark Ages, and in doing so he speaks for many Americans.

After Virtue begins engagingly enough with a science-fiction scenario and the dismissal of analytical philosophy as a tool for living. The scenario provides what may be a better picture of his ideas than the complex historical, literary, philosophical chapters that follow. MacIntyre's metaphor proposes a world suffering from a series of natural disasters. The public blames science. Massive riots take place. The rioters destroy everything connected to science: laboratories, university buildings, libraries, and then they kill the scientists. A Know Nothing political movement comes to power, removes science from textbooks, and forbids the teaching of it in schools. After some time passes, fragments of books are found, along with pieces of instruments; words that had been connected to science are reintroduced. People use the words but do not understand them. The various branches of the sciences are reestablished, people speak of relativity, evolution, and so on, but they do not quite know what the words mean or how the science was meant to be done. The language of science—boson, meson, genome, etc.—reappears, systems are formed around the words, but the meaning of them is not the same as it was before the catastrophe. Children study this incomprehending science.

And who would save the world after these disasters, riots, and mis-

understandings? Much of the rest of *After Virtue* is devoted to identify-
ing the analogues of the opening metaphor. Who destroyed virtue
ethics? The Enlightenment philosophers. Who will save the world for
ethics? It could be Alasdair MacIntyre in his role as Aristotle's radical
warrior. To be fair, MacIntyre is not so arrogant as all that, although
prescriptive philosophy is the most perfectly hubristic thing any person
can do (short of writing about prescriptive philosophy).

The world he describes in the metaphor and the book it forecasts at
first seem more curious than tragic, almost funny, but MacIntyre does
not laugh or suggest laughter. The love of life, the forgiveness of foible
expressed in wholehearted laughter, does not appear in his work. He
has a sense of how to approach the world more carefully and yet more
daringly than mere seriousness, but it does not include laughter. When
a man who holds that the Roman Catholic Church is God's community
on earth writes about virtue, it is grim stuff. There are no jokes in the
Lives of the Saints.

Near the end of *After Virtue* he arrives at the question that reaches
beyond personal virtue to judgment of the modern state, which he
appears to find beyond repair. That being the case, he had to suggest a
way to replace the state. He could not simply leap to a solution like St.
Benedict's abandonment of society, the end of hope for both "modern
politics" and the "modern state." MacIntyre looks to Aristotle for advice
on human conduct; that is, ethics.[21] He sees Aristotle's idea of friendship
in the *Nicomachean Ethics* as a means to bind up some of the more egre-
gious wounds in our American democracy. He is not the first to take
that position. In *Habits of the Heart,* a book that generated great interest
in the 1980s, Robert Bellah, a communitarian not entirely like MacIntyre, also depended on Aristotle's idea of friendship to show how a large
society can be held together. "Without civic friendship," he wrote, "a
city will degenerate into a struggle of contending interest groups
unmediated by any public solidarity."[22] MacIntyre is less optimistic. He
thinks the Athenian *polis* in the fifth century B.C.E. was already too large

---

[21] For an interesting exploration of Aristotle's concept of friendship, see Danielle Allen,
Talking to Strangers (Chicago: University of Chicago Press, 2004).

[22] Berkeley: University of California Press, 1985.

for such friendships, having more than 10,000 males who qualified as citizens. Hundreds of millions of Americans make the idea of community, as MacIntyre tells it, impossible. Bellah, whose ideas influenced President Clinton, seeks a vast community, a national community; "our friends, our fellow citizens," are the words he uses to end *Habits of the Heart*. And like MacIntyre, he worries about consumerism and power for the sake of power. He criticizes the modern state, but he, like the sociologist Alan Wolfe, sees possibilities within it. MacIntyre reads Aristotle differently and takes another road. He concludes that the argument is finally between "liberal individualism" and "the Aristotelian tradition."

MacIntyre lists the ills of the modern state from the manipulations and false faces of contemporary national politics to the breaking of promises to the way the modern state mitigates against the Kantian *sapere aude* (dare to think), the backbone of Kant's answer to the question "What is enlightenment?"[23] Furthermore, MacIntyre says that advanced Western democracies are not democracies at all, but oligarchies, which is true in many respects, but also deeply pessimistic. Having eliminated the possibility of changing these states through democratic means, MacIntyre comes to the conclusion that participation in them is useless. He proposes a different form of social organization, one that rids the community of the pernicious aspects of institutions. In such communities people may seek their own happiness and the happiness of others; that is, they may live virtuously because they have developed good character. What other conservatives have named "family values" will be restored, people will live on small family farms, and be able to "engage together in systematic reasoned debate."[24]

---

[23] MacIntyre blames the ills of the world on the Enlightenment, but admires some aspects of Kant's work.

[24] Given his political journey from Communist to Catholic, it is interesting to compare MacIntyre's utopia to the one Marx described in *The German Ideology*: ". . . in communist society, where nobody has one exclusive sphere of activity but each can be accomplished in any branch he wishes, society regulates the general production and thus makes it possible for me to do one thing to-day and another to-morrow, to hunt in the morning, fish in the afternoon, rear cattle in the evening, criticize after dinner, just as I have a mind, without ever becoming a hunter, fisherman, shepherd or critic."

Such societies must be small-scale and, "so far as possible, as self-sufficient as they need to be to protect themselves from the destructive incursions of the state and the wider market economy." In the end, he posits a utopia within the dystopia of the modern state, and like all utopians he wins over his audience with the charms of paradise, but only for a moment, for he is not dreaming. His radical response to the ills of the modern state does not differ in many ways from the ideas held by Grover Norquist of Americans for Tax Reform or those that underlay the policies of Barry Goldwater, Ronald Reagan, and Jerry Falwell, and now inform the thinking of George W. Bush and the right wing of the Republican Party. They are all enemies of the modern state. They all view (or viewed in the cases of Goldwater and Reagan) the state as inefficient, intrusive, and immoral, a failure of the Enlightenment. Their solution to oppression by the state has been to starve it through lower taxes and a reduction in the bureaucracy, by which it means the state's workforce. The concept is unworkable, which has not deterred conservatives, from Goldwater to MacIntyre, from championing it. Lower taxes resulted in higher debt, and Reagan and Bush produced more bureaucrats, not fewer. Reagan had an adversary in the Soviet Union, which he used as an excuse to operate contrary to what he said he believed about the state. Bush inherited Clinton's Qaeda problem. Then came a second attack on the World Trade Center,[25] which terrified the nation, but a clandestine enemy was insufficient reason for Bush to expand the state through debt even as he told his conservative allies he was starving it through lower taxes; he followed the advice of Dick Cheney and the neoconservatives in his government and created a visible threat in Iraq.

Then what role does MacIntyre play? He said philosophy had a connection to politics in the seventeenth and eighteenth centuries, but not since. Having come to that conclusion, why would he continue to pursue philosophy? Why not buy a small farm somewhere, join the community, act upon the virtues he learned from the traditional Gaelic

---

[25] The first came in 1993.

and European narratives that had formed him when he was still a child? Or is it no longer possible to retreat to the life of "an everyday plain person" once having risen to the role of philosopher? Is that what has led to his popularity among so many highly educated people: the simple fact that a group of thoughtful and pessimistic people wants some idea, some possible solution for an anchor? Are they like Bill Clinton, who adopted communitarianism because he could not find another way? Does MacIntyre, along with other communitarians, supply an answer that is no answer at all to the key question of virtue ethics: how to live?

MacIntyre is a peculiar kind of utopian; he does not imagine a world that could never be, but a world that could never be again. He comes very close to acknowledging reality: "Any worthwhile politics of local community will certainly have to concern itself in a variety of ways with the impact upon it of the nation-state and of national and international markets. It will from time to time need to secure resources from them, but only, so far as is possible, at a price acceptable by the local community."

Who then are the poor bastards who live in that dreadful nation-state and supply resources from time to time to the local community? The local community will have to join the nation-state now and then to fight National Socialism or Stalinist Communism, but "it will always also have to be wary and antagonistic in all its dealings with the politics of the state and the market economy. . . ." Like Plato's Republic, MacIntyre's world is a world we will never see, unless the modern state we call the United States of America collapses. Like Plato failing to install the rule of a philosopher in Syracuse, MacIntyre is unlikely to remake the modern American state. Only a few philosophers have had sufficient influence to remake a government. Marx, if we consider him a philosopher rather than an economist, remade many governments. Or we could grant Rousseau credit for the French Revolution. Jefferson and the other founders represented philosophers, but were not themselves philosophers. MacIntyre is correct when he describes the modern disjunction of political philosophy and politics, but only if he means a direct connection, tutelage, otherwise the statement is disingenuous.

Philosophy has been part of the political world since the inception of politics.

It would be interesting to know how the small communities he promotes in his works will choose whom to admit and whom to exclude. MacIntyre does not say who will make and enforce the laws that do not permit discrimination within the communities. He raises the issue of the Bakke case in which a white applicant to a graduate school at a state university claimed to have been refused admission because his place was given to a black, but offers no opinion about a just decision. What does he think? Where does he stand?

The right embraces him as a conservative. He favors what the right would call "family values," opposes what they call "statism," will not countenance abortion under any circumstances, is guided by religious values, and most of all, he detests the Enlightenment, which the right blames for the rise of godlessness in the world, and MacIntyre adds to that blame for all the ills of liberalism as it now applies to capitalism, corporations, and the enormous, oppressive, wasteful modern state. MacIntyre offers thoughts that will seem revolutionary or at least disconcerting to many readers: he says the idea of natural rights is a fiction, the conflict between natural rights and utility cannot be resolved. The only way to proceed is to follow Aristotle's *telos*, to understand that ancient "end," to take the journey from man as he is to man as he could be, if only "he realized his essential nature." And virtue ethics is the guide to this rational happiness. MacIntyre holds with Aristotle that good habits build good character and people of good character can be trusted to make good decisions.

Can he be a follower of Aquinas and the precepts of heaven's community on earth and still be a revolutionary, a man who finds all political traditions in our society exhausted? When ideas conflict, can both or either be correct? Revolutions from the right have occurred before; to be a reactionary is, in a sense, to be a revolutionary.

Setting aside the labels, the thrust of his work is finally not so much about ethics as about politics, and a very special kind of politics, escape from the destructive tutelage of the modern state through the partial secession of many small communities. He is as clear as he can be about it. Near the end of *After Virtue* he compares the modern state to the Roman Empire. This is the way he puts history to use in his argument: ". . . men and women of good will turned aside from the task of shoring up the Roman *imperium* and ceased to identify the continuation of civility and moral community with the maintenance of the *imperium*." They constructed new forms of community "so that both morality and civility could survive the coming ages of barbarism and darkness." Then he asks for the construction of similar communities to survive "the new Dark Ages which are already upon us."

He reminds us that we survived the last Dark Ages, and concludes: "This time, however, the barbarians are not waiting beyond the frontiers; they have already been governing us for quite some time. And it is our lack of consciousness of this that constitutes part of our predicament. We are not waiting for a Godot, but for another—doubtless very different—St. Benedict." How are we to read the preceding statement, which is more or less a summation of his views? Samuel Beckett's character Godot is often thought to mean "God," but Beckett refused ever to agree to this interpretation. Nor did he accede to ideas about the play as a modern retelling of the crucifixion of Jesus, with the two characters, Vladimir and Estragon, as the thieves. If Godot is not God, Godot is surely some hope of rescue from the uselessness and tedium of life, a savior of some kind, perhaps a nonexistent savior. Benedict may be the Godot of MacIntyre's hopes, someone who abandons Rome as hopeless and goes off to lead the life of a hermit, taking only his old nurse with him into his mountain retreat. Benedict chooses a way of life that some would say is no life at all. In this sentence about Godot and Benedict it becomes fairly clear that MacIntyre sees no solution to the contemporary human predicament, no use waiting for someone or something to change it; the only answer is to escape. Like many conservatives, he judges the modern state as Benedict judged sixth-century Rome. It is the conservative concept of America as Rome and the eventual fall of the United States. I heard it at an Americans for Tax Reform party and a Republican National Convention; it expresses in a few sentences the pessimism of the national political movement.

Assuming that his criticisms of the modern state are mainly justified, what exactly is it that MacIntyre wants us to do? Can a man who interrupts his disagreement with David Hume to tell the reader that Hume was a Calvinist devise small *ecumenical* communities? Or is his allegiance to Aristotle, the early Christians (which is what I think he meant about the small communities that survived the fall of Rome and the Dark Ages), the Roman Catholic Church, and St. Thomas Aquinas too strong to permit ecumenism? Does he really expect the collapse of the modern state? Does he want to usher it in through the creation of small communities, a series of secessions that will suck the remaining life out of the state? Is that what Kelvin Knight means when he says MacIntyre is a revolutionary?

In August and early September 2005 the Bush Administration shamed the nation with its bureaucratic bungling, general incompetence, and, according to many, racist motivation in the handling of the hurricane disaster along the Gulf Coast, particularly in New Orleans. On September 2, Bill O'Reilly, on the Fox News Network, told his listeners: "If you rely on the government for anything, you're likely to be disappointed." A column by liberal-left economist Paul Krugman in the *New York Times* the preceding day bore a headline with the same sentiment. Only a few weeks earlier the *New Yorker* (July 25) carried a long article about New York City Police Commissioner Raymond Kelly and his antiterrorist efforts in which Kelly and the author of the article said over and over that the federal government was unable to deal with terrorism as well as Kelly and his sophisticated staff. MacIntyre's concept of the failure of the modern state had quickly come to seem less a Swiftian dystopia than an accurate and not uncommon assessment. People read MacIntyre, and not just reactionaries, not just cranks. To many people his ideas are proving out in practice. He seems to many a prophet as well as a philosopher. He is the great pessimist, the philosopher of the fall. Follow St. Benedict, he said; it is the only way.

One aspect of the modern state that MacIntyre deplored had grown far worse during the Clinton Administration: the income gap between rich and poor. And Bush policies exacerbated the gap, the poverty level worsened during his first five years in office, but 30 percent of the population of New Orleans did not fall into poverty in only four years. An economic basis for racism had been described by Gunnar Myrdal in 1944 in his *American Dilemma*,[26] and it was there for the world to see in New Orleans: the poor were almost all black. Michael Brown, the director of the Federal Emergency Management Agency (FEMA), who came to the job prepared by his management experience as counsel for the International Arabian Horse Association, blamed the poor for remaining in the city during the hurricane; in other words, for being too poor to have the means to leave. Four days after the hurricane came through the city, while tens of thousands of people were suffering inside the Convention Center in New Orleans, watched by people around the world, the director of FEMA said on television that the agency had been unaware of the problem until that day.[27] The appointment of Brown, apparently arranged by the man who managed Bush's first presidential campaign, was understood in America and the world not merely as a sign of stupidity, corruption, cronyism, and carelessness in the Bush Administration, but as an indication of the fall from military, economic, and moral grace of the United States. Bush had done what Al Qaeda could not.

The crisis following hurricane Katrina may presage the further weakening of the state. Its immediate political effect was to weaken the Bush wing of the Republican Party; it may be the event that gives credence to the idea of small communities. No city government, no gulf state government, or the national government made an adequate response in an emergency. Until then, those who subscribe to the idea of revising government downward had held on dearly to the idea of a policing as well as a military function for the federal government, but it had failed to perform the policing task, and its emergency relief work had been abominable. Wayne LaPierre, executive vice president of the National Rifle Association, was widely quoted on his response to pictures of the aftermath of the hurricane: "Americans saw a collapse of

---

[26] London: Transaction Publishers (reprint), 1944.

[27] After resigning in disgrace, Michael Brown became a consultant on emergency management.

the government's ability to protect them. That burnt in: those pictures of people standing there defending their lives and defending their property and their family, where one source of comfort was a firearm." LaPierre's view carried through the Congress, which soon after the hurricane passed a bill exempting gun manufacturers from suit by a victim or class of victims of gun violence.

On the geopolitical level the government had been even less effective. The invasion and occupation of Iraq had been the result of the incompetent execution of an idiotic plan. What advice would the Scotsman give for the next election? What tiny town, what cluster of white wooden houses on the vast prairie would satisfy his hope for the future?

Nine

SAFETY

Speaking generally Émile will have more taste for the
books of the ancients than for our own, just because
they were the first, and therefore the ancients are
nearer to nature and their own genius is more distinct.

— ROUSSEAU

The problem inherent in the surface of things, and only
in the surface of things is the heart of things.

— LEO STRAUSS

In the academy, Straussians have provoked suspicion of
sectarianism . . . clearly lobbying to help "their own"
for what seem more ideological than academic reasons
and by creating in students a sense of (false, unearned,
in my view) superiority, that "we have got it" and "they
don't get it. . . ."

— ROBERT B. PIPPIN
Chair, Committee on Social Thought
University of Chicago (1994–1997, 1998–2001)

In the last year of the nineteenth century a boy born to a Jewish family in Kirchheim, Germany, could look forward to a decent life, perhaps a small business, a large one if he was ambitious; or a job in the
civil service if he was so inclined. If the child was gifted, there were no
limits to what he might accomplish in literature, science, philosophy,

music, economics, psychology, modern or ancient history. Every possibility was open to the gifted, the diligent, and the truly blessed, those
who were born lucky. Leo Strauss was such a child, born with a brain
of surpassing capability, diligent from his early years, and lucky enough
to have parents who cared for him, professors who delighted in him,
and universities that chose him. He was a Zionist as a young man, an
Orthodox Jew who found a place in the academic pursuits of Jewish
organizations as he grew up. We do not have a full biography of
Strauss, he did not leave a memoir, and his personal history did not
appear overtly in his work. Germany's greatest philosophers invited
Strauss to study with them. The neo-Kantians, who were popular at
the time, took him under their wing. At the age of thirty Leo Strauss
was one of the two or three most brilliant young philosophers in
Europe. It was a glorious period for the humanities: Philosophy was all
the rage. Art, literature, psychology, science, were in full bloom. The
time was an especially good one for Jews: Kafka, Wittgenstein, Arendt,[1]
Benjamin, the most important neo-Kantian philosopher Hermann
Cohen, Einstein, and young Leo Strauss, who was to have a great effect
on one current of American political thinking. It was not Athens in the
fifth century, but the air was rich with beauty and disputation and the
scent of imperialism and war, as Athens had been in its moment of
greatness.

   Strauss became a student of Martin Heidegger, the existentialist
philosopher who captivated his mind as well as the mind (and body) of

---

[1] Hannah Arendt is mentioned only briefly in this book, although there are certain parallels
between her career and Strauss's that would lead to interesting speculation. They were both
students of Martin Heidegger, both German Jews, both brilliant, and both studied at the
University of Marburg and taught at the New School for Social Research in New York City
and the University of Chicago. They did not like or admire each other. Arendt was seven
years younger than Strauss. She was very beautiful as a young woman, handsome as she
aged. A mutual acquaintance said of her during her years at the New School, "She had good
legs, and she was very proud of them." In some photographs, Strauss looks like the comedian Jack Benny. Strauss left Germany in 1932; Arendt did not get out until 1941, barely
avoiding the death camps. She married Heinrich Blucher, a Communist; Strauss became a
conservative. Since this is not a biography, it does not attempt to closely align their political
philosophies with their life experiences, but it is interesting to note that Arendt, who had
seen Jews categorized as a race, deprived of their rights, and sent to death camps, could not
understand the plight of American blacks and did not sympathize with their desperate
efforts to improve their situation in America.

Hannah Arendt. Young Strauss declared Heidegger the most brilliant and original thinker of the twentieth century, a view he maintained until his death. On his way to a brilliant career in Germany, the young political philosopher, possessed by some strange prescience, left his native country for France in 1932. From there he went to England on a Rockefeller grant to write a book on Hobbes. In 1933 the news arrived in England of an event that haunted Strauss all the rest of his days: he saw philosophy betrayed. On German Armistice Day of that year, Martin Heidegger, author of *Being and Time*, rector of the University of Freiburg, had delivered a pro-Nazi speech and allowed himself to be photographed in the company of uniformed Nazi officers and Nazi thugs in business suits. Strauss was not alone in the way the shock of disappointment affected him. No one writing about Heidegger since then has been able to avoid the problem of the existentialist's capitulation to the Nazis. An entire world of culture was shattered by the inability of the wise to resist evil.

Heidegger survived the defeat of Germany, but refused until the day he died to discuss his actions during the years leading up to the Second World War. Hannah Arendt defended her former lover and lifelong friend, claiming his Nazi sympathies were simply the flaws of a philosopher who entered into worldly affairs. She compared his membership in the Nazi Party to Plato's folly in Syracuse; it was not Arendt at her best. She was not alone. Yale Professor Paul de Man turns out to have been a journalist on a Nazi newspaper, and French philosopher Jacques Derrida defended him; it was not Derrida at his best.

Heidegger had been openly anti-Semitic as a young man, but Strauss may not have known about his professor's character while he studied with him, which could account in some measure for the effect of the revelations about Heidegger in Strauss's life and thought. Arendt, only nineteen years old when she fell under Heidegger's influence, must have learned about his anti-Semitism at some point early on in their affair. Why she continued to warm the bed of her married professor, who hated her categorically even as he was attracted to her intellectually as well as physically, is difficult to comprehend; perhaps it later provided an entry point for her major work, *The Origins of Totalitarianism,* or more tellingly for the concept of the banality of evil in her *Eich-*

mann in Jerusalem. Heidegger's effect must have been mesmerizing, for Arendt and Strauss, his brilliant students, came to despise each other— Arendt, the doyenne of citizenship, and Strauss, the advocate of superiority, cultural, intellectual, and national—but they were never able to put aside their involvement with the man they idolized. The 1933 photograph produced a less loving, more troubled reaction in Strauss, and as with Arendt, his lifelong fascination with Heidegger cannot be separated from the effects of the Holocaust, emigration, the sense that never left them of the world as a dangerous and unpredictable place. Separately they fled from Europe to the United States. Strauss found work at the New School for Social Research in New York City in 1938. The faculty, rich with brilliant émigré scholars, was a university in exile.

War in Europe broke out in September of the next year with the German bombing of Poland . Strauss was forty, and he had already witnessed the beginning of two world wars, the roots of the Holocaust, and the takeover of the Soviet Union by Joseph Stalin. He had himself escaped the whirlwind, which he saw as the collapse of the liberal democracies, but the effect of the experience on the minds of émigrés, especially those with extraordinary talent, is incalculable. Theodor Adorno, who left Germany and the neo-Marxist Frankfurt School and settled in the United States until nostalgia drew him back home after the war, may have come close to defining a measure of the effect when he said, "To write lyric poetry after Auschwitz is barbaric." Strauss took a different, more aggressive position: he blamed the weakness of liberal democracy, in this instance the Weimar Republic, for the Holocaust and theorized that liberal democracies must have external enemies if they are to be strong. Although Strauss never proposed preemptive war, the idea of the necessary enemy, a response to what could have been his own death, emerged as the philosophical basis for the American invasion of Iraq and may lead to war with Iran.

In the summer of 1948, Strauss traveled to Chicago to be interviewed for the vacant post of professor of political philosophy. Robert Maynard Hutchins, then chancellor, talked with Strauss and immediately appointed him a full professor. Strauss stayed on at Chicago for twenty years. In the late 1940s and into the next decade, the University of Chicago was the most left-wing university in the United States, and there, hidden among the graduate divisions, the accidental father of much of neoconservatism taught Plato and Montesquieu, Spinoza, Machiavelli, and Hobbes. Leo Strauss arrived at Chicago when the hard sciences were in their ascendance, not many years after the first nuclear chain reaction was created under the old West Stands of the abandoned football field. The newcomer was outgunned by the big-time Aristotelians, such as Richard McKeon, but Hutchins had appointed him, and he could hold his own as a scholar with anyone in his field.

There were other key figures of the time at the University of Chicago, many of them in the physical, biological, and social sciences and mathematics: Fermi and Szilard worked on nuclear physics, Watson and Crick found the double helix that gave birth to the comprehension of DNA. Rosalie Wax, David Riesman, and Robert Redfield had major reputations in the social sciences. One of these figures, with little or no public reputation, Albert Wohlstetter, a mathematical logician, was largely responsible for the Cold War theory of mutually assured destruction, although MAD, as it was known, had many inventors.[2] Wohlstetter's specific contribution was more in the area of targeting: as targeting became more accurate and the area within which a rocket was likely to hit was more tightly defined, the explosive power required to destroy the target decreased. Thus, if the rocket was expected to land within a mile of the target, enormous explosive force, probably nuclear, was required. If the rocket was expected to land within a few yards of the target, conventional explosives were sufficient.[3] Wohlstetter was also the "genius" behind Reagan's Star Wars idea. If Wohlstetter and Strauss, the theoreticians of the Cold War, knew each other at all during those twenty years, it was to nod in passing.

---

[2] Wohlstetter later became involved in theories of Mutually Assured Survival. He had great influence on the views of Paul Wolfowitz, who wrote his doctoral dissertation on nuclear weapons in the Middle East.

[3] This is, of course, a vast oversimplification of Wohlstetter's calculations. Hardened targets deep underground present different problems.

Strauss was not a popular figure on campus. Many students did not like him at all. More than a full generation later they spoke to me of his arrogance and elitism, and asked not to be identified by name.[4] Strauss and the social scientists found each other unbearable, for he took pains to attack Max Weber, and they hated him for it. In worldly things Strauss suffered from arrogance and timidity, partly the result of the Platonist's anxiety—the fear that, like Socrates, he would be put to death for being a philosopher—and the other fear, the one taught not by slow reading, but by the Holocaust. The university's renowned Committee on Social Thought never included Strauss, yet he had disciples, and disciples have two duties: to sit at the feet of the master and to spread word of his wisdom. The "Straussians" excelled at their work: Leo Strauss has become one of the most widely discussed writers on political philosophy in our time.

The career of Strauss's teachings is one of the wonders and the dangers of the book, as the master himself might have said, knowing that the long life of books, unlike newspapers or television, is bound up with history in a process of indirection. The ideas in books somehow manage to wiggle through the morass of individuals and information in large societies and become effective. The way is not clear. Strauss was more or less content to write books in obscurity and to convey the ideas in them to a few students and a small number of readers. The students carried on the work, and their numbers multiplied. They found places in the universities and in the government. A cadre of Straussians appeared in both places, and the cadre soon began to think of itself as a class, that class for which Plato could find no more apt name than gold.

There are three distinct aspects of Strauss's work and legacy. One of these, the wondrously scholarly mind of Leo Strauss, has produced work that will continue to be read and admired for many years; it is represented by Seth Benardete. Another, resulting from a flaw in Strauss's

---

[4] They have good reason. Straussians who have achieved positions of power in the academic world have become adept at intellectual street fighting. They have a reputation for ending careers. Their influence is somewhat less now, but empires in decline have always fought hard, anticipating the pain of the alternative, and the Straussians are no exception. The academic world is already hostile to them; their political world has fallen from public favor; they survive on invective and tenure, but they survive.

conception of democracy,[5] gave us the character of the Straussians described by Professor Pippin in the epigraph; it is represented by Allan Bloom. The third is the political Strauss, which he may or may not have intended; it is represented by Paul Wolfowitz and many of the neoconservatives who have wounded America at home and abroad and who may, by their arrogance and stupidity, have caused a catastrophe that will engulf much of the world in fire and death. After long consideration it is my opinion that had Strauss lived to see this last group of Straussians he would have detested them—not for the exercise of aberrant will, but for the inability to think even one move ahead in the games of national and international politics; Strauss was an elitist, and the neoconservatives have not measured up.

Nuts

At times Strauss and his disciples, including Benardete, seem to have been a bit, well, nuts. According to Benardete, one day when Strauss was discussing the *Republic* he said that Socrates had given seven examples in an argument and the middle example was the most important. He went on to say he had found that in any odd number of examples the one in the center was always the most important. Instead of greeting the observation with a polite chuckle, Benardete offers another example, as if to prove Strauss's case: A skeptical friend "went home, took down from the shelf a copy of Montaigne's *Essays* from his library, counted

---

[5] I find this flaw especially disturbing since more than ten years ago I founded the Clemente Course in the Humanities to teach the humanities at the college level to the poor. The course is now taught in seven countries, at sixty sites, a fourth of them in conjunction with Bard College. The faculty comes from the University of Chicago, Sungkonghoe University (South Korea), Northwestern University, Harvard University, National Autonomous University of Mexico, Reed College, University of British Columbia, Dalhousie University, University of Ghana, Mount St. Vincent University, St. Mary's University (Halifax), King's College, Franklin and Marshall College, University of Science and Arts of Oklahoma, Oklahoma City University, Bloomfield College, University of Wisconsin, UNAPEC (Dominican Republic), University of Ottawa, University of Illinois, Autonomous University of Yucatán, University of Alaska, Lakehead University, Australian Catholic University, Victoria University, San Andrés University (Argentina), Georgetown University, Trident Technical College, University of Massachusetts (Dartmouth), New York University, and so on.

their number, and looked up the central one. It was entitled *On Vain Subtleties,* and its theme was the importance of being in the middle."[6] Induction was not a strong suit for Strauss. In this case, the particular from which he argued was apparent, but the general idea he drew from it was closer to revelation than reason. And it is not a very good revelation. Is the middle book always the most important? My Oxford Bible lists thirty-nine books in the Old Testament. The middle book is Proverbs.

Benardete was an eccentric as a young man, a quality that grew more pronounced in his writing throughout his life. Strauss was not a public eccentric. He responded to the sense of homelessness life had thrust on him—émigré, Jew, philosopher—by a mix of assertiveness and profound conservatism. Strauss could not make a journey home like Odysseus; he had no home. He presented himself as a man of reason, but choosing the importance of an example by its place in a series of numbers belongs to the Kabbalah or a comedy club. Strauss and Benardete both appreciated a good joke.

Benardete

The reputation of one of the Straussians continues to rise even as events, age, and serious consideration by people on the right as well as the left bring about the decline of the neoconservative followers of the master. By far the most brilliant of Strauss's followers, Seth Benardete, who died in 2001, was interested in the connection of philosophy to poetry as well as to politics. He applied Strauss's method of slow, deep reading of old texts to Plato, Homer, and the Greek playwrights, producing brilliant translations and dense, difficult, occasionally weird, exegetical essays. In one sentence Benardete found the essence of Strauss at his best: "The first thing Strauss was always doing in his study of Plato was to be a beginner. He knew how to start again, not as if he were starting for the first time, but really starting for the first time."[7] Two aspects of

---

[6] *The Argument of the Action* (Chicago: University of Chicago Press, 2000).

[7] Ibid.

Plato's thinking on the idea of rethinking or thinking anew occupied Strauss and Benardete. There is, in Plato, a "second sailing," another way of looking at the world. Socrates, on the verge of death, offers a brief philosophical biography in the *Phaedo* that became a method for Strauss, but even more so for Benardete. The second aspect comes from the allegory of the cave in which the prisoner, chained, and facing a wall of shadows, is freed, brought up to the surface, and sees the sunlight, the world of ideas. It is also a method. Strauss and Benardete could find the structure of each dialogue and all the dialogues in it.

Strauss read Plato brilliantly, as did Benardete after him. They wished to understand Plato as he had been understood in his own time. If Strauss had been content with essaying the dialogues of Plato, if the side of him that produced Benardete had been all of him, his contribution to scholarship would have been grand, but quiet. His followers would have been few, but excellent, and there is no telling what might have come of the quality of mind produced by this effort to think through Plato as one might have thought of him in his own time. But it was not to be. Strauss set sail for the troubled waters of the political life of man; his mind was captured by the worst in Plato. As he was timid in life, he was bold in thought, an adventurer into thinking so complex that even his most brilliant disciple said he could not always understand him. Perhaps as an irony or in an unintended revelation of his arrogance, Strauss said that esoteric writing might not be necessary, because so much work was not understood anyway.

The difference between Benardete and the others—Allan Bloom, Harvey Mansfield, and so on—shows most clearly in the field of interest of the disciples. Benardete was a scholar who inspired scholars; the others, whom we know as Straussians, were concerned with power and inspired war. While a student at the University of Chicago, Benardete established close relationships with Strauss and the classicist David Grene. Benardete had a quality then that other Straussians lack. He could laugh. His best pal was Severn Darden, a legendary figure on campus, brilliant, funny, a member of the improvisational *Compass Theater*. He and Benardete enjoyed philosophical jokes and great odysseys in Darden's ancient Rolls-Royce. Given his friendship with Darden, the lapses into strangeness in Benardete's work are not surprising. He and Darden were part of a nest of laughers and philosophers in and around the university. Even the owner of the tavern that housed the theater where Darden, dressed as usual in a long cape, did improvisations, was a philosopher; he opened the business immediately after receiving his doctorate.

Allan Bloom was different. He was a nasty man, vicious in the classroom,[8] a misogynist, publicity seeker, closet homosexual, elitist, opponent of the poor. He did not laugh at the world; he sneered. Benardete, who knew how to laugh, knew Bloom and worked with him, but chose his own direction in scholarship and life, and he gives every indication in *Encounters and Reflections*[9] that he did not like Bloom very much. Perhaps they were too different by temperament; because he could laugh, Benardete made the connection between philosophy and literature as Bloom and the other Straussians could not. Strauss himself could laugh. Benardete described him "laughing his head off" on more than one occasion. The unpleasant side of their laughter, like Darden's, is that it was almost always a matter of laughing *at* someone.

There was another side of Strauss that his stepson and the orphaned niece he adopted and raised as his own child must have known. It was Strauss the romantic, who met his future wife while she was still married to another man and immediately announced that he would marry her. It was Strauss the timid American immigrant, who upon being invited to go from New York to Chicago for an interview asked a taxi driver how much he would charge for the trip. Benardete tells this last to remind us that Strauss had been sent into exile, which for the ancient Greeks was tantamount to a death sentence. Thus we have a man terrified, in a Greek sense dead, in a Jewish sense in yet another diaspora. While Strauss wished to read the Greeks in their own time, Benardete tells us to read Strauss in his own time.

Benardete dressed in black and said death was his chosen field of

---

8 Students who attended Bloom's seminar reported that he chose Norman Podhoretz and Midge Decter's son John for a victim, torturing him with sarcasm and insult.

9 Subtitled *Conversations with Seth Benardete*, with Robert Berman, Ronna Burger, and Michael Davis, ed. Ronna Burger (Chicago: University of Chicago Press, 2002).

study.[10] A Sephardic Jew, he came of a distant experience of persecution, one remembered across more than four centuries. Strauss, had he remained in Germany, would most likely have died in a Nazi concentration camp. Perhaps that accounts for the differences of mind in the teacher and his star pupil. We know only that Benardete and his college friends, George Steiner among them, did at some time in their lives enjoy the rib-tickling tragicomedy of existence. Steiner, who was born in France and came to the United States at the age of eleven, wrote fiction, essays, an interesting book on *Antigones*,[11] and a useful little book on Heidegger, in which he devoted many pages to his disgust with Heidegger's Nazi past. Steiner noted Benardete's work in *Antigones* and elsewhere. Bloom made no mention of Benardete in his best-seller, nor did Thomas L. Pangle speak of him in his introduction to a collection of Strauss's essays and lectures, and there was no word from Joseph Cropsey about him in the vast tome he and Strauss wrote as a textbook on political philosophy. There was no obituary for Benardete in the *New York Times*. Harvey Mansfield, who brought Straussian conservatism to Harvard, wrote an appreciation of Benardete in the *Weekly Standard*, but the political conservatives could not really claim him for their own. In fact, Mansfield is reported to have said in response to a question about Benardete as a conservative: "Perhaps he was above conservatism, if such a thing is possible."

Bloom

William Kristol wrote that "Strauss, chiefly by way of his students, is in large part responsible for making the thought and principles of America's founders a source of political knowledge and appeal, and for making political excellence more broadly a subject of appreciation and study." America's founders thought it self-evident that all men are cre-

---

[10] In *Encounters and Reflections: Conversations with Seth Benardete* (Chicago: University of Chicago Press, 2002).

[11] *Antigones* (New York: Oxford University Press, 1984).

ated equal,[12] and yet increasing inequality has been the hallmark of the Bush Administration, as it was of the Reagan and Clinton administrations. Donald Rumsfeld's primary task under Ronald Reagan was to rid the country of the Great Society programs of the early 1960s. Irving Kristol, an early Straussian, advised Reagan and Rumsfeld and their staffs of the need to stop coddling hungry children, educating the poor, and helping the aged, the infirm, and victims of prejudice. The current conservative government works more boldly toward inequality. It has adopted a tax system suggested by Grover Norquist, another Straussian, a man who publicly compared the inheritance tax to the Holocaust. It marries the idea of small semiautonomous communities advocated by MacIntyre with the strict definitions of class that come from the Bloom embrace of Strauss's idea of limiting the use of the great books to a small elite.

In 1959, in a commencement address in Rockefeller Chapel at the University of Chicago, Strauss said, "Liberal education is the necessary endeavor to found an aristocracy within democratic mass society." In one sentence he had stated his elitism and his distaste for what he called the vulgarity of democratic society. The speech was a mess, probably written in haste; in it Strauss called for "a universal aristocracy," which is a contradiction in terms. Three years later he made clear that the phrase was unthinking, a burlesque of political philosophy. He made the ruling elite permanent: "We must not expect that liberal education can ever become universal education. It will always remain the obliga-

---

12 The problems connected with a literal reading of Jefferson's phrase in the Declaration of Independence are limitless. Clearly he did not say that he meant all persons, without regard to gender, race, ownership of property, and so on. The document was to serve as an announcement of the separation from England, but Jefferson had read Francis Hutcheson and been inspired by his ideas. The pursuit of happiness may well have come from Hutcheson's idea that the greatest good is the happiness of others. A fundamental understanding of the intent of the founders would seem to mean the extension of the equality provision in pursuit of the greatest good. Reading the minds of the founders has been an American sport since the founding, and in a democratic republic it should, of course, continue for as long as the republic lasts. The idea of equality has often served as a goal for political groups in the United States, resulting in equality to a greater or lesser extent over the years. The Civil War was fought in one respect to establish a country more closely aligned with the ideal. The Women's Suffrage Movement, the New Deal, and the Civil Rights and Voting Rights acts all followed the same direction. To a great extent it has been possible to define major political groups in the U.S. according to their will to put the idea of equality into practice.

tion and the privilege of a minority." It was a mean-spirited reading of Book VI of the *Republic,* which is in itself a mean-spirited work. The following excerpt is from the Paul Shorey translation.

> "... *just as men escape from prison to take sanctuary in temples, so these gentlemen joyously bound away from the mechanical arts (trades) to philosophy, those that are most cunning in their little craft. For in comparison with the other arts the prestige of philosophy even in her present low estate retains a superior dignity; and this is the ambition and aspiration of that multitude of pretenders unfit by nature, whose souls are bowed and mutilated by their vulgar occupations even as their bodies are marred by their arts and crafts. Is not that inevitable?" [Paragraphing inserted.]*
>
> *"Quite so," he said.*
>
> *"Is not the picture, which they present," I said, "precisely that of a little bald-headed tinker who has made money and just been freed from bonds (prison) and had a bath and is wearing a new garment and has got himself up like a bridegroom and is about to marry his master's daughter who has fallen into poverty and abandonment?"*
>
> *"There is no difference at all," he said.*
>
> *"Of what sort will probably be the offspring of such parents? Will they not be bastard and base?"*
>
> *"Inevitably."*
>
> *"And so when men unfit for culture approach philosophy and consort with her unworthily, what sort of ideas and opinions shall we say they beget? Will they not produce what may in very deed be fairly called sophisms, and nothing that is genuine or that partakes of true intelligence?"*
>
> *"There is a very small remnant, then, Adeimantus," I said, "of those who consort worthily with philosophy. . . ."*[13]

In the preceding passage the reader will find the essence of the Leo Strauss–Allan Bloom (and to a considerable degree Seth Benardete)

---

[13] New York: Loeb Classical Library, 1935.

theory of education and their argument in defense of practically anything they say. The Straussians see the world in terms of themselves and the baldheaded tinkers. They are wrong, of course. Anyone can read the preceding passage. People in prison can read Plato; I have taught Plato to classes in a maximum security prison. Professors from Reed College are teaching a full academic year course in "the Greeks" to men in the Pendleton (Oregon) Correctional Facility. Bard College has a prison education program.[14] A group led by Professor Michael DeWilde of Grand Valley State University has been teaching philosophy to men in a state prison in Michigan. To have the Strauss-Bloom view makes one the enemy of philosophy: to withhold philosophy from the people is to cheat philosophy of its *telos* or final cause, their happiness. Strauss, who was the Robert Maynard Hutchins Distinguished Service Professor, and the man for whom the chair was named had contrasting views. Hutchins, the founder with Mortimer Adler of the Great Books program, had said, "The best education for the best is the best education for all."

By the time Strauss gave the commencement address, he had nothing to fear about this basic opposition to the thinking of the man who had hired him. Hutchins had been forced out of the university in 1951, replaced by Lawrence A. Kimpton, who announced immediately that he was going to get rid of the "queer kids." Years later, I asked Hutchins about it. He said, "He meant the Jews." Did Strauss know? If so, did he fear it was the beginning of Germany again?[15]

Bloom comes directly out of this flaw in Strauss's understanding of democratic education. The flaw determined Bloom's character (at least in part; according to Saul Bellow, he had other problems) and that of the Straussians described by Professor Pippen in the epigraph (above). As might be expected, arrogance or elitism leads to cruelty, the capability,

---

[14] I chair the Advisory Board of the Bard College Clemente Course in the Humanities, but am not involved in the Bard College prison program.

[15] I do not know if Strauss ever visited Hutchins at the Center for the Study of Democratic Institutions in Santa Barbara. Hutchins did not mention Strauss to me, and there is no reference to Strauss in Harry S. Ashmore's exhaustive biography of Hutchins, *Unseasonable Truths* (Boston: Little, Brown, 1989).

perhaps even the desire, to use people, to make them into things. No follower of the Bloom school of Strauss can agree with Kant's description
of human dignity. Kant wrote in the *Metaphysical Foundations of Morals*
that "whoever transgresses the rights of men intends to use the person
of others merely as means without considering that as rational beings
they shall always be regarded as ends. . . ." The Straussians assign dignity to the few, and those who are deprived of dignity cannot pursue "the
natural end . . . all men have (which) is their own happiness." William
Kristol has a point: The study of Strauss's work does lead to thinking
about the founders; not how they would agree with the Straussians but
how they would oppose them. History has shown that the work of the
founders produced a republic capable of overcoming its flaws, while the
Bloom branch of Strauss's thinking leads to a return to one of the most
significant flaws, which is an end to intellectual mobility. This idea of a
permanent sorting of people by intellectual class based on race and various inherited social and economic deficits has recently found defenders. There was an attempt to resurrect the reputation of Bloom among
"liberals" in the newly conservative *New York Times Book Review*.[16]

I have quoted Bloom on the subject elsewhere, but it is useful to listen to his objections to any effort to achieve fairness in the society. Following Strauss, his project proposes to deprive all but the most
fortunate of the possibility of the liberal arts and to limit the group of
the fortunate even further by expelling the children of divorced parents
and nonwhites. Like Strauss, Charles Murray, and the right wing of the
Republican Party, Bloom detested the egalitarian implications of American democracy. This is some of what he wrote on the question of fairness in his best-selling book. On his "sample" of students fit to study the
liberal arts:

---

[16] September 4, 2005. Some newly conservative people in the academy now speak of Bloom's
"love for his students" as part of this revisionist view of Bloom's writings. Bloom was in
some ways a tragic figure, betrayed by his friend and "biographer" Saul Bellow, but Bloom
was often unpleasant in and out of the classroom. He died of AIDS but could not bring
himself to say more than two tepid sentences about the plight of homosexuals in the course
of a dozen pages under the rubric "sex" in *The Closing of the American Mind*, written more
than five years after the 1969 Stonewall Uprising.

> *It consists of thousands of students of comparatively high inteligence, materially and spiritually free to do pretty much what they want with the few years of college they are privileged to have— in short, the kind of young persons who populate the twenty or thirty best universities. There are other kinds of students whom circumstances of one sort or another prevent from having the freedom required to pursue a liberal education. They have their own needs and may very well have different characters from those I describe here.*

He had written on the subject before, and he quoted himself without giving the source: "I am referring to . . . those to whom a liberal education is primarily directed and who are the objects of a training which presupposes the best possible material. These young people have never experienced the anxieties about simple physical well-being that their parents experienced during the Depression. They have been raised in comfort and with the expectation of ever increasing comfort." Bloom then paraphrased Strauss: ". . . these students are a kind of democratic version of an aristocracy."[17]

Since Plato was, in the vulgar language of modern neoconservatism, "mugged" by the death of Socrates, there has been a web of consistency in conservative thinking. While Strauss was not interested in specific social problems, Plato's idea in the *Republic* of immutable classes of men (gold, silver, bronze, and iron) and the proper education of each class was carried on and made even more strict by the Straussians, beginning with Bloom. Plato permitted some mobility in that children born to one class might be educated into another, but Bloom would have none of it. Nor did he have any hope for affirmative action changing the situation of people of African descent. He wrote: "Affirmative action (quotas), at least in universities, is the source of what I fear is the long-term deteri-

[17] Lest there be even the slightest doubt about the inaccuracy as well as the ugliness of Bloom's view of proper students, Mary Ann Mason, dean of graduate studies, and Genaro Padilla, vice chancellor for student affairs, have both told me in personal conversations that 20 percent of the students at the University of California at Berkeley come from families earning less than $30,000 a year. UC Berkeley is surely among the twenty or thirty best universities, if not the best two or three. Bloom was, quite simply, an indefensible man.

oration of relations between the races in America." Since the need for affirmative action is not caused by nature but by poor relations (slavery, prejudice, etc.) between the races, Bloom is arguing that the effect of an action is the same as its cause. If his thinking is correct (and there are not many people other than perpetual-motion-machine theorists who would go along with it), affirmative action simply maintains the status quo ante. Fairness was not on Bloom's mind, as it was never on the mind of his mentor. Nor is Bloom here following the advice of Socrates "daily to discourse about virtue." In the contest between racism and reason, he chose racism. This is what he wrote on the preceding page: "The fact is that the average black student's achievements do not equal those of the average white student in the good universities, and everybody knows it. It is also a fact that the university degree of a black student is also tainted, and employers look on it with suspicion, or become guilty accomplices in the toleration of incompetence."[18]

Blacks are not the only group Bloom wants to exclude from the liberal arts. He made another observation during his years in the classroom, and the conclusion he draws from it is astonishing. "A university teacher of liberal arts cannot help confronting special handicaps, a slight deformity of the spirit, in the students, ever more numerous, whose parents are divorced. I do not have the slightest doubt that they do as well as others in all kinds of specialized subjects, but I find that they are not as open to the serious study of philosophy and literature as some other students are. I would guess this is because they are less eager to look into the meaning of their lives, or to risk shaking their received opinions. In order to live with the chaos of their experience, they tend to have rigid frameworks about what is right and wrong and how they ought to live. They are full of desperate platitudes about self-determination, respect for other people's rights and decisions, the need to work at one's individual values and commitments, etc. All this is a thin veneer over boundless seas of rage, doubt and fear." Bloom is more severely classist than Plato not

---

[18] Compare this stereotyping to Nietzsche's in *Human, All Too Human:* "The whole problem of the *Jews* [his italics] exists only in nation states, for here their energy and higher intelligence, their accumulated capital of spirit and will, gathered from generation to generation through a long schooling in suffering . . ."

only in the case of blacks (and Latinos, if he had given them a thought), but these poor wretches whose parents have divorced.

He goes on about their lack of courage and how he pities them. "They are indeed victims." And then he administers the *coup de grâce*: "An additional factor in the state of these students' souls is the fact that they have undergone therapy." Again he paraphrases Strauss, putting them in a place below "the cave (of the shadows), or the world of common sense." It is an argument in favor of what are now called "family values" to go along with the case for limiting the educational mobility of people of color. Bloom went well beyond anything Strauss had said, and the Straussians after Bloom have gone beyond him in their arrogance. They have raised what used to be thought of as the ideas of ignorant people to the realm of academic respectability.

Once the poor, blacks, and the children of divorced parents have been barred from studying the liberal arts, there is no place for them in governing the society. Plato made a ferocious argument on the point. He believed the wise should rule—and who could quarrel with that? But who then decides among competing wise men, and what should be the limits of the wise statesman's power? It is instructive to listen to Strauss: "It would be absurd to hamper the free flow of wisdom by any regulations; hence the rule of the wise must be absolute rule. It would be equally absurd to hamper the free flow of wisdom by consideration of the unwise wishes of the unwise; hence the wise rulers ought not to be responsible to the unwise subjects." Strauss explains that this would result in the subjection of what is by nature higher to that which is lower. His reading of Plato comes down to this: true democracy is an act against nature and must be prevented at all costs. How to reconcile this with Strauss's concern for strengthening liberal democracies is one of the problems his followers must constantly confront.

A careful reader of Plato soon comes to understand that he did not lay out his ideas in the flat form of a newspaper article, but created dramas in which the action—the interplay between the participants—goes on at the same time as the argument. Each of the players has a personality, a history, and a physical presence, like the characters in a play. The dramatic action and the argument inform each other. It makes reading Plato interesting and difficult. Plato, who wanted to kick the poets out of his imagined *Republic*, is recognized by his readers as something of a poet himself, another contradiction. This is the modern reading of Plato, and Strauss and Benardete make much of it.

Quite a lot of Benardete's and Strauss's writing on Plato has to do with these elements. The dramatic action and the second sailing, or beginning anew, are the basis of their methodology. It must have excited students very much when they first encountered it, but any teacher who has used the Socratic method in a classroom and used it even passingly well comes to the same recognition. The classroom is filled with people, each of whom is a complete and complex human being, and if it is a class in philosophy or literature, the discussion will be filled with contradictions, ending with the final contradiction from which the students cannot escape, bringing them to understanding. It is, for the professor, the glory of teaching, the reason why there is no sameness in the work of the good teacher. It was a commonplace in Athens. Socrates and the Sophists used it. And the method gave Plato a dramatic structure for most of his writings. Strauss, Bloom, and Benardete made much of the method; at times they implied that they just might have discovered it. Their genius was not in the discovery of the structure of Plato's work, but in the obfuscation of it.

Since Strauss was not Plato, but a commentator on Plato, a reader might expect that his work would be closer to a newspaper article than to a Platonic dialogue, which is by nature a series of contradictions leading to more contradictions and eventually to the aporia, the contradiction from which there is no escape, when the disputant concedes the error of his thinking and Socrates triumphs yet again. Strauss did not write in dialogue. He did not speak of accepting the work of great minds, but of the interplay among the ideas of great minds. Instead of a dialogue within a work, he posited a dialogue among many works. An unfriendly reader might infer from that position an awe-inspiring arrogance: to have such a project Strauss must have considered himself one of the great minds orchestrating the grand dialogue among great minds. Such arrogance is not unusual among philosophers. Nietzsche, to whom Strauss is married in many ways, suffered from it more than most. Walter Kaufmann, who said, "Nietzsche's books are easier to read but harder to understand than those of almost any other thinker," went on to explain that "in Nietzsche's books the individual sentences seem clear enough and it is the total design that puzzles us."[19] In the case of Strauss neither the total design nor the individual sentences are clear. His use of contradiction, perhaps unwittingly, has become the intellectual hallmark of Straussians and through them the Bush Administration, which spoke in increasingly contradictory language as its policies failed and it fell in the estimation of the people.

There are two kinds of contradictions—those in dialogue and those in declarative sentences. The former are a dramatic strategy and a fine classroom tactic. The latter are not lies, but nonsense. An axis of evil that cannot be connected along any imaginable axis is a nonsense statement. Compassionate conservative in the Bush lexicon is nonsense. An imposed democracy is nonsense. And such nonsense is dangerous. A democratic government would collapse if it spoke only nonsense. Under George W. Bush the government has learned to speak on two levels at the same time. What appears to be nonsense to most people makes some sense to those who are initiated into a way of thinking and a certain set of references, many of them biblical. From the constant use of the word "evil" to subtle references to the book of Revelation, the favorite text of end-time thinkers, Bush's speeches and remarks have carried an esoteric message. The language of his administration runs from deception, which is a form of lying, to saying the opposite of what they know to be a fact, to calumny.

All politicians lie. "I will not raise taxes," said Roosevelt. "Read my lips," said the elder George Bush. "I am not a crook," said Richard Nixon. "I did not have sex with that woman," said Bill Clinton. "Weapons of mass destruction," said Bush. "See the weapons of mass destruction," said his Secretary of State Colin Powell to the United Nations Security Council. The difference between the current Bush and his cronies and past administrations is in both the way the various forms of lying have permeated their actions and in the Straussian justification of it, which is quite different from self-preservation or realpolitik.

---

[19] *Nietzsche: Philosopher, Psychologist, Antichrist* (Princeton: Princeton University Press, 1950).

In the only book he wrote in anything close to plain English, *Persecution and the Art of Writing*,[20] Leo Strauss advised his readers not to write in plain English, and he followed his own advice. Convoluted, contradictory, arcane, clubfooted writing was his game. He worked at it. He skulked in the dark corners of exposition, making it all but impossible for anyone, including his acolyte Benardete, to discern exactly what he thought. In all the history of the English language, there had never been a man—not merely a man, a professor at a great university—who so publicly opposed clarity and so brilliantly demonstrated his talent for obfuscation. In his chosen field he was a giant, and the best scholar he produced, Benardete, stood on the shoulders of the giant.

Bad writing, unintelligible, contradictory writing, and systematic lying raise a moral question, as Strauss well knew, but denied. He ascribed his advocacy of bad writing, which he called "esoteric writing," to the possibility that a writer could be persecuted for what he said. If the writer lives in danger of death or imprisonment because of speaking his ideas clearly, to write as if in a code addressed to a small coterie of followers is not unreasonable. Strauss based his argument on the work of Moses Maimonides, a Jewish physician and philosopher of twelfth-century Spain, who concerned himself with the conflict between faith and reason. Maimonides's *Guide of the Perplexed* was addressed to one of his students, himself a highly educated man. In the preface to the book Maimonides clearly divided the world into those who could read the complex ideas of philosophy and those who could not.

On the surface the *Guide* could be read for its interpretations of Scripture and its ethical prescriptions. But Maimonides said that a reader would have to be conversant with many philosophers and other commentaries on Scripture to fully understand the work. The same might be said of an essay by William Gass or a sermon by John Donne. Strauss went beyond that; he revived the long-forgotten idea of the "secret" meaning of Plato's work, and he argued that the *Guide* too contained secret teaching, a metaphysics contrary in some respects to the

---

[20] New York: The Free Press, 1952.

literal teachings of the Bible, one that must be concealed from the masses, who would be unable to comprehend why God, for example, must necessarily be devoid of attributes. According to Strauss, the poor organization of the *Guide* and its obvious repetitions and contradictions were not merely lapses on the part of Maimonides, but a secret to be discovered by some very small number of readers. It was not, as Maimonides said, that his book was written for a knowledgeable reader, but that there was something more, something cabalistic about the work, not metaphors in Scripture, like those Maimonides interpreted, but secrets, the kind one finds by adding up the numerical values of the letters in a name or counting the eyes on the wheels of a chariot.[21] It was secret, Strauss claimed, because such knowledge might turn the masses away from religion; it was dangerous. He took the example of Maimonides and applied it not to commentary about metaphors and other difficult passages in the Bible, but to contemporary political philosophy. He became midwife to the method of the American right.[22]

Strauss claimed that clarity in a philosopher's work endangered not only the philosopher, but the world as well. Perhaps. Although he was born in Germany, Leo Strauss wrote all but one of his books in England and the United States, and he was not a homosexual, a Communist, or

---

[21] Ezekiel 10:12.

[22] The back cover of the paperback edition of *Persecution and the Art of Writing*, above the quote from Irving Kristol's review in *Commentary*, offers as an enticement to the reader several lines from the following paragraph on p. 25 of the book: "Persecution, then, gives rise to a peculiar technique of writing, and therewith to a peculiar type of literature, in which the truth about all crucial things is presented exclusively between the lines. That literature is addressed, not to all readers, but to trustworthy and intelligent readers only. It has all the advantages of private communication without having its greatest disadvantage—that it reaches only the writer's acquaintances. It has all the advantages of public communication without having its greatest disadvantage—capital punishment for the author. But how can a man perform the miracle of speaking in a publication to a minority, while being silent to the majority of his readers? The fact which makes this literature possible can be expressed in the axiom that thoughtless men are careless readers, and only thoughtful men are careful readers. Therefore, an author who wishes to address only thoughtful men has but to write in such a way that only a very careful reader can detect the meaning of his book. But, it will be objected, there may be clever men, careful readers, who are not trustworthy, and who, after having found the author out, would denounce him to the authorities. As a matter of fact, this literature would be impossible if the Socratic dictum that virtue is knowledge, and therefore that thoughtful men as such are trustworthy and not cruel, were entirely wrong."

a person of color. Who would drag him out of his bed in the middle of the night to accuse him of adoring Plato or snuggling up to Aristotle? Who would put his small body on the rack to force a confession for the crime of promoting bad writing? Philosophers are not endangered in America, but if by philosophers we mean Straussians, especially those in government, the world may very well be in danger from philosophers.

The president of the United States told the world that Iraq had weapons of mass destruction. His secretaries of defense and state made the same assertions. They claimed to be telling the kind of truth that enables good countries to go to war against evil ones. Secretary Powell showed drawings of mobile biological weapons factories to the United Nations Security Council, and America went to war. From time to time after the occupation of Iraq, the reason for going to war changed, for there were no weapons of mass destruction, only a miserable dictator and the remains of a once prosperous country. As a result of the war, the Iraqi people went from fear to fear and anger; the contradiction of imposed democracy failed, and killing and group hatreds that could be characterized as civil war took place. As American soldiers were killed and maimed and no weapons of mass destruction were found, the administration no longer spoke of the chimerical weapons; it changed to the celebration of a terrible dictator deposed, the sweet flower of freedom planted in Babylon.

One of the great services that Strauss and his disciples performed for the Bush regime was the provision of a philosophy of the noble lie, the conviction that lies, far from being simply a regrettable necessity of political life, are instead virtuous and noble instruments of wise policy. The idea's provenance could not be more elevated: Plato himself advised his nobles, men with golden souls, to tell noble lies—political fables, much like the specter of Saddam Hussein with a nuclear bomb—to keep the other levels of human society (silver, brass, iron) in their proper places, loyal to the state and willing to do its bidding. Strauss too advised the telling of noble lies in the service of the national interest, and he held Plato's view of aristocrats as persons so virtuous that such lies would be used only for the good, for keeping order in the state and in the world. He defined a modern version of the noble lie in the use of esoteric messages within an exoteric text, telling the truth to the wise while at the same time conveying something quite different to the many.

For Strauss, as for Plato, the virtue of the lie depends on who is doing the lying. If a poor woman lies on her application for welfare benefits, the lie cannot be countenanced. The woman has committed fraud and must be punished. The woman is not noble, therefore the lie cannot be noble. When the leader of the free world says that "free nations do not have weapons of mass destruction," it is a noble lie, a fable told by the aristocratic president of a country with enough nuclear weapons to leave the earth a desert less welcoming than the surface of the moon.

Wolfowitz

The third aspect of Strauss is represented by Paul Wolfowitz. It comprises esotericism, lying as a virtue, and some scholarship, but the most important and dangerous feature comes of magisterial self-regard, for it raises the vulgarity of Bloom's social thinking to the level of geopolitics. Wolfowitz and his fellow Straussians in government are the architects of what is, so far, the political error of the century. To lay the damage that Wolfowitz, Rumsfeld, and Bush wreaked upon the world in this generation and generations to come at the feet of Leo Strauss may be no more reasonable than assigning responsibility to Nietzsche for the Nazis, but the adherence to their version of Strauss's ideas cannot be overlooked even if Strauss merely provided, like Nietzsche, work so unclear it could become Scripture for scholarship or villainy.

The Straussian neoconservatives in the U.S. government sometimes describe themselves jokingly as a "cabal." A cabal, however, implies a level of shrewdness about worldly things they do not possess. They might better be called a ship of fools. The chief fools—and history will not use such a gentle word to describe them—were in the Department of Defense, most notably Paul Wolfowitz, whom George W. Bush rewarded for the disaster he helped to bring on the world by promoting him to head the World Bank, where he would be able to do yet more damage. Richard N. Perle resigned as chairman of the Defense Policy Advisory Committee after Seymour Hersh disclosed his business dealings with companies whose products and services he championed to the committee. Perle called Hersh a "terrorist" and threatened to sue him for libel, but settled for promoting a silly book Perle wrote with former Bush speechwriter David Frum. Douglas Feith, undersecretary of defense for policy, was also a Straussian and no more adept at his job than Wolfowitz or Perle; Feith[23] is reputed to have sold the war and Straussian thinking to Vice President Dick Cheney. Cheney's chief of staff, I. Lewis Libby, Jr., who had been one of Wolfowitz's students at Yale, was convicted of perjury.

The Straussians penetrated Defense, State, and served twice as chief of staff of the vice president of the United States, once for Cheney, and before that when William Kristol worked for Dan Quayle, with whom he may have shared insights into Plato, but not the spelling of "potato." Leon Kass was a member of the President's Council on Bioethics, as was Francis Fukuyama, author of *The End of History and the Last Man*. Gary Schmitt became executive director of the Project for the New American Century. Alan Keyes exercised his logorrhea as assistant secretary of state and as a candidate for the presidency and the U.S. Senate. Stephen A. Cambone was undersecretary of defense for intelligence; Abraham Shulsky headed the Defense Department Office of Special Plans. Many of the Straussians studied at Cornell and the University of Chicago with Strauss's disciple, Allan Bloom, others with Harvey Mansfield at Harvard and Paul Wolfowitz at Yale. They were not philosophers or classicists: not one claims to have studied at New York University or the New School for Social Research with Seth Benardete.

The Straussian concentration on the value of studying the liberal arts has unfortunate and disturbing parallels in Europe during the period leading up to the Second World War. In prewar Germany study was often connected to a feeling of moral revulsion at the behavior of large parts of the German population during the Weimar Republic, which is not very different from the current feeling toward Hollywood, homosexuality, and abortion of the Christian right in the United States. Germany in the early twentieth century was one of the most sophisti-

---

23 Feith is now associated with Georgetown University and the Kennedy School of Government at Harvard University.

cated countries in the world. Leo Strauss was born into a society richer in the knowledge of the humanities than perhaps any other in modern times. Among those people who rose to the top of the Nazi government were students of the humanities, former scholars. Joseph Goebbels had studied history and literature at the University of Heidelberg. Reinhard (Hangman) Heydrich was the child of a pianist and an opera singer who founded a conservatory. Ernst Kaltenbrunner studied law at the University of Prague. More than a third of the members of the Vienna Philharmonic belonged to the Nazi Party. Albert Speer, who ran the business side of the Nazi war machine, was an architect. Rudolf Hess studied political science at the University of Munich; his mentor there, Karl Haushofer, thought to be one of the philosophical influences on Nazism, came from a family of scholars and devoted much of his early academic life to the study of Schopenhauer. Strauss has never been accused of Nazi sympathies; the accusation would be absurd. He has been accused only of writing a criticism "from the right," meaning a Hobbesian perspective, of attacks on liberalism by Carl Schmitt, who later became an important jurist in the Nazi government.[24] The nature of the horror in Germany is not that Strauss was a Nazi. Schmitt was. But Strauss, the student of the liberal arts, was thirty years old, beyond the excuse of innocence, when he attacked Schmitt from the imperialist right. Much later Strauss wrote about the idea of Athens as a "totalitarian state," saying that it had all the aspects of totalitarianism (it did not), but that it permitted philosophy, which kept it from fitting the definition (he does not offer one) of totalitarianism. He contradicted himself elsewhere on freedom in the ancient world. And of course, it is not Athens the imperialist real city that has the aspect of totalitarianism, but the imagined city of Plato, and even the imagined city lacks the technological capabilities of a totalitarian state.

That Strauss does not feel at all uncomfortable with certain aspects of Plato's city leads to the possibility that the liberal arts studied by the brightest of students is no guarantee against the worst kind of thought or action. In his 1959 commencement speech on liberal education,

---

[24] *Logos*, Spring 2004.

Strauss could not muster a defense of democracy, only a criticism of it as "the hard shell which promotes the soft mass culture." As he had attacked Schmitt from the imperialist right almost thirty years earlier, he attacked democracy from the right in the great stone hall of Rockefeller Chapel at the University of Chicago. He left a strangely contradictory legacy; Zionist and atheist, defender of what he called liberal democracy and its enemy, champion and abuser of the liberal arts.

How Wolfowitz and the Straussian neoconservatives came to their view of the world and their method of operation requires a brief venture into some of Strauss's ideas. There are, according to Strauss, two ways to read or write a philosophical work. There is the "exoteric" text—that is, what is on the page—and the "esoteric" text, the secret meaning that only certain careful readers can understand. For example: in the preface to his *Theologico-Political Treatise*, Spinoza addresses his work to Christians; that is the exoteric text. Strauss reads the esoteric text, which says to him that Spinoza addressed the work to Jews, perhaps basing his view on the excommunication of Spinoza from the Jewish community in Holland. The Straussian method is to see what does not exist except to a Straussian. Applied to Spinoza, it is harmless enough; anyone can make a mistake. Applied to Saddam Hussein's weapons by an administration influenced by Paul Wolfowitz, it can lead to war. The Straussians in the Bush Administration read the world as Strauss read Spinoza. They whispered what they divined into the ear of the president, and the president went to war. Over the last few years, some Straussians in the academy have made a point of denying their teacher's influence in matters of policy. Aside from the fact that such denials are in perfect keeping with the Straussian approach to public discourse, we need not be concerned with proving direct lines of influence. A brief summary of Straussian doctrine suffices to demonstrate its affinity with what one might call the "mind of the regime," whether any particular member of the Bush Administration has read Strauss or not.

The Straussians made some of their intentions known. Perhaps they thought they were acting according to right reason. Perhaps fear drove them to read secret meanings into what they saw in the world. Wolfowitz, like Strauss, had personal connections to the Holocaust and the Cold War. Wolfowitz grew up in a time when people learned to build shelters to combat the radioactive fallout from nuclear weapons. His father, a mathematician, had emigrated from Poland in the 1920s, but many of his relatives who stayed in Poland died in the Holocaust. And both he and others in the Defense Department saw as part of their mission the protection of the United States and the maintenance of its superiority (Strauss's word) in the world. Unfortunately these men, who thought of themselves as patriots defending the great liberal democracy, acted in a way that put the very democracy they wanted to protect at great risk from both internal and external forces.

Long before the events of September 11, 2001, the Bush Administration—goaded on by Wolfowitz, Kristol, the American Enterprise Institute, the Project for the New American Century, and others on the right—had made a decision to oust Saddam Hussein. Bush seems to have had a personal vendetta, but the others had more philosophical reasons. There was nothing Machiavellian about the attack. It was based on principles the planners derived from natural law. One suspects that President Bush, with his simplistic messianic mind-set, was attracted to this line of reasoning: natural law derived from the concept of natural right, the innate ability to know right from wrong, took precedence over mere convention. And so the Bush regime violated the contract that was agreed to when the United States joined the United Nations; it flouted the U.S. Constitution, which is also a contract, by attacking without the required declaration of war by the Congress; and it disregarded the Geneva Conventions in its treatment of prisoners at Guantánamo Bay, Cuba, in Iraq, and in secret detention camps around the world.

The administration's wise men held up Strauss's version of natural law as the model, dismissing contracts as mere laws of men. Natural law, interpreted by Bush's "wise counsels," gave the president permission to launch a preemptive war through an appeal to the higher power. Natural-law theory assumes that men seek the good and that by asking the perennial questions—what is virtue? what is justice?—they will come to wisdom. Straussians, like Kristol, hold that the founding fathers espoused natural-law theory, saying that natural law was both divine and self-evident. But the founders were concerned with unalienable natural rights. After much debate in their convention, they wrote a contract.

There were many factors in the corruption of the country, but Strauss's work, twisted into a Nietzschean scheme by his political followers, played a significant role. The Straussians who have access to the public media have never denied it. William Kristol and Steven Lenzner wrote in the *Public Interest* (Fall 2003): "President Bush's advocacy of 'regime change'—which avoids the pitfalls of a wishful global universalism on the one hand, and a fatalistic cultural determinism on the other—is a not altogether unworthy product of Strauss's rehabilitation of the notion of regime."[25] Strauss spoke of the "central significance" of "regime." It is worthwhile to see what he meant by the word. Here follows a series of quotations from his writing on the idea of "regime," which Kristol and Lenzner so admire in the Bush Administration. The ominous tone comes from his view of democracy as a hopeless system of government. Strauss wrote often of saving the "liberal democracies," but he offered no evidence of understanding how these democracies came about or could be maintained. He and his followers have an imperialist attitude; they simply do not think the "common people" are capable of wisdom.

- *The probability that all human societies should be capable of genuine freedom at the same time is exceedingly small. For all precious things are exceedingly rare.*
- *If restraint is as natural to man as is freedom, and restraint must in many cases be forcible restraint in order to be effective, one cannot say that the city is conventional or against nature because it is a coercive society.*
- *The classics called the best society the best* politeia. . . . politeia *is not a legal phenomenon. The classics used* politeia *in contradistinction to "laws." The* politeia *is more fundamental than any law; it is the source of all laws.*
- *The American Constitution is not the same thing as the American way of life.* Politeia *means the way of life of a society rather than its constitution.*

---

25 In *Natural Right and History* (Chicago: University of Chicago Press, 1953), he explained his use of the term. The quotes above on "regime" are all from chap. 4.

- *We shall translate* politeia *by "regime," taking regime in the broad sense. . . . The thought connecting "way of life of a society" and "form of government" can provisionally be stated as follows: The character, or tone, of a society depends on what the society regards as the most respectable or most worthy of admiration.*
- *"Civilization" is the modern substitute for "regime." It is difficult to find out what a civilization is.*
- *The best regime, which is according to nature, was perhaps never actual; there is no reason to assume that it is actual at present; and it may never become actual. It is of its essence to exist in speech as distinguished from deed. In a word, the best regime is . . . a "utopia."*
- *The best regime is that in which the best men habitually rule, or aristocracy.*
- *The political problem consists in reconciling the requirements for wisdom with the requirement for consent.*

Given the effect of his work on the world, even as proof of the geopolitical error of his neoconservative followers plays out in Iraq, and the moral failings of the conservatives in such things as limiting health care for the poor through passing Medicaid on to private health insurers grow more serious every day and the old guard of the Straussians sinks into the weaknesses of age, it is useful to know something about how they got there, for I do not think the Straussians will disappear anytime soon. The national political movement owes much of its philosophical underpinning to them. They are not traitors, nor do I think they have formed a cabal; they inherited the terrors of history: the Holocaust, Hiroshima, and the Cold War. The error of their thinking comes of the knowledge of the death of deaths, the end of all of immortality's humanizing forms, the time when there may be no one to examine the markings made in stone. The objective of Hitler, Stalin, Mao, and Pol Pot was to obliterate enemies, to leave no history of them; a totalitarian society could not exist without the will to control memory as well as the moment. If we look back very carefully at Strauss, whose brush with nothingness came not when his heart failed in old age but when he saw Heidegger, "the most brilliant mind of the twentieth century," at home among the Nazis, we can see how the awful discovery should have confirmed in his mind the profound role of history on human thought. Was that also part of the reason Strauss denied the value of historicism in the work of Heidegger and countless other philosophers? Did Strauss have a premonition about what was to come in Germany? Benardete, whose ancestors escaped the Spanish Inquisition to carry on their language, memory, and tradition, and Wolfowitz, much of whose family died in the Holocaust, took very different paths. Death is personal, but in our last moments we may console ourselves with the idea that we will be remembered, if only in the genes of our successor, but annihilation is the end of social and genetic immortality; it is inconsolable. The way we understand the difference between the two kinds of death may determine the way we read and write: what we are willing to dare, how public we may be in our loves and languish-ings. Strauss feared the fate of Socrates, and in *Persecution and the Art of Writing* he read Maimonides as if it were Tadeusz Borowski's story of the Nazi death camps, *This Way for the Gas, Ladies and Gentlemen.*

Strauss despised the Weimar Republic for its weakness in allowing the rise of Hitler. He thought the Russians who had permitted the Marxist-Leninist takeover were equally weak and despicable. The Nazis and Communists had driven him out of his home, had murdered his fellow Jews. He feared the Marxists would take over the world. He said that Marxists, socialists, and what we now call liberals aimed toward the same goal. Only strength could withstand the onslaught of these ominous forces, and the only way for a liberal democracy to remain strong was to have external enemies. Strauss provided a ration-ale for the will to power, the only means left of maintaining the pursuit of virtue by noble men. The Straussian rightists took in his reading of the history of philosophy, manipulated it to fit their own version of his-tory, and went to work. They began just after the Cold War and soon focused on their former ally, Saddam Hussein, who provided an oppor-tunity for testing Albert Wohlstetter's ideas about smart bombs and precision targeting. As the rockets fell on Baghdad, the two old Uni-versity of Chicago professors, Strauss and Wohlstetter, had joined forces at last.

Historical events as such had little to do with the U.S. invasion of Iraq. Wise men advised the president to do what he thought was right, according to principle. Bush consulted with heaven, not with events on earth, and heaven, as he often said in the esoteric part of his speeches, told him what to do. That Richard Perle and William Kristol were his prophets and the Christian right his congregation was the American misfortune. The misreading of the events of 9/11 led to an attack on the wrong enemy for no other reason than the presumed need of a clearly defined enemy to make our liberal democracy strong. This triumph of principle over history initiated a series of contingent events, not only in the Middle East but also in large parts of Asia, that may not be resolved for decades. Strauss, buffeted by history in his own life, railed against historicism, which holds that meaning can arise only from within a particular historical context. The Straussians contend that historicism leads to relativism and thus to nihilism, finally to the crisis that could bring about the destruction of the American liberal democracy—a crisis, as Strauss himself said, that comes of the loss of the American sense of superiority.

Strauss wanted to return to the ideas of the ancient world, to think exclusively as they had thought, but unlike Nietzsche and Heidegger, he did not want to go back to the pre-Socratics, only to Plato, and now and then Aristotle. In this, Strauss and MacIntyre meet. MacIntyre opposes the modern state and the Enlightenment that gave birth to it, Strauss opposes modernism entirely. According to Strauss, Heidegger was the end of a progression of modernism that began with Machiavelli, whom Strauss regarded as the first modern philosopher. He denounced Machiavelli as a "teacher of evil," not so much for counseling his prince to be ruthless in pursuit of worldly power as for betraying the principles of ancient philosophy. "His discovery," Strauss wrote, "is implied in the principle that one must take one's bearings from how men live as distinguished from how they ought to live." Prior to Machiavelli, philosophy had taken its bearing by the eternal truths; after him, philosophy was concerned with the ignoble reality of how men actually live. It was a crisis of modernity, he said. And if this world had become intolerable, if history had gone wrong, the only solution lay in the old books. Only the ancients could be trusted, only the perennial questions were worth considering. One had only to read them carefully, slowly, uncovering their secret teachings. Only students who thought themselves brilliant were attracted to Strauss; they worshiped him. How disappointed his acolytes in the Department of Defense must be at the fact that Strauss once published a sentence in which he opposed preventive war!

Was that one of the principles derived from pursuit of the eternal questions? St. Augustine had defined the idea of a just war, but a just war was not preventive war. There was no way that Strauss could twist principle around to see preventive war as the act of noble men. He never argued for a first strike. Yet his followers did just that. Strauss made a principle of the idea of the enemy. While he lived, it was the Communists. Now it has become the Muslims. He held on principle that having an enemy was the prerequisite for strength, but he did not think principle should change based on history. He did not think ideas that differed from what he understood to be principle merited consideration. He spoke of the interplay between great minds, but his followers understand themselves as the masters of the interplay, like puppeteers manipulating the little dustups between Socrates and Aristotle, Burke and Rousseau, Smith and Marx. There is one way, and they know the way. I think Strauss, for all his Nietzschean proclivities, would have despised Cheney, Wolfowitz, Kristol, et al.

During his lifetime Strauss had a great intellectual antagonist, Sir Isaiah Berlin. They represented the polar opposites of political philosophy, the one and the many, the idealist conservative and the pluralist liberal. To Berlin there was no one true answer to any of the great questions of political philosophy, and if there were true answers, we might well never know them. He saw political philosophy, which he described as ethics applied to society, as an attempt to negotiate conflicts among the virtues, none more clear than the conflict between liberty and equality. The Oxford don put it with remarkable clarity: "Liberty for wolves is death to the lambs." The principle of equality must limit the liberty of the strong if the weak are to be fed and clothed. Berlin agreed with Hegel that the essence of freedom was to be at home in one's own culture. He carefully drew the distinction between relativism and pluralism: "'I prefer coffee, you prefer champagne. We have different tastes. There is no more to be said.' That is relativism." Pluralism, he wrote, is "the conception that there are many different ends that men may seek and still be fully rational, fully men, capable of understanding each other and sympathizing and deriving light from each other, as we derive it from reading Plato or the novels of medieval Japan."

The pluralist wrote, "Ends, moral principles, are many. But not infinitely many: they must be within the human horizon." Strauss had a far narrower horizon, and he believed there must necessarily be no more than one true and unchanging answer to each of the perennial questions. Nature willed it so. Nature willed everything, even the superiority of the capitalist West over all the rest of the world. The crisis of our time is the failure of the West to believe in its own superiority. He took that view during the Cold War. With the collapse of the Soviet Union, his followers applied it to the Middle East.

Strauss saw the fundamental questions of human identity and survival exemplified in the Jewish question. And he believed it had no resolution, for the answer to the Jewish question was assimilation, unless the Jews had a land of their own—and with a land of their own they would be assimilated into the society of nations. One way or the other, they would disappear. The Jewish problem, like the human problem, was insoluble. He offered no exoteric answer. He quoted Gershom Scholem's work on the Kabbalah, sounding more literary than philosophical, much like Jorge Luis Borges. Strauss spoke of what could not be known, the mystery of the Aleph, the first letter of the Ten Commandments. Had he become a Kabbalist, wrapped in the mystery of revelation? His embrace of esotericism was not, I think, theological; his method was to use reason to understand religion. His personal history, the history of philosophy, and the history of the world in his time were mixed in him in esoteric, perhaps impenetrable fashion; he was, despite the chill mask of arrogance, human, and it is the human who remains hidden. Unlike Socrates, he does not reveal himself in a brief autobiography, as in the *Phaedo*, nor is there anything in Strauss even vaguely like the beloved, human Socrates of the *Apology*. Derrida was correct. We must know something about our philosophers, we cannot understand them as mere abstractions, thought devoid of life. Strauss looked back, but never inward, for answers to the questions of the unfathomable present. He sought a method and found it in Plato's perfect city, the city Strauss said would never be. He gave us the life of the mind but never the life of the man. He could laugh at situations, but never at life;

he could not overcome the barrier to human greatness, the sense of life that was available to the very people he and Bloom and all those who came after them rejected as unworthy. He gave his followers no ethical guidance; he made the Platonist's error of thinking aristocrats are virtuous. He gave his political followers a method: to usurp the power of revelation in the service of their idea of reason. They coddled the minds and coerced the wills of their leaders, whom they must have considered the shrewdest of simpletons.

In the mind of George Bush, the ancient problem of the conflict between faith and reason was resolved by force.[26] Bush was hardly the first man to learn the comforting character of power, or the first to abuse its use. In itself power poses no danger to the country or to the world. It may be used in constructive or destructive ways, and it can be legitimate or not depending upon its origins. Historically the crisis comes in the resolution that has now been made in America. Faith has a poor record in the exercise of power, and the contemplation of the perennial problems has not done much better. The Bush regime relies on faith when it can and reason when it must, not in the cause of peace or justice but in pursuit of dominion. In its use of violence and secrecy, the stick and the lie, it has no end in mind but power.

That is not the *telos* of a constitutional democracy. There is a movement in the country now, still inchoate, that flirts with the transmogrification of democracy into a controlling society based on secrecy and disinformation, and devoted to the accretion of power without end, which is the definition of totalitarianism.

The present American government follows Wohlstetter's last logic and Strauss's esoteric morality. Judging from the number of quotations and references to the philosopher in their writings, the Straussian worldview appears to have come straight from Plato. But the legacy of Strauss fits better with the ideas of Friedrich Nietzsche.[27] This may

---

[26] The problem occupies Maimonides, who was influenced by his reading of Al-Farabi, the tenth-century Arab philosopher. Maimonides's writing about it in the *Guide* is important to Strauss's views about exoteric and esoteric writing.

[27] MacIntyre argues against Nietzsche in *After Virtue*.

seem curious, because Strauss blamed "the second crisis of modernity" (the crisis of our time) on the author of *Beyond Good and Evil*.

When Strauss wrote about Nietzsche, he used the word "public" again and again, perhaps betraying something close to envy. Nietzsche had found the style and the daring to say what lay in the depths of Strauss's soul. Nietzsche's aphoristic love letters to power were the image of Strauss revealed in the aesthetic mirror. Nietzsche ensnared the timid professor who passed on the ideas to his disciples, who taught them to the men and women who held power. Straussian thinking agrees with Nietzsche on historicism and trumpets the master morality over the slave morality.

No one more than Strauss (and now his followers) has greater contempt for the weakness of humility or puts more credence in the arrogance of the overman (*Übermensch*). The Straussians, like their mentor, say the greatest danger to the United States comes from weakness in the face of its enemies and from the failure to believe in its own superiority. It is a theoretical problem, they say. The alternative to superiority is the end of ideals, a descent into the comforts of mere being. Nietzsche called the feckless creature who cares for nothing more than preservation of his own skin, wishing only comfort and universal equality, "the last man." He wrote in *Thus Spake Zarathustra*, "'We have discovered happiness'—say the last men, and they blink." He called them the most despicable men, those who despise themselves. It was his warning to the world. The only alternative to the last man is the will to power, which Nietzsche said is the will to life itself, the will to overcome, to control, to be master of all things.

History belongs, Nietzsche wrote, to "the man who fights one great battle," the man who looks to the past only in order to find exemplars, other great figures who attempted to shape the clay of humanity for a "higher purpose." History is filled with such figures and with nations that, to their sorrow, put their faith in them.

Tomorrow

Machines and mechanistic campaigners grow old; the statistical probability of failure increases; photons go increasingly awry; they lose the constancy that was their most beloved virtue. The question of what Bush will do has already been succeeded by the need to decide who he was, what he did, and if he and those who surrounded him will be exemplars for yet another round of men and women who believe they must fight one last battle. The importance of a president has to do with the ideas he invented or endorsed, not with the women he bedded or the alcohol he consumed, or the mixed-race children he fathered, or the cold rain on inauguration day that killed him. Presidential details fade, but the half-life of an idea is very long.

We are now in a period based on political philosophy just as we were in the eighteenth century when Arthur Lee, under the pseudonym Cincinnatus, wrote on November 29, 1787: ". . . give me leave to recommend to you to read Mr. Locke. . . ." It was a time when Thomas Jefferson published a translation of Montesquieu's *Spirit of the Laws*, when Madison in *The Federalist*, No. 10, could argue the difference between a tiny pure democracy and a great republic almost as if he were arguing against MacIntyre's opposition to the modern state. The debates on the Constitution used Plato and Sir Thomas More as examples of states that could never be. The founders were mostly thoughtful, if harsh, men, who wanted to turn ideas into realities. They were amenable to compromise, sometimes in bizarre ways, as in the three-fifths rule regarding the personhood of black people.

It was all these educated, imperfect men could do to lay the foundation for a society that became egalitarian enough to merit the name democracy as we use it now. The difference between the way ideas affected them and the current national political movement has to do more with the quality of the men and women who interpret ideas than with the ideas themselves. Tom DeLay, who led the Republicans in the House of Representatives, is a shrewd man but not an educated man; he was trained as an exterminator. The former Senate majority leader, Dr. Frist, was trained in the practice of medicine but not educated in the practice of government. The outgoing president was trained as a mechanical man, a pilot of very high-speed fighter jets. Religion spared him from a life dominated by alcohol, and he thinks of himself as a metaphor: he is the world. He suffers a kind of Wilsonian madness, a mechanistic willing, without the intellectual wherewithal to know the meaning of his obsession. Like the machines whose constancy he emulates, he lacks judgment, which must be learned, but he learned only to rely on the judgment of others. Had it been good judgment, had Karl Rove and Paul Wolfowitz been Harry Hopkins and George C. Marshall, the tattered world he leaves behind would have been different.

In *Rationalism in Politics and Other Essays*,[28] Michael Oakeshott offered an often-quoted definition of conservatism: "to prefer the familiar to the unknown, to prefer the tried to the untried, fact to mystery, the actual to the possible, the limited to the unbounded, the near to the distant, the sufficient to the superabundant, the convenient to the perfect, present laughter to utopian bliss." The right wing of the Republican Party relies now on him, Adam Smith, Burke, Hayek, Strauss, and MacIntyre, and through them interpretations of political philosophy from as far back as the theological-philosophical ideas in Scripture. The question that has to be raised in considering the actions of the right, from Goldwater to what they will suggest in 2008, is if, in the realm of political life, thinking leads directly to acting. That is, should philosophers be kings? The idea is more tempting than any other in all of political philosophy. Like many people, I can remember reading the *Republic* for the first time and being so excited by the promise of the philosopher as king that I could not catch my breath. The idea floods the mind with dreams more beautiful than freedom, with the possibility of perfection. Then the realization that perfection permits no freedom falls over the mind like night and begins the struggle against the darkness of a world without substance or history. Plato had no love for what may, despite its flaws, have been the best real city, if we judge real cities more by the duration of their brilliance than by the hubris that inevitably comes of *kudos* (glory). He invented a countercity, one that could never be, where the ills of slavery and misogyny could never be overcome. He knew that a perfect city could not be democratic. Perfection implies stasis, and democracy moves. It comes out of the endless conversation of the marketplace. It is spoken by hawkers and hagglers

---

[28] New York: Basic Books, 1962.

and all those who by nature desire to know. It belongs to a disputatious citizenry with no tolerance for aristocrats or kings. And over all this tumultuous, continuously evolving system that is no system at all, there still lingers the sound of human laughter and the potential for happiness. We have to fear only elitists, separatists, perpetual war, and the promise of perfection.

Ten

RIVERS

"No," said the priest, "it is not necessary to accept everything as true, one must only accept it as necessary."

"A melancholy conclusion," said K. "It turns lying
into a universal principle."

— FRANZ KAFKA
Parables and Paradoxes

Norquist: I think we've done sufficient damage to the
jerks who want to hurt us that they won't
throw another punch.
Question: What if they do throw another punch?
Norquist: We get pissed and blow up Cuba.

— INTERVIEW, SEPTEMBER 7, 2004

Generally, an S corporation is exempt from federal
income tax other than tax on certain capital gains and
passive income.

— INTERNAL REVENUE SERVICE

Every person in a large, pluralistic society has a unique set of
responses to public life. It is the antithesis of the way people think
in an autocracy, where everyone has to choose a positive or negative
response to government. For major change to take place in a country as
diverse as the contemporary United States, there has to be a confluence
of the streams of thoughts and feelings into rivers and rivers into one

river so broad it overflows its banks and becomes a flood. It does not happen often, because the country is so big and there are so many people. The argument about size dates back to James Madison in the debates over the Constitution. He had a vision of a great, stable country, like a slow-moving river, never a flood. And he has been correct, mostly. Size did not deter the country from Civil War; to the contrary, the growth of America in the middle of the nineteenth century exacerbated the moral and economic differences that led to the war. Almost 150 years later the effects of the war remain, not yet fully resolved. At times they become a backwater, at other times, as now, they push the current of the river to run fast.

In a big country, with a long-standing Constitution and a tripartite national government designed to balance the powers within, war and catastrophe have been the only events to change the country quickly, and in unexpected ways. Of the two, war has sometimes been desired,[1] catastrophe never. The people fear catastrophe, have a limited tolerance for war, and do not respond well to radical change. The framers of the Constitution, who knew the people then and perhaps imagined what they might become, created a republican democracy, a design for gradualism. Radical change requires something very different, a broad political movement, the river that overflows its banks, a flood. And a flood is very difficult to manage. The prospect of the flood worried the framers, who made every effort to bar the possibility.

A New Deal

The Constitution limited the response to the catastrophe of the Depression in the 1930s, but it could not hold back the flood. The country was gripped by a desire to change; it was willing to accept almost any change that would enable it to survive. There was a movement in favor of security, and Roosevelt responded with the New Deal. The movement, which had roots in late-nineteenth-century American Protestantism

---

[1] The Revolutionary War, Polk's Mexican War, and for some the Civil War. After Pearl Harbor, World War II. And for a time the current war in Iraq.

and socialism, lasted for thirty years, and declined because the fear of hunger and revolution was pushed aside by other fears, even more profound. Since the end of the Johnson Administration in defeat and perhaps regret, the inheritors of the New Deal, who played an important role in ending the Vietnam War, have been unable to sustain their social and moral positions.

Many things contributed to the demise of the New Dealers, none more than time and mortality. The New Dealers died. The traditional base of the left-liberal coalition, the union movement, shrank toward irrelevance. Membership declined as new businesses, some from overseas, settled in low-wage states and set up nonunion shops. Reagan had paved the way in 1981, firing the air traffic controllers who went out on strike. Only three years earlier, the airlines had been freed of federal regulation. For what seems like only a moment now, everyone was delighted; fares went down, profits and payrolls went up. Then came the fall in profits and the bankruptcy of major airlines. The union workers who kept their jobs gave back advances in wages, pensions, and benefits. In 2005 the United Auto Workers, which had won the most generous contracts for factory workers, agreed to give back part of its health-care benefits to General Motors. In 1980 the Auto Workers and other union members had been Reagan Democrats; they accepted Reagan's promise to protect their salaries, their savings, and their lives.[2]

The working class, often described as the economic bottom third of the country (slowly becoming the bottom half), has been pitied and scorned by the liberal-left for "voting against their own interests." In fact, people are still Democrats or Republicans to a considerable extent according to their economic interests. There is no credible evidence to the contrary, although the distinction was more marked in the past. The difference is that in these fearful times people have other interests

---

[2] There were 1,446,000 members of the United Auto Workers in 1980. Ten years later their numbers had fallen below a million, and by 2004 the union had 623,000 workers. Toward the end of 2006, Ford announced plant closings and buyout offers to union workers. Ford offered the buyout to 76,000 union workers; 38,000 accepted the $35,000-to-$140,000 one-time payment. Auto workers were at the top of the middle class in 1980. It was difficult for a person with two cars, a boat, a second home, paid health insurance, and a lifetime pension to identify with the poor.

that challenge the primacy of their economic concerns. A CNN exit poll in 2006 reported that the 40 percent of voters earning less than $50,000 a year in pretax household income said they were Democrats, while those above split their votes between the two parties. Those earning between $50,000 and $100,000 were Democats by a slight majority. At the lower and upper extremes, voters were respectively more or less Democratic or Republican. A question now is, Will I live? And if I die before my time, what will be my destiny? Can my life affect my destiny, and if so, what must I do?

There is no personal connection now between the leadership of the Democratic Party and its traditional base among working people. FDR ran against unemployment and hunger and with the influence of the Social Gospel. Kennedy ran against a stumbling Nixon and with the help of the electoral shenanigans of the mayor of Chicago, who was so close to the people he still lived in a small house within smelling distance of the stockyards. The chairman of the Democratic National Committee now is a physician who grew up on Park Avenue in New York. The Democratic presidential candidate in 2004 was married to the billionaire widow of a prominent Republican, and the vice presidential candidate was a trial lawyer who had made millions by suing corporations on behalf of the sick, the wounded, and the dead, taking a staggering percentage of the awards made to those he said could not defend themselves. Democrats spent almost as much money as Republicans and used great numbers of paid campaign workers in 2004 and 2006. In the eyes of the electorate, there appeared to be two parties of the rich and influential. For many people in what is said to be the Democratic Party's base, there was no one with whom they could identify— no Roosevelt to turn to in their hour of need, no Kennedy to reassure them that there was a great future for America, no New Deal, no New Frontier, no ideas. All they had to motivate them was a failed war and the corruption within the Republican Party; it was enough. In New York City, Michael Bloomberg switched from the Democratic to the Republican Party and hardly anyone noticed the difference; they voted for the six-billion dollar man. In 2005, Bloomberg ran for reelection against Fernando Ferrer, a Latino who could not even hold his Latino base against Bloomberg. The liberal-left, which once had a base defined by race, economics, and two religious groups—Catholics and Jews—had lost its way.

Results of the 2006 elections pointed to a complex election in 2008. There would be two political contests. One would, of course, be between the Democrats and the Republicans, but the other would be within the Democratic Party. It would pit the liberal-left remains of the New Deal against the new national political movement represented by the Clinton wing of the party. The party owed control of both houses of Congress to the Clinton wing, which had recruited and supported candidates who had moved very far from liberal-left ideals. While the politics of the Democratic Party had been blurred, the Republicans had resolved many of their internal party conflicts in 2006 by sharpening the party's social and economic conservative character. Some examples of the changing character of American electoral politics and the growth of the national political movement follow.

The new U.S. senator from Montana belonged to the NRA, favored a harsh immigration policy, and was pro-choice.

Jim Webb barely defeated Republican incumbent George Allen in Virginia. Webb was himself a former Republican. On October 31, 2006, the *Virginian-Pilot* of Hampton Roads said about the two candidates for the U.S. Senate, "Who would Virginians find more objectionable?" Before his disastrous campaign Allen had been considered a potential Republican candidate for president.

In Connecticut, bloggers and antiwar Democrats defeated longtime U.S. senator and former vice presidential candidate Joe Lieberman in the primary, only to see him win the general election by 10 percentage points. Exit polls showed Lieberman carrying only 27 percent of the "liberal" vote, but 55 percent of the "moderate" vote. Liberal-left Democrats had defeated Lieberman in the primary by publicizing a photograph of him being kissed by President George W. Bush.

In elections for U.S. representative, scandal helped the Democrats almost as much as politics. By some counts Republicans lost nine seats to scandal, including Mark Foley in Florida, Tom DeLay in Texas, Bob Ney in Ohio, Don Sherwood in Pennsylvania, and John Sweeney in New York.

Joe Donnelly, a social conservative, won a seat in Indiana, defeating a Republican incumbent mainly because of a toll road and daylight savings time. He is a social and fiscal conservative.

Former Sheriff Brad Ellsworth won an Indiana seat based on family values and his opposition to crime, immigrants, and abortion.

Baron Hill won an Indiana seat he had lost in 2004 by campaigning on family values, fiscal conservatism, and anti-immigrant positions. The press described him as a moderate.

Heath Shuler, a social conservative, won a seat in North Carolina.

In Pennsylvania, Jason Altmire won a seat from a Republican by claiming to be a pro-life, pro-NRA, anti-immigrant social conservative.

In Rhode Island, one of the most liberal members of the U.S. Senate, Lincoln Chafee, who refused to vote for George W. Bush in the 2004 election, lost to a Democrat. Chafee's defeat was but one instance of the moderate-liberal wing of the Republican Party losing power in both the Senate and the House.

Michigan's Seventh Congressional District moved from the right to the far right as Tim Wahlberg defeated moderate incumbent Joe Schwarz in the Republican primary and went on to win the general election. Walberg is a social and economic conservative.

At the same time, conservative Republicans were able to hold on to their seats against some of the most able challengers from the liberal wing of the Democratic Party. One of these was extreme conservative Jean Schmidt of Ohio. In a state in which Republican officeholders at both the state and national level were involved in scandals, Schmidt defeated Victoria Wulsin, M.D. Wulsin, a physician who also earned a doctorate in public health at Harvard, had a long record of service both at home and in Africa, where she started an organization to help AIDS patients. She also did work in Africa for the Heimlich Institute. When Wulsin cautioned against unsupervised experiments in Africa, in a situation reminiscent of the heroic battle in John Le Carré's *The Constant Gardener*, she was fired from her post at the Heimlich Institute. She reported the dismissal in an article in *Radar Online* (November 11, 2005).

There were other signs of the increasing power of the national political movement despite the Democratic victory. Seven more states voted to ban same-sex marriage, raising the total to twenty-seven of the twenty-eight states in which a ban had been on the ballot.

Several issues that at first glance seemed at odds with the national political movement passed, most prominently stem-cell research, but public attitudes about the use of stem cells may have more to do with fear than with politics. Four states raised cigarette taxes, which has little to do with social justice.

Arizona, a state with a large Latino population, passed a law making English the official language.

In Michigan—a state with a Democratic governor, two Democratic U.S. senators, including the current chairman of the Senate Armed Services Committee, Carl Levin, and one of the most powerful members of the House of Representatives in liberal Democrat John Conyers—voters passed a ban on the use by the state of race or gender to determine college admissions, hiring, and the selection of contractors.

In her victory speech Hillary Clinton, who won reelection as New York's junior senator, stood next to her husband, who was impeached as a result of his affair with Monica Lewinsky, and spoke of "family values."

Less than two weeks after the 2006 elections, John McCain opened an official exploratory committee to enable him to raise money as he considered running for president in 2008. He urged Republicans to return to the "principled leadership" of Ronald Reagan.

Seventy-two percent of white evangelical Protestants voted for Republican candidates in 2006, roughly the same percentage as in the last midterm election in 2002, according to the Pew Research Center. Scandals involving homosexuals in the Republican Party, corruption of Republican state and federal elected officials, and a failed war in Iraq caused only a 3-percentage-point drop in loyalty to the Republican Party. The base of the national political movement remained solid. There are two views of the meaning of the vote. Pew says there are 76 million white evangelical Protestants in the U.S.; the Gallup Poll puts the number at 146 million. If the real number is somewhere between the two estimates, perhaps 33 percent of the voters in the United States are white evangelical Protestants. They are part of a long history of the coming to power of the new national political movement.

Economic forces had been joined in the South to leftover social and political effects from the Civil War and Reconstruction to move the country to the political right. An even deeper influence had come during the Second World War and its aftermath. The fear of death, once as personal as a heartbeat, had become a national mania. Into this confluence came Richard Wirthlin, who did for the unraveling of the New Deal what Roosevelt's observers of the national political mood did for the making of it. FDR's man was Harry Hopkins, and his idea of how to understand the world outside Washington was entirely different from Wirthlin's. This is the way the news was gathered and reported to Roosevelt:

> *"What I want you to do," said Harry Hopkins to journalist Lorena Hickok in July, 1933, "is to go out around the country and look this thing over. I don't want statistics from you. I don't want the social-worker angle. I just want your own reaction, as an ordinary citizen.*
>
> *"Go talk with preachers and teachers, businessmen, workers, farmers. Go talk with the unemployed, those who are on relief and those who aren't. And when you talk with them don't ever forget that but for the grace of God you, I, any of our friends might be in their shoes. Tell me what you see and hear. All of it. Don't ever pull your punches."[3]*

Wirthlin had come to affect national politics through the recommendation of a defeated client. One night over dinner, Barry Goldwater told Ronald Reagan, who had begun his 1966 campaign for the governorship of California, about a very bright young fellow out of Brigham Young University, a college professor who had earned a doctorate in economics from the University of California at Berkeley. Richard Wirthlin had been Goldwater's pollster, and Goldwater thought Reagan ought to meet him; he would need someone like Wirthlin at his side if he was planning a political career. Reagan agreed. He and Wirthlin began working together. By 1980, Wirthlin had become Reagan's strategist as well as his pollster. Wirthlin had read the work of Max Weber and taken from it an idea about values and how it

---

[3] Richard Lowitt and Maurine Beasley, eds., *One Third of a Nation: Lorena Hickok Reports on the Great Depression* (Urbana: University of Illinois Press, 1981), quoted in David M. Kennedy, *Freedom from Fear* (Oxford and New York: Oxford University Press, 1999).

could be applied to political campaigns. It suited Reagan perfectly. He had the sense of narrative that Wirthlin said was the ideal way to connect to the deeply held views at the top of the ladder of a person's thoughts, the values.

Reagan followed Wirthlin's advice on strategy, but Wirthlin told me many years later that Reagan had done something during the campaign that was not part of the strategy he had prepared for him. It was a move Reagan had made entirely on his own, and like the notion of values, it came to dominate American politics. According to Wirthlin, Ronald Reagan was the first Republican candidate in the twentieth century to go to Baptist churches in the South; he had divined something about America that neither Richard Nixon's "southern strategy" nor Wirthlin's interviewers had turned up. Reagan did not limit his meetings to churches. During the planning of the campaign he and the Reverend Jerry Falwell, founder of Moral Majority, met in the back seats of limousines.[4] Goldwater had not only set political policy for the Republicans that would last into the next century, he had often referred to God in his speeches. Reagan took the ideas of Barry Goldwater and added a powerful ingredient, the profession of love for Jesus Christ. He had stumbled upon the route to power in America.

In his method Wirthlin did not have one Hickok, he had many, and he did not necessarily send them out to enter the houses of the electorate, look them in the eye, and attempt to understand the world. His interviewers used the telephone, and they listened as the people talked and talked and talked. He believed forty minutes to an hour, sometimes longer, was required to know what people thought. It was a long way from Hickok's reports to Hopkins, but it was different from the brevity of most polls leading up to an election. Like Hopkins, Wirthlin was seeking the signs of a movement, the river that could be turned into a flood, overcoming everything, denying the Madisonian principle of size as a guarantor of stability. The gradualism built into a Constitution that was so difficult to amend could be overcome at flood tide. Roosevelt thought so. He tried to pack the U.S. Supreme Court to accomplish his

---

[4] Conversation with Dr. Ronald Godwin of Jerry Falwell Ministries.

goals, but the country resisted his efforts, and the courts forced him into a more gradualist approach, even as the feelings of the moment flooded the country. The best way to circumvent the gradualist limitations of the Constitution was to control all three branches of government. And Roosevelt knew that gaining control of the Supreme Court was the stickiest problem. Appointments are for life, ensuring that the character of the court can only change over decades, perhaps generations. It is the last, best check against the flood. Only when the court is lined up with the executive and legislative branches of government does the greatest danger arise: the flood can become unstoppable.

If that happens, a movement may no longer be contained within the limits of a gradualist democracy. In extreme times the nation has only the Constitution to hold on to, and the Constitution can be interpreted to become part of the flood. When that happens, the country comes under the control of something other than a compromise between political parties; it falls into the grip of a political movement, which then has the capability to overthrow the limitations of gradualist democracy. Then the movement can amplify what it wants the country to hear and lower the voice of dissent by shouting down the strident dissenters and silencing the others through manipulation and fear. At that point what began as a movement may become a coup.

The Origin of the New Movement

Historians may locate the beginning of the present movement on the day the U.S. Supreme Court accepted the Florida vote count that elected George W. Bush in 2000 or the day in 2006 when the Senate voted to seat the last Supreme Court justice required to produce a majority more closely aligned with the executive and legislative branches of government. But those would be signs of the culmination of the movement's rise to power, not of the movement itself.

The movement may have begun the night of Ronald Reagan's televised speech in support of Barry Goldwater. A more likely date, however, is August 6, 1945. The *Enola Gay* arrived over Hiroshima at 7:25 that morning. At 8:16 the bomb was released from an altitude of 26,000 feet and detonated a few thousand feet above the city. As instructed,

Colonel Paul Tibbets put his plane into a radical turn to avoid the blast. The crew, wearing special dark glasses, saw a blinding light and a mushroom cloud that rose more than 60,000 feet into the air. The world changed. By 1981, when Ronald Reagan took office, the movement, which may have begun on that morning in 1945, had America in its grasp. Or the movement may have begun on Kristallnacht, November 9, 1938, when the Nazis implemented the policy that demonstrated the capacity of a technological society to eliminate an entire people in a short time. It would be useful to be able to mark the day when one event initiated a national movement in America, but there was no Reichstag fire, no arrival at the Finland Station; there was a series of events.

An American political movement has many beginnings; it lacks the singularity commonly associated with radical change. Pluralism still describes much of the American national character. Many of Tocqueville's observations about equality still apply today. Gordon Wood's understanding of the economic basis of the radicalism of the American revolution in the early nineteenth century revealed one of the streams of the American confluence that still affects the county. And Sean Wilentz's view of the rise of American democracy in his book of that name[5] shows the political evolution of the country into what we now think of as a democracy, which is very different from the fearsome beasts of political organization that so worried Plato and Aristotle and moderns like J. L. Talmon. Wilentz and Wood alike place the time of change into modern democracy between the presidencies of Jefferson and Lincoln. Neither of them names a day, a year, a decade, although they would not argue with Arthur Schlesinger, Jr.'s idea that Andrew Jackson was emblematic of what happened. They are historians—Wilentz and Wood and Schlesinger, Jr.—but their understanding of the confluences of earlier times enables us to grasp what America is now as a new movement captures it; they tell us what is at risk.

In a country of 300 million, with a political tradition more than two hundred years old, the establishment of a movement takes place slowly, rising and falling and rising again, growing stronger over

---

[5] *The Rise of American Democracy* (New York: W. W. Norton, 2005).

decades, more than a single generation, unless a great catastrophe causes an irrepressible change of mood. And even then the seeds of the movement must have been germinating for many years, like those of the New Deal. It was the catastrophe of the Great Depression that permitted that movement to take power, but the New Deal had its American origin in settlement houses and churches almost half a century before the economic collapse. Barring a catastrophic period that propels it to sudden prominence, a contemporary American movement requires a cadre that will not be dissuaded from its goal of turning the feelings of a large part of the nation into political power. The cadre need not include only ideologues or true believers, for in a democracy people are constantly seeking a direction. The cadre that brings an American movement to power is bound together more deeply than a coalition, less so than a brotherhood; the members of the cadre are not comrades, certainly not willing to die for each other; the depth of their connection is strong but not necessarily permanent. Rousseau could have imagined such a movement as an expression of the general will; the same movement would have made less sense to Lenin or Hitler, both of whom formed sharply defined political movements in the turmoil of catastrophe.

When democracy fails, it is almost always because there is broad dissatisfaction with the government, which becomes unstable, like one of the jittery atoms of immense destructive power. A leader suddenly emerges to propose a single unifying idea, there is a coup d'état, and a new kind of state, perhaps fascist, more likely totalitarian, rises in its place. An American national movement does not have only one idea for a guide. It grows out of a plurality of desires, solutions, fears, certainties, loyalties, disloyalties, oppositions, rages, and many varieties of pessimism. It has no song, no slogan, few philosophers, many operatives. It has no constitution, no rules, no standards, innumerable leaders. Like a religion, it has lay members, deacons, priests, bishops, and there its organization ends, without a synod, a cardinal, and certainly no pope. Movements have been inspired by presidents, but not controlled by them; to think a president controls a movement or even leads it is to mistake the American form of government for some other.

Fools and philosophers, scientists and fundamentalists, Wall Streeters

and street vendors, and politicians of all parties and their friends and enemies in the social and economic worlds may join an American political
movement, and many of them will not be able to say why, except that it
"feels right." A movement is a river, it is created, like a river, out of the
confluence of many raindrops, rivulets, streams, tributaries, and finally
becomes a great river; it has a clear current and like some rivers it is prone
to flood. A movement is not history. It is more like an accident of nature,
which gives it a reason for being, a final cause, as Aristotle would say;
and one day it may flood, overcoming every obstacle in its path: dikes,
berms, ditches, and diversions. Yet it is not a mob, not disorderly, not
defined by class or education, not prone to rages or madness, and not
immune from error.

For an American national political movement to succeed it must be
based on elemental feelings; that is, the movement is more like religion
than politics. In the common definition most religions have these key
elements: a God-given moral code, a sense of purpose, rituals and
prayers, and belief in something beyond this world (the supernatural).
Religion has one more aspect not generally described in textbooks or
hymnals. A religion, like the current American political movement, is a
continuously revised series of bargains. Individual belief systems exist,
but for a belief system to be a religion it must comprise many individuals: hundreds, thousands, millions, more than a billion in several
instances. William James, whose *Varieties of Religious Experience*
remains one of the key texts on the subject, found all religions basically
the same. He wrote, "The fact that we *can* die, that we *can* be ill at all, is
what perplexes us; the fact that we now for a moment live and are well
is irrelevant to that perplexity. We need a life not correlated with death,
a health not liable to illness, a good that will not perish, a good in fact
that flies beyond the Goods of nature."

His interest was in religion as "feelings, experiences, acts of individuals in their solitude." If there was any religion other than the religion
of "feelings," James did not acknowledge it. In that respect, a broad-
based political movement in America is like his idea of religion, because
it is about feelings and experiences. Like the religion described by
James, the present American political movement is "private and dumb
and unable to give an account of itself." The movement, again like reli-

gion, revolves around one's "personal destiny." It is not a collective movement, not a mob, but many individuals moving in the same direction, driven by feelings they cannot explain.

In a 1961 introduction to a new edition of James's book on religion, Reinhold Niebuhr suggested a different source for religious feelings: "Our generation is bound to be anxious, not so much about the brevity of our individual life (though that anxiety can never be suppressed) but about the chance of the whole world escaping a nuclear catastrophe." Niebuhr was not "private and dumb" about the feelings of that time. It was not then known how those feelings would be manifest in a political movement, nor would Niebuhr's complaint that James had missed the importance of history ring hollow forty-five years later. The current American political movement had only just begun to gather force. Driven by the feelings associated with sudden death, the *mors repentina* that terrified people in the Middle Ages, the feeling of the imminent death of everything as in the great plague, herds the nation in its present direction. The diversity of America—capitalist and worker, hedonist and ascetic, hoarder and hellion—is herded in one direction, some believing everything must be spent before the end and others certain that the accumulation of capital is God's will. To move from one politics to another transcends ordinary life and once cherished beliefs; it is the acceptance of a new religion.

"To be converted, to be regenerated, to receive grace, to experience religion, to gain an assurance, are so many phrases which denote the process, gradual or sudden, by which a self hitherto divided, and consciously wrong, inferior, and unhappy becomes unified and consciously right, superior, and happy, in consequence of its firmer hold upon religious realities," said James. "This at least is what conversion signifies in general terms, whether or not we believe that a direct divine operation is needed to bring such a moral change about."

As one nears death, like Tolstoy's Ivan Ilyich, whose dying is long and ugly and not hidden from view, or in the lonely, antiseptic, hospitalized death of our time, the belief in an afterlife increases. At the end one seeks a beginning. For the faithful, death is the beginning of life in Christ, and when the end appears imminent for everyone, death and the beginning become the driving force in daily life. Johan Huizinga said there has never been as much stress on death as in the plague-ridden waning years of the Middle Ages. Philippe Aries[6] said of the same period, "An atmosphere of anxiety seems to have taken hold," almost exactly the same language Niebuhr used to describe the world after Hiroshima. Now there is the age of terror, which the president of the United States has declared may last for many years. And all the while the ability to make nuclear weapons spreads from country to country. The miracle of science has become the anxiety that drives the specter of extinction in the only country that saw fit to detonate nuclear weapons over enemy cities without warning, to kill 140,000 civilians on an ordinary August morning. Along with the fear, there is a curious moral question: if we are good and we did this to our enemies, why should our enemies, who are not good, hesitate to use a nuclear weapon against us?

Fear

The historian David M. Kennedy described the politics of the period between the Great Depression and the end of World War II as *Freedom from Fear.* He used it as the title of his book about the period because those three words represented the essence of the movement of that time. The movement of this time could be described as "Fear Without End," but the fear, except in a few cases, has remained "private and dumb and unable to give an account of itself." One of the exceptions came in 1982 when Jonathan Schell wrote about nuclear weapons in the *New Yorker*:[7] ". . . the world has declined, on the whole, to think about them very much. We have thus far failed to fashion, or to discover within ourselves, an emotional or intellectual or political response to them." Schell was writing at the height of the Cold War, when most of the thinking in the country had to do with mutually assured destruction (MAD). By that time Terry Southern had approached nuclear war with satire in the book and film *Dr. Strangelove*, and philosophers, including Karl Jaspers, as well as the mathematician Albert Wohlstetter, had attempted to

---

[6] *The Hour of Our Death*, trans. Helen Weaver (New York: Knopf, 1971).

[7] The article also appeared in book form, *The Fate of the Earth* (New York: Knopf, 1982).

come to terms with it. Yet, Schell was correct in his assessment: at the time there had been no response within the American people themselves. The Cuban Missile Crisis had passed with no serious event, the Vietnam War had produced no nuclear confrontation, and there had not been a serious accident. Yet the threat had established itself in the American consciousness. Schell's essay gave voice to it in words touching on the deepest beliefs: "According to the Bible, when Adam and Eve ate the fruit of the tree of knowledge God punished them by withdrawing from them the privilege of immortality and dooming them and their kind to die. Now our species has eaten more deeply of the fruit of the tree of knowledge, and has brought itself face to face with a second death—the death of mankind." And he concluded the thought: ". . . we have altered the human condition."

Schell, like others before him, had connected nuclear weapons to a biblical punishment. He ended the work with a plea to cleanse the world of weapons. It was still too early in the history of the weapons and their ultimate spread to less and less stable governments to know that their effect would not be to send Americans toward reason. They would move instead to faith and scurrying. Even as Schell was writing that Americans had discovered no political response within themselves, a political movement had manifested itself in the 1980 election. Ronald Reagan had been the first Republican in the twentieth century to connect to Baptist churches in the South. The movement both contained many religious conservatives and was, in itself, more like religion than politics. Reagan had intuited its character with exactness.

The plea to rid the world of nuclear weapons has gone unheeded. The worm of what Schell called "the second death" exists inside almost every American. When asked about it, members of the movement almost always answer in the same way. "No, I don't think about nuclear weapons," but then, as the conversation goes on, the subject comes up again. Their lead-in to nuclear weapons is usually end-time or the book of Revelation or simply the word "fear." "I think nuclear weapons will be used," said a woman member of the movement who had spent fourteen years in the Army and then worked as a supervisor at Time-Warner. "We'll wipe each other out." The "second death" in the form of the loss of the ability to retain the intellectual valuables of our own time, is the parable at the beginning of MacIntyre's *After Virtue* and the knowledge of the Holocaust that tortured Leo Strauss. The feelings engendered by fear of the several kinds of holocausts created the movement and continue it.

Something terrible will happen; the secretary of homeland security, the cochairs of the 9/11 Commission, the entire federal government, have assured us it will happen. They say it is not a matter of "if," but "when." They know there will be no end to nuclear or biological or chemical or conventional weapons. As much as any other single attribute, the possibility of mass destruction describes contemporary life. A person today may reasonably expect to die before his time. Yet responses to fear were not uniform during other terrible periods: the plague years, the Civil War, the Great Depression and World Wars I and II, and they are not now.

Antithetical positions not only survive in an American political movement, they are at the heart of it, enabling people to go along with the movement while thinking ambivalently about one or many of its attributes. A single member of the movement, personally devoted to the care of the less fortunate, may oppose government aid to the same group of people, although depriving them of aid will cause them to suffer and perhaps to die. The owner of a tiny store, deeply in debt, at the bottom 20 percent of family income, and sinking, favors an end to the estate tax, and with good reason, for the moment a person concludes that he will never succeed, never get rich, never have anything to leave his children, he is done for, a dead man, and he knows it.[8]

In the view of the liberal-left that man or woman who votes for a conservative promise of capitalist hope or the hope of heaven or both is voting against his or her economic interests. A more thoroughly researched view shows that voters in the lower third of the economic scale are as Democratic as ever in their party affiliation, but it does not measure which wing of a deeply divided party commands their loyalty, nor can it predict the strength of the bond between the voters and the party. The American idea of economic and social mobility, no matter how chimerical, creates multiple views inside one person. This internal plu-

---

[8] The store is in Grand Rapids, Michigan. The person asked not to be identified.

ralism makes many Americans vulnerable to a movement that has no single thesis. They can belong to it today and tomorrow, on the day when business is good and the next day or week or month when business is bad. The movement is not like National Socialism or communism in its structure and discipline, but something vague, a dissatisfaction movement, an opposition. The members do not know what they oppose in general; they have a plurality of dissatisfactions. At the core, they fear an untimely death, and it need not be tomorrow or next year, or in ten years, but it is inevitable. They expect catastrophe. And if enough people expect a catastrophe, no real catastrophe need occur; the expectation is a catastrophe. The politics of heaven becomes the only given in an otherwise many-faceted movement.

Misperceptions

There have been no other national political movements in recent American history. The archetypal person in the current movement cannot be described. The movement is too broad; it encompasses too many different kinds of people, too many different ideas. On the liberal-left, which has not intellectualized the existence of an American movement even while being stung by it, studies begin with a thesis and then massage the data to make it fit. There is no admonition like that of Harry Hopkins to Lorena Hickok. A good example is the view that some members of the movement vote against their own interests, a thesis both absurd and arrogant. The absurdity is that people would vote against their own interests and the arrogance is that the journalist or scholar who advances the theory knows the interests of the voters better than the voters themselves.[9] The only way to support such a thesis is to

---

[9] Presidential elections are notoriously poor measures of party loyalty. Despite the Bush victory in 2004, the Pew survey found more Americans still identified themselves as Democrat than either Republican or Independent. While it is true that Republicans made some inroads among middle-class Americans, the numbers fluctuate. By the end of 2005, following a series of political mistakes, the gains reported in preceding years had largely evaporated.

Kansas is the state the liberal-left despises most. Tom Frank chose it as the place to prove that people with low incomes vote against their own interests, and he wrote a lively bestseller about it: *What's the Matter with Kansas?* (New York: Metropolitan Books, 2004). The relation of some of the thinking to the elitism of Leo Strauss or Allan Bloom is unexpected

assume the voters are stupid. It is an antidemocratic thesis, more in keeping with the ideas of Allan Bloom than with those of Thomas Jefferson. Contemporary liberal-left thinkers have, perhaps inadvertently, perhaps because of what they perceive as their intellectual superiority to *hoi polloi,* come to the same conclusions reached by Leo Strauss. The people are not respected. There is a liberal-left version of Leo Strauss's fear of "the unwise leading the wise."

The greatest surprise to preconceptions in looking at this movement comes in finding that evangelicals are poor no more. The stereotype of Baptist and Methodist evangelicals living up in "hollers" in Appalachia or Missouri is at least one full generation out of date. It is equally anachronistic to think all those evangelicals who have escaped poverty have miraculously found their way into middle- and upper-middle-class jobs and small businesses without scientific knowledge and with very little other education, that they remain ignorant "rednecks." In fact, evangelicals design sophisticated jet aircraft, serve as technical advisors to national security groups in the government, do the most advanced computer engineering, teach philosophy at secular universities, and one evangelical is a nuclear engineer and the best-loved former president of the United States. Reinhold Niebuhr was a member of the German Evangelical Synod of the Lutheran Church. Walter Rauschenbusch, one of the theologians whose work gave rise to many of the ideas of the American political movement that we know as the

---

in a book written by one of the brightest and most accomplished liberal-left writers in America. In 2002, Kathleen Sebelius, a Democrat, won the Kansas gubernatorial election. Sebelius, the daughter of former Ohio Governor John Gilligan, was born in Ohio, is Roman Catholic in a state supposedly dominated by fundamentalist Protestants, concerns herself with health care, education, and budget questions. She speaks of government "as a protector" and said people should "demand more of government." Sebelius is married to the son of Keith Sebelius, a popular Republican congressman from Kansas in the 1970s. After three years in office, she had an approval rating close to 60 percent in a state where there are almost twice as many Republicans as Democrats.

A professor at the Woodrow Wilson School of Government at Princeton, Larry M. Bartels, published an article in which he demonstrated that white voters in the lower third economically, whose real income had fallen, had become more, not less Democratic in their political party identification. The article generated quite a lot of comment in the liberal and academic press, but the commentators neglected even the possibility that liberal-left intellectuals (certainly not Bartels among them) were susceptible to the blandishments of elitism; i.e., they misread the data to prove the error of the voters.

New Deal, was a Baptist minister. The reason why the economic and social situations of evangelicals are misunderstood comes of evangelicals not having followed the classic American economic path. The majority of evangelicals are not recent immigrants or the descendants of recent immigrants.[10] They are mostly from English or northern European stock, unlike the descendants of the great nineteenth- and early-twentieth-century waves of immigrants from Ireland and southern and eastern Europe.

Evangelicals do not yet commonly have a history of working in city, state, and federal government jobs, like many of those immigrants who came in the great waves. And "evangelical" is a term so inclusive and so variously defined that it is not useful for understanding their economic role in America, because we are never quite sure whom we are talking about. Anyone who spreads the Good News is an evangelical. An evangelical Protestant from El Salvador living in the poorest part of Washington, D.C., and an evangelical Protestant of the same age and gender whose family owns Amway Corporation (now Alticor, Inc.) have very little in common other than evangelical Protestantism. Harry Hopkins, the soul of the New Deal, was an evangelical Protestant. A person may pastor an unaffiliated evangelical church without formal training in theology, perhaps without any formal training at all; the only requirement being the ability to read the words in the Bible and more or less know their meaning. Another evangelical may be one of the country's leading theologians. The same difficulty with definitions comes of Midge Decter, a member of the neoconservative Committee for a Free World, and Victor Navasky, for many years editor and publisher of *The Nation*, both being Jews, or John XXIII and Benedict XVI, both being Roman Catholics.

---

[10] This is a rapidly changing situation, since several evangelical groups, most prominently Pentecostals, are recruiting large numbers of Latinos. But the new members are not just Latinos. Jeff Lane, a young pastor of a Nazarene church in Massachusetts, said his church was working closely with recent immigrants from Vietnam. Lane is a gentle fellow, who looks younger than his years, like the clean-cut college football hero of America in its innocence. Long before the 2004 election, he said, "I'm not a war person." Lane was unhappy about the war while the *New York Times* was still justifying it. He married a young woman with Celtic eyes named Keli. Her favorite author is Toni Morrison.

An American political movement may include rich, middle-class, and poor people, and members of any religious group or sect or those who think of themselves as agnostics or atheists. A single-issue movement, like the anti–Vietnam War movement of the 1960s and 70s or the women's movement can generate a lot of noise and even win its case, but it can never be more than a stream joining the great confluence, it cannot become a river. The American Revolution presented itself as a single issue, but it was really the beginning of an American movement that lasted unabated, although not unchanged, for a hundred years. It was the movement that defined the country—gradualist, open-ended, so utterly pluralistic it could include urban and rural, rich and poor, Federalist and Republican, yeoman and aristocrat, and move eventually from a purely political revolution to a second, Jacksonian stage driven by economic freedom and a new sense of equality. By the time the movement came to an end in a more settled country after the Civil War and the turmoil of Reconstruction, party politics had replaced it. Only during the Great Depression did another American movement surface, and it was short-lived. The current American political movement became manifest in the 1980 presidential election and exhibited real power after 2001. Republicans Reagan and Bush held office for twelve years before being replaced by a conservative Democrat, who held office for eight years but won the presidency with the help of a third-party candidate and held on to it for a second term by tagging along on the coattails of the movement. In 2005, in Virginia, the power of the movement and the willingness of the Democratic Party to become part of it showed up in the gubernatorial election. Tim Kaine, a conservative Democrat, replaced another conservative Democrat, Mark Warner, who had been a popular governor. Kaine campaigned as "the faith and values candidate."[11] Yet, the American Progress Action Fund's Web site called Kaine's win "a victory for progressives."

The failure of George W. Bush as president has had surprisingly little effect on the national political movement. A small liberal wing of the Democratic Party briefly gained control of the party machinery after

---

[11] *Roanoke Times*, October 13, 2005.

the loss in the 2004 presidential election, but Tim Kaine had to run against that wing of the party. The component parts of the national movement, which includes many Democrats, among them former vice presidential candidate Senator Joseph Lieberman, did not lose their enthusiasm. In 2006, conservatives in Congress, pressed to do something as the cost of Hurricane Katrina rose into the tens of billions, pushed through cuts in services to the poor, the elderly, children, and the disabled rather than rescind tax cuts for the wealthy. California and Ohio voted against redistricting, which would have opened more opportunity for opposition candidates. Intelligent design won out in Kansas, Texas voted for an antigay marriage law, and Bill Clinton and George H. W. Bush became a vaudeville team on behalf of good causes.

With the occupation of Iraq going badly, the movement turned against it. But support for the war in Iraq had never been its defining tenet. Grover Norquist, one of the movement's leading operatives, said in an interview in 2004 that he did not support the American adventure in Iraq. It was not a general antiwar position—Norquist had been involved in the Afghani war against the Russians and in a right-wing rebellion led by Jonas Savimbi in Angola—it was opposition to the Iraq adventure of the Bush Administration. Kristine Greenhaw, a devout evangelical Christian still in her twenties, working in the College of Education at the University of South Florida, is as sweet and subtle and winning as Norquist is brusque and blunt and aggressive. She said she voted for George Bush but that it was a difficult decision for her because of her concern for the poor. On the subject of war, she said, "I don't think anything good can come of war." Evangelical Christians said frequently in our conversations that they opposed war, although they feared terrorism and thought Muslims were an implacable enemy. The movement was not so much driven by Iraq as torn by it. From the outset people in the movement had problems reconciling war with their Christian beliefs.

A full year before the 2006 midterm elections it was generally conceded that Democrats would take more seats in the House of Representatives and the Senate for several reasons: the "out" party almost always makes large gains in midterm elections, especially in time of war, Bush is one of the most inept presidents in American history, some of the key figures in the party and the administration were indicted for corruption, the war had gone very badly, and there is a limited tolerance for polemic in America. Beset with problems, Bush simply didn't know what to do. On a trip to China in November 2005, he made a televised speech, and when it was over, he turned to leave by one of the doors at the side of the stage. It was locked. He tried another door, and it too was locked. Confused, he looked around for help. Someone beckoned to him from the far side of the stage, and he was finally able to make his exit. It was symptomatic of his presidency. He could not deal with simple issues, and the complex problems were beyond his comprehension. He did not have young Kristine Greenhaw's grasp of the meaning of life. The go/no-go mind of the twenty-first-century man, which had seemed so attractive during the 2004 political campaign, could not deal with the subtleties of a world that required thinking in the middle ground. He disappointed the movement that had thrust him into power. Bush floundered, succumbed to manipulation by a series of advisors, each of whom failed him: Paul Wolfowitz, Dick Cheney, George Tenet, Donald Rumsfeld, Rudy Giuliani.[12] Bush fired Tenet less than a month after publication of the 9/11 Commission Report in May 2004, but waited until after the 2006 elections to fire Rumsfeld, whose ouster had been demanded by Republicans as well as Democrats for months preceding the election. Worse for Bush, his personal hero, Karl Rove, proved to be not so bright after all. Rove had been riding on the coattails of the movement and presenting himself as a genius for doing so. During Bush's second term Rove was under suspicion for leaking the name of a classified CIA agent and giving the kind of advice to his client that brought the president's "approval rating" to 30 percent

---

[12] Giuliani's judgment becomes more questionable as revelations about ties between the man he urged on Bush as secretary of homeland security, Bernard Kerik, and the mafia continue to appear in the newspapers. On June 30, 2006, Kerik pleaded guilty to ethics violations and was fined $221,000. Prior to the fifth anniversary of the World Trade Center bombing, allegations began to surface about Giuliani's failure to provide proper equipment to police and firefighters, which may have been the cause of many deaths. Giuliani had more than enough time to ascertain the needs after the first bombing in 1993. It was not a failure attributable to party politics. The Clinton Administration was no more effective in discharging its responsibilities following the 1993 attack. Giuliani was simply more distasteful because of his preening as "America's Mayor."

in some polls and only a few points higher in others.[13] And Rove worked no magic in the 2006 elections. A president and his administration are not, however, a movement. They are the implements a movement uses to exercise its will, as is the Congress, and indirectly the judiciary. The implements must serve the demands of the movement or be cast aside. Liberal and moderate Republicans in contested districts began criticizing the Bush Administration well in advance of the 2006 election, demonstrating to the movement that they were still useful even if Bush had become a liability. Their newfound voices failed them.

Concessions

To win House and Senate seats and even the presidency, Democrats believed they would have to make concessions to the national political movement. Former President Jimmy Carter told them what he thought they had to do. He said they could not win unless they embraced the idea of a "right to life."[14] Said differently, in order to win, the Democrats would have to lose, they would have to join the movement, if only at the fringe. Rahm Emanuel, head of the 2006 Democratic Congressional Campaign Committee, showed how far the Democrats had moved toward membership in the movement in an interview on the Charlie Rose PBS program on August 21, 2006. To prove that Demo-

---

[13] While uncomfortably low for any president, they were not extraordinary. Other presidents had similarly low approval ratings:

Truman: 22% mid-February 1952
Eisenhower: 49% mid-July 1960
Kennedy: 56% mid-September 1963
Johnson: 35% early August 1968
Nixon: 24% mid-July 1974, and early August 1974
Ford: 37% early January 1975, and late March 1975
Carter: 28% late June 1979
Reagan: 35% late January 1983
George H. W. Bush: 29% late July 1992
Clinton: 37% early June 1993
George W. Bush: 34%* March 2006
* To date.

Source: Gallup polls, 1952–1991; CNN/USA Today/Gallup polls, 1992–present.

[14] "I think for the Democratic Party to get identified as being completely pro-choice, with no attention given to the rights of the fetus, is very self-defeating policy." UPI, November 4, 2005.

crats were not "extreme liberals," he pointed out, with some pride, that Bob Casey, Jr., who had defeated two other men to win the Democratic primary for a U.S. Senate seat from Pennsylvania, was "pro-life." He had taken Carter's advice. They did not think the Democrats could win without some connection to the movement. Casey's victory over Rick Santorum, a ferocious defender of "the right to life," was understood by the Clinton wing of the party as a vindication of their position.

On the other hand, the encompassing movement could appear to lose an election and go on getting stronger, as it had after the Clinton victories. The movement would not lose political power on any single issue despite many arguments, including Carter's, that the right to life alone would be the deciding factor. At the Republican National Convention in 2004, some of the delegates and alternates talked about their views on "the right to life."

I'm pro-life. I think liberals are hypocritical on this issue. We have to save the dolphins, but what about the baby humans? I believe in birth control. If you don't want the child, put it up for adoption. I've voted for pro-choice candidates. For me it would not automatically disqualify a candidate.

—RALPH McGEHEE
Chairman, Falls Church (Va.)
City Republican Committee

I'm a moderate. I have basic Republican values. I'm pro-life, except in cases of rape.

—MARY PAULINE JONES, 18
Youngest (Alternate) Delegate

I'm conservative. Her (Mary Pauline Jones's) father was a very extreme conservative. You cannot support a candidate if they're not pro-life.

—SUSAN JONES
Consultant on Retainer to U.S. Rep. Tom Davis

If it was me, I could never choose abortion. On the other hand, I can't judge. I wish so many people were not bogged down in that issue. I don't know if I could live with it. If I had a friend who had to make that choice, I would try to talk her out of it. It's always a gray area for me.

— RUTH CLEVELAND

Wife of vice mayor of Alexandria, Va.

[As the days of the convention wore on, the speakers got far more applause with anti–gay marriage lines than with pro-life comments.]

I'm a spiritual person. I feel, in good conscience, I could not vote for a person who favors abortion. Partial-birth abortion is infanticide. What we do on earth is a speck in time. [She repeatedly offered variations on the "speck in time" phrase.] Life passes so fast; we'll be judged on those decisions.

— MARISA MARY RUMMEL

Owner, manufacturing plant, Spring, Tex.

In the South people are very pro-life to the point of obnoxiousness.

— ROBERT C. CAHALY

Political consultant with clients in nine states

In other interviews with evangelical Protestants, including the pastors of both affiliated and unaffiliated churches, the answer was often, "I vote for the man. If a man was pro-choice, I could still vote for him, if he was a better candidate on other issues." Abortion is, as some observers have said, "a menu option"; one can choose from any of a number of positions, ranging from Mrs. Rummel's Roman Catholic absolute ban on abortion to Ruth Cleveland's "gray area." At the convention some delegates and alternates said, "I'm a fiscal conservative, social liberal." But social liberalism did not mean they condoned abortion; it meant there were certain circumstances in which abortion was acceptable. These social liberals, and there were very few, existed on the fringe of the national political movement. They belonged to the all-but-forgotten liberal wing of the Republican Party, which had been represented by George H. W. Bush in the 1980 Republican presidential primaries. He was defeated by Ronald Reagan for the nomination and chose to abandon his old Republican liberal stance to join the movement and become Reagan's running mate. At the 1980 convention the movement showed its strength, booing the name of Nelson Rockefeller, sneering at Jacob K. Javits, the liberal senator from New York.[15] The boos were triumphant, like the sound that accompanied the expulsion of the controversial filmmaker Michael Moore at the 2004 convention, with the same kind of hatred, but not the threat of violence, not jack-boot rage. The Rockefeller wing had no official representative in the convention hall in 2004.

After a quarter of a century in power the movement had become sophisticated, as had the party. Delegates to the convention said they had been "media-trained." And it was true. For the first few minutes of a conversation the answers they gave were remarkably similar. After an hour they confided the whispers about Cheney that had been going around the Convention, the hope that he would not run again, that it would be John McCain, a hero, a man of the movement, yet different from the archetype imagined in the newspapers; one of them, but not Zell Miller, not a screamer. McCain had suffered imprisonment and torture, but gave no sign of having lost control of himself, like Miller screaming or Schwarzenegger preening, or Giuliani swaggering, or like the crowd when it heard the name of Michael Moore. They saw in McCain the decency Cheney lacked. Their judgment would be borne

---

[15] I was squatting in the aisle next to Javits, conducting an interview with him, when the convention jeered at the late governor's name. Javits, whose health was failing, turned away from me and stared stonily ahead. When he thought his gesture of defiance had been noted, he turned back to the interview. I saw that the gesture had drained him. His eyes had gone dead. He had no strength to hold up his head. The great nose, the shiny dome, no longer dominated the moment. He had no more interest in the interview. Neither did I. Javits had been one of the pillars of the Rockefeller wing of the party, and it was over. I said I was sorry for what had happened, and went on. Reagan's "kitchen cabinet" was there on the floor in the California delegation.

out a year and a half later as Cheney and McCain contested over the question of torture. Cheney argued hard against McCain's position that the U.S. government should not torture people under any circumstances. Cheney wanted to exempt the CIA from McCain's moral position. The whispered opposition to Cheney, which appeared to have spread out of the delegations from the southern states, revealed the complex moral character of the movement. Senator John McCain is an ideal presidential candidate to serve an American political movement. He is a man of a multitude of internal bargains. He is for the war and against the war, for lower taxes unless . . . in which case he will be for higher taxes. He is for abortion, but only in some instances. And so on. He is a natural implement of the movement. Cheney is not. The delegates did not wish Cheney ill; they wanted him to use his heart condition as a graceful exit line. McCain was their dream candidate. Giuliani had not yet entered the race.

The movement could not see itself in Cheney. He could be employed by the movement, but he could not embody it; he could be the dark side of it, but not all of it. He could not lead, nor could George W. Bush, who misunderstood the very movement he claimed to represent. He killed its children, wounded its grandparents, and shamed the nation by his incompetence. In his first term he made massive death seem less likely by his computerlike demeanor, for there was a sense in the country that technological superiority could protect it. In his second term it became clear that he made massive death more likely; he even predicted it. In his second term he betrayed the movement. McCain said he could save the party; he knew the Republicans would suffer a serious defeat in 2006. Everyone knew. History told them that presidents are reelected in time of war, and then repudiated two years later.

McCain bore no resemblance to Bush or Cheney; he was more like Bill Clinton, who did not have to consciously change himself into a man of the movement, but who embodied it in his persona. Clinton was the patriot who would not go to war, the liberal who saw the gap between rich and poor grow until it defined two nations under his presidency, the boy born poor who signed a bill to take women off welfare and yet leave them in poverty, the man who courted blacks and let them twist in the wind on affirmative action and crime and welfare, who won the black vote with words and the white vote with his actions, the one who claimed the Republicans pasted in the chads on Florida ballots and traveled the country time and again with George H. W. Bush. Clinton had calmed the fears of the country by pretending the 1993 attack on the World Trade Center was without portent. Yet he could not lead the movement because he needed the support of people outside the movement. He was a man who was neither here nor there.

McCain does not suffer Clinton's debilitating division. He belongs to the movement. If he becomes president of the United States, it will not be based on political maneuvering, shifting here and there, like a tailor taking tucks in a suit to make it fit. He need not shift; perhaps he cannot. It makes little difference, because he and the movement are not contiguous; they are congruent. They suffer the same conflicts. He will offer the movement what neither Bush nor Clinton could. He will not be killed—he is a killer; in a world at risk of massive death the members of the movement believe they must now choose between killing and being killed. He is a man of angers and memories. If elected, he will come in riding on a tiger, and he will be so astonishingly certain, so thoroughly proven in so many fields, that the movement will take his name for its own, and think of him as themselves. He will be the master of oppositions, who is not likely to tolerate opposition. But first he must be elected, and to do that he will have to run in opposition to his party and the other; he will have to be the movement candidate, the one who transcends parties. And to be both inflexible and electable is a rarity in America. But this is not America as ever before; the role of the oceans, which stood for so many years like two great moats between this country and the world, has vanished. The movement asks, What now?

The conflicts within the movement appeared in almost every member. They were individual mirrors of the great conflicts inside McCain. J. Don George, the pastor of a Pentecostal church with 7,000 members in Irving, Texas, just outside Dallas, said "homosexuality is an abomination, abortion is an abomination" but George went on to say that it was God's challenge to love the homosexual and the abortionist, to hate no man. "As a matter of fact," he said, "there are three or four homosexuals who are members of this church." When I asked how he knew their sexual preference, he said, "They came to me and said they were homosexual, but [they did not say so] before they came into membership."

In his views on various social issues J. Don George is an excellent example of the moral complexity of the movement. He talks in a matter-of-fact way about abortion and homosexuality, speaking slowly, in the calm, deep, sure, Texas hill country voice of *that old time religion*. Only when he speaks of poverty in Irving and its effect on schoolchildren does he become passionate. He cites detailed statistical information about the problem and the work Calvary Church's members have done for the children. He has traveled with Jerry Falwell, attended all four of George W. Bush's inaugurations as governor and president, was a member of one of the small groups of pastors who met with Bush when he was trying to decide if he should run for president, yet he speaks of "a growing disconnect between the very rich and the very poor."

No single characteristic defines the person who becomes part of an American political movement, which gives the movement both strength and durability. One person or a million can leave the movement without vitiating it. A movement requires the same of its philosophy: it must have moral, political, and religious philosophers to rely on, and they need not be entirely in agreement. Leo Strauss, Adam Smith, Alasdair MacIntyre, Plato, Michael Oakeshott, Edmund Burke, John Calvin, and the ultrarightist Roman Catholic Opus Dei have many areas of disagreement, but no disagreement is serious enough to push any one of them out of the movement. What holds them together is a more interesting question than what separates them.

William Saroyan said, "Everyone needs a little bit of paranoia."[16] Leo Strauss made paranoia a key feature of his politics: the necessary external enemy. This American political movement is better defined by the Saroyan-Strauss point of view than by any positive program. It depends on its enemies—real, imagined, human, or theoretical—for energy. For one part of the movement the modern state, which is the United States of America itself, is the enemy. In that sense, someone

---

[16] Personal conversation.

like Grover Norquist is an enemy of the state, a political position in regard to one's country for which there is the harshest term. For another part of the movement—those young men and women who went to fight in Iraq because they believed it was their duty—there is the sweetest term: they are heroes. If there is one thing they hold in common, Norquist and heroes, it is the expectation of the end. At an Americans for Tax Reform (ATR) party prior to the opening night of the 2004 Republican National Convention, a member, insisting that he spoke for himself, not for the organization he represented, said, "The country will die of a thousand nicks, being deprived of freedom. All societies die, sooner or later, at some point in time, for some reason." He went on to speak of Rome and what he believed was the role of conservatives in America: "to hold off the death of the society for as long as possible."[17] Tom Readmond, federal affairs manager of ATR, told me he thought the country would not last forever, that the fall of the American nation, the end, was inevitable. The disjunction of the two ways of considering the end defines two of the boundaries of the movement. Heroes think of glory, others think of the long dying of the sick or the agonies meted out by terrorists. No theory binds them, only a preoccupation with the varieties of death. And death is not a theory.

A Definition

An American political movement does not require a theorist, nor can its existence depend on the ideas or personality of a single leader. It is not a totalitarian movement, which must be based on the leader being at the top of a standard pyramidal management structure and also at the center of an onion structure of personal relations.[18] An American political

---

[17] Richard Gose is vice president for political affairs of a national organization. We did not speak about Alasdair MacIntyre, but I do not think his agreement with MacIntyre comes from having read *After Virtue*; rather it is that both men are what MacIntyre might describe as "plain people" when it comes to the common kind of pessimism.

[18] See Hannah Arendt, *The Origins of Totalitarianism* (New York: Harcourt, Brace & World, 1951).

movement will include the president, the courts, and at least part of the legislature to wield power most effectively, but the president is not the leader of the movement. The movement follows the pattern of bureaucracy more closely than that of any other form of organization. "A bureaucracy is the rule of nobody," as Hannah Arendt wrote. When Kafka's nameless protagonist in *The Trial* encounters the bureaucracy, he cannot find out who has accused him; he does not even know the nature of his crime. Kafka knew exactly what he was writing about. He himself had worked inside a bureaucracy.

To establish the rule of nobody in the United States requires more than 50 million people of voting age. It would be impossible to name all or even a small portion of the members of the movement of nobody except in the most general terms. The movement can be characterized as Protestant, which is to say it is an American movement, all Americans being Protestants. On the list in the following paragraph there is probably no group in which all the members belong to the movement, because of the pluralism within individual Americans and the separation of communities. The movement is an affiliation of the fearful, each group expressing its fears in a different form.

All evangelical Christians do not belong to the movement. Narrowing the category to evangelical Christian *conservatives* eliminates most of the members of the first group who are not swept along on the river. More than half of all Roman Catholics have ties to the movement based largely on papal pronouncements on abortion and homosexuality. Jewish neoconservatives want to lead the movement as a way to alleviate the fears that sent them to neoconservatism in the first place. Fundamentalists of many varieties participate in the movement: Protestant, Catholic, Jewish, Muslim, Hindu, Buddhist, and Sikh. Some mainline Protestant denominations have split into those whose beliefs on social or economic questions do or do not separate them from the movement. Pentecostals and Nazarenes, who share many of the same beliefs and practices as the fundamentalists but are experiential rather than fundamentalist, form a large and increasingly important part of the movement. Pentecostalism is the fastest-growing religious denomination in America and the world. The great majority of the remaining thousand or more sects and unaffiliated churches[19] in the United States also participate in the rule of nobody. Many of these are "megachurches," like Rick Warren's church in California, which has the most members— 23,000 (or 27,000, depending on who is doing the estimate). Warren makes a loud case for the size and influence of his rapidly growing church, although the pope's church, with 1.1 billion members, is still in the lead. Warren would like to be a leader of the movement, and he has certainly sold a lot of books, but not nearly so many as Tim LaHaye (the Left Behind series had passed 60 million at this writing), and LaHaye does not lead the movement.

The movement practices the politics of heaven, but there are many Americans whose love of God separates them from this movement. Religious differences are an old story in America. Democrats and Republicans are often separated by opposing interpretations of Scripture. The problem was more serious in the mid-nineteenth century, when competing interpretations of Scripture fortified the abolitionists and proslavery factions as they prepared to tear the country apart. The role of religion in America worried the founders into writing a Constitution wholly separated from religion; neither the word "God" nor the name of any religious denomination or sect appears in the document. Nonetheless, religion was a powerful force in American life then, and it is, if anything, even stronger today. Yet America is not a theocracy. A national political movement is not a religious movement. It has both religious and secular components, and the spheres are not distinct, but overlapping. Fear sets the tone.

The secular components have a fervent and negative cast. Their advocates understand disagreement as if it were sin rather than politics. A good example is the Iraq War. The core belief is to preserve the lives and livelihoods of citizens in the United States by extending "democ-

---

[19] Many of these unaffiliated churches are experiential, like Pentecostalism—meaning they are concerned with the personal experience of faith, including possession by the Holy Spirit in various forms, from talking in tongues, which is all but universal among experiential churches, but may also include such arcane practices as snake-handling and eating poison— but do not follow the rules of the large Pentecostal organizations. Assemblies of God and other national and international Pentecostal organizations have rules requiring formal study and interpretation of Scripture that are binding on their pastors.

racy" to the rest of the world. There are varying opinions on how best to do this, what is worth sacrificing to accomplish this goal, when war costs more than it may gain, and so on. To renounce the core belief is not opinion, but sin, and the sinner must recant in order to be saved. There is no middle ground, no purgatory; there is only heaven or hell, yes or no, positive or negative. It combines a modern sense of the Manichean (1,0) machine with biblical certitude; every component has its own sense of inerrancy. When the movement contains opposing views, they are always about method or degree, which the movement treats as opinions not beliefs; disagreement in these instances is not sinful.

These are some of the many views included in the movement:

antiabortion
anti–gun control
anti–big government
anti stem cell research
antieuthanasia
anti-Darwin
antiatheism
anti–government regulation
antigovernment
anti–separation of church and state
antitax
anti–graduated income tax
anti–inheritance tax
anti–dividend tax
antipornography
antinudity
antiprostitution
antiliberal
anti–*New York Times*
anti–New York
anti–gay marriage
antigay
anti-immigrant
anti–undocumented immigrant

antibilingualism

anti–citizenship for children born here of foreign parents

antimulticulturalism

antidivorce

antiwelfare

anticorruption

anti–flouridated drinking water

anti–public education

anti–political correctness

anti–national health care

anti-Muslim

anti-Marxist

anti-communist

antipluralism

anti-Hollywood

antioutsourcing

anti–United Nations

anti–foreign aid

anti–trial lawyer

antijudiciary

anti–international environmental standards

antienvironmentalism

anti-ACLU

antidrug

antialcohol

anti–affirmative action

antiblack

anti-Jewish

anti-Catholic

anti-Mexican

antidancing

anti–Thomas Jefferson

anti–Tom Paine

There are also some subjects on which the movement holds divided opinions. Many people are antiwar yet still support the war in Iraq for reasons of patriotism and fear of terrorism. Pro-McCain and anti-McCain members must balance many issues to make a decision about him, not the least of which is the question of power. Few issues trouble the movement more than the power of large corporations and their ability to escape taxation as they crush small businesses, but the movement is largely funded by big business; members of the movement shop at Wal-Mart even as they despise it. Owners of small businesses (S-corporations) make up much of the cadre of the movement. The purpose of forming an S-corporation is to avoid corporate income tax, yet the owners of S-corporations, who pay taxes as individuals, still claim the rate is too high. There are more than 4 million S-corporations in the United States, with gross receipts in the trillions of dollars. At the 2004 Republican National Convention the owners of these corporations were over-represented. They seemed to be everywhere, constantly complaining at having to pay at the maximum Federal tax rate of 35 percent, meaning they earned more than $326,000.[20]

The ambivalent attitudes of members of the movement show up most clearly in Grover Norquist, whom the press has made a leader, but who in reality is merely another operative. Norquist depends on his alliance with the Christian right to support his claim of leadership. The Christian right has a hard pro-Israel stance. Rev. Jerry Falwell, who says there are 70 million people on the Christian right who support Israel, told CBS in 2003, ". . . the Bible Belt in America is Israel's only safety belt right now." Yet Norquist, who includes the Christian fundamentalists in his "leave us alone coalition," wrote: "George W. Bush was elected President of the United States of America because of the Muslim vote. . . . Muslims in Florida favored Bush over Gore by 20 to 1."[21] That gave Bush 55,000 votes, according to Norquist. He went on to describe Muslims as "natural conservatives," while saying Republicans would never get enough of the Jewish vote to matter. If his support of Muslims and Falwell's support of Israel should come to a head over

---

[20] The 2006 rate at the margin. For the IRS definition of an S-corporation see the epigraph at the beginning of this chapter.

[21] *The American Spectator*, June 1, 2001.

issues in the Middle East, it could either be the first sign of a crack in the movement or simply an organizational misjudgment. When we talked, I asked Norquist if he knew his forerunner, Morton Blackwell, who had mentored Karl Rove, among other conservatives. He said he knew Blackwell, but did not know much about him. I said Blackwell, founder of the Leadership Institute, which "prepares conservatives for success in politics," had been a young Democrat in Louisiana who became a Republican when Raymond Moley,[22] turned against FDR and became one of the most ferocious critics of New Deal economic policies. Norquist, whose undergraduate degree is in economics, had never heard of Raymond Moley.

Norquist characterizes the movement as the "leave us alone coalition"; that is, a coalition of communities of people who are against something, but not one another. Their interests do not conflict: for example, those who oppose abortion do not conflict with those who want lower taxes. He is correct when he says that each of the interest groups wants to be left alone. That is characteristic of the movement. A coalition of people who want to be left alone is a paradox. Either they are alone or part of a coalition; they cannot be both (in the language of logic P and not P). Politics, however, does not always follow the rules of logic. Logically a leave-us-alone coalition should not exist (it is a contradiction in terms), which is why it has proved so difficult to combat or even to consider. Most of the effort of students of politics has gone into seeking to understand the methods used to implement the will of various constituent parts of the movement rather than into considering the movement itself.

The movement, which needs a name to legitimize it, should, I think, have a name that includes or implies fear, death, racism, and capitalism, those being its key components. (I have not given the movement a name in this book to avoid the appearance of sloganeering.) Perhaps it is the sign of the times in which we live. Perhaps we have entered an Age of Opposition, a period when nothing suits us or our destiny, when the radical oppositionists no longer have confidence in American insti-

---

[22] Moley is widely credited with having invented the term "new deal."

tutions, envisioning the eventual collapse of the country. The lobbyist drinking and gorging himself on hors d'oeuvres at the Americans for Tax Reform party before the 2004 Republican National Convention may be that kind of radical oppositionist. He may represent something beyond his own judgment when he speaks about the not-quite-imminent fall of the state. And at the same party a young black woman, the prettiest woman in the crowd, stood beside her friend, the only other person of color in the room, and hiding in laughter, said, "Perhaps they only want to help me because of my color."

It was the loneliest room, the loneliest convention, the loneliest community. Death and capitalism, both of which have the capacity to distance one person, one community from another, dominated the rooms; they were everywhere, as if they were the whispers of the wine. They made for a war convention. In 2004 a cacophonous cheer for killing shook the hall. There is no sound like it. The cheer has no music, no rhythm, no organization; it is a roar of the voices of strangers, neither a marching song, nor a hurrah, but a growl of discontent, as disordered and deafening as battle, an imitation of the chaos of war. The delegates and onlookers roared in a different, unified voice for McCain, the real hero, and for Giuliani, who proclaimed himself a hero, but they exhibited a kind of madness as Zell Miller, the former Democrat, spoke, and when they had finished with Miller, they were sheepish about what they had become, and they wanted to be civilized again. I saw them blushing, looking away, but there was nothing civilized to give them solace. They love the idea of war, but only political war not bloody war; the community comes and goes, forming and reforming; they are an army of disjunction, with no central theme but opposition. By 2004 the people in the convention hall still favored the Iraq war, but outside the circle of delegates and alternates, the cadre, war had little appeal; the people told me so, even the people who would vote for Bush.

This was not a Nazi Party rally at Nuremberg in 1936. At Nuremberg there had been unity in madness, and that was how it was sustained. There was no unity in this assembly. It did not even enjoy the binding comfort of a mob. Capitalists make a poor mob and a worse army; they go about their lives separated from each other by envy. It was apparent among the delegates: the slightly-too-helpful man who runs the limousine service in Virginia eyes the wallet of the factory owner from Georgia. A question arose in the many-tiered auditorium of Madison Square Garden: how could they make war without endangering themselves? This was no English "band of brothers" ready to die for God and Harry at Agincourt. The former Marine from West Texas who did a tour in Iraq said he had trained the men who were training the next generation of Marines—he was not going back to Iraq; he was now a member of the Chamber of Commerce of his hometown.

The brigades in the army of those who want to be left alone are too separate to form ranks. They do politics as William James said people practiced religion. The politics in the hall were about feelings, and they were not good feelings. The conventioneers did not need Rudy Giuliani or Arnold Schwarzenegger to tell them this was a dangerous world, replete with terrorists and nuclear weapons. They were already convinced of the lurking death that will surface suddenly in an airplane or in church, and they do not have to read about Ivan Ilyich or commune with Heidegger to know they are going to die alone. They understood that every person owns his death. In a curious way the first capital is one's own death. And it is coming. The security forces in and around the hall reminded them. They had seen the black SUVs with the blacked-out windows coming up out of the garage under the very building in which they were sitting. And they had also seen the men in black warrior's uniforms carrying automatic weapons, prowling the perimeter of the hall, especially the darkened street on the west side of the building. They understood the security to mean death was waiting. It could be in this hall, on the street, in the airplane departing. They could all imagine the faces of the killers. If only Jesus would embrace them when their time came, if only death was truly the beginning of life, if only they could be alone together. It was a touching and terrible reunion.

A Political Party Is Not a Movement

The difference between a political movement and a political party as the terms are used here can be illustrated in several ways. The key difference is simply categorical: a national movement can contain political parties. It has been so since the inception of the United States. The movement that favored independence from the British crown comprised two well-defined groups, which soon became two political parties: Federalist and Democratic-Republican. It resulted in the contest between John Adams (Federalist) and Thomas Jefferson (Democratic-Republican).[23]

A political party in a democratic society represents a part of the society. At times the party will represent fewer people, at other times more. If the party represents everyone or almost everyone it can no longer be described as a party, but becomes the beast Plato and Aristotle described as a mob. Both philosophers said the rule of a mob results in despotism, which is why they opposed democracy. A constitutional democracy is less likely to become a mob and choose a despot to lead it, but the advent of totalitarian democracy in the twentieth century shows that constitutional democracies are not immune to the Greek prediction.

In a constitutional democracy a political party selects candidates for elections, develops theories of government into policy proposals, and serves as a guardian of the public interest by contending with the other party or parties over interpretations of fact, hierarchies of need, adequacy of solutions to both domestic and foreign issues, and the qualities of officeholders and candidates.

A single-issue political movement organizes people either to defend or oppose an ongoing or proposed thought or action. The Vietnam War and abortion have both engendered single-issue political movements. Some movements combine thought and action. Evolution is an action, but organizing a movement to put a stop to it presents some problems; reversing the action is even more difficult, so antievolutionists have no choice but to make war on the thought.

A national political movement comprises many issues, parties, people, ideas. The movement selects candidates for public office, but not in a formal way. It expresses its frantic pessimism through the ballot box, books, magazines, broadcast media, Web sites, church sermons, donations of money and time, attendance at public and semipublic gather-

---

[23] In 2001, David McCullough's best-selling biography of John Adams lauded the conservative Federalist and fueled the growing anti-Jeffersonian sentiment in the country.

ings (school boards, PTAs, civic commissions, etc.) schools, colleges, universities, lectures, films, songs, demonstrations, and even violence (beatings, burnings, bombings, murders, terrorism, the Ku Klux Klan, skinheads, right-to-life groups, etc.), military service in peace and war, and charitable acts both at home and abroad.

What Does the Movement Want?

The mind is its own place,
and in itself,
can make heaven of Hell,
and a hell of Heaven.

— JOHN MILTON

The last national political movement and this one have the same goal: security. The difference between them comes in the definition, not the desire, for the components of security and the character of the movement have changed. One side would as gladly hang the other based on definitions now as when Henry Barrow could not agree with his persecutors on the difference between a schism and a sect and was executed in Jacobean England for being a Puritan separatist. The definition was complex and important to the core belief about life and the afterlife then as it is now. The change from the New Deal to the current movement could not be more profound. The current movement cannot reasonably seek "freedom from fear" as its primary goal. On January 15, 1940, one day after Paris fell to the Nazis, Franklin Delano Roosevelt signed a letter to Vannevar Bush. The subject of the letter, most of which had been dictated by Dr. Bush, was "the relationship to national defense of recent discoveries in the field of atomistics [*sic*]." It authorized the beginning of the work that would produce the atomic bomb. Five and a half years later, after Hiroshima, the definition of security had to be revised.

Slowly at first, then with increasing speed as the prospect of safety declined, the current movement redefined the meaning of security and the character of the nation. It abandoned the ethical aims of the Social

Gospel, which were at the heart of the old movement, and instead took up a harsh new kind of security in which America contended with other nations and Americans contended with each other. The world had changed. The idea of security for all forever became anachronistic. In the new environment the definition changed to security for the fittest.

Perhaps the best way to understand the goal of the current national political movement is to look at the one it replaced. The New Deal took its ethical view from the Social Gospel. Like the current movement, it was driven by fear. The rich feared revolution and the rest of the country feared hunger. No one was safe. In response to the will of the movement, Roosevelt chose a fellow Social Gospeler for his right hand man. Harry Hopkins, who had little experience other than working in New York settlement houses and public welfare at the municipal level, took on the task of making Roosevelt's promise of safety a reality. He set about putting everyone to work, poets as well as plumbers, composers as well as construction workers. It was a massive, expensive task.

Roosevelt began a Social Security program in 1937, and by 1940 the first checks were paid to the elderly. In 1933 an estimated 31 million people were living at a bare subsistence level, and state and local welfare programs could not cope. More than 200,000 boys dropped out of school and left home to make their way in the streets. At least 20 percent of schoolchildren were malnourished.[24] In 1935 the members of the national political movement applauded a federal welfare program to care for them.

Not everyone agreed with the federalizing of ideas that came out of the Social Gospel. Opposition mounted as the Depression years went on. Business interests argued that New Deal policies on taxes, labor, and public spending impeded recovery. In 1938 an economic setback and a rise in unemployment to 19 percent gave new energy to the anti-Roosevelt faction, but opposition to the idea that safety meant safety for everyone was minimal. Motives and ends were not seriously questioned except by a few; most opposition was to the means. A great majority of the people had come to believe that safety for one meant safety for all. However,

---

[24] The percentage of children living in poverty is not markedly different today, but the response to their suffering is emblematic of the new definition of security.

this did not cause racism or regionalism to disappear. Blacks, Mexican-Americans, people in Appalachia, and many recent immigrants did not enjoy the benefits of the federal response to the national movement. No one ever said the New Deal was perfectly ethical, but the nation did make sacrifices for the sake of fairness as well as survival. As the Jacksonian democracy had resulted from a national political movement, so the New Deal came from a national movement. One was driven by inequality, the other by fear.

The country grew more fearful as the Depression wore on. War seemed inevitable. Many feared that Great Britain and then the United States would be defeated by the Nazis. Although Congress wanted the United States to stay out of the war, Roosevelt increased production of military goods. For the first few years after the United States entered the war, it went badly in both Europe and Asia. Safety from military attack was added to safety from revolution and the collapse of "the American way." Safety had been Woodrow Wilson's slogan—"To make the world safe for democracy"—and safety was FDR's slogan, phrased as "Freedom from fear."

The war ended with the atomic massacres in Hiroshima and Nagasaki. Soon enough the capacity to make atomic weapons spread. Thoughts of disarmament gave way to plans for mutual assured destruction (MAD) and then to mutual assured survival, but survival for whom was a question never answered. Star Wars, protection against nuclear missile attack, failed every test.

The logic was inescapable: If one could be safe from war and revolution, an ethical nation and universal security were conceivable. If no one could be assured of safety, no other assurances mattered; fearful people contended for the remains. The objects of contention were determined by the sudden rise in the standard of living at the end of World War II. Along with the euphoria of victory came the realization that even without more than 5 million of its most able citizens in the workforce America was the greatest productive engine in the history of the world. And when most of the 5 million came home, the economy boomed. The standard of living rose almost in spite of the growing danger of nuclear war and the series of limited wars. The Korean War cost the lives of more than 36,500 Americans and left over 100,000 wounded. More than

58,000 were killed in Vietnam, and the numbers of the physically and psychologically wounded "survivors" horrified the nation, but the standard of living continued to rise. Lyndon Johnson announced a policy of "guns and butter." As Wilson's slogan had morphed into Roosevelt's, Lyndon Johnson had found the language to describe the goal of the next movement. Guns and butter fit the definition of a different kind of security. Johnson accomplished his civil rights goals, but all the rhetoric, the arm twisting, and embraces; all the dreams of being another Roosevelt, gave way to the counted bodies, the draft cards burning, and the children screaming. It was a time when adult Americans pretended they were safe inside the shopping malls while their children were stoned out of their minds on dope bought with daddy's dollars. Alas, the sixties! It was the madness of a generation at the end of a movement, very like the Roaring Twenties had been at the end of the Gilded Age. The most authentic voice of the time, Bob Dylan, who was born Robert Allen Zimmerman, said "the times they are a-changin'."

Slowly Johnson came to see what Dylan meant. A villain when it came to foreign wars, LBJ was not yet a complete fool about politics. He knew what the people wanted: security. He said he would give it to them—guns and butter—but he could not deliver on his promise. When he finally understood that the people did not think anyone or anything could make them safe, that sacrifice belonged to an earlier time, he had to face the one sentiment he had avoided all his life—pessimism—and he quit.

He and Nixon after him belonged to a prenuclear world. Anachronism made madmen of them, for they still believed in Wilson's hope and Roosevelt's promise. They still believed that wars were fought in trenches and bloody victories could be won. They still believed in glory. And there is no glory in the new wish for security. It is a pessimist's prayer. Ronald Reagan, who presented himself as an optimist, believed the world would end in fiery Armageddon, according to Richard Wirthlin. He sold the idea of security until that day, he put off the end of everything, but he did not tell people to put off gratification. In a curiously Calvinist way, he thought good acts made no difference. He let the ethics of the old movement lapse, he made racism and inequality acceptable in America.

In the 1984 campaign against Walter Mondale, he followed the advice of his strategist Wirthlin, who understood what the new movement wanted. Wirthlin's research produced what he calls a "voter decision map." (He was kind enough to provide me with a copy of the map.) It showed the differences between Reagan's and Walter Mondale's paths to what Wirthlin had defined as the ultimate value: "Make U.S./World a Better Place for Future Generations." He drew his chart rising from the level of "Issues" to "Policies, Programs, Traits" up to "Values" and the ultimate value. By 2005, Wirthlin had changed the ultimate value to "security." He did not say "safety," and Richard Wirthlin is a very careful man with words, especially when the tape recorder is running. He made a companion point that goes a long way toward explaining what Americans want when they think of security. He said the people of the United States were pessimistic, interpreting the "going in the wrong direction" answers in many public polls, including his own, as a sign of pessimism. He gave the ratio of pessimism to optimism as 2 to 1. It was as good an estimate of the size of the national political movement as we are likely to get. There is a spate of pessimistic books now in support of the movement, not all of them by people who identify themselves as Republicans. Ann Coulter is the most pessimistic, Kevin Phillips the most statistical, Thomas Frank the liveliest, Victor Davis Hanson the cruelest, David Horowitz the least palatable, Rush Limbaugh the loudest, and so on.

A movement based on fear and fallen into pessimism may turn into a search for a hero, a secular savior to care for the people until such time as heaven bids. Even a still hopeful nation held the danger of totalitarian democracy in 1933, the same year that Adolf Hitler became führer and Reich chancellor. The movement that chose FDR to lead it, with Hopkins at his side, wanted to be safe from military attack, shielded from complete economic dissolution (revolution was a real possibility in a country with 25 percent unemployment), and perhaps most of all the politically astute among them wanted to be safe from fascism. This is Robert Sherwood, in *Roosevelt and Hopkins*:

> . . . *some Americans who had read* Mein Kampf *and had taken seriously its implications were frightened as they tried to peer into the heavily clouded future.*
>
> *There is deep rooted in our consciousness the conviction that a*

*great President will appear "whenever we really need him," and in
the years 1929–33 the question being asked, constantly and appre-
hensively, was "Where is he now?"*

*No cosmic dramatist could possibly devise a better entrance for
a President—or a new Dictator, or a new Messiah—than that
accorded to Franklin Delano Roosevelt.*

. . .

*Roosevelt rode in on a wheel chair instead of a white horse, but
the roll of drums and the thunderclaps which attended him were pos-
itively Wagnerian as emotional stimuli and also as ugly warnings of
what might happen to American democracy if the new President
should turn out to possess any of the qualities of a Hitler or even of a
Huey Long.*[25]

In FDR's First Inaugural, he addressed the problem in a way that
indicated he might seek extraordinary power, but would not use the
country's suffering to become a despot. In the most memorable phrase
of his long career, he said, ". . . we have nothing to fear but fear itself."

Despotism rides a different horse. The old Athenians knew. They
understood how fear could change a democratic society into a mob.
The danger in the United States now is not the Bush Administration,
for all its incompetence and all its killing of innocents and violations of
the rules of war, decency, and civil rights. The danger is the arrival of
the man or woman who accords perfectly with the wants of the
national movement, the one who can serve the conflicting desires
within the definition. Perhaps that person would be no more dangerous than FDR. Perhaps not. When the next act of terror occurs in the
United States, if it is a big one, or there are many attacks at the same
time, there may come a man or woman on a white horse or a green-
eyed tiger who will say "Follow me," and it will be the beginning of the
end of liberty in the United States of America.

This is what the movement wants. The definition differs from that
of the previous movement in both order and content:

---

[25] New York: HarperCollins, 1948.

1. Certainty of eternal life in heaven after death or by ascension during one's life
2. Safety from physical harm
   a. by a disease; that is, a flu pandemic
   b. by an attack on one's person; i.e., mugging, robbery, murder
   c. by accident
   d. by a nuclear attack
   e. by attack with harmful biological or chemical agents
   f. by attack with a nonnuclear bomb
3. Assurance that economic needs and desires will be met
   a. absolute needs of food, shelter, clothing, medical care
   b. relative to other people's goods
4. Certainty of superior social position by virtue of
   a. race
   b. income
   c. occupation
   d. education
   e. associations; i.e., social circle, business connections, rank
   f. church membership
5. Availability of pleasure
   a. physical; e.g., sexual, athletic
   b. joy; e.g., family, religious experience
   c. cultural; e.g., music, films, books, etc.
6. Guarantee of autonomy
   a. freedom from federal rule
   b. freedom from local rule; that is, not accepting public education, recycling rules, fluoridation of water[26]

Neither Roosevelt nor Hoover nor Wilson could have understood the fears that drive this movement. Its definition of security would have baffled them. What has not changed from their time to this is the danger that the man on the white horse will come riding in, tall in the sad-

---

[26] Not in the strict libertarian sense of eliminating such rules, but of having the ability to choose the rules and if chosen by others to follow or flout them.

dle, soldier and saint, grand enough in himself to contain all the contradictions in the movement, and the people give up everything to him if
he will only make them safe, at least for a little while, long enough for
their children to be born and the size of their houses to increase. What
has changed is that the love of God and one's fellow man has given way
to the fear of God and one's fellow man.

The Paradox Solved

Some paradoxes cannot be solved. The structure of the current national
political movement is not one of them. By definition, an interest group
and a national movement are not the same. There is a hierarchical relation of communities of the fearful to a national political movement.

This movement is not like any that went before. The King James
love of language is gone, and there is no great excitement like the beginning of an American culture separate from Europe, nor does the excitement of modernism and movies connect the people. This movement is
different: it has no cultural center but the business of marketing, no
connectedness other than the chill electronics of the Internet and the
promise of ashes. This is the loneliest time in America. The thought of
death has not been so common since the seventeenth century and never
so likely to be massive, obliterating everything, even memory. This time
the operative who assembles the convivial oppositions speaks proudly of
a "leave us alone coalition," mistaking the worst for the best, as if the
loneliness of small, populous islands in a great ocean were the only credible freedom. This time the fastest-growing religion is the one in which
people speak in tongues, in an ecstasy no other group alive can understand. This time people pray together to be possessed by the spirit of
holy loneliness.

> *A nation committed to a democratic way of life, but which prescribes
> for its citizens a set of beliefs concerning the nature of the cosmos and
> man's place in it, is a contradiction in terms. When permitted to
> reflect freely upon fundamental questions, men are stimulated to
> thought by diverse experiences and divergent traditions; and under
> these circumstances the world comes to be viewed from many differ-*

ent perspectives and portrayed in many different colors. But the freedom to develop alternative conceptions of nature and man, even though some of them may be grossly inadequate to their subject matter, is an essential part of the liberal, democratic tradition. There is accordingly no official American philosophy.

—ERNEST NAGEL

Sovereign Reason and Other Studies in the Philosophy of Science

Eleven

PESSIMISM

"Yes, I know the New Right. I may as well tell you my
qualifications. I'm policy director for Senator Gordon
Humphrey [Republican] of New Hampshire. That
means I'm over the whole legislative staff.

"I was a Goldwater delegate in '64 from Louisiana.
And a Reagan delegate in '68. I wrote a substantial portion of the delegate allocation formula in '72.

"From '65 to '70 I was executive director of National
College Republicans. I was national vice chairman of
Young Republicans and on the executive committee for
fifteen years. My wife, Helen, was a county chairman in
Virginia, where we moved in '72.

"I went to work for Richard Vigucric in '72. I'm editor of the *New Right Newsletter* and contributing editor
of *Conservative Digest*. I founded Conservative Youth
Politics. Its purpose is to locate, recruit, train, place, and
finance youth coordinators for candidates. I would say
I've trained virtually all the youth in the New Right.

"As a member of a senator's staff I am not permitted by law to belong to organizations that finance candidates. But I'm still president of the Leadership
Institute, which trains, but does not support, candidates. Every other Monday for six and a half years, I've
hosted a luncheon for activists interested in House and

Senate campaigns. It's social—Dutch treat. We don't make any group decisions.

"New Right is hard to capsulize because it's not a membership organization. It is best described as an approach to getting things done—different from the way conservatives used to go. There's hardly any difference between the Old and the New Right. We are all New Right now.

"Being right in the sense of being correct is not enough to win. Victory will not fall into our deserving hands like a ripe fruit. We have studied the political process from a realistic viewpoint. If there is a single dominant characteristic of the New Right, it is that they are out studying how to win.

"One thing we've done is to observe what the Left is doing. All things we have done organizationally have predecessors on the Left. We have mirror-image committees. We've studied what has worked.

"What determines success is not so much political philosophy or party but the organizational technology you employ. We owe it to our political philosophy to learn how to win. There is an immense amount of cross-pollination. It's not unusual to have right-to-work people speaking at a right-to-life congress. You see, most technology is philosophically neutral. For someone who is totally committed philosophically that's hard to believe. Now, I think the Left has fallen behind us in technology. In some areas we're way ahead—direct mail, for example.

"We are obviously not at the end of the up-cycle for conservative action. People who say we are on the verge now of coming to power in this country are not correct. We've got a long way to go. The Reagan Administration is going to be a battle for us. We are a major influence, but we don't have a lock on it. We don't dominate the Reagan Administration by any means. We are in a building process.

"I'll oversee the national youth organization in the Reagan campaign in the fall. The Reagan group is shot through with New Right people. I have no doubt that there will be people who are simply congenial to the platform in a substantial number of roles in the Reagan Administration. He didn't exclude strong conservatives from his administration in California."

I told Blackwell I was interested in the philosophy behind the New Right and asked what he thought of this quote from Edmund Burke: "Those who have made the exhibition of the 14th of July are capable of every evil. They do not commit crimes for their designs; but they form designs that they may commit crimes. It is not their necessity, but their nature that impels them." Then I asked, "Do you agree with that view of man?"

Blackwell said he was not the theologian of the New Right. "I'll tell you something people in the New Right are fond of saying: 'Don't let them immanentize the eschaton.' In other words, no Heaven on Earth. It's a paraphrase of Ludwig von Mises, an Austrian economist and a colleague of Hayek, who wrote *The Road to Serfdom*."[1]

His wife, Helen, explained, "You know, the Utopian heresy, the belief that perfection can be found on earth. It's impossible. . . ."

---

[1] Among other works, von Mises published a tract against the use of state power to solve problems of multiculturalism, which he said was a cause of German imperialism. He opposed socialism, defended capitalism, and in his later years, when he taught at New York University, became the darling of libertarians.

Friedrich Hayek, also an Austrian, was a member of the Committee on Social Thought at the University of Chicago. His work was mainly in defense of laissez-faire economics, claiming that any kind of collectivism would lead eventually to totalitarianism. Hayek, who won the Nobel Prize in 1974, shared it, ironically, with Gunnar Myrdal.

And he finished the sentence for her: ". . . because man is inherently evil."

—*Conversation with* MR. AND MRS. MORTON BLACKWELL
at the 1980 Republican National Convention[2]

A national political movement can not be imposed, much as people like Morton Blackwell would like to think so. It can only grow out of the will of the people. The will itself imposes the methods and conditions upon the body politic, a process that bears more than a little resemblance to the way Schopenhauer understood the world; i.e., will trumps reason. The optimism of the Enlightenment had no place in Schopenhauer's understanding of the way the world works. He thought human beings could expect no more than doom and darkness, and nothing they could do would change that prognosis. Social and legal rules were of some use in protecting people from outside forces, but nothing could protect people from themselves. No social programs, no philosophical or theological solutions, nothing could alter the will. He said the will arises from the unconscious, a physiological monster making a world of eternal misery. The life in art he recommended as a way to get along in the world had no sense of optimism about it. Schopenhauer could not imagine that the revolutionary aspect of art gives—no matter how gloomy its content—testimony to optimism simply because a person chose to create it. In his own life he had not been

---

[2] Morton Blackwell has remained an almost unknown soldier in service of the national political movement. His place in movement politics was praised by Rev. Ronald Godwin, president of Jerry Falwell Ministries and dean of the Jesse Helms School of Government at Liberty University, and president of Moral Majority during "most of its existence." He left the Falwell Ministries for a time to work for Rev. Sun Myung Moon as senior vice president of the *Washington Times*. Godwin said, "Morton Blackwell, among all the leading conservative activists in the nation has done more practical good in training the next generation of conservative activists than all the others combined. Morton, quietly, year after year, has continued to train young conservatives in practical political skills." He characterized Blackwell's work as "practical, not just theoretical or conceptual." He said that Blackwell had worked on 250 college campuses. "All successful political leaders have taken courses from Morton over the years at his Leadership Institute."

witness to good news, real or implied. His mother committed suicide, the Prussian Army conquered Danzig, where he was born, and his family fled to Germany. As if to prove the pessimism of his major work, completed when he was barely thirty years old, *The World as Will and Idea* went largely unnoticed. Schopenhauer saw only the worst and expected only the worst. The idea of the perfection of man may have been the one thing that could make him laugh. Or turn his mind to the most dangerous kind of thinking.

The philosophical pessimism of Schopenhauer differs from the political pessimism of our time in that it was, in large measure, a response to the optimism of Enlightenment thinking. It was a philosophical argument, and one philosophical argument can be countered with another. The pessimism of the national political movement in this time is not a response to ideas or personal life. It originated in historical events and now pervades much of the thought and action of the country. The bleak view followed a long period of optimism.[3]

The events of the Second World War and its aftermath support seven kinds of pessimism in our time: biological, theological, social, political, environmental, cultural, and philosophical. The categories overlap, as they have since the first human beings or their ancestors faced their mortality. And there is always the same question at the root: What do we do until we die? And then? Pessimism is about the aftermath here and there, wherever here and there may be.

The Hebrews were optimists in that they concerned themselves with life on earth, not with the next life, although the Old Testament is filled with accounts of slavery, war, betrayal, destruction, and sin. Jews survived enormous suffering in part because they had no world but the world in which they lived.

---

[3] Danzig had enjoyed a period of "liberty" from foreign domination prior to the Prussian takeover that affected Schopenhauer, but it cannot be compared with the great optimism of Americans that survived wars and the Great Depression, only to begin to decay after World War II and sink into pessimism during the Cold War, the Vietnam War, and Watergate, becoming the grim emotional situation that President Carter described as "malaise." After 9/11, American pessimism grew more pronounced, but it was mixed with sadness, a funereal sense. As the failure of the Iraq invasion and occupation became clear, pessimism became the salient American emotion.

To the west of monotheism (and slightly to the north) Socrates went to his death believing in the possibilities of a wobbly, imperialistic, but nonetheless democratic city. He died an optimist, interested in this world, vague about the next. Plato, who matured in the shadow of the death of Socrates, held out no hope for the real city. He proposed an idea that was, he thought, superior to any reality; his city was intellectually clean, the perfect city, not like the raucous, bumbling, uncertain, contentious, egotistical, capricious marvel of self-government. Plato was a pessimist about the real city, as if the disorder of democracy had an odor of uncleanness about it that repelled him. Leo Strauss and his followers carried the pessimism of Plato as well as the imperialism of Pericles in the DNA of their political philosophy.

The Hebrews, although continually besieged by enemies from Pharaoh to Falwell,[4] live in the only world imaginable to them; optimists perforce in life, pessimists because they are still so far from Eden. Christianity was the end of all that. Christians took the pessimistic view, devoting themselves to the next world. Theological pessimism regards life in this world as meaningless, a brief passage on the way to eternal life either at the side of God or in the fires of hell. No other philosophical, political, environmental, cultural, or social concept can match the power of theological pessimism. It concerns itself with the end of the world through individual death or the death of everything. Theological pessimism transcends the petty differences among religions; it motivates Muslims and Aztecs as well as Hindus and Christians. Heaven and hell have many names, death has only one; it is as clear as that. No one can entirely escape the pessimism of mortality, as Jesus knew in his mortal life. And what could Christians think of this world in which the most beautiful, perfect, loving creature was made to die upon the cross?

The social and political pessimism of ancient times came of historical collapse or conquest: the end of the Homeric Age, the dispersion of

---

[4] Falwell, who had been dickering with death in a hospital watched over by his daughter, a medical doctor, during much of 2005, announced soon thereafter that Jews could not enter heaven unless they converted to Christianity. Senator John McCain, the candidate best fitted to the national political movement, agreed to speak at Falwell's Liberty University.

the worldly Jewish optimists from their ancestral home, the failure of the greatest political invention—democracy—and the suffering at the hands of the Romans of Him, who was said to deserve no less than Paradise. And certainly the political pessimism of Plato came in the wake of the failure of the Athenian democracy. History betrayed reason. The will of the people betrayed reason. There was no hope for this world, and then came the Enlightenment: "Dare to think!" Only to be followed by Schopenhauer.

Death never relented. It only grew worse: death in mortal combat with beasts; angry combat with fellow creatures over food or mates; organized territorial and theologically motivated death between tribes; the military death of more politically advanced societies; and always biological death; then came the slaughter of the innocent firstborn of Egypt by the angel of God, the inexcusable death; and finally the complicity of God in the death of his own child. After that, only the death of everything, technological death, could be worse. And by early August 1945 it was no longer inconceivable. It had been prophesied.

Fear of environmental catastrophe came much later and increased more slowly. The original inhabitants of the hemisphere, although theological pessimists, followed a plan of harmony with nature. The Europeans who came to the hemisphere believed the natural world (including its inhabitants, whom they called "naturals") was for conquest. They were theological pessimists who could not have cared less about this world or its future; their way of life left an ugly mark on the land, and eventually in the air and sea as well. No one but the natives noticed for most of 470 years.

By the end of the sixteenth century large swaths of the land had been irrevocably damaged. On the Yucatán Peninsula the Maya revolted, attempting to destroy all imported fauna and flora, as if they could look into the future and see the coming ecological destruction. They were the first environmental pessimists. In their book known as the Popol Vuh (Pop Wuj) the men of wood, who could not speak (in Mesoamerica speech was thought to be the defining human characteristic), were destroyed by their things. Their plates and spoons and pots, all the products they had made out of the earth and the things that grew on it, rose up, attacked and destroyed their faces. It was, thought the

Maya, the end of the world. Then came yet another world and another creation. This time humans could think. They cut down the trees to raise sisal, and when no one wanted to buy sisal, they turned to raising vast quantities of pigs.

The native peoples of what is now the United States fought to preserve the land on which they had lived for thousands of years, but the Europeans who came to the United States were theological pessimists. They followed the same pattern. Instead of sisal and pigs, they killed the buffalo and plowed the plains.

Machines produced more than humans could and steam engines were far more efficient and reliable than water wheels or oxen for powering machines. It was the beginning of the process the Maya had observed among the men of wood. Soon enough, the machines, belching smoke, fouled the air, and the chemicals required to make the materials worked by the machines ruined the water. In the early twentieth century humans started to think the natives had known something about the land; Theodore Roosevelt brought the idea of conservation to the presidency. As the century entered its final decades, scientists spoke of the way human inventions had risen up like the plates and pots and spoons of Mayan mythology, and attacked them. Rachel Carson was the first modern environmental pessimist. In 1962 she wrote in the dedication to *Silent Spring*,[5] "Man has lost the capacity to foresee and forestall. He will end by destroying the earth."

Although Carson's work gave great impetus to the single-issue ecological movement, which read her book as a call to action rather than a prediction, her message did not interest people in the slowly developing national political movement. They did not reject it for reasons of politics or optimism, they simply thought Carson was wrong. Environmentalists produced laughter in the national movement. Ronald Reagan really did say in response to arguments about saving California's redwoods, "If you've seen one tree, you've seen them all."

Environmentalism began as the most optimistic of single-issue political movements. Its proponents believed they were "stewards of the

---

[5] New York: Houghton Mifflin.

earth," and its opponents believed environmentalism was a foolish attack on the industrial heart of the nation. The pessimistic policy issue of the time belonged to people who feared nuclear power, claiming that accidental meltdowns at nuclear power plants would kill vast numbers of people, some of them immediately, others with cancer resulting from radiation. A release of radiation into the air on March 28, 1979, from the Three Mile Island nuclear plant in Pennsylvania gave credence to the arguments of the nuclear pessimists.

Organizations like the Sierra Club saw their work as pure optimism: making the earth a cleaner, more healthful, still beautiful (in some areas) place to live. In the decade after Three Mile Island, optimism faltered. The difference between the optimists and the pessimists grew out of the way the signs of an endangered earth were read. The pessimists now understood Carson's work differently. The optimistic response had failed. Love of the earth was replaced by fear. They spoke of poisoned earth and air, of vast deposits of nuclear waste buried in the ground, and by the end of the century the rate at which ice was melting at the top of the world became apparent. The most fundamentalist of Christians embraced the pessimism of the Maya and the scientists. A group of eighty-six prominent evangelicals, including presidents of evangelical colleges, formed the Evangelical Climate Initiative. Political conservatives like Kevin Phillips, who helped to vitiate clean air standards through his work for the Nixon Administration, joined with the followers of Rachel Carson.[6] Phillips, who had become the crier of jeremiads against the very causes he had strengthened, turned on the oil industry, neoconservative war policies of the government, and the Christian Right. Chemical poison, nuclear poison, the choking air of Los Angeles, Mexico City, and Chinese industrial cities had been replaced by the fear of heat. Only Rush Limbaugh argued against the dire consequences of the deterioration of the environment. For the rest, theological pessimism had been joined to environmental pessimism; man's own inventions would destroy him and all that he had made. It had been prophesied.

---

[6] *American Theocracy* (New York: Viking, 2006).

The history of social pessimism predates all but biological and theological despair of this world. Athens thrived on slave labor. Social pessimism appeared in Deuteronomy 15:11: "For the poor shall never cease out of the land: therefore I command thee, saying, Thou shalt open thine hand wide unto thy brother, to thy poor, and to thy needy, in thy land."[7] A different interpretation came from the Calvinists of the Reformation. Exploitation of the poor was not only without sin; it was the work of good Christians. And in any event, there were those who were the elect of God and there were all the rest, and nothing the rest could do would change God's will. Social pessimism carried on through the early years of the settling of the United States until the advent of Jacksonian democracy, which blurred the social categories but did not eradicate social pessimism. Then came the Civil War. Lincoln opposed slavery, but when it came to class, he spoke of men born poor having the chance to become wealthy. He did not propose a time when there would no longer be poor men; he spoke of poor men working hard, opening their own establishments, and hiring other poor men to work for them. "That is the true system," he said.[8] When the war came, he did not make it illegal for a man to buy his way out of service in the federal Army. Nor did he suggest that freed slaves would achieve economic equality with whites. Whether he liked the "true system" is not clear. He accepted it.

There was a respite from social pessimism during what should have been the most pessimistic of times, the Great Depression. Roosevelt promised a New Deal, and as much as anything, it meant an end to social pessimism, to the suffering of the poor, the aged, and the residents of what had long been the most economically depressed areas of the country. His promise did not extend to blacks, Mexicans, and American Indians. After the Second World War, social pessimism did not decline despite Harry S. Truman's racial integration of the military and his willingness to cast aside the southerners in the Democratic Party. The

---

[7] And in another context in Mark 14:7.

[8] March 6, 1860.

Southern Strategy that elected Richard M. Nixon and gave the South to the Republican Party was built on social pessimism, not on states' rights. Barry Goldwater promoted social pessimism in the form of racism and classism, as did Ronald Reagan, although both men presented themselves as optimists.

The current intellectual foundation for social pessimism was laid during the last part of the twentieth century. It began with a group of former Marxists,[9] all but a few of them Jews, all very bright and all terrified by the Holocaust, willing to think almost anything, do almost anything, to avoid a similar fate for themselves and their loved ones. They thought they would be safe if they allied themselves with the powerful, became the "court Jews" of their time. Irving Kristol defined a neoconservative as "a liberal who had been mugged by reality." Norman Podhoretz wrote about his fear of "Negroes" as a boy growing up in Brooklyn. The neoconservatives were scholars and writers, but they could not grasp the difference between FDR and Stalin. They advised Donald Rumsfeld on how to unravel Great Society programs, they studied Leo Strauss, and when they were appointed to government posts, they pushed Straussian foreign policy ideas and were drummers for war. The founders of neoconservatism were the children of immigrants and Holocaust survivors. They had emigrated from poverty only yesterday, yet they were without mercy for the poor.

Charles Murray codified social pessimism in several books, especially *The Bell Curve*,[10] a racist tract in the form of sociology, which he wrote with Richard J. Herrnstein, a Harvard professor. Earlier on, Murray had devoted a book, *Losing Ground*,[11] to attacking the social

---

[9] Earl Shorris, *Jews Without Mercy: A Lament* (New York: Anchor Press/Doubleday, 1982). The title was a gloss on Michael Gold's famed novel *Jews Without Money* (New York: Liveright, 1930).

[10] New York: Free Press, 1994.

[11] New York: Basic Books, 1984. The back cover of the book carries the information that it was supported by the Bradley Foundation, among the wealthiest of many foundations supporting conservative causes, with assets well over half a billion dollars. The Walton Family Foundation is about the same size.

character of the poor and to the destruction of the welfare system. It was praised by the neoconservative *New Yorker* writer Ken Auletta, who invented the term "underclass," which he described as violent, drug-using, sexually out of control, criminal, and nonwhite. Social pessimism became the American way of thinking. Newt Gingrich embraced it. He and his fellow Republicans called it a Contract with America. The Democratic president, William J. Clinton, agreed and signed legislation to make social pessimism into law. It was Clinton's "bridge to the twenty-first century."

George W. Bush and the Congress took money from the poor and gave it to the rich, because they did not think the poor could be stewards of the wealth of the nation. It had been the Clinton policy too. As he capitulated to social pessimism, the gap between rich and poor in the United States eclipsed that of any other industrialized nation. The people too were pessimistic; they accepted the decline of the middle class[12] and the punishment of those who had been on welfare; they did not notice that 2 million Americans languished in prisons and jails. They were pessimistic about one another. They bought lottery tickets.

It had been prophesied.

Political pessimism inevitably references Edward Gibbon's *Decline and Fall of the Roman Empire*, and it is no matter whether the pessimists have read the entire million and a half words of Gibbon or never opened the book at all. For those whose patience was worn out before the end or who did not get to the beginning, this is part of the final paragraph:

> . . . *of every reader, the attention will be excited by a History of the Decline and Fall of the Roman Empire, the greatest, perhaps, and most awful scene in the history of mankind. The various causes and*

---

[12] In 2004 about 7 percent of U.S. households had assets other than a personal residence of more than $1 million. About one-half of the millionaires were retired. Many had earned the bulk of their money from real estate investments. More than 7.9 million families lived in poverty (37 million people). Both the number of millionaires and the number in poverty increased from the preceding year.

progressive effects are connected with many of the events most inter-
esting in human annals: the artful policy of the Caesars, who long
maintained the name and image of a free republic; the disorders of
military despotism; the rise, establishment, and sects of Christianity;
the foundation of Constantinople; the division of the monarchy; the
invasion and settlements of the barbarians of Germany and Scythia;
the institutions of the civil law; the character and religion of
Mohammed; the temporal sovereignty of the popes; the restoration
and decay of the Western empire of Charlemagne; the crusades of
the Latins in the East; the conquests of the Saracens and Turks; the
ruin of the Greek empire; the state and revolutions of Rome in the
middle age.

Gibbon's work, published in 1788, still produces a sense of déjà vu
in some people, as if the United States were the Roman Empire. One
might expect political pessimism on the left, their politics in a long and
severe decline, unable to hold out against the tide of the national movement. By definition, however, the left is not pessimistic; theirs has
always been the hopeful politics, dreaming of earthly paradise, of the
sweet life of socialism described in Marx's *German Ideology*. Political
pessimism comes from the other side; part of the foundation of the
movement. Alasdair MacIntyre, despairing of a successful route to an
earthly paradise, spoke of heaven's work on earth and of the failure of
the modern state. He did not specify the state, perhaps he means all
modern states, but the reader is invited to suspect that he means the
United States. The political pessimism of Leo Strauss has roots in Plato,
Stalinism, fascism, and Nazi Germany. MacIntyre and Strauss offered
opposite responses to the problem. The Scotsman wants to break up the
state into little communities and the German wanted the liberal democratic states to strengthen themselves by defending against external
enemies, real or, if necessary, imagined. Strauss had no interest in corporations or their effects on the citizenry.

The United States remains hostage to the pessimism of the people.
William Schneider, a fellow at the American Enterprise Institute, spoke
of American pessimism about the economy as part of the national polit-

ical picture in 2005. Reuters confirmed the view on March 16, 2006, citing the polling numbers that had concerned Wirthlin. They consistently showed that two out of three[13] Americans thought "the country was headed in the wrong direction." Pessimism about the war in Iraq was surely a factor, but Schneider was speaking of an economy producing as many as 200,000 jobs a month, a rising stock market, and low interest rates; he was not asking about the war. True, real wages had been falling, but not very much and not for two-thirds of this country. Yet whoever looked at the American people saw little besides pessimism. Latin America was turning leftward, the Middle East was in political tatters, there were demonstrations that turned into rioting in Europe, genocide had become all but endemic in many African nations, terrorist attacks were expected to continue and probably increase, and the country had turned its full attention away from the disaster of the Iraq War to look at immigration from the south, another problem with no apparent solution. Stopping foreigners, mainly Mexicans, from crossing the border into the United States to do work that did not appeal to American citizens had the effect in 2006 of causing a shortage of labor in California's vast agricultural industry. If the broadcaster Lou Dobbs and the professor Victor Davis Hanson had demonstrated impressive cruelty, economic ignorance could now be added to their résumés.

People who had supported George W. Bush and favored the war quickly turned against the president and the war. Pessimism had gone far beyond party politics. Democrats as well as Republicans were thought to be corrupt, the entire Congress inept, all likely presidential candidates hypocritical. China was expected to surpass the United States in economics, technology, and military capability. Political pessimism was based on a series of suppositions: immigration would weaken the country internally, China would threaten it militarily and economically,

---

[13] Some polls showed the number at more than 70 percent. The Pew survey asks different questions, and gets less pessimistic answers. Republicans are more optimistic than Democrats on economic questions, which may now be due to higher income levels among Republicans. Many other surveys show the country more pessimistic.

India would be a serious competitor in every area of enterprise, both economic and political freedoms would decline, and terrorists would
launch more sudden massive attacks. The commission known as (James)
Baker–(Lee) Hamilton reported to the president on December 6, 2006,
its long-considered conclusions on solving the problem of a failed war
in Iraq. The report spelled out the pessimistic possibilities: "collapse . . .
catastrophe . . . clashes . . . al Qaeda could win a propaganda victory . . .
the global standing of the United States could be diminished." The
report offered no innovative solutions. The great decline had begun.
Two-thirds of the people thought so. It had been prophesied.

Cultural pessimism has existed since human beings first became
self-aware enough to consider the origin and future of their human
attributes. And unlike death, pessimism has no certain resolution. This
idea about human endeavor arrives at the present through the two
defining lines of modern Western culture.

In Hesiod's *Works and Days*, Zeus speaks these lines to Prometheus:[14]
"Son of Iapetus, surpassing all in cunning, you are glad that you have
outwitted me and stolen fire—a great plague to you yourself and to men
that shall be. But I will give men as the price for fire an evil thing in which
they may all be glad of heart while they embrace their own destruction."

In Genesis 3:17, God tells Adam: "Because thou hast hearkened
unto the voice of thy wife, and hast eaten of the tree, of which I commanded thee, saying, Thou shalt not eat of it: cursed is the ground for
thy sake; in sorrow shalt thou eat of it all the days of thy life." According to both myths, the gift of culture does not lead to happiness or salvation. Human beings generally feel pessimistic about culture. The
end is always coming, the city is never quite worth saving; Sodom and
Gomorrah deserve to be destroyed. No glory, no golden age, no renaissance is ever glorious enough or enduring enough. A dark age is
always coming, a rebirth will always be needed but not expected. This

---

[14] His name means "forethinker." Prometheus is the culture bearer in Greek mythology,
like Adam and Eve in Judeo-Christian mythology, Quetzalcoatl in Mesoamerican mythology, and so on.

is not a perfect world. If it were perfect or even the "best of all possible worlds,"[15] as Voltaire said—using Leibniz's own words to satirize his justification of the existence of evil in a world created by a good and omnipotent God—pessimism would make no sense at all. In the "best of all possible worlds," people would be satisfied, if not happy. They are not. The idea underlying cultural pessimism or perhaps the result of it is that a perfect world is possible. One version of perfection belongs to religion: the return of Jesus Christ to reign for a thousand years. The other involves secular activity: a National Socialist millennium or the end of history in communism. Cultural pessimists believe the world as it is must be overturned to arrive at happiness, for nothing but corruption exists. To save the world it must be cleansed of imperfect people and bad ideas. Pessimists accept as their life's work the invention of the "best of all possible worlds," and beyond mere invention—implementation.

It is the implementation that kills—in Germany, the Soviet Union, the People's Republic of China; in the westward push of the Europeans; in wars to save the world for Christianity, democracy, or Western civilization. There can be only one perfection. If there were two, they would have to be identical. In a perfect world there can be but one god, one politics, one economics, one aesthetics, one science, one morality; that is, one truth, one way. Whatever deviates from the standards the pessimists set is itself cause for pessimism. To the pessimist the world is unbearable, a Promethean punishment, banishment from Eden; it must be rescued.

In response to his pessimism about the real city, Plato described an entire culture; education, music, mathematics, political philosophy, the concept of the ideal (the forms) itself, but no poetry. The ideal city itself was an aesthetic creation; he would permit no dreamers within the dream. To ensure that no one deviated from the ideal, Plato's Republic had a class of guardians to monitor the behavior of the residents. The great philosopher instructed pessimists how to think, he showed them that the *telos* of pessimism is perfection.

---

[15] Spoken by Dr. Pangloss in *Candide* and coined by Leibniz in *Theodicy* (1710).

Cultural pessimists, modeling themselves on biblical prophets or Plato's philosophical descendants, energize the current national political movement on both religious and secular grounds. Religious pessimists insist upon their set of morals, which they claim to have interpreted as God's desire for human behavior according to His instructions in Scripture. Deviation from Scripture, according to some religious cultural pessimists, results in human error. Naturalism leads to Marxism and everyone knows that the atheists in the Soviet Union came very near to destroying the world during the Cold War. They point to the way the world is now: The unborn are dying, sucked out of their mothers' wombs at what cost to the search for the love of God? Pornography is rampant on the Internet; for enough money a child will be raped before the cameras. Homosexuals not only commit unspeakable acts, but are sanctioned by the state, as if their acts were acts of love. Marriage fails, families are destroyed; the movies show a constant double bill: sex and murder. Stockbrokers cheat. CEOs earn millions for failing, while workers and investors languish. And the price of gasoline keeps going up. For some there is the sign of Satan too in dancing, lipstick, short dresses, and bright colors. All the abominations of this world are cultural.

Secular pessimists have other reasons for despair: the level of education all across America has fallen, art has come to an end of discovery, the novel is dead, the printed book is all but over, audiences have disappeared, whatever was not ruined by television was killed by the computer; whatever survived technology has capitulated to marketing,[16] science has given way to technology on the one hand and to religion on the other. Moreover, the secularists and the pious find one another's existence reason for despair. Passion belongs to the pessimists, whose vehemence leaves little place for the voices of the disinterested.

The world is coming apart, they say, ruined by culture. Who knows what will happen next at some nightclub in New York City? What is on

---

[16] I am among those who have criticized, in the strongest terms, the effect of marketing on culture. See *A Nation of Salesmen: The Tyranny of the Market and the Subversion of Culture* (New York: W. W. Norton, 1994).

the presses? Satan and sickness will make monsters of us all, unless . . .
some person, some idea, gathers America just in time and makes everything clear. It can happen. There is heaven. And history too may have a
happy ending. Or maybe not. It has been prophesied.

The history of philosophy contains but few tales of optimism. If we
think of Buddhism as philosophical rather than simply religious, it
could not be more pessimistic, for the revealed truth was the misery of
man. That is what came to Gautama under the Bo tree, the revelation
of a state of being so miserable that only the negation of everything, of
consciousness itself, could cease the desires that result in misery.

For Freud pessimism grew out of the idea of the id and the ego, not
so different from Schopenhauer's will and Gautama's desire. Like
Rousseau, he found disastrous results in civilization. Augustine is generally considered an optimist, yet the last four books of *The City of God*
deal with war and suffering without end. If Augustine is an optimist,
he is history's grimmest optimist, from the beginning of his *Confessions*,
when he declares that infants are not innocent, they just lack the
strength to do harm, to the books of war and death, and then finally his
truly wonderful description of heaven at the end of *The City of God*.
Lovely as it is, it belongs to the dead, not to the living.

And Kant, even Immanuel Kant, dean of the Enlightenment, could
not maintain his sense of optimism as he grew older. By 1784, in his
Idea of a Universal History, Kant wrote: "In the course of human affairs
a vast amount of hardship awaits man." He had not yet reached the
depths of his pessimism, for he spoke of later generations living in the
building made by the labors of their ancestors. A year later his pessimism could not be assuaged by hope for the future. He said there was
really nothing to do other than to have courage in the face of the grim
existence of human creatures. In the nineteenth century Charles Darwin published a theory of the struggle for survival and innovation that
had been going on without letup since the advent of life forms on earth.
Entire species died out, replaced by newer, better-adapted species. He
envisioned no respite for any species for all the rest of history.

At the end of World War II, Karl Jaspers, psychiatrist and philosopher, abandoned hope for human reason and turned to religion when he came to believe that even the threat of massive retaliation could not put off a nuclear holocaust. His fellow philosopher of the brief period between world wars of the twentieth century, Martin Heidegger, had what many consider the most pessimistic philosophy of his time. Heidegger was obsessed by the idea of death. He wrote that the only authentic existence was in "being-toward-death."

In an interview in the German news magazine *Der Spiegel* in 1966,[17] Heidegger said, "Philosophy will not be able to bring about a direct change of the present state of the world. This is true not only of philosophy but of all merely human meditations and endeavors. Only a god can still save us. I think the only possibility of salvation left to us is to prepare readiness, through thinking and poetry, for the appearance of the god or for the absence of the god during the decline; so that we do not, simply put, die meaningless deaths, but that when we decline, we decline in the face of the absent god."

Out of pessimism, not for any other known reason, Heidegger joined the Nazi Party. Like Freud, he had been deeply affected by the horrors of World War I and the punishment of his country written into the Treaty of Versailles. German pessimism turned Heidegger to the search for the one answer. He complained later that Germany had many political parties in the 1930s; it was this situation, he said, that led him to join the party that could be the one. He chose a politics that could permit no other: out of pessimism—perfection.

In the wake of the attacks on the World Trade Center, the failed adventure in Iraq, the foreseeable end of American economic and military dominance, Americans have come to expect the worst. The idea of constancy to which George W. Bush turned for lack of a coherent sense of either the past or the future cannot survive the endless pursuit of failed policies. The national political movement seeks a new response to its desires. The danger lurks in the growing pessimism of the move-

---

[17] Günther Neske and Emil Kettering, eds., *Martin Heidegger and National Socialism* (New York: Paragon House, 1990).

ment, for pessimists have historically sought strength in the one, the person or idea that answers all fears, all questions, the perfect answer, heaven or the ideal city. They think, with Heidegger, "Only a god can still save us," and look in many faces to find the face of a god so that they need look no more.

Twelve

METHOD

A great hope fell
You heard no noise
The ruin was within
Oh cunning wreck that told no tale
And let no Witness in

— Emily Dickinson (1123)

We deliberate not about ends but about means.

— Aristotle
Nicomachean Ethics III:3

The national political movement is not an abstraction. It exists. It has form, but not a permanent form; it has an opportunistic form: the parts of it can change or reproduce with astonishing speed. The phrase "national political movement" describes a gathering of forms, all of which have motives, means, and ends; that is, a national political movement can be understood as an ethics as well as a politics. It wins adherents more in the manner of an ethical system than in that of a standard politics.

To see how it works as an ethics, we should probably start with the end the movement has in mind. All the parts of the movement know more or less where they want to go. We can say with some degree of certainty that security is the end (*telos*) of the movement and that of all the aspects of security heaven is the most important. Why its adherents have chosen that end and how they intend to get there are the next questions. The motive comes out of a complex of fears, mostly fears of death and discomfort. What remains to be considered is the means of creating and maintaining a movement. Religion would seem, at first, to be the most effective means; its methods, the many varieties of the promise of heaven, have been known for many centuries. If religion provided the only means for the national movement to succeed, the nation would have to be a theocracy, and it is not a government by a religion. All Americans are Protestants, which catches the way they live and think and work in the world, but not exactly how they hope to get to heaven, if they believe in heaven at all. This all-encompassing Protestantism gave the country the New Deal as well as many aspects of this security movement.

Clearly, a movement in America needs other methods besides a foundation in sixteenth-century religion. And no one method can succeed without the others; the security movement requires affinity between persons and groups as well as religion, and the social and economic health of the movement's white adherents rely in part on the exploitation of nonwhites. How all this work gets done depends in some measure on the public media, although the splintering of the media into great numbers of radio and television stations and innumerable blogs makes media more important to the maintenance of the movement than to its ability to grow. People choose the television network or newspaper or magazine or blog that agrees with their political and social views. New ideas enter the public realm slowly, if at all. Half a century ago, when there were fewer alternatives, one magazine had great effect. William Rusher and William Buckley set out many of the ideas of conservatism in the *National Review*. No magazine has such force in American politics now. The national political movement has taken its stand, instructed its adherents, and raised a cadre so committed and so powerful that it can ignore new ideas and, using shopworn versions of conservatism, raise an army for any election or referendum. The movement remains more easily stirred to opposition than to anything positive.

Democrats who would like to be chosen for public office have now conceded that the only way to get elected is to join the movement. The liberal-left press has taken a similar position. Politics outside the movement has become a mirror of the movement. Al Gore travels around the country predicting environmental doom while describing himself as an optimist, because he believes he is on a moral crusade. He is almost certainly right about the environment, but why a "moral" crusade? Isn't self-preservation sufficient reason? Gore lost one election to the people who claimed to have a lock on morality; he surely doesn't want to lose this one. Only by redefining the issue so that it fits with the national political movement can he hope to succeed. He must make earthly politics into the politics of heaven. The carefully designed capitulation to the movement by a man who served in the Senate, was twice vice president, and was once the candidate for president on the Democratic ticket is another indication that the movement no longer has a need for Republicans to win elections; both parties belong to the movement now. Hillary Clinton, Barack Obama, Howard Dean, John Kerry, Joseph Lieberman, and of course the Reverend Al Sharpton pray for your vote. As has often been said, "There are no atheists in foxholes."

The movement has many methods. It grows by accretion, inclusion, and reinforcement. It adds whole groups of people who have a particular interest and includes more people as each of those groups grows. Since no two people have quite the same feelings about the aspects of security, spokesmen and spokeswomen for the groups that have been added to the movement continually work to strengthen feelings that agree with its general direction. The movement is a continuously changing confluence of groups, members within groups, and force of conviction in the individual members.

Grover Norquist organized a coalition, but a coalition is not the same as a confluence. In a confluence each of the streams becomes an integral part of the river, which flows in this instance toward security. In a coalition the parts move separately. A "leave-us-alone coalition" contains the seeds of its own destruction: the member groups may actually decide to leave one another alone. A confluence cannot separate out its constituent parts; once joined, they remain a part of the whole. New parts may enter the confluence, but a national political movement, like history, cannot rid itself of its past. Norquist may find the members of his coalition throwing chairs at each other in their next meeting, like Stalinists and Trotskyites in earlier coalitions.

The movement will be very difficult to supersede. Keeping to the metaphor of the confluence of streams into rivers and rivers into one great flow toward the goal, new streams, by which I mean new policies for achieving security, could become dominant. A new understanding of the best route to heaven could change the course of the movement entirely. A great event would almost certainly initiate changes in the country that would produce a new movement, but only a catastrophe is likely to do that quickly. Discoveries, economic or population changes, a new attitude as important as the recognition of global warming, even terrorism, could take decades to produce a new movement to supersede this one. That has been the lesson of history about national political movements in America. But history does not always predict the future.

Following are the key methods that gave rise to the security movement and now maintain it.

Racism

The Black Caucus had been waiting anxiously for the appearance of Governor Reagan, when he strode into the room more than an hour late. He was introduced as "the man who will save Black America." As he prepared to leave the room, he looked out over the audience and said, "I see a lot of old friends in the crowd." The governor's mind appeared to go blank. His gaze swept the audience, looking for a clue, someone, something familiar, among the mostly black faces. But there was no one; not one name came to mind. Finally he saw someone he knew: he greeted Daniel J. Evans, former governor of Washington. Silence came over the room. Reagan thanked the caucus for their work, asked for their votes, and aides escorted him from the room. The members of the caucus filed out after him, and there in the hallway just outside the meeting room they saw Ronald Reagan embracing a short black man wearing a loud sport coat: Lionel Hampton.[1]

---

[1] The press did not attend the meeting. I was advised of it by my dentist, Dr. Henry Lucas, who was one of the few blacks appointed to national commissions during the Reagan

During the 1980 presidential campaign Reagan had to make his views on race clear to the movement. After all, he had once been a Hollywood leftist. He went to the Neshoba County Fair in Philadelphia, Mississippi, not far from the spot where James Chaney, Andrew Goodman, and Michael Schwerner, three civil rights workers, had been murdered in 1964. At the fair Reagan proclaimed his belief in states' rights, the code word then and now for racism. Instinct told him he was the movement candidate running against an evangelical Christian Democratic president who still worked his peanut farm in Georgia; Reagan had to do something to carry the South. Racism was a tried and true movement method. He did the most racist thing he could; he dishonored the three young men in the very place where they died.

Racism remained a part of the Reagan strategy throughout his career.[2]

The movement was fully aware of the power of racism and the unwillingness of Americans to confront it. For example, in Chicago, on September 6, 1955, a little more than a mile from the site of the first atomic chain reaction at Stagg Field, tens of thousands of people

Administration. Lucas, a staunch Republican, was named one of the ten best dentists in the country in 2004.

Lionel Hampton played with Benny Goodman's orchestra and then with Goodman's small groups as well as leading groups of his own. The great jazz musician had come to the convention to support the son of Senator Prescott Bush, whom he had met during World War II at a rally to promote the sale of War Bonds. That was when Hampton became a loyal Republican. He worked in Richard Nixon's California political campaigns, and somehow he became convinced that Nixon had started the Small Business Administration to help blacks. Hampton must have been disappointed when Bush had to settle for second billing, but he worked hard for the ticket, which won a smaller percentage of the black vote than Gerald Ford had in 1976. He must have been even more disappointed by Reagan's racism.

[2] Wirthlin's "Voter Decision Map" for the 1984 campaign makes no mention of race, but concedes the issue of "fairness" to the Democrats. The Mormon Church at the time, according to Wirthlin, whose father headed the church, had many racist practices. A former elder of the church himself, Wirthlin does not hide that aspect of the history of the church and is not at all happy about it.

watched the funeral procession of Emmett Till, a fourteen-year-old boy who was beaten and murdered by two white men in Mississippi. The murderers said they killed the child "to teach him a lesson." He had whistled at a white woman. They were tried by an all-white jury, which acquitted them after deliberating for sixty-seven minutes. One of the jurors said the decision would have come more quickly if they had not taken a break to have a soft drink. Fifty thousand people filed by the open casket to look at the battered body. His mother had wanted the world to see the result of racism. It did not occur to anyone then that the proximity of the funeral to the site of the first nuclear chain reaction hinted at the confluence of fear and the anxious hatred of racism in a national political movement.

One would think, given the press coverage over the last few years, that religion is the most important method of the movement. Surprisingly, racism is more influential and far more widespread. The shift of the locus of racism from the New Deal to the current movement has been the most important appropriation of a powerful method. Almost 150 years after the Civil War, racism in America still ranges from the most elegant subtlety to brutal murder. The nature of racism is best demonstrated in relation to blacks, but it applies to other groups as well, more openly now to Latinos, especially those who appear to the racist as "illegals."[3] The most brilliant subtlety of the movement's method is that nonwhites have learned intramural racism from the white majority. Blacks and Latinos are at each other's throats.

No matter who makes the case about justice in America, inequality is a question of who deserves the blame, God or man. Theologians framed the question as a matter of Scriptural justification for slavery or abolition and hotly debated it in the years leading up to the Civil War. Said another way, if slavery is immoral and God made certain beings fit only for slavery, either God is immoral or Africans are not humans.

---

[3] Lawyers for the Mexican American Legal Defense and Education Fund (MALDEF) and California Rural Legal Assistance challenged what was then known as the Immigration and Naturalization Service (INS) for arresting people because they looked "illegal." The MALDEF attorney, a Mexican-American graduate of Harvard and Harvard Law School, asked in U.S. district court if the color of his skin made him look "illegal."

The question has not been fully resolved in America despite educational, legislative, and judicial efforts. In 2004, George W. Bush won 11 percent of the black vote and 67 percent of the white Protestant vote. The importance of racism to the movement merits a brief overview of the use of religion in racism and racism in politics.

Abolitionists and proslavery clergy cited many passages in Scripture to support their cases; often the same passage was interpreted as pro- or antislavery by the two sides. Some abolitionists were so unhappy about biblical arguments in support of slavery they declared the Bible immoral, although they did not go so far as to attack God on those grounds. They remained deists.

E. Brooks Holifield offers no less than twenty examples of theological arguments on race.[4] Here are but a few:

> *Abraham owned slaves, yet the Old Testament forbids the people of Israel from enslaving their own.*
>
> *In the New Testament both sides found comfort in the Epistle to Philomen. Paul sends Onesimus, apparently a runaway slave, back to his master Philomen, but then says Onesimus, having been converted to Christianity, is now a "beloved brother."*
>
> *Ephesians 6:5 was difficult for abolitionists to deny. It reads: "Servants, be obedient to them that are your masters according to the flesh, with fear and trembling, in singleness of your heart, as unto Christ." Nevertheless, the abolitionists cited Ephesians 6:9, "And, ye masters, do the same things unto them. . . ."*

The most powerful argument made by the proslavery theologians came from something not stated in the New Testament. Although half the people under the control of Rome were slaves, Jesus never condemned slavery. In parables like the healing of the Roman centurion's palsied servant (Matthew 8:6) Jesus speaks of lord and servant, by which we understand slave, without commenting on the institution of slavery. The abolitionist response was that there was no need for Jesus to con-

---

[4] *Theology in America* (New Haven: Yale University Press, 2003).

demn slavery specifically since he was opposed to oppression in any form, *including slavery*. Churches split into north and south over the issue. With no exegetical resolution to the problem, the Yankees and the Rebels took up their weapons.

A hundred years after Lincoln signed the Emancipation Proclamation, the Reverend Martin Luther King, Jr., speaking to the Second Methodist Conference on Human Relations (August 27, 1963), told his audience: "At 11 o'clock on Sunday morning when we sing 'In Christ there is no East or West,' we are in the most totally segregated hour of the week, and the most segregated schools in America are the church schools."[5] Race and religion were tied together in America. No one understood it better than Martin Luther King.

Important attacks on antiblack racism began shortly after the end of World War II. The black leadership demanded desegregation of all branches of the military, and President Truman complied, ordering desegregation in July 1948. That same year disputes over civil rights tore the Democratic Party apart. At their 1948 National Convention there was a floor fight over the civil rights plank in the platform. The southerners had been able to control the platform committee, but a strong civil rights movement led by Senator Hubert H. Humphrey defeated them on the floor, and the southerners walked out. They held their own States' Rights Party (Dixiecrat) convention in Birmingham and nominated Strom Thurmond, the governor of South Carolina, for president. Truman won the election despite the loss of Alabama, Louisiana, Mississippi, and South Carolina. That was the year the movement was conceived. The next year the Soviet Union exploded a nuclear device and the new national political movement was born. Conceived in hatred and born in fear; it was not a good beginning.

There is a myth about America and the methods of the current political movement. It holds that the Goldwater-Reagan revolution,

---

[5] Donald E. Collins, *When the Church Bell Rang Racist* (Macon, Ga.: Mercer University Press, 1998). Collins is also the source for much of the information about the Alabama–West Florida Methodist Conference. Collins is a fourth-generation Methodist who was ordained a minister in the Alabama Methodist Conference in 1952. He left the pastoral ministry in 1969.

which began in 1960, was about taxes, the size of government, and defense. Southern- and border-state conservatives, who account for a good part of the current political movement, deny that Goldwater had found a series of code words for race when he spoke about welfare, soup kitchens, local control, and the power of the federal government.

The managing partner of a Birmingham law firm, who asked that I not use his name, recalled the Goldwater campaign differently. He said it was not about taxes or the size of government; it was about race. A political consultant in South Carolina disagreed,[6] he said the shift from Democrat to Republican in the South was a direct result of southern opposition to interference in local matters by the federal government; southerners wanted their independence. The political consultant's argument was intended to recall the southern position a full century before the Goldwater campaign, but it was not just a matter of states' rights in 1864 or 1964; in fact, the interference the South still found untenable had largely to do with race. Washington had already begun to ensure voting rights and civil rights for blacks. The sly reference to the preceding century was exactly right—it was Reconstruction all over again, instituted this time by Democrats instead of Lincoln's Republican successors. Goldwater knew. Nixon knew. Reagan knew. Lyndon Johnson knew and flouted the rules of the movement. Senator Robert Byrd of West Virginia knew; a former "Kleage" and "Grand Cyclops" in the Ku Klux Klan, Byrd was still defending the Klan when Martin Luther King was sitting in the Birmingham jail. In 1964, Byrd voted against civil rights legislation. In 1969, almost a decade after Goldwater first employed the strategy, Kevin Phillips described the emerging Republican majority.[7]

When Richard Wirthlin and I talked about Goldwater and race, at first Wirthlin insisted that Goldwater was not racist. He pointed out Goldwater's Jewish ancestry as if it were some sort of proof. As we continued our conversation, Wirthlin thought back to his work with the man who had introduced him to Ronald Reagan and said, "Maybe I was oblivious."

---

[6] Robert Cahaly. See more of his views below.

[7] *The Emerging Republican Majority* (New Rochelle, N.Y.: Arlington House, 1969).

No one could have been oblivious to the voice of Alabama Governor George C. Wallace as he delivered his 1962 inaugural address: "In the name of the greatest people that have ever trod this earth, I draw a line in the dust and toss the gauntlet before the feet of tyranny, and I say: segregation now, segregation tomorrow, and segregation forever."

The next year, in Birmingham, Dr. Martin Luther King put Wallace's resolve to the test. The head of the Birmingham law firm remembers the confrontation between civil rights and racism in the city: "I was never frightened by the riots. I was concerned about civility and morals and the economic climate. It was obvious that things were being done that were unfair and illegal against the blacks. We had restaurants that wouldn't permit blacks to enter. When the bombings began, the character of things changed. The area close to downtown was called Dynamite Hill. Then there was that awful church bombing at 16th Street Baptist. It changed the character of the situation. It was no longer fun; it was serious.

"The churches didn't help matters on the race issue—at least Protestant churches. Businesspeople were more progressive. The Episcopal bishop supported segregation." He went on to speak of race problems in Charleston, of an uprising at Sewanee, Tennessee, over admission of blacks to the University of the South.

A year after Dr. King spent his night in the Birmingham jail and two years after Wallace's segregation-forever speech, Barry Goldwater was the Republican candidate for president of the United States. He carried six states, one of which was his home state, Arizona. The other five were Louisiana, Alabama, Mississippi, Georgia, and South Carolina. It was the first time since Reconstruction that the five states of the Deep South had voted Republican. And the first time a candidate (Goldwater) had said he would use tactical nuclear weapons. Goldwater won 27 million of 70 million votes cast for president in 1964. A movement that had been inchoate began to develop its themes as Goldwater and Reagan articulated them. Racism was the most widely held value in America. Unless it was racist, an American movement could not claim to be national.

One of the leading figures in the "new South" describes present-day Birmingham as a highly segregated city, no longer officially so, but de facto just as segregated as it had been in 1963 when the Reverend Martin Luther King wrote his famous letter from the Birmingham jail. A young partner in the same firm said that a white person could not be elected in Alabama unless he or she was racist.[8]

Racism supports the movement in several ways, none quite so crude as George Wallace's blunt declaration of "segregation forever." Wallace had lost a political contest when he did not declare himself a strong segregationist. He learned from his mistake. The movement, which has strong racist views, especially at the middle and lower economic levels, where a fair distribution of income according to intelligence would have the greatest effect, demands support for its feelings.

Now these feelings, once known as hatred, are supported in more subtle ways. Segregation in housing, the level and quality of education, employment, medical care, longevity, and hope are no longer de jure, they are now simply de facto. Racial inequality is necessary to both the economic and psychological needs of the members of the movement. One of the real dangers to the movement and its members exists in the possibility of racial fairness. To defend against that possibility, racists hold that equality is disproved by psychological testing, rates of success in higher education, economic differences, and the prevalence of social problems among nonwhites other than Asians. Their bible is Charles Murray's *Bell Curve*.

Murray and others provided an intellectual foundation for racism in the twentieth century just as the French anthropologist Joseph Artur de Gobineau had in the middle of the nineteenth century. They comforted a movement that had to be racist to hold power at the federal level. Their intellectualized version of racism was subtle, brutal, and acceptable. It strengthened the movement by allowing its adherents to include racism as part of what they saw as a rational political movement.

For a brief time at the end of 2005 during Hurricane Katrina and its aftermath, the racial politics of the movement seemed shameful. Racism needed a defender, and Barbara Bush, wife of one president

---

[8] Artur Davis lives in Birmingham and represents Alabama's 7th Congressional District, which is a black-majority district created under the Voting Rights Act. Davis is a moderate-conservative Democrat.

and mother of another, stepped forward. She stated the movement position with startling clarity as she considered the suffering of thousands of black families who had been uprooted by the hurricane and crowded onto the floor of an indoor sports stadium. "And so many of the people in the arena here, you know, were underprivileged anyway, so this—this [she chuckles slightly] is working very well for them."[9] Charles Murray could not have said it better. George H. W. Bush, whose election to the presidency turned on an overtly racist commercial about a black criminal, must have smiled.

In political campaigns the movement still makes its will clear on the question of race, and political candidates succumb, either because they are themselves racist or because they acquiesce to the power of the movement. As George W. Bush and John McCain battled for the Republican nomination in 2000, Bush lost to McCain in New Hampshire, then faced him in the South Carolina primary. McCain and Bush both worked the race issue in South Carolina, being subtle, using code words about the question of flying the Confederate flag over the State House. McCain had said: "Some view it as a symbol of slavery. Others view it as a symbol of heritage. Personally, I see the battle flag as a symbol of heritage." Karl Rove and his staff spread rumors about McCain having black children, but the rumors were not sufficiently credible; they needed something like the Reagan speech at the Neshoba County Fair. The most overtly racist institution in South Carolina was Bob Jones University, which said in its published policy statement: "Students who date outside of their own race will be expelled . . ." At the beginning of February 2000, Bush spoke to the students and faculty of Bob Jones University and won the South Carolina primary. Racism works. The movement rewards it. And it rewards the movement. The unemployment rate among young black men in America is as high as the rate of unemployment in Iraq, which is in the middle of a civil war. Racism means jobs for whites. In the last half century the situation for black men has only grown worse.

Religious groups have many missionaries in Africa, Latin America,

---

9 *Editor and Publisher,* September 5, 2005.

the Pacific, and Southeast Asia. At the international level the move-ment supports a smoldering holy war on the one hand, and on the other it competes with Islam for converts. Pentecostalism, which had its ori-gins in black churches and became a largely white sect, now grows faster than Islam. Racism does not prohibit conversion of nonwhites; racists have always seen their role as superior to others, who must be saved because they do not have the sense to save themselves.

Racist feelings about blacks have been augmented by nativism, focused mainly on people from Latin America, whom the movement calls "illegals." The movement benefits from these feelings by a sense not only of superiority, but of belonging, of being "American." It sup-ports and is supported by a group of intellectual and journalistic ratio-nalizers for its hatred of "browns." Samuel P. Huntington, chairman of Harvard's Academy for International and Area Studies, and a propo-nent of anti-Muslim as well as anti-Mexican attitudes in the United States, is the most prominent racist in the academy. Huntington claims to be saving "American" culture, the English language, and your job. Victor Davis Hanson of Stanford's Hoover Institution gave as an exam-ple of the need to limit the number of Mexicans in the United States the tragedy of his large property in California's Central Valley: a group of Mexican laborers sat on the side of the road that runs past his land to eat lunch, and they left some trash behind. For such crimes Hanson said Mexicans should be barred from U.S. territory. With almost admirable deftness, the movement attacks blacks who have been here for centuries and still suffer unemployment, poverty, and have an astonishingly dis-proportionate and unfair number of their young men in jails and pris-ons; and on the other hand attacks Latinos for being newcomers who take jobs and public resources from Americans, especially those in the working class.

Religion

The nature of fear has changed since FDR set the poverty level at "one third of a nation." We cannot measure it the way he did, nor can we cal-culate hunger using the curious methods of Jacob Riis, who counted the number of people who got a pauper's burial in New York between 1885 and 1890 (10 percent). Absolute poverty in America has decreased, replaced by relative poverty. Starvation is rare, malnutrition is common; smallpox is practically unknown, asthma is epidemic; housing is heated, housing projects are nightmarish. We live longer and we are not satisfied. All Americans are Protestants, devoted while on God's own earth now to thoughts of acquisition and death.

The political wars in Europe and Asia are long past, the United States is now at war with Islam over the question of who will win God's love, what kind of death will come, who will sit at the right hand of God, Jesus or Mohammed? And if it is one or the other, what will be the place of the defeated? This does not characterize the entire method of the American political movement. Death is not a politics, but an engine of politics as of religion, and it has not been certain for a very long time—more than half a century—what kind of death drives the preachers and philosophers who manage the mind of the national movement.

The news that drives politics appears in the form of obituaries: dead by this or that or, in the movement's most beloved fiction, Tim LaHaye's books about the "rapture," accorded the arrogant death of those few of faith, made members of a holy crowd and assumed into heaven like the Virgin Mary herself. At the core of the national movement the faithful live, so fearful they cannot imagine a politics devoid of faith, ever mindful of the other death, the catastrophe they call endtime. They are as certain of the coming end of the world as the atomic scientists who watch their clock move ever closer to midnight or the environmentalists who say it will soon be too late to reverse the trend of global warming and save the earth.

Measurements of faith-based politics, one of the main engines of the movement, put its influence at 35 percent or some other all-but-arbitrary number, but every mention of nuclear weapons in Iran, nuclear arrangements with India, the instability of Pakistan, North Korea's nuclear threat, the still low-level project in Brazil, Israeli nuclear capability, the uncounted enriched uranium in the former Soviet Union, the dirty bomb, the germ that cannot be contained, the poison powder, revises the size of the movement's engine.

If the third of Americans who respond to the term "evangelical" were content to live quietly with their religion, the movement might have remained no more than an aspect of a complex democratic politics, but evangelical does not mean quiet or contemplative. By definition the evangel is the Good News and evangelicals are those who bring the Good News to others. Evangelical conservatives not only spread the good news of the Christ, they spread and strengthen the national political movement, they evangelize for Christ and for the movement. They hold a specific definition of a Christian country and see their work as the conversion of the country to that definition. They focus on death, examining this life in light of it. They are discontent, as all Protestants are discontent, generous in their discontent, believing faith will save you as it saves them. The itch in certain kinds of evangelism is predestination, the Calvinist belief that God has made his decision and if you are not among the elect, nothing will save you. No human can tamper with the will of God. He will not be bribed with good works or cajoled by prayer, or convinced that he erred in separating you from the elect. Some evangelicals, mainly Baptists who follow Calvinism in what they believe is its purest form, oppose the involvement of evangelical Christians in the power politics of the movement. Theirs is an uncommon position. The prevailing view is argued by Tom Minnery, a former journalist who has become director of public relations for Focus on the Family. He favors fierce political activism by evangelicals. His boss, James Dobson, takes that position to great lengths, meddling in everything from electoral politics to the confirmation of justices for the U.S. Supreme Court. His political activism has led to questions about the tax status of Focus on the Family—nonprofit organizations are not permitted by law to engage in electoral politics.

Minnery has a particular kind of activism in mind, because activism per se does not affect the movement. Activism need not be political; it may also be the kind advised by Jesus, such as days spent working with evangelical Christian Jimmy Carter's Habitat for Humanity or serving food to the homeless in a church-run soup kitchen. The political activism of the army of the movement reeks of arrogance, not goodness. It wishes to establish a set of rules of behavior that will carry it to heaven, although many of the members of that army will have to ask forgiveness of Jesus for violating the very rules it propounds. The religious battalions of the army have a quid pro quo relationship with God and government: politics for salvation, salvation for politics. The payoff is not so quick or certain as the reward for racism. Racism pays now. Faith doesn't pay until you're dead, but then it is expected to pay and keep on paying forever.

The execution of evangelical conservatism in contemporary America would appear to have but little relation to the idea of "the salt of the earth" in Matthew 5:13. The belief in the movement is that good acts by government on behalf of those beloved of Jesus do not accrue to seekers of eternal life. A church group may feed the hungry on Wednesdays but will not favor the government feeding or educating or housing the poor and the meek on the other six days. They cannot imagine a quid pro quo in the case of government caring for the poor. The execution of the policy of loving God is thus the maintenance of the poor in a state of desperation so they can be given a bag of bread and cheese at the close of a Sunday morning sermon.

The notes in the Geneva Bible (by John Calvin, John Knox, et al.)[10] and in Falwell's Liberty Bible, which follows the Geneva Bible but lacks its eloquence, offer an insight about the soul of the movement. Here follow the verse and the notes from the Geneva Bible (John Calvin first suggested that the verses be numbered).

> *5:13 Ye[2] are the salt of the[d] earth: but if the salt have lost his savour, wherewith shall it be[e] salted? it is thenceforth good for nothing, but to be cast out, and to be trodden under foot of men.*
>
> *(2) The ministers of the word especially (unless they will be the most cowardly of all) must lead others both by word and deed to this greatest joy and happiness. (d) Your doctrine must be very sound and good, for if it is not so, it will be not regarded and cast away as a thing unsavoury and vain. (e) What will you have to salt with? And so are fools in the Latin tongue called "saltless," as you would say, men that have no salt or savour and taste in them.*

---

[10] Published in 1560. The notes are from the 1599 revised edition. The Geneva Bible, like the King James Version, owes much to the earlier translation (1526) by William Tyndale. For his troubles Tyndale was convicted of heresy, strangled, and his corpse burned in 1536.

Religious activists take their cue from the passage following the beatitudes, interpreting it to mean they should play a role in national politics. There may be some question as to whether the Sermon on the Mount and the unforgiving character of the army of the national political movement have the same behavior in mind.

A better case can be made for the actions of conservative Christians as the contemporary version of machine politics. Where once the big city ward heeler promised food or rent money for votes, the evangelical ward heeler promises salvation. He or she delivers votes to government in return for the promulgation of laws that comport with evangelism's view of goodness. The role of evangelical-versus-opportunist is a serious one in the politics of the movement. Richard Wirthlin and others have said that suddenly speaking out on religious principles after a lifetime of silence, as Hillary Clinton has done, may cost a candidate far more votes than it wins. It will not sit well with the faithful, especially those workers in the fields who can change the outcome of an election: they are very serious about their religion.

The well-trained troops of the Christian Right, with death riding on their shoulders like Coleridge's albatross, work the neighborhoods to deliver the votes that elect the people who make the laws that produce the behavior that will cause God to reward them now and at the hour of their death. Not all religious conservatives follow this rule of a reward in heaven. Many do not agree with Minnery and Falwell about political participation. There are still Christians of all political views who believe in "justification by faith alone." And there are still many evangelical Christians—members of the mainline denominations—liberal Catholics, and Jews who form a bulwark against the advance of the movement.

Affinities

If there is a man who understands in microcosm how affinities work to produce a national political movement and elect its candidates, it is Robert Cahaly of South Carolina. Cahaly, who owns Bonnie Blue Public Relations and works at the point of contact, where affinities are both found and made. His small firm has offices in Atlanta, Georgia, and Columbia, South Carolina, and a room in an employee's house in Washington, D.C. He advises candidates in many parts of the country: in the South, Midwest, and a growing number of mid-Atlantic states. Cahaly says he has won 72 percent of the campaigns he has worked on, including primaries. He is quick to say he is more conservative than many of his clients, but that doesn't seem to bother him. "I really would like to see much stronger state and local government and much weaker federal government. And I'm much more pro-life." He says people like him are perceived to be cynical, working for any kind of candidate, but he never could see himself that way. Cahaly works for people with whom he has an affinity: conservatives. He is part of the movement, and he makes alibis for racism, converting hatred into the demand for states' rights. He works a lot of small contests, usually local. Sometimes he works statewide contests; he has worked Congressional races, but not yet for U.S. Senate or gubernatorial candidates. Cahaly does his business where Tip O'Neill said politics takes place; for him all politics really is local.

Cahaly does politics by affinity. That is generally all he has to sell. In his races he would never be so stupid as the Democrats who thought they could win Ohio in 2004 with paid campaign workers brought in from distant states. When the Democrats complained later that the election had been stolen, movement operatives, from Ken Mehlman and Morton Blackwell to Blackwell's student, Karl Rove, on to Robert Cahaly, must have laughed at the whining naïveté. They might have said, had they wanted to put their methods on display, "It's the PTA, stupid." The PTA and the coffee that is held every Sunday after church is where elections are won and lost. As Cahaly said, it was something the Democrats had known seventy years ago but had forgotten. Now, as the party became separated from both ideas and energy, the Democrats thought they could rely on blogs, money, computer programs, and acquiescence to the national political movement. Unlike the conservatives in 1964, the Democrats of 2006 gave up, gave in, and won by losing.

And how exactly does affinity work at the grass roots? What is it the group outside the movement has forgotten? Cahaly said that in the cities and towns where he works—and he doesn't separate the Midwest and mid-Atlantic from the South—religion and politics are intricately entwined. "I've had candidates who go to a different church every Sunday. I've had candidates speak to the congregation from the pulpit, but it's more common for the deacon to invite a candidate to a church cof-fee afterward. You start from a network, often they know each other, or this guy knows this guy. Often there's a church strategy. Say there's seven churches in the town. Who do you know who goes to this church? Who do you know who goes to that church?" In local races, he said, the church strategy is often employed, but in bigger races only occasionally. "I was in a race—it wasn't my candidate—it was a con-gressional race, and that candidate was in a different church every weekend. And he won. He beat my candidate, because in county after county where my candidate should have had the advantage, the movers and shakers who went to the big churches, in many cases were lined up behind this guy, because this guy employed the strategy two years out. He is a great politician."

"You have to know somebody in the church. Every campaign is organized by what's called a kitchen cabinet. Part of what I do is I help to put together a kitchen cabinet. We're sitting around and the kitchen cabinet is this rich guy who's kind of in touch with all the money people in town. And maybe somebody involved in some capacity with inter-faith ministry. You have somebody from different walks of life all there. Let's say you have these eight people sitting around and you bring up the subject of church. Which church can you get into? And they say something like, First Pres is really huge, they have something like two thousand members. Who do we know from First Pres? And one guy sitting at the table says, 'My buddy Joseph goes to First Pres.' Well, why don't we see if Joseph will take the candidate to church with him? What we'll do is we'll set up Joseph to meet the candidate. Then he goes to that church and he meets twelve other people and obviously he's met them in some other walk of life.

"In the race that I'm talking about I had a candidate who thought that was absolutely wrong. I didn't think it was wrong. There is a tak-ing advantage, but simply meeting people who share ideology, an out-growth in many cases of values anyway—I don't see a problem with it. I'm not crazy about [candidates] speaking from the pulpit, even though I know it happens. In that particular race my candidate refused to do it. He went to his own church every Sunday. He lost. It cost him. It was a congressional race.

"I've known candidates to switch churches, move to the biggest church in town. I think not to have a mention of church anywhere in any of your literature is a nail in the coffin. In the average district you can't have nothing on there [the campaign literature]. I've had candidates, when I asked them did they go to church—it took them a long time to answer—taught me they really didn't. They said, 'Well, I really don't go that often.' But I said, 'You don't put that down there, put that at least you're Presbyterian. You need to put something down.' South Carolina's one of the few states where you don't have to be a certain religion, but you have to at least believe in a Supreme Being, you have to believe in something. Belief in a Supreme Being is in the [State] Constitution.

"I've had a candidate who I told you're about to sit down with three ladies who are extremely devout Christians and they're gonna ask you questions about what exactly you believe about abortion, and about the death penalty, and about this and about that and about this, and sometimes they ask very specific questions to the religious nuances even within Protestantism. What do you believe here? What do you believe there?"

He drove his point home with a grotesquerie: "The really hard-core pro-lifers carry a little plastic fetus in their pocket. Have you ever seen one?

"People believe they die and go to heaven. They believe in hell too, absolutely. You find somebody in this part of the country [the South] and they say they don't believe in hell, everybody questions them being a Christian. That's like saying 'I'm a Christian, but I don't believe in Jesus.' I mean, if you believe it, you gotta believe it."

On national issues, he said, only terrorism has taken "any hold." But even terrorism lives next door or not at all in his world. There is a nuclear plant not far from where he lives, and people there are afraid of an explosion.

Suddenly, apropos of nothing, he broke into the thread of the conversation to speak about himself and how he differs from some of his candidates and the people whose votes he seeks to win. "The thing I have the biggest problem with is: you know this concept of the Lord helps those who help themselves. That has no basis in religion. That's from

Poor Richard's Almanac. I think too often the Republicans are like, the government shouldn't do this. But then do we as individuals get involved in private charities to do it? It's easier to condemn than to actually do it. I have to consider what every candidate's like, and [one], I can't expect everyone to take my position on issues, and two, every district is different. I think my job is to pick out what someone's core values truly are and build a campaign around them, but not try and change them."

Cahaly is a complex man. Once a high school football player, he broke his leg, and now he's very heavy, his cheeks permanently flushed, as if rouged by the history of the broken leg. He is the necessary man of the national political movement, the affinity man. And there are tens of thousands like him, not all so quick or observant, not all so willing to see a role for government. Cahaly has no wish, at least not yet, to make policy, to mold candidates. He executes the will of the movement, he enhances affinities. The world is not forever, he thinks. He sees an end coming, a long decline for America, the world, and then the end. Like his neighbors and clients, Cahaly speaks optimistically about the fight of the moment, but understands the difference between battles and wars; the war cannot be won.

He thinks in terms of connections, not of subtleties. Social justice, although he would shrink from the sound of the words, means connection to him. It lies interred with the old movement, the neglected thing that Jesus said. If he were to set aside the work of affinity for a moment, forget the poll-watchers and the subtle and not-so-subtle suggestions of preachers and the way neighbors win elections, and think of the way death drives God and politics, he would realize that the little plastic figure in the antiabortionist's pocket does not only represent the right to life of the fetus; it signifies the claim to eternal life of the bearer.

Constancy

"You shook your head at my acknowledging that I should not like to engage in the duties of a clergyman always for a constancy. Yes, that was the word. Constancy, I am not afraid of the word. I would spell it, read it, write it with anybody. I see nothing alarming in the word. Did you think I ought?"

"Perhaps, Sir," said Fanny, wearied at last into speaking—
"perhaps, Sir, I thought it was a pity you did not always know your-
self as well as you seemed to do at that moment."

"... You think me unsteady—easily swayed by the whim of the
moment—easily tempted—easily put aside. . . . But we shall see."

— Jane Austen
Mansfield Park

And without constancy all the other virtues, to some degree lose
their point.

— Alasdair MacIntyre
After Virtue

Constancy has been a vital element of the current movement as it grew from fearfulness to action over the last sixty years. Constancy describes the patience of the movement, the long, slow creation of affinities. It also refers to the wholeness of the movement, the integration of its many parts, the way affinities are bound to each other. Jane Austen attached great moral value to the idea of constancy, implying that without constancy the other virtues could not exist. Yet constancy itself has no moral component. Constancy is not a virtue, not in the sense of virtue being within a person, as Aristotle would have it, and constancy does not come from knowledge, like the Socratic origin of virtue. Constancy has no tie to motive or end. It belongs in the category of means. Nevertheless, the role of constancy should not be underestimated. Movements may operate for the better or worse of a society or the world, but they must be constant. When they begin to waver, to have some internal worm, some new definition of security, some failure in God's name, like the failure of a president in war, they must purge themselves of inconstancy or the inconstant one if they are to survive.

They can do so with difficulty, but without seriously harming the movement. The constancy of a movement does not depend on labels or party politics. Political parties may gain or lose power and the movement can still be constant. The incompetence of George W. Bush and the failed foreign adventures weaken his political party but not the national movement. A national political movement transcends political parties. Like the idealized person of a Jane Austen heroine's dreams, a movement embraces those whom it loves with "warm and faithful feelings." Yet like a novel, it must have conflict to move the story along; constancy must be in opposition to something—better yet to many things.

In Plato's famous misquote, Heraclitus says that we can never step twice into the same river, for the river is always changing. What Heraclitus really said is that while the waters are always changing, the river remains the same—an apparent contradiction. Constancy also appears to violate the rule of noncontradiction. Within the movement, which remains the same, the affinities are always in flux. It is not a comfortable idea to deal with in our contemporary go/no-go manner of thinking, but it is the case. The movement remains; parts of it may be Democrats today, Republicans tomorrow, yet the definition of security, the list of oppositions, the confluences that make a movement, do not change. Until a stream of devastating effect enters the river and the river itself changes. What that stream might be, other than catastrophe, is perhaps the most important political question of our time.

Meanwhile, the movement remains constant. It holds to its oppositions and creates affinities where there would appear to be none: to oppose abortion and favor the death penalty are contradictory propositions about death. It is also a contradiction to oppose abortion and withhold health care from infant children. That kind of thinking does not destroy the constancy of the movement. The embrace of contradiction is a primary function of constancy. Within the movement a group that feels alone, like a Jane Austen heroine thinking she has passed marrying age, will compromise its expectations for the sake of affinity. In that way groups (religious, fraternal, familial, industrial) in the lower middle class can be part of the movement that wounds them, because they are willing to trade rational expectations to be counted among the faithful.

The movement comforts the compromised by giving them a sense of working for the greater good, it embraces them with "warm and faithful feelings." Constancy means showing this generosity of spirit to those within the movement, but it does not extend to people or groups outside. Poor children, who have no power to offer and few, if any, legal rights to pursue, fall farthest from the generosity that integrates the movement. The idea of taking money away from public schools to use for vouchers to send children to private, mainly religious and for-profit schools, enhances affinity in many ways: it weakens big government, abets racism, favors religion, and supports the conversion of education to business.

Media

Movements infiltrate a society through various media, the most effective of which are personal affinities. These include churches, neighborhoods, Parent Teacher Associations, fraternal organizations, town meetings, union meetings, work contacts, barber shops, beauty salons, exercise classes, coffees with candidates, and so on. Mass affinities, created and maintained at a distance through public media, do not have the same effectiveness, but work far more efficiently. These are not created through paid media. The movement has no funds and no other access to paid media (advertising) except through some of its constituent parts. Early on, Goldwater, Reagan, Rusher, Buckley, and others used paid media to explain movement policies as the best way to attain the kind of security desired during the Cold War. By 1980 paid media were used to elect candidates who supported movement policies, most of which had been defined by then. Advertising for single issues such as "right to life" continues apace, and is supportive of the movement. Attack media directed at a single candidate, like the commercials claiming Senator John Kerry had not merited the medals he received as a Swift boat commander during the Vietnam War, can turn an election, but they have little or no effect on the movement.

In the 2000 and 2004 presidential campaigns personal affinities were far more important than all the attempts at massified affinity. But that was not the case in 2006, when massified antipathy played a significant role. It differed from the preceding presidential campaign years when personal affinities were used to increase the influence of the movement in two ways: people were brought to the polls through the influence of acquaintances and friends, and others (mainly blacks and students) were prevented from voting by illegal or unethical actions at the personal level; that is, subtle decisions to violate the spirit of the Voting Rights Act of 1965 were made "on the spot."

Personal affinities place limits on behavior that do not exist in mass communication; in a democratic society they depend upon civility. However, in a democratic society losing its hold on the civility of democracy, personal affinities can turn brutal. We have evidence of this in the history of democracies undergoing a metamorphosis into totalitarianism: betrayal of parents and friends, switching parties, abandoning artistic endeavors, physically attacking "enemies of the state," burning books. Politics done in close proximity leads either to a certain decorum or a punch in the nose. On the other hand, distance has protected the noses of speakers since Aristophanes savaged his enemies from behind the mask of theater in ancient Athens. Aristophanes enjoyed laughter and satire, but he was not above polemic, which belongs to mass media rather than personal contact. Insulting a candidate to her face is more difficult than doing it in the newspapers. Lying on a blog happens so often no one bothers to censure dishonest bloggers, but lying in a PTA meeting may result in anything from a black eye to ostracism.

The use of lying or (perhaps more gently said) misinforming the public in the media is that people still believe some of what they read in the papers. The varieties of lying are so great that the two main categories, omission and commission, which apply to other sins as well, do not suffice. The distinction between opinion and the retailing of observation, which has become less and less the task of the news, is not quite the distinction between lying and truth, but opinion in the media is completely market-driven. Any deviation from the views the market expects will send readers or listeners to some other station or magazine or newspaper. That means a loss of revenue since advertisers pay for space or time according to the size and composition of the audience, and advertising pays the bills.

Charm, amusement, sex, violence, or a carefully planned mix of all four can be used to increase the audience for lies or opinions. In one version *The O'Reilly Factor* uses sex and violence, in the style of the *New York Post* or the *National Enquirer,* to increase the audience for its opinions and variations on reasonable reporting. In another, *Vanity Fair* uses stories about movie stars and other celebrities to bring readers to its liberal views. There are no media without opinions. Some attempt to keep opinion out of what they describe as news, but the choice of what to publish in print or broadcast is an expression of opinion.

The uses of media as method (the movement is far more adept than its detractors at this) continually evolves. During the invasion of Iraq the Bush Administration chose to "embed" reporters with the troops. It also embedded reporters, like Judith Miller of the *New York Times,* with key administration personnel in Washington. A national political movement relies on this kind of mass media, but not mass media alone. In addition to personal affinity and affinity with broadcasters like Rush Limbaugh, a circus performer with opinions and an addiction to the powerful narcotic OxyContin, the movement is supported by the Internet and by a relatively new form of interactive media. Focus on the Family, under the guidance of former National Security Agency advisor Del Tackett, has been developing CDs to mail out to people who respond to Focus on the Family materials in mass media. Focus on the Family asks for fees from those who can afford them or sends the materials out free to those who say they can't afford to pay. It is a form of in-home electronic revival meeting, and it may be very effective. Neither Tackett nor Marc Fey, a very bright and winning young man who works with him, could offer an estimate of the effectiveness when I spoke with them, but they were both optimistic. If their idea works as planned, it may demonstrate that the use of interactive media is a way to integrate personal and mass affinities. A CD and the Internet may offer the same material in the same way, but the CD is real, it does not disappear when the machine is turned off, it is "my" CD; no one thinks about "my" Internet.

Considerable parts of the movement's media work do appear on the Internet, which is not a mass medium, like television or radio, although like both television and radio the profusion of possibilities requires most of the audience to have made some previous media contact. Public media are becoming more and more the means to maintain the movement rather than to expand it. At one time, media friendly to the movement amused their audiences by inviting guest politicians, writers, or other discussants from outside the movement to serve as foils, but the possibility of introducing the audience to different opinions and media came to seem like free advertising. Now a program on Fox News is more likely to use sex or violence, always shown in the light of opprobrium (Look at the way this immoral starlet bares her breasts! Shameful!), to attract new members of the audience and hold their attention. Books also belong in the category of preaching to the converted. Like journals of opinion, they must cater to their market. The number of people who can be persuaded to spend their time or money on an unfriendly opinion could not support a magazine or keep a blogger in venom. Books, films, plays, television programs, music, even blogs, are open to review and now and then to serious criticism. Reviewing is a dicey business at best, intellectually corrupt far too often; that is, biased politically or artistically. Thomas Mallon, deputy chairman of the National Endowment for the Humanities, who claims to be a friend to both Vice President Cheney and the editor of the *New York Times Book Review*, published a vicious attack on, of all people, Harper Lee in the *New Yorker*.

The *Times Book Review* invited Robert Alter, a noted translator of the Bible and a frequent contributor to *Commentary*, to review a collection of articles and essays on Leo Strauss by Stephen B. Smith. In the review (June 25, 2006) Alter wrote that the "admirably lucid, meticulously argued book, persuasively sets the record straight on Strauss's political views and what his writing is really about." Alter then quoted the book's epigraph, which was written by Joseph Cropsey, whom he described as "the political scientist," who set the keynote for the book. Cropsey might better have been identified as Strauss's coauthor of a history of political philosophy and the author of a foreword to one of Strauss's other books. It was what is sometimes referred to in the trade as a "put-up job." And not a very good one. Alter wrote, "Smith is right to associate Strauss with cold war liberals like . . . Isaiah Berlin. . . ." Two more different views of political philosophy would be difficult to find; Strauss and Berlin detested one another's work.

The same kind of selection of reviewers is found in *The Nation* and the *National Review*, which are admittedly journals of opinion with distinct political views. It is the "objective" media, like the *New York Times*, mercilessly battered by the government, media, and corporate resources of the movement, that have begun to waver. To its credit, the

Times, pulling itself out of the mire after the Judith Miller fiasco, has responded with revealing stories about the way the Bush Administration flouts constitutional guarantees, especially the right to privacy.

While the public efforts of the movement go forward, others happen less openly. Some years ago the Scaife Foundation[11] made the following deal with Lewis Lapham, then in his conservative phase, to hire an editor of its choosing at *Harper's Magazine*. Scaife said it would pay the new hire's salary and benefits. When the publisher of *Harper's*, John R. MacArthur, realized what they had done, he pulled the plug on the deal. Scaife's plan failed at *Harper's*, but various parts of the movement use concentrated economic power to subvert the media in various ways. Editors who subscribe to many of the precepts of the movement have now entered what were once considered "objective" media and not as columnists hired for "balance," but as editors. Their hire was sometimes a quid pro quo; more often a marketing decision by an organization, hoping to expand its audience to include at least some part of the movement, which has grown so large and powerful that it dominates much of the market for mass media. The movement and the media live in symbiosis; each is a market for the other. But even in a circular relation the movement has more power; it is a buyer's market.

A national political movement that has chosen the majority of office-holders at all levels of government cannot escape scandal or hide every foolish act, as many Republicans in Congress learned, but it can go very far toward shutting out disagreement. In the style of Dick Cheney it can simply refuse to speak to the media. No longer beholden to public media, the movement grows by affinity, under its own momentum. Media may be instrumental in removing officeholders from one party and replacing them with people from a different party, but the replacements and the people they replace may hold the same opinions on most issues. Membership in the conservative Blue Dog Coalition and the New

---

11 There are several Scaife foundations. The Sarah Scaife Foundation is the largest. The foundation is run by Richard Mellon Scaife, an ultraconservative, who inherited banking and oil money. Scaife put up much of the money ($2 million or so) for the *American Spectator*, a journal of very conservative opinion, until something about the magazine displeased him and he dropped it.

Democrats combined grew by 20 percent in 2006, a higher rate of increase than the overall Democratic gains in Congress.

The movement endures because it belongs to many closed circles: the elected are the electable; the readers determine what they read, and the listeners decide what they will hear. No arrangement is more likely to settle on the eternal questions and the only acceptable answers. The flaw in democracy is the same as its greatest virtue: "the people shall judge." History's cruel truth is that democracies fall by democratic means. And in history's light the methods of this movement bear comparison to the early stages of movements that brought down democratic societies in the last century.

Thirteen

AMERICANS

O sweet spontaneous
earth . . .

. . . .

. . .   .how
often have religions taken
thee upon their scraggy knees
squeezing and

buffeting thee that thou mightest conceive
gods

—E. E. Cummings

At 7:52 A.M. Saigon time, April 30, 1975, a CH-46 helicopter rose from the roof of the U.S. embassy carrying the last 11 Marines of the 800 who had guarded the embassy compound. Hundreds of South Vietnamese clambered up the now unguarded walls and gate, and rushed toward the building and the rooftop where the helicopters had been landing. They waited for the next helicopter, the next red smoke grenade that would guide the chopper down. But there was no more red smoke, there were no more helicopters. It was over.

The American people, stirred to action by tens of thousands of dead young men in the jungles and cities of a distant country that some—the older ones—still thought of as Indochina, had stopped the war. The effort to end the killing was led by the fallen, whose bloody deaths appeared on television, and by a revolt of the youth of the country. The young were angry, radicalized, emboldened by their fear and sufficiently middle-class to think they were able to change America. They did not change America, and they did not remain radical for the most part except in the way they listened to music or went to bed. They did not end the Cold War or revoke the Holocaust. The dead of Auschwitz, Hiroshima, the gulag, and the Cultural Revolution did not rise. Pol Pot went about his grisly work in Cambodia. The national political movement in America did not end, did not weaken. A lost war seemed to the movement only to hasten the fall of the civilization and the final end of everything.

The American adventure in Iraq presages an even more profound defeat. As the Baker-Hamilton Study Group said, if no sudden change occurs, the entire Middle East will become more unstable and the great fools who represent the American national political movement and its maniacal philosophers will have become the great villains. Americans will grow more pessimistic. Like Vietnam, Iraq may have no lasting effect on the national political movement, except to strengthen it as the people become more fearful and less affluent. Or the war itself could alter the character of the movement, making it even more pessimistic, as more of its members decided the invasion of Iraq had been ill-conceived and poorly executed. It has begun to seem more like the Vietnam War, in which Americans were caught between conflicting principles. At first Vietnam was a conflict between national security (Kennedy's anticommunism) and nonintervention (anti-imperialism). And then between constancy (stay the course) and wisdom (withdraw and end the killing).

After months of study the group headed by James A. Baker III and Lee H. Hamilton offered seventy-nine recommendations on war policy but did not call for withdrawal of American forces. The study group, which was composed of conservative and moderate former elected and appointed officials and Vernon E. Jordan, Jr., will be remembered for having declared bankruptcy—its own and that of the administration. William Kristol, Paul Wolfowitz, Donald Rumsfeld, Judith Miller, and others, Straussians and fools without mentors, had pushed America into a war far more dangerous than Vietnam. And no one, military or civilian, had found a reasonable road to resolution. Not even the Democrats who gained control of both houses of Congress in 2006. The Republican minority stymied the Democrats in the Senate. The House was more aggressive, but could not bring itself to cut off funding for the war. Republicans realized the timidity of the Democrats, and led by John McCain began to ask the critical question by March 2007: If the Democrats really believed the war was wrong, why didn't they use "the power of the purse" to put an end to it? The Democrats did not respond. They were afraid of the result of doing what they believed.

Given the war, the unfair distribution of wealth, the suffering of poor children, racism, religious intolerance, pessimism, and the willingness to starve its national government into desperate weakness, the character of the country and the quality of its constitutional democracy are open to doubt. The ability of the American people to rule themselves is now in question.

A Flaw

The national political movement contains a flaw deep in its construction. A hint about the flaw came from Dr. John Phelan, dean of the Evangelical Covenant Church's Seminary in Chicago. Phelan, who said he found much to agree with in the politics of Dennis Kucinich, the most radical of the Democrats in the 2004 presidential primaries, certainly has little in common with the other members of the 750 congregations of the Evangelical Covenant Church. The other members I talked to had all voted for Bush in 2000 and 2004. A staff member at the church's national headquarters said many of the members questioned Phelan's politics. Yet there was no sense in his conversation that the dean was at all concerned; he knew very well who he was and what he believed.

To define himself, the Evangelical Covenant Church (ECC), and the problem of religion in the United States, Phelan quoted the Reverend Will Willamon, who told a student at Duke University, "We're evangelical, but we're not mean." Willamon's statement raises the question of antinomy precisely for evangelicals, and by inference for the entire national political movement. Parsing it will occupy the rest of this section, and Phelan will help.

The Pietist origins of the ECC set the tone for Phelan. He put it this way: having seen the Thirty Years' War, the Pietists advised their membership to move away from ideological fighting over doctrine: "What you believe is not worth killing someone over." Phelan took the same position. He opposed the war in Iraq, and not after 70 percent of Americans thought it was a mistake. He made his decision much earlier; he did not want war at all.

Phelan said the ECC has a long tradition of trying to feed the poor, going back to its migrant roots in the United States: "In the nineteenth century we were the poor. It was the same during the Depression." But then he raised a central problem of American Christianity: "For most people it is either the Gospel or social justice, and never the twain shall meet." Phelan does not think that position is correct. It is a problem for evangelicals, whom Phelan said voted for Carter and Clinton, adding, "We have always been nervous about the Republican Party." He and I did not talk about a definition of "always."

"Some of my friends voted for Bush," he said. "They were not happy about the war or the cutbacks in social services. Abortion and gay marriage were the issues for those people—a pretty thin basis for a (presidential) decision." And then he said something surprising about the two issues the movement had chosen as key: "Abortion and gay marriage are a stand-in for the perception that Christianity is losing its power. There is a general sense that Christian morality is declining." But he is not pro-choice: "I don't think anyone likes abortion—how can we find common ground?"

Having been the pastor of a church for seven years before coming to the seminary, he has a sense of what people think "when sitting around a table in a small town in Illinois." They are not oblivious to the world. "I think that in spite of the fall of communism people still live with a shudder in the back of their minds. And now terrorists may be getting atomic weapons. In theology we say you can't do it the same after the Holocaust; there is a crisis of Providence after the Holocaust and the bomb. I think 1945 changed everything; why did Bonhoeffer[1] become so popular after the war?"

The crisis of Providence is very much on his mind. He talks with his European counterparts about it. "American triumphalism is a part of our lethalness," he said. "As a person of faith, I am less hopeful and more cynical because I recognize our capacity for self-deception."

Phelan is far better educated, more contemplative, than the men around Jerry Falwell and Liberty University, yet even there the tough guys of fundamentalism practice decency among their own kind. Ronald Godwin calls himself "a street fighter" and says he often has to "clean up after Falwell." Godwin travels with Falwell, giving him outlines for his talks or preachments. He said Falwell needs no more than a few notes to speak for hours. Yet completely unscripted, he is prone to making self-destructive statements. Falwell's projects were short of money at the time Godwin and I spoke, because Falwell had said homosexuality and other sins caused the attack on 9/11. Donations dried up,

---

[1] Dietrich Bonhoeffer is one of the Christian martyrs of the last century. There is a statue of him and the other martyrs at Westminster Abbey in London.

Bonhoeffer was born in Germany in 1906. He became a Lutheran minister, spent time in the United States and England before returning to Germany where he along with Karl Barth was one of the founders of the Confessing Church, which should not be confused with the present-day Confessing Movement of the United Methodist Church. In Germany, Bonhoeffer headed an illegal Confessing Church Seminary. The Gestapo banned him from preaching and working in the seminary, after which he became involved in helping Jews to escape from the Nazis and in plotting with a group of German officers to kill Hitler. Bonhoeffer, who was already in prison when the 1944 plot failed and the plotters were discovered, was transferred to the concentration camp at Flossenburg.

On April 9, 1945, less than a month before the liberation of the city, Dietrich Bonhoeffer, his brother and two brothers-in-law were forced to walk naked through the prison to the gallows, where they were hanged. In his books Bonhoeffer wrote about "religionless Christianity," which many liberal theologians interpret as making Christianity relevant to social needs, an extension of Christian ideals to the secular realm. Although Bonhoeffer had come to the United States prior to the outbreak of World War II, he returned to Germany to work against the Nazis despite the urging of friends to remain in the safety of America. "When Christ calls a man," he said, "He bids him come and die."

After the war, there were two paths open to Christians: the one chosen by Bonhoeffer, who understood the secular application of Christianity and chose to return to Germany and die because of his faith in Christ, and the new conservative Christians who choose faith to save themselves. Phelan's reminder of the importance of Bonhoeffer's idea of Christianity is the most trenchant criticism one could make of the theology of Pat Robertson or James Dobson or Jerry Falwell.

but not expenses. Godwin, the toughest of the tough guys, bore much of the responsibility for keeping the many projects out of bankruptcy. He must have been exasperated with Falwell, he must have known that their time was nearing the end, that there was no successor, but he gave no hint of it, not when he talked about the man he calls "Doc."

Falwell was seriously ill in 2004. He couldn't sleep at night, had trouble breathing. Something had gone wrong with his lungs, his coronary arteries, or the heart itself. He was taken to a hospital in Richmond, where his daughter is a physician on staff, and while he was there, according to both Godwin and Reverend Ed Hindson, "Doc" did not know how to deal with people visiting *him* and praying for *him*. He had spent most of his life visiting the sick and praying for *them*. "When the tables were turned, he was very uncomfortable," they said, using almost exactly the same words, as if it had been scripted.

There are apparently several Jerry Falwells, as there are several Falwell ministries. One is feisty, arrogant, and unthinking; the other is an old-fashioned, small-town Virginia pastor. One had dangerous political ambitions, the other shrank back fearfully when I first spoke to him, although he is much bigger than I am, I was wearing press credentials, and Duke Westover, his executive-assistant-*cum*-bodyguard, was at his side. There is something wrong, not merely the temperament, although the lack of control was always a factor. Falwell could not have been Bonhoeffer despite his claim to love Jews. It is not fair perhaps to compare the two, but Falwell and his followers lay claim to be stewards of American morality, the role Bonhoeffer has played for many Christians and non-Christians during all the years when the American national political movement was developing. Falwell could not have been Bonhoeffer, although both men did not hesitate to enter the political life: one to oppose Hitler, the other to press the Cold War, promote the not-so-subtle racism of Ronald Reagan, and support the occupation of Iraq. One did not put his name on the Confessing Church; the other called his work Falwell Ministries. One died for his love of Jews, Christians, Communists, gypsies, homosexuals, and those who were born with less than perfect bodies. The other detests homosexuals, thinks Jews may not be allowed into heaven, and hates Muslims and Communists. No, Falwell could not have been Bonhoeffer. The idea that faith permits the violation of moral law, the supreme antinomy,[2] was anathema to Bonhoeffer. Moral Majority, which was led by Falwell, supported racism, war, and lying during the Reagan Administration.

The signal antinomy of the national political movement can be found in Matthew 5:13, in which Jesus says, "Ye are the salt of the earth. . . ," which, as we saw earlier, is generally interpreted to mean that those who minister to His followers must lead both by both their words and their actions. Bonhoeffer and Falwell and James Dobson and the Southern Baptist Convention and Pat Robertson all dedicated themselves to following that admonition. Only Bonhoeffer was clear about it, only Bonhoeffer was an ethicist as well as a theologian. The others are all antinomians; that is, they are men of faith, believers in the moral law, which allows them to violate the moral law. Antinomianism is that kind of blatant contradiction. For example, the Bible says very clearly, "Thou shalt not kill," but the Christian Right supported war in Iraq and still supports the death penalty at home on the principle that it is good to kill people they deem bad. Their faith—that is, their acceptance of the moral law in the Bible—is absolute; yet their actions are in conflict with their faith. Bonhoeffer held to the proposition "But wilt thou know, O vain man, that faith without works is dead?" (James 2:20). In the conflict between Paul's saying that there could be justification by faith alone and James's understanding of the need for good works, Bonhoeffer embraced both faith and works.

The Christian Right suffers the problem of a conflict between faith and works, as Phelan said. To hold such conflicting principles may lead to bad acts without necessarily making evil persons of them. Here

---

[2] Antinomy has several definitions. Antinomianism has a strictly religious definition: a state of grace achieved through faith or election by God permits one to violate moral law. This definition has a long history; Roman Catholics accused Protestants of antinomianism during the Protestant Reformation and various periods after it, including the present. Many Catholics hold that one earns the right to a good afterlife through deeds and cannot be justified by faith alone. The secular definition is, if anything, more complex. In the main it means contradiction between two principles or rules. Slavery and the racism left in its wake are the most apparent secular antinomies in a society that holds "all men are created equal." Immanuel Kant discussed "the antinomies" as conflicts between reason and experience. Antinomy and hypocrisy differ in that hypocrisy is a pretense of acting on or speaking of a principle; antinomy is a conflict between principles. Hypocrisy has nothing to do with the Grace of God and very little to do with reason.

again, Bonhoeffer's work is helpful. He drew a useful distinction between evil acts and a disposition to evil, saying it was worse for a liar to tell the truth than for an honest man to lie. It was the disposition to evil, bad character, that concerned him most, just as it did Aristotle.[3] If there is evil connected to the members of the national political movement, it would be in the actions, not in the character of most of them. A conflict of principles may lead to evil actions, but it is not a sign of a disposition to evil.

The conflicting principles of the movement have done great harm, and its theologians and philosophers as well as its political advisors bear responsibility for that harm. The Christian Right follows Jesus, who said, ". . . go sell your possessions and give to the poor . . ." (Matthew 19:21), and supports a tax system that rewards the very rich and takes from everyone else. The movement opposes the killing of fetuses and condones capital punishment. It believes in the divinity of Jesus, who said, "Whoever welcomes one of these little children in my name, welcomes me. . . ." (Mark 9:37), yet opposes health insurance for millions of American children. It adores the Prince of Peace and promotes war.

As Phelan said, the movement claims to follow the Gospel, which contains the social philosophy of Jesus, but when the private acts of citizens cannot serve the needs of the poor the movement believes it is better to let children suffer than to have their suffering alleviated by the government. It is the same with the profession of peace and the willingness to make war. The movement's chosen national leaders lavish praise on the Constitution and on the need to violate it through illegal wars, searches without warrants, detentions without trials, a hidden government. The movement opposes murder and defends the right to carry weapons that have no use but murder. Its chosen leaders oppose high gasoline prices and make laws to increase the profits of oil companies. It embraces freedom of religion on constitutional principle and questions

---

[3] I have used Bonhoeffer's "evil" and Aristotle's *kakos*, which is usually translated as "bad" when used as an adjective and "evil" when used as a noun, as largely synonymous. To devote pages here to discussing the difference between the two concepts does not seem fruitful when they would be tangential to the character and behaviors in question. Bonhoeffer's "disposition" is Aristotle's *hexis*.

the loyalty of Muslims on the principle of the right to self-defense. While venerating the history of immigration in America, the movement sees newcomers as a "threat to American customs and values."[4]

So many conflicts of moral principle raises the question of the disposition to evil. Much of the answer about the character of human beings both collectively and as individuals depends on the definition of evil. If one subscribes to the idea of total depravity (the T in Calvin's TULIP), meaning every part of every human, mind and body, body and soul, will, spirit, desire, every act and thought of every description, then man is sinful and only God can choose to save him, as in "there but for the Grace of God. . . ." This leads to the idea of unconditional election (the U) and theological antinomianism; that is, perseverance of the saints (the P), meaning one cannot lose the election of God. The criticism of this idea of grace through faith is that all acts are permitted in this life, for they will make no difference in the afterlife for the elect. If this does not dispose men to do their worst, the idea does not inhibit avarice, greed, cruelty, deceit, selfishness, even killing. When evil describes the human disposition, pessimism is warranted.[5]

As for Satan, John Milton had this to say in the Argument of Book IV of *Paradise Regained*: "Night comes on: Satan raises a tremendous storm, and attempts farther to alarm Jesus with frightful dreams, and terrific threatening spectres. A calm, bright, beautiful morning succeeds to the horrors of the night." It may not be "Morning in America these days,"[6] but I think Satan is probably not skulking about in the dark corners of America except in metaphor. The definition of evil here has to do with harm to others, either physical harm or the making of them into a means, which robs them of their human dignity.[7]

---

[4] Pew Survey, April 26, 2006.

[5] In *The Brothers Karamazov*, Dostoyevsky presented a different view. Smerdyakov, who killed the patriarch Fyodor, had learned from Ivan, his tutor in atheism, that without God, everything is permitted. Neither Calvin nor Dostoyevsky offer proof of their theories; the only conclusion one can draw from the contrasting views is that human beings are intent on proving that in this world everything is permitted. And the nihilistic obverse: nothing is permitted.

[6] Reagan campaign slogan in 1980.

[7] See Kant, *The Metaphysical Foundation of Morals*.

American corporations have done serious harm to the physical environment (pollution, global warming, etc.), to the culture (driving the culture below its lowest common denominator through marketing), to the health of the citizenry (high fat, unclean foods, dangerous prescription and over-the-counter drugs, high-sugar drinks marketed to children, and tobacco marketing), to the health and welfare of workers (unsafe working conditions in factories, mines, construction, agriculture, and offices), and to the cause of international peace (economic support through trade and sales of strategic goods and weapons to oppressive regimes and war profiteering). To think there is a character flaw, Bonhoeffer's "disposition to evil," in some American businesses is undeniable, especially if the problem of moral blindness (the Greek *apate*)[8] as well as greed is included under the definition of "evil."

The question of a disposition to evil, the character question of Bonhoeffer, with a bow toward Aristotle, is raised yet again by the linkage between business, government, religion, politics, and foreign affairs; that is, by the movement itself. David Keene, head of the American Conservative Union, is now a managing director of the Carmen Group, which worked with Jorg Haider's ultrarightist Austrian Freedom Party. Norman Podhoretz, whose "My Negro Problem—and Ours" told the origins of his racism, has received the Medal of Freedom from George W. Bush. The public relations person at the American Conservative Union is a young woman who graduated from Jerry Falwell's Liberty University. Richard Perle, a lobbyist and advisor to the federal government, was or is part of the Committee on the Present Danger. Perle is a long-time associate of Paul Wolfowitz, who was one of the architects of the invasion and occupation of Iraq. And Wolfowitz, who was one of the chief promoters of Straussian ideas in government, was named by Bush to head the World Bank. Without friends, said Aristotle, one might as well be dead.

If these men and women who lead the movement intellectually, politically, spiritually, and economically have done so much harm to the

---

[8] Or more often translated as "deceit." According to Laszlo Versényi in *Socratic Humanism* (New Haven: Yale University Press, 1963), the meeting of *ate* (human blindness) and *logos*, as in *Agamemmnon*. Plato used the word in this sense in his *Phaedrus*.

poor, the shrinking middle class, the Middle East, the military (so many dead and maimed), the Iraqis (even more dead and maimed), the people of Darfur, the city of New Orleans, the very air we breathe, can they be said to have a disposition to evil? If not all of them, some of them? Wolfowitz, Cheney, Perle, Abramoff, Rumsfeld, Bush, and Rove? The school of government at Liberty University is named for Senator Jesse Helms. How should the character of Helms be described? What meaning does the naming of the school have for the movement? Or was Helms inconsequential, an aberration?

The question of character is constantly being asked by journalists, scholars, and pundits for each of the outstanding figures of the national movement. Many of them—Bush, Cheney, Senator Sam Brownback, former Congressman Tom DeLay, Senator Trent Lott, among others— appear to fit the definition of a disposition to evil.[9] In themselves they are both interesting and dangerous, but in a democracy they stand in the second rank of importance. The five mentioned above were all elected and reelected by the people; that is, after their actions betrayed their character, the people judged them and still found them acceptable, perhaps admirable. They were not accidental choices, nor were they chosen out of ignorance.

According to the definition of democracy, the government reflects the character of the people. Plato and Aristotle found democracy a less-than-desirable form of government because they assumed the character of the people was not sufficiently good. Few people have disagreed. Raw democracy, purely mathematical democracy, rule by the majority, has little to recommend it, especially to those likely to find themselves in the minority. Aristotle said that democracy without the rule of law is subject to the rise of demagogues, who lure the people from democracy into tyranny. Hannah Arendt, J. L. Talmon, and others found a new danger in democracy beside those that occurred to the Ancient Greeks: the possibility of democracy sliding into totalitarianism. A constitution; a balance of powers among the executive, legislative, and judicial branches of government; a set of guarantees against oppression by gov-

---

[9] Doing evil as part of one's character.

ernment; free elections; free exchange of ideas; the right to criticize the actions of government, are among the bulwarks against the totalitarian, despotic, oligarchic, and anarchic dangers to a democracy. All these guarantees, which are often said to be "the rule of law" are not the rule of law at all, only the rule of laws made by people. In the end, the Greeks were right, a democracy is not beholden to a constitution, only to the will of the people.

By the will of the people a national political movement has been growing in the United States since 1945. Among the men and women it has chosen to lead, from 1948 on, more than a few have been of inferior character, their actions opening them to the question of a disposition to evil. And the events that gave rise to the movement cannot be construed as excuses for its actions, freeing the people from responsibility. The movement is about the fear of extinction, extraordinary death, the death without memory. But all death, even the death of death, the end of everything, offers choices in life: both heaven and politics are at hand. The movement is not then a passing thing, but the choice of a life. If we choose to think the possibility of heaven has already been decided for us, life has no meaning. And if nothing other than the hope of heaven determines our actions, we live a pushcart life, bargaining with God over every act.

A noble life can also be a response to death: Jesus or Socrates. Saints tend to be boring, and neither saints nor saviors demonstrate quite the same quality of nobility as a dairyman in New Hampshire or a laborer in the fields of California, or a businesswoman in Kansas who has cultivated the habit of virtue through a lifetime of good actions, although any of them may have smoked cigarettes and enjoyed a dalliance or two in a proper time. The dairyman and the businesswoman and the laborer prove the possibility of a noble life, but only if they do not belong to the national political movement and they do not share a will to security based on moral blindness or deceit. They have a different sense of security, one based on life and fairness; they belong to the minority. Death calls to them to venerate their lives among others; they are given to noble laughter. Perhaps they will always be in the minority now, after 1945; perhaps it is asking too much to expect a disposition to nobility to be common in a democracy.

If people live by the complex definition of security that drives the movement, nobility may lie somewhere beyond reach; the movement may be death's misdirection, a disposition to choose leaders who propose to satisfy the movement's desire for security. In a democratic society, a long-lived majority movement and the leaders it chooses mirror each other. The shadows of history flee across the surfaces, but do not disturb the mirroring relation; a national political movement becomes more stable as it increases in size and duration and a disposition to evil may hide in the mirroring surfaces.

Character

A woman who had been raised on the Lower East Side of New York City when it was still mainly a Jewish ghetto, a Workers Circle liberal-leftist, moved to a small southern city. She soon learned that her neighbors were all conservative Christians. At first, she was wary of them. After a few months, however, she reported that she liked her neighbors. They were good people, she said, solid, and if ever she needed them, she knew they would help her. Statistically, they were not so likable. They hated blacks, Mexicans, homosexuals, abortionists, Muslims, liberals, Communists, taxes, Hollywood, and the federal government, and they were certain the end of the world was coming, if not tomorrow, then soon, and if not soon, then sooner or later. Statistically, they would rather a child went hungry than receive what they called a "handout" from the federal government. Yet they would share their last piece of bread with the same child. As time went on and she came to know her neighbors better, she felt close to them. She did not abandon the statistical portrait of people like her neighbors, but it did not make sense to her when she thought of them in their houses or watering their lawns or playing with their children. She saw them as a paradox.

Her experience will come as no surprise to anyone who has spent much time with evangelical conservatives or other people who call themselves conservatives: seen from afar, they are a troubled and troubling group, but up close they are good friends and neighbors. After years spent talking with people in the national political movement, I too found that I liked many of them. They were like conservative friends I had known for many years. They talked a lot about their children, they worried over the high divorce rate among evangelicals, they wanted to help the poor, and they were against war. They thought they lived as Jesus would have liked. Heaven was on their minds, as was hell. One or two had shaky ethics, but that is the human condition. A philosophy professor worried about the mistakes of his past. A young man in Focus on the Family talked about being teased for his Christian beliefs when he attended a secular college, but understood that it was quite alright in America if Focus on the Family was picketed on the same day by people on the right and left. The confrontation pleased him, it made him feel American. The young man did not think the world would end soon; nuclear annihilation was a metaphor, he said. He loved his children.

There was also a question to be raised about evangelicals and their work of spreading the Good News of the Redeemer. The conversion of the heathens has always resulted in the destruction of culture, which is almost always intertwined with religion. There were too many missionaries to the heathens, working in third-world backwaters, stumbling in some language they could not understand, destroying cultures and original languages like locusts devouring ancient fields. They said God told them to do it. God visited one girl when she was three years old and told her to convert her parents, which she did. God came to help another man make a success of his store. They could not explain why God caused the tsunami in the Pacific Ocean that killed so many people, but they went to Indonesia to do God's work. They were evangelicals, and that is what evangelicals must do, according to God—they said. For the love of God—they said. They brought Christian Bibles to convert the tsunami victims to Jesus and win heaven for themselves. The bargaining with God over the question of grace is a grim business; that is, death plays an unseemly part in their lives. They never offered earthly reasons for helping the poor and suffering; their eye was on the next world; death was never far from their thoughts.

Perhaps it is not a good idea to fish for causes in other people's lives; it would be better to concentrate on what they do. A Pentecostal congregation took a weekend to repair a public school in a poor neighborhood in a midwestern town. Nazarenes in Massachusetts care for Vietnamese refugees. A Baptist group took in an Evangelical Covenant Church family on a planting mission. Catholics and Protestants build and operate homeless shelters; every religion runs retirement homes. Jews tend to build hospitals. The movement is made up almost entirely of people who say they want to be good, who know the spiritual and secular rules of life. They are generally honest enough to admit their failures in the small things, but they hold on to the big ones. They say they want to be guided by principle, seeking the good, the fair, the decent; they follow Jesus and the American Constitution, and a great many of them believe both the Bible and the Constitution are true and not to be sullied with doubt or interpretation.

But Wisdom (or Prudence), Moderation, Courage, and Justice may be more virtue than anyone can expect in the Lower East Side lady's neighbors. They are not ancient Athenians following Plato's cardinal virtues (neither were most Athenians). They learn the Christian virtues—faith, hope, and charity (First Corinthians 13:13)—before they learn to read. They want to practice these virtues, of which the Apostle said, "charity is the greatest of them."[10] Considering the role the Lower East Side lady's neighbors and the millions of Americans like them play in the movement, there is a disjunction between their neighborly and their political character. It may be that the disposition to evil hides in proximity, and none of their neighbors, including the lady from the Lower East Side and me, can see this part of the American character when we are in its presence. Perhaps there is some minimal moral distance at which evil is revealed, and the lady from the Lower East Side and I are too close. Perhaps we can only recognize this failure of character in distant villains: Perle, Rumsfeld, Bush, and the like. It may be that this disposition is only apparent in a person like Wolfowitz or Cheney who promotes war and takes the food from the mouths of hungry children; it may be too subtle to recognize in the people who gave power to those who are disposed to evil. It is almost impossible to comprehend. The movement has chosen leaders who demonstrate a disposition to evil, yet the people who did the choosing did not will evil. Or

---

[10] The Geneva Bible notes: "And among these, charity is the chiefest because it ceases not in the life to come as the rest do, but is perfected and accomplished. For seeing that faith and hope tend to things which are promised and are to come, when we have presently gotten them, to what purpose would we have faith and hope? But yet there at length we will truly and perfectly love both God and one another."

did they? That is the terrible conundrum presented by the politics of heaven.

The problem of the person who knows what is right and yet does otherwise has dogged philosophers since Socrates. He thought a person who had sufficient knowledge could not act badly. And if that person did something bad, it was because he had not really gained knowledge. It was only opinion. If fact, the problem stumped Socrates; he could not wriggle out of it.

Aristotle looked at the same problem and devised a better answer, one that brings to light the human flaw in the national political movement. He said acting badly was a failure of wisdom. Not grand wisdom about universal things. That was not the problem then or now. People in the American political movement read the Bible, know something about the Constitution, may have read Plato or Aristotle, even Kant. Certainly, Wolfowitz and the vast majority of Straussian academics did, perhaps Rumsfeld too. Aristotle said the flaw was a failure of practical wisdom (*phronesis*),[11] wisdom about how to live. A person who has practical wisdom knows what ought to be done and does it. He called that person continent and said the incontinent person, knowing what he does is bad, does so out of passion.[12] Incontinence affects the way people live, how they govern, what they mean by their prayers. Incontinence is not like vice, he said; an incontinent person is not a criminal, but his actions have the same consequences.

Think of the senators who voted in favor of war in Iraq, knowing full well that it was not what St. Augustine described as a "just war." Their actions had the same effect as those of criminals: looting, destruction, torture, and death. The fear of death now and an eternity of horrors to come led them to act contrary to what they knew ought to be done. Fear is the great passion of the incontinent; it matters more than sex or greed, but it does not eliminate them. Its has biological and social roots, and it does politics. Americans are cultural and economic Protes-

---

[11] *Nicomachean Ethics*, bks. VI, VII.

[12] Incontinence (*akrasia*) seems comical to us, because we associate it with peeing in our pants. For those who suffer the problem it is not funny. But that is one meaning of the word: physical incontinence, the inability to control bodily functions—urination or sexual desire.

tants, followers of an ethic that leads to brilliant critical thought and industrial, technological, and scientific gain, but in excess the Protestant ethic leads to exploitation in the workplace, deceit in the marketplace, an unfair tax system, and the willingness to eat a hungry person's lunch. Famous examples show up in the newspapers almost every day.

Dennis Kozlowski went to prison because of an excessive desire for money and honor.[13] The WorldCom and Enron scandals grew out of the same excesses. The financial corruption of members of the Congress and executives of almost every part of government, from the White House down through ranks of the federal agencies, was no different. The once-honored Navy ace who survived a fall to the sea after a direct hit by a Russian-made missile—California Congressman Randy "Duke" Cunningham—knew it was wrong to accept more than $2 million in bribes, but he did it, the incontinent ultraconservative hero had a passion for money and the pleasures corruption could buy; he was an influential member of the movement who had been reelected seven times. He wore a wire to betray those who thought he was their friend, and his prison sentence was reduced to eight years.

An incontinent person may love and desire what Aristotle called "the class of noble and good things," but an excess of the same love and desire will cause him or her to go beyond fit and proper limits, with bad results. A person may agree that the Constitution provides for the right to bear arms but believe it so deeply that he insists people be allowed to own weapons that have no use except for war or mayhem. It is a matter of excess. To love honor is good, but for a president to so desire honor that he stands on the deck of an aircraft carrier in front of a gigantic banner reading "Mission Accomplished" while people are dying as a conquered country descends into chaos is incontinence. Or it may be that Bush did not know what he did was bad; the cause may have been ignorance or a disposition to evil. It will be up to the historians to say.

To seek gain is good, but when Hillary Clinton bonds with Rupert Murdoch, who heads some of the most reactionary news organizations in the world, it comes of an excess of the love of honor on her part and

---

[13] Kozlowski confused the conspicuous display of wealth with honor.

an excess of the love of gain on his; they are both incontinent, if either is a good person. Again it has to be left to the historians to decide. Bush may not have a disposition to evil; he may be so drawn to evil acts by his passion for honor and heaven that incontinence has become his permanent state. Murdoch represents the riches of wretchedness. Hillary is ambitious. When National Democratic Party Chairman Howard Dean told the Christian Broadcasting Network that the Democratic Party platform said "marriage is between a man and a woman,"[14] it was clearly his passion for both honor and gain that led him to betray the gay allies of his party in the hope of winning over the Christian Right. When John McCain spoke at Liberty University standing beside Jerry Falwell, whom he had earlier accused of being "an agent of intolerance," it was clearly an excess of desire for honor—meaning the presidency of the United States. McCain embodies the national political movement, an incontinent man hoping to represent an incontinent majority of the country.

Incontinence should not be confused with ignorance, and the kind of incontinence discussed here has only to do with good people, those who know what they ought to do; that is, the great majority of Americans, including most of those who subscribe to one degree or another to the national political movement and even some who, like Howard Dean, are not a part of the movement. When religious and cultural leaders like James Dobson or Pat Robertson or D. James Kennedy speak about church and state and the framers of the U.S. Constitution, they are ignorant but not incontinent: the framers and the document they gave us, however flawed, left no room for dispute about church and state. For a person to be incontinent requires having practical wisdom and being led by passion to act badly.

Ignorance is much less dangerous than incontinence, because one can be cured with knowledge, but the other, carried out in full knowledge of what ought to be done, is a surrender to passion and excess that infects a person's life and can be cured only with temperance, which is a rare attribute in the formerly incontinent. In some people, especially the

---

14 Associated Press, May 12, 2006.

very sophisticated, the question of ignorance or incontinence takes a strange course. Senator John Kerry, asked about his vote on a supplemental appropriation for troops in Iraq, said, "I did actually vote for the $87 billion before I voted against it."[15] Ignorance about the war (he had voted for it), or a passion for honor (he hoped to be president)? Or could he have been incontinent on both sides of the question? It would seem that way.

Leo Strauss is a more interesting anomaly. Can esoteric writing, which is open to interpretation, be incontinent? Strauss reveled in *sophia* and stumbled about like a blind man without a stick of reality to guide him when he walked in the world of practical wisdom. He became the godfather of neoconservatism, which has demonstrated a disposition to evil.

Francis Fukuyama, a more or less ex-neoconservative, provides another interesting case. Fukuyama signed letters urging both Presidents Clinton and Bush to overthrow the government of Iraq, then after the invasion and occupation turned out to be a disaster decided it had been a bad idea. Had he but known! Fukuyama now compares neoconservatism to Leninism. He has developed a variation on the Hegelian progression in which ignorance informs the thesis, failure the antithesis, and vacillation the synthesis. Fukuyama thinks neoconservatism was a good idea that went wrong when it was pushed to excess. If neoconservatism had been a good idea at the outset, Fukuyama's description would be interesting, if not original.

Losing candidates and mistaken philosophers make for curious examples, but incontinence is both more interesting and of greater importance in the majority of people in a society teetering at the edge of democracy. They still have control of the internal politics of the country. Who they are and what they think matters. Aristotle's notion of incontinence offers an astonishing evaluation of their character: If the movement and all the people who belong to it are incontinent, they must be good people who know they are doing bad things, but cannot control their passions. The opposite would be true for bad people: incontinence

---

[15] CBS News, September 29, 2004.

would result in good acts. Since that is unlikely, Aristotle did not give much time to it.

The important insight he gives us about the people in the movement is that they do not have a disposition to evil, they are not bad people, they are incontinent; they have chosen (or permitted) people with a disposition to evil to lead them. At the 2004 Republican National Convention I did not meet anyone who did not think Dick Cheney had a disposition to evil. They did not say it that way, but neither they nor anyone else in the movement wanted him. Of all the people I interviewed, including several still in the military, not one thought war was a good thing, but they all voted for the man who started the war. Racists say racism is bad. And all Christians must either think the suffering of the defenseless is bad or renounce Jesus. The difference between the people in this national political movement and those who remain outside it does not depend on the wish for security alone. All Americans want to be secure. Some Americans, perhaps still a majority, have a passion for security that drives them to do what they know is bad. They do not know what else to do; they feel desperately pessimistic about this country, this life, this world. No one speaks to them of a reasonable alternative.

Americans in this political movement are as dour as Puritans, as unhappy as Calvin would have them. The passion that produces incontinence offers no pleasure. It makes money, wants to put off "my death" and the death of everything. It trades the happiness of others for the hope of heaven. It corrupts, destroys, ruins, makes desolation of what were once nations in pursuit of some mirage of democracy. It condones torture. Fully 70 percent of Americans tell pollsters they think the country is going in the wrong direction, without recognizing that a majority of Americans set the direction with their opposition to ideas other than their own and their pessimism about the American future.

Incontinence is a gloomy business. It wears Dick Cheney's assassin's grimace in the form of a smile. Incontinent people have no friends, because friendship demands loyalty and incontinence is in itself a betrayal of one's own sense of what a person ought to do. If a person can betray the practical wisdom that creates virtue, there is no limit to the perfidy he can commit; he is a friend to no one, not even himself. And without friendship no community can exist, for a community is no more or less than a collection of friends.

The national political movement is not a community, not made up of friends. Membership in the movement requires incontinence. Members must betray themselves to belong; that is, they must actively promote what they know is wrong if they are to get whatever it is they passionately desire: gain, honor, and most often heaven at the end of their own limited time in a world with a foreseeable end.

This generalized incontinence is the gravest error in a society. It confuses aims, weakens hope, and permits betrayal of the small things of life and the most important. When incontinence becomes the rule instead of the exception in the lives of individuals and societies, it awaits only some terrible event to bring down a small country or one of the world's great democracies. When incontinence becomes the rule, all sense of limits disappears: there is no bad thing that cannot be done. It is the end of practical wisdom. Neither history nor law any longer affects the course of a nation. It floats on its passions, and death is foremost. The central idea in a death-obsessed nation is that there is no laughter in heaven and nothing but bitterness on earth.

Fourteen

OPTIMISM

Martin Luther King, Jr., in search of a mentor for his political ideals, found him in Walter Rauschenbusch, a German-born Baptist minister who died in 1918. The man who would lead the Poor People's March on Washington wrote this in 1958:

> *Rauschenbusch had done a great service for the Christian Church by insisting that the gospel deals with the whole man, not only his soul but his body; not only his spiritual well-being but his material well-being. It has been my conviction ever since reading Rauschenbusch that any religion which professes to be concerned about the souls of men and is not concerned about the social and economic conditions that scar the soul, is a spiritually moribund religion only waiting for the day to be buried.*

Marketing

The national political movement will be very difficult to replace. It cannot be defeated at the polls like a political party. The movement does not even have a name to put on a ballot or register in any jurisdiction as a political party or lobbying organization. It has candidates, but they may belong to any party; there is no movement line on any ballot. The movement does not respond to standard political marketing techniques for those reasons and many more, among them:

1. Negative campaigning works, but it is virtually impossible to run a negative campaign against a nameless thing that has no

official existence. No political party or organization has as yet put forward an alternative to the movement.

2. Since no one is quite sure about who belongs to the movement, an attack on some presumed aspect of the movement may turn out to be a shot aimed straight at the negative campaign's foot.

3. Market research methods designed to determine the appeal of laundry soap or automobiles do not apply to a national movement. The focus group, which has been in use since the 1930s and became the major method for determining policy under the Clinton Administration, has not yet been able to penetrate to the profound thoughts and feelings of participants, where the strength of the movement lies. And any comparison of the focus group, a one-time encounter, to group psychotherapy, which deals with the kind of profound feelings that power the movement, is ludicrous.

4. Interview methods, either by telephone or face-to-face, which reached a high level of sophistication during the Reagan presidential campaigns, can only gain some understanding of people's views about various situations or contested issues, but cannot discover what people think about life and death, what is a true feeling and what is only symbolic of some hidden feeling.

5. Standard marketing techniques, which have dominated American politics for more than thirty years, appear to work very well for the movement, but not for the other side. Marketers can discover what people want and sell it to them, although they are much less effective at selling new ideas. Marketing is an essentially conservative encounter with the world. It discovers what people want, and then provides the product that satisfies their wants. It may be a candidate for president or a can of beans. The process is circular, and the circle has little room for novel goods or ideas. The market can only demand what it knows and the marketers sell only what the market demands. The competitive aspects lie in finding out precisely what people want and promising and sometimes delivering the policy, the candidate, or the can of beans that best satisfies the demand. A market is both

sluggish and tyrannical, insatiable and wary of change. Once set in motion, the inertial force of the market tends to increase. Like a market in motion, the body politic continues on its path, resisting change. National political movements endure. But not forever. History tells us that they can be replaced by events (usually catastrophic) or great ideas that capture the fear or hope of the majority of a nation.

The market has often been compared to democracy by people who do not understand either the market or democracy. The market has to do with consumption; it has hungers, but not for freedom or justice. It cannot distinguish between satiety and happiness, competition and dialogue. For those reasons the application of marketing methods to democratic processes humbles democracy and impedes progress. It would seem unlikely then to be able to replace the current political movement by using marketing methods.

If the market cannot be moved, the market must be changed. Americans have done so from time to time by adding or subtracting large numbers of people from the voting roles, creating a very different market each time. When I was a boy, I saw how Texas, like many former Confederate states, used the poll tax to control the market, by barring people of color and poor people from voting. When the poll tax was abolished, the market was changed. The inverse of the poll tax could be used now to change the market again. If a negative poll tax in the form of a payment of a significant amount of taxable money[1] were paid to each voter in a federal election, the poor, minorities, and the young might find the payment an inducement to go to the polls.[2] The negative tax would make the vote more democratic, especially when combined with other ideas

---

[1] By making the payment taxable, the somewhat graduated income tax would make the negative poll tax a graduated tax as well, since the portion returned to the federal government through income tax would be calculated at the margin. The size of the payment would probably not be large enough to significantly change the lives of any voter, including the poor; however, the proper amount could be quickly determined by test marketing methods.

[2] It is illegal to pay people to vote, but the law could be changed without harming the intent of the current law if *all* voters were paid.

used to increase voting, such as changing election days to Sunday, allowing people to vote on more than one day, and using the driver's license
as voter registration. Candidates would have to campaign differently, and
if elected they would have to propose laws with more regard for those
groups that are less likely now to vote. The idea is not far-fetched. Other
countries have dealt with the problem of voting skewed toward wealth
by making voting compulsory, as in Australia, or levying a fine on non-
voters, as in Brazil. The negative poll tax, along with other methods to
increase the percentage of people who vote, could not guarantee the victory of any candidate, policy, or party; it would guarantee nothing more
than greater democracy, which could overwhelm the movement or
strengthen it. As everyone knows, democracy is always a risk.

A more democratic society may not affect the way the majority of
Americans have come to think about death, which is at the core of the
national movement. A catastrophic event: nuclear war or a horrendous
act or series of acts of terrorism could as well strengthen the movement
as lead to its replacement. The ongoing catastrophes of global warming
and the ruin of the lives of millions of people through globalization and
such globalizing policies as the North American Free Trade Agreement
have so far had no effect on the movement, which is more likely to
respond to sudden and violent acts of destruction. If we are fortunate
enough to avoid that kind of event, the task will fall to ideas, which means
questioning the deeply held beliefs of the national movement. And that
requires challenging some of the standard thinking about politics.

Politicians have known instinctively for a very long time that no
matter what they say they cannot change what people hold most dear.
They can only affect opinions. Richard Wirthlin, who adapted Max
Weber's ideas about values[3] and opinions and codified them for use in
the Reagan 1980 campaign, thought opinions could be changed but not
values. What follows attempts to go beyond what he said is possible in a
short-term campaign. If this movement is to be replaced by another less
concerned with death and pessimism, a change of opinions, a switch to
a different political party, will not suffice. What Americans truly value

---

[3] Ideas impervious to rational argument. Popular media and political operatives have
changed the popular idea of "values" to mean opinions about social issues.

has been undergoing a long, slow shift from the loving ideas of the Social Gospel to a gospel of fear and avarice.

There may be some points at which the deeply held ideas of people in the movement are vulnerable to incremental change. Which philosopher, preacher, politician, publicist, or president speaks to the questions raised below is impossible to predict. Perhaps no one will want to take the risk. Perhaps someone will come along with a far better list than I have made here and that person or another, a willing woman or man of great stature, will begin the work. It will probably not be a political candidate, because a movement is made of a series of confluences, and political candidates do not think in terms of confluences. They win or lose. In order to win, a political candidate must now be constantly aware of the movement even in those jurisdictions where the movement seems to be weaker than its alternative; a candidate who seeks the support of a minority of voters anywhere in the country invites irrelevance now, and if not now, soon, perhaps in the next election or the one after that.

Part of the movement is vulnerable to rational argument: A coalition of people who want to be left alone will come apart sooner or later, because it has no common principle. The movement generally opposes same-sex marriage, but the vice president has a gay daughter who stood with her longtime partner as she announced her pregnancy in 2006. The dissolution may be speeded up by revealing conflicts among the members. For example, people who desire lower taxes may also believe abortion is a matter of personal choice rather than the choice of the state; the probability of the dissolution of the coalition follows the internal contradiction in Alasdair MacIntyre's argument against voting in 2004.

The reasonable religious cohort is the most likely segment of the movement to change. It is made up of good people who want to do good things. As long as people outside the movement fail to recognize the best character traits of these fundamentalists, Pentecostals and other evangelical sects, the estrangement between good people in and out of the movement will continue. Teaching people in the movement how to act virtuously through their elected government may be exactly what they want to know. On the other hand, it would be self-defeating to follow Hillary Clinton, who began playing the politics of heaven on the very day George W. Bush was inaugurated for his second term. In a speech in Boston she said, "There is no contradiction between support for faith-based initiatives and upholding our constitutional principles."[4] She had adopted the single most cynical attitude anyone can hold in politics or in life: If you can't beat 'em, join 'em. It was a textbook case of incontinence.

The desire for economic security cannot be debated, but it can be harnessed. If it is true that the national debt burden will damage the country and lessen the security of every citizen, the question of the debt can be framed in human terms rather than belabored in the bald quantitative language of the dismal science. An economic version of a little girl, a daisy, and a nuclear explosion is a more effective way to speak to the debt than to drone on about unimaginably large numbers. No one alive can count to a billion, let alone a trillion.

Moral arguments against racism have been made since the first non-whites came into the colonies, and before that arguments were made against racist policies toward the original inhabitants of the land. Racists have never responded to moral argument as evidenced by the Civil War, the Dixiecrats, Goldwater's Southern Strategy, and the reliance of the national political movement on racism as its foundation. Racism has always been understood as an economic benefit to the white majority. Blacks always did the jobs whites did not want, even though the blacks were intellectually and physically capable of holding better jobs now held by whites. The same situation now exists with Latinos. Whites still believe that racism prevents their fellow whites from falling to the economic bottom, but in a world of global competition the continuation of racist policies in the United States, effectively barring most of the African American and Latino population from full participation in the educational and entrepreneurial aspects of the society deprives the rest of the country of the best of 80 million black and Latino minds.

Assuming that the real Bell Curve[5] of intelligence, not the racist curve argued by Charles Murray, is correct, a significant number of

---

[4] *Boston Globe*, January 20, 2005.

[5] The Bell Curve represents a normal distribution, with the greatest number at the average and fewer at the extremes.

these people have intelligence above normal. In IQ numbers that means they would score 130 or higher. In other words, of the 80 million blacks and Latinos 3 percent or 2,400,000 have considerably better-than-normal innate intelligence. About 0.1 percent of this same group have innate intelligence that measures over 145. That means there are about 80,000 people in America who have superior capabilities for science or art or business or government whose horizons are limited at birth because of racist social, educational, and economic policies.

Moral appeals to end racism may still be ineffective, but if the counterproductive character of racism can be demonstrated in a way that touches the American desire for security, especially economic security, one of the core attitudes of the movement may be weakened. Two million people with superior mental capacity and eighty thousand with superb capacity could reverse what many in the movement think is the inevitable American decline. The people of color whose talents are now wasted may be the very ones who could produce or certainly contribute to the often-referenced rising tide that lifts all boats. The economic basis of racism, which provided a foundation for the movement as it began to take clear shape in the late 1950s in the South with Barry Goldwater's first campaign to win the Republican nomination for president, no longer makes sense. In a globalized economy racism may be the racist's worst enemy. Yet who will explain the future of racism to the racist? What skinhead freshly released from prison? What bullet-headed southern deputy sheriff? What New York or Chicago or Los Angeles patrolman in his radio car? What Texas hanging judge? What vigilante calling himself a "Minuteman" and lying in wait on the Mexican border for the heart of an innocent to appear in the crosshairs of his sniper scope? Which of those trusted social scientists will relieve the movement of its immoral foundation?

The political theories that underlie the economic foundations of the movement and its attitude toward the government should be shown in a clear light—not in rage, but in some emotional as well as intellectual context. In the philosophical world, Alasdair MacIntyre has proposed weakening the "modern state" by relieving it of any functions but policing and war; and in the world of avarice, groups like Americans for Tax Reform advocate bringing down the government by starving it of taxes.

The good people of the movement deserve to know the true meaning and the likely consequences of the ideas promoted by their economic and philosophical leaders. To incite the overthrow of the Government of the United States of America by economic means is a violent act that should be considered treason. These people who seek to strike down the government by economic means are far more dangerous to the country than Julius and Ethel Rosenberg or Sacco and Vanzetti, all of whom were executed for what they did or did not do. This is not to suggest that MacIntyre and Norquist or Dick Cheney and Sam Brownback should be hanged or electrocuted, only that their work be seen in light of every American's sworn love of country.

The most perturbing example of the difference between a political party and a movement—the willingness of people in the lower-middle class to vote for candidates who support tax cuts for the rich—accounted in no small part for the victory of the movement in the 2000 and 2004 elections and even helped elect some conservative Democrats in 2006. The seemingly unnatural voting pattern led some observers to say these people vote against their own interests. The more likely explanation for the voting suggested in an earlier chapter is that people who belong to the Christian Right did not vote against what they believed were their interests. They supported candidates who opposed abortion and gay marriage and by so doing the voters believed they demonstrated their love of God and improved their chances for a sweet eternity.

If lower-middle-class and working-class voters do not really vote against their own interests, but like many others of all economic classes, vote according to what they believe are their profound interests over the course of eternity, it will be very difficult to dislodge them from the movement. They are good citizens and good people and they should not be asked to abandon their God but to serve Him by abandoning the political precepts of the leaders of the Christian Right. And to ask them to do that is a difficult but not impossible request to make;[6] there is an ethical argument, as Jesus was an ethicist; and a political argument, as

---

[6] Jim Wallis has done more than ask people to make that change. He has worked at it diligently and with a good heart for many years.

Jesus was a political philosopher whose miracles had to do with healing the sick, distributing food to the poor, forgiving those who had committed crimes. What has to be said of the leaders of the Christian Right and all the pastors who follow them into a politics of antinomy and incontinence will sound cruel and perhaps unwarranted, and it would not be a decent thing to do if the Christian Right did not promote policies that ruin the lives of millions of people. They have gloried in war and condoned torture; they oppose policies that would bring health care to children, the aged, and immigrants; they foster racism and sexism and religious hatred; they prefer antinomy to clarity and incontinence to ethics; they impose the teaching of unreasonable ideas about the evolutionary routine of the planet; and they are unforgiving of those who have trespassed against their variant readings of Scripture. These are not the gentle followers of Jesus, but hard people like D. James Kennedy and Richard Viguerie and James Dobson and Jerry Falwell and Pat Robertson and the leaders of the Southern Baptist Convention and the followers of Roman Catholic dogma on abortion and homosexuality and the Jewish fundamentalists who practice even more narrowly defined policies on similar issues.[7] If it is evil to promote suffering, these leaders and others like them have shown a disposition to evil. The good people who follow them should be aware of the darkening storm their leaders have made and ask them to explain their choice of angels. As it stands, those religious leaders of the movement,

---

[7] According to Matthew 6:15, ". . . if ye forgive not men their trespasses, neither will your Father forgive your trespasses," which puts the unforgiving leaders of the Southern Baptist Convention in something of a bind.

The pamphlet on homosexuality published by the Southern Baptist Convention's Christian Life Commission reads:

Discrimination against gays and lesbians is proper, in the areas of:
Employment
To protect the [presumably heterosexual] "family" [sic]
To protect other social institutions

The Roman Catholic Church has raised the possibility of excommunication for those who do not follow its rules on abortion and homosexuality.

Fundamentalist Jews expel people from their communities for having abortions, practicing homosexuality, and so on.

who profess belief in the divinity of the admonitions of Isaiah, Micah, and Jesus yet make a religion of incontinence, are the enemies of God.

American Gospel

There was much success and little happiness, and death stalked the days and nights of the first Europeans in America. The Puritans quoted Luke 6:25, in which Jesus said, "Woe unto you that laugh now! for ye shall mourn and weep." And so it must have been. They wept for their dead children and for the wives or husbands taken from them when they were still young. The dour men and women who first came to New England must have expected the stones that literally rose up out of the earth as if to punish them for clearing the fields, but they did not expect the woods rich with game and the fast-growing summer corn or the bushes laden with blackberries in autumn. They came from difficult times in England to an unknown place to live among "Heathens . . . who might in one houre have made a dispatch of us. . . ."[8] And they suffered a din of preachments from men like Thomas Hooker, who published his sermons in book form, telling his readers in 1640, "There is a sobriety required in the soul. . . ." They sat in unadorned churches and listened to sermons spoken in flat voices, intoned, as cold as the breeze from Satan's wings in Dante's last, worst, deepest circle of Hell. Finally, Samuel Finley, an Irish immigrant, put emotion into preaching, but he preached a grim afterlife and a miserable present, embodied in his quotation of Proverbs 14:13: "In the midst of Laughter the Heart is sorrowful, and the End of that Mirth is Heaviness."[9]

American society eventually could not abide the miserable preachments of these men who carried the harsh view of human destiny into the middle of the eighteenth century. The other strain coming to the

[8] Robert Cushman, "A Sermon Preached at Plimmoth in New-England," December 9, 1621.

[9] Finley, a Presbyterian, came to America in 1734. He was one of the key figures in the First Great Awakening. From 1761 to 1766 he was president of the College of New Jersey, now Princeton University.

fore in America was the sense of optimism, of righteous angers, and great joys. Weeping must have seemed a foolish response to God's gifts of plenty; worse than foolish—ungrateful. If Providence had smiled on America, America had to smile back. To one powerful stream in the American confluence the grim metaphysics of the Puritans came to seem inappropriate. The country developed a bawdy, satirical streak in the face of death.

In 1777, in the darkest days of the Revolution, Tom Paine wrote, "There is not such a Being in America as a Tory from conscience.... A woman's virtue must sit very lightly on her who can even hint a favourable sentiment in their behalf. It is remarkable that the whole race of prostitutes in New York were Tories."

Imagine a group of men in 1773, all in costume, pretending to be Mohawk Indians, boarding three British ships at anchor in Boston Harbor, breaking open crates of tea and dumping the contents overboard. Those *faux* Mohawks established an aspect of the American character that would not disappear in dark times. They connected their laughter to the politics of optimism and the will to be free. Optimism came with armloads of pumpkins; baskets of corn; a deer slung over the hunter's shoulder; gamebirds on a string; the fisherman's creel heavy with trout, bass, perch, walleye, whitefish, crappie, and pike.

The Great Awakening of the early eighteenth century in America does not refer only to a miraculous awakening to the rules of Puritanism. It was, as George Marsden said in his biography of Jonathan Edwards, the end of the established hierarchy of the church.[10] People gained a sense of themselves as individuals, free to choose their own way to worship, their own way to live. Americans attended revival meetings and came away awakened. If they attended a revival led by James Davenport, one of the youngest graduates of Yale University, they might be awakened indeed. According to Marsden, the meetings went on late into the night. "At one of these late night commencement-week gatherings, as one critic described it, all order had disappeared, 'some praying, some exhorting and terrifying, some singing, some

---

[10] *Jonathan Edwards: A Life* (New Haven: Yale University Press, 2003).

screaming, some crying, some laughing and some scolding, made the most amazing confusion that ever was heard.' "

The country seemed limitless, a West that went on forever. Who but the most daring could traverse its grand spread, and in the hard life of pioneering, find fulfillment? Happiness lost its sinful character. A cadre of classicists came to the fore, no more lively mind than Jefferson's, no more sensualist and capital-loving soul than Franklin's. They were out for having a good time in a good country even if it meant dying for the sake of sovereignty and the accompanying exercise of freedom. By the early decades of the nineteenth century, democracy included the little guys as well as the greats, and the Jacksonian White House was a raucous response to all the sour preachments that had ruled the minds of Americans during the early years of the Europeanization of the continent. The teetotalers and the prophets of hellfire and damnation had not disappeared, but the tavern had gained respectability as the place where revolutions were born, and the hard-won wealth conferred on rough men and their stalwart women by the Wild West had infused the country with roaring optimism. There had never been such boisterous, optimistic, democratic laughter until there was American laughter.

The whole country grew looser, livelier; Ralph Waldo Emerson went from town to town preaching "Self-Reliance," telling Americans to give up their adoration of Europe. His friend Henry David Thoreau practiced "Civil Disobedience" on grounds of his personal moral objections to the actions of government. They thumbed their noses at the Old World, the old ideas, the old sobriety. And in their freedom from the bonds of the old Calvinism, they turned to the question of freedom for all. Harriet Beecher Stowe wrote *Uncle Tom's Cabin*, and her brother Henry Ward Beecher preached about a gentle, loving God in contrast to his father's grim Calvinist deity.

No man was more emblematic of the marriage of religion and optimism than Abraham Lincoln. Standing on the battlefield at Gettysburg, where 45,286 men had died, Lincoln spoke the words that generations of schoolchildren have learned as if it were an American catechism: ". . . this nation, under God, shall have a new birth of freedom, and . . . government of the people, by the people, for the people, shall not perish from the earth."

He was a religious man in a way that is no longer common. When asked if he thought God was on the side of the Union, Lincoln replied, "Sir, my concern is not whether God is on our side; my greatest concern is to be on God's side. . . ." He was a melancholy man who told stories to amuse his friends. He understood the roles of camaraderie and reverence in American life, and although he did not belong to any church, Lincoln held some of the same views of the relation of man to God that would be the foundation of the idea of the Social Gospel, which became widespread only a few years after his death.

After the prayers for the war dead, the country had to move on. There was a vast economic expansion. The railroad barons and steelmakers and other industrialists amassed enormous fortunes. America entered the Gilded Age. At the end of the nineteenth century the discrepancy between the corporate rich and the working poor produced angry unions and terrible slums. In New York City, the immigrant poor, barely clothed, malnourished, unwashed, suffering every sickness that could spread through the crowded warrens in which they ate, slept, made love, birthed their children, and died were within walking distance of the vast mansions of Fifth Avenue. It was no different in Boston or Philadelphia, and the South still struggled to overcome the destruction of the war and the terrible mismanagement of Reconstruction. The sound of careless laughter was heard in the ballrooms and gardens of the rich. Newport, Rhode Island, boasted a row of ostentatious mansions along Bellevue Avenue. It was a cruel time for most Americans, for it was not a time when everyone was poor: poverty was a relative thing, and relative poverty wounds most deeply, because it adds to the discomfort of meager rations of food, clothing, and shelter the pain of failure, of knowing others are doing better. In the language of Calvinism, relative poverty proves that some few are the elect of God and all the rest may expect their suffering in eternity.

In 1873, a major banking firm collapsed, taking down almost a hundred railroads with it. President Ulysses S. Grant responded to the bankruptcy by tightening the money supply, and the panic only grew worse. The New York Stock Exchange closed for ten days, unemployment grew to 14 percent, and in a two-year period 18,000 businesses closed. Wages fell, workers went out on strike in 1,200 factories across the country. On May 1, 1886, workers in Chicago marched in what was to become known as the celebration of May Day, but the celebration went sour: May Day led to a riot in Haymarket Square. A bomb killed a policeman, and the police opened fire on the crowd. The country turned against labor, afraid of anarchists, five of whom were sentenced to death by hanging for their part in the Haymarket Riot. The movement for an eight-hour day collapsed. Yet the new, liberal churchmen would not accept the evidence, they would not return to the grim theology of Calvinism.

In the shadow of the great gulf between luxurious laughter and the suffering of those who worked or searched for work, the liberal churchmen sought to overcome the idea that the poor in America endured a life of endless labor and little reward because God had willed it so. Phillips Brooks, the Episcopal bishop of Boston in the 1880s, refused to accept the idea of unhappiness as the lot of man. The bishop said, "Happiness is the natural flower of duty." And that conception of the role of religion in the happiness of others traveled far beyond Brooks in Boston and the other liberal theologians in the East and Midwest. In Iowa, Ohio, and New York, churchmen combined socialism, progressivism, and the idea of the Kingdom of God. If they could make a world of Christian goodness on earth, they believed, it would invite the return of Jesus, who would reign for a thousand years. Beginning at about the time of the Haymarket Riot, these liberal churchmen, influenced by British Anglicans, German Baptists, and Roman Catholics, put forth the ideas behind the great social and political movement that emerged in the darkest times to revise America. The Social Gospel responded not only to poverty itself, but to the brutal methods of those with economic power.

There were three distinct versions of the Social Gospel. At the First Congregational Church in Columbus, Ohio, Washington Gladden, who is often called the "Father of the Social Gospel," preached the gospel of physical as well as spiritual need; that is, he cared for the poor. Gladden was a Progressive, one who advocated some government intervention to better the lives of the people, but not political socialism. The radical in the mix of Social Gospelers, known earlier as "social Christianity," was George Herron, who taught at Grinnell College in

Grinnell, Iowa. Herron belonged to the Socialist Party, was a man of great certainty about the coming kingdom of God on earth, and for a brief time this Congregationalist who eventually turned away from his church was one of the most influential of the Social Gospelers. Herron's influence made Grinnell College the center of the "kingdom movement," and home to a conference that was attended by many of the leading Social Gospelers in the waning years of the nineteenth century.

Like Herron, Walter Rauschenbusch believed Christians could bring about the Kingdom of God. In *Christianity and the Social Crisis,*[11] he wrote, ". . . the essential purpose of Christianity was to transform human society into the kingdom of God by regenerating all human relations and reconstituting them in accordance with the will of God." And later in the book, he raised the question of "why the Christian Church has never undertaken to carry out this fundamental purpose of its existence." His answer was socialism, a fair distribution of the wealth, decent working conditions, pacifism, and labor that was not alienating but gave workers a sense of usefulness in the world. Unlike Herron, who was willing to accept violent change, Rauschenbusch could not accept the idea of a society torn apart by radical acts. He preached a form of Christianity that was both social and christological; i.e., it argued for social justice for its own sake as taught by Jesus and for the existence of a divine Jesus as proof of the existence of God. His love of the people who, it might be said, taught him the principles of the Social Gospel, was unending. In *Christianity and the Social Crisis* he wrote:

> For eleven years I was pastor among the working people on the West Side of New York City. I shared their life as well as I then knew, and used up the early strength of my life in their service. In recent years my work has been turned into other channels [teaching theology], but I have never ceased to feel that I owe help to the plain people who were my friends. If this book in some far-off way helps to ease the pressure that bears them down and increases the forces that bear them up, I shall meet the Master of my life with better confidence.

---

[11] London: Macmillan, 1913.

That is who he was: A Baptist born in Rochester, New York, in 1861, deaf from the age of thirty, devoted to the poor who came to his church in New York's Hell's Kitchen, a brilliant theologian, and a great optimist—some would later say, utopian[12]—Rauschenbusch concerned himself less with heaven and more with human life. He was a friend of John D. Rockefeller, who was also a Baptist, but Rauschenbusch never let his friendship with Rockefeller move him away from his concern for the poor, his hostility to the exploitation of the working class by corporations, and his opposition to war. For a time, at the beginning of the twentieth century, he and the other Social Gospelers were the strongest and most loved religious force in America. They were not the only religious group, of course. Fundamentalism began to spread with the publication between 1910 and 1915 of 3 million copies of the books known as "The Fundamentals."

More than an opposing theology, the murderous war in Europe tested the faith of the Social Gospelers in the possibility of the kingdom of God on earth, and when Woodrow Wilson sent Americans overseas to die in the foul trenches and bloody fields, the idea of the Social Gospel went into decline. Like young Sigmund Freud in Europe, Americans could no longer hold on to their hopeful view of man. The joy of optimism, the glorious sense of the perfectibility of man on earth, could still be heard, but no longer with the same certainty. After the war and the chill of Woodrow Wilson's highly abstract reasons for

---

[12] During the rise of the Nazis and the Cold War, Reinhold Niebuhr took Rauschenbusch to task for being too optimistic, believing that Christian love could settle the problems of war and exploitation and poverty. Niebuhr claimed to be equally concerned with the poor and the dangers of war, but more realistic. He is sometimes considered one of the sources for neoconservatism in that he was not opposed to first-strike options in war. Niebuhr moved away from the Social Gospel for many reasons. He said it was sentimental, unrealistic, and the horror the Social Gospelers felt at news of World War I made no sense to him. He thought pacifism was foolish, because wars could not be avoided. In our time the "just war" theory of St. Augustine is being replaced by the notion of religious war, a repeat of the pattern of the Crusades, when the Roman Church joined an ongoing war.

The Reverend Jim Wallis has been trying desperately to break through into the popular consciousness with his nineteenth-century evangelical version of Christianity, arguing that he is not a promoter of the Social Gospel, only a good Christian promoting Christian values. Wallis does not take strong positions on theological questions. He is a sweet man and surely a good man, but cautious.

sending young men to die, the Social Gospelers could not take part in the brassy music of American triumphalism, nor could they invest their churches any more with the full-throated song of the expectation of the Kingdom of God.

Martin E. Marty, one of the great scholars of religion in America, sees World War I as the end of the Social Gospel of Walter Rauschenbusch, Washington Gladden, and all the others who paid more heed to social problems and less to religious questions. But I do not think history works that way. Ideas do not disappear; they have their own social immortality; they grow quiet for a time, but memory is not the same as silence—the difference between them was one of the most profound questions of the twentieth century, as the Nazis sought to destroy all memory of Jews, Gypsies, and heroes. Nuclear weapons threatened a similar although more widespread destruction. The Social Gospel did not sink into silence without memory after World War I. It was called upon again, only a dozen years after its supposed demise, when a disaster worse than the Panic of 1873 descended on America. International economic problems roiled American markets, there was a glut of commodities, prices fell, factories closed. Hoover did not know what to do. If we think of history as a series of events in America, accepting the theory that ideas disappear into the silence of reaction, it was the end of the optimism that began with the Social Gospelers in Grinnell, Iowa, and with Rauschenbusch in Hell's Kitchen. If we think of American history as a series of confluences, it will seem perfectly ordinary for Harry Hopkins, who studied with the Social Gospelers at Grinnell College, to have gone to New York City, where he came to the attention of Franklin Delano Roosevelt, who had learned his Social Gospel ideas from Endicott Peabody, the headmaster of the Groton School.

The Democrats could not help but feel the optimism of the Social Gospel when New York Governor Franklin Delano Roosevelt, who could not walk or even stand without holding on to a person or a podium, but whose managerial talents were already widely known and appreciated, went to the Democratic National Convention in 1932. Hoover's policies, which would today be called "trickle-down economics," had been unable to lift the country out of economic depression. Unemployment was at 25 percent. The suddenly poor Americans were worse off than they had been when Rauschenbusch preached in Hell's Kitchen at the turn of the century. The number of jobless men and women was close to that of Dickensian London. And Roosevelt chose for his theme song at the convention "Happy Days Are Here Again." The country was not optimistic, not happy, it was Roosevelt who was optimistic, and he intended the optimism of his great laugh and his straightforward rhetoric, delivered in his Brahmin accent, to be heard across the country and around the world. This was a rich man—Groton, Harvard—another Roosevelt, the American aristocracy announcing that he was on the side of the poor and hungry.

Harry Hopkins went to Washington to present the newly elected president with a plan to alleviate suffering from lack of shelter, food, clothing, and self-esteem, all attributable to joblessness. Hopkins, who had been a social work administrator in New York, had impressed Governor Roosevelt, and his plan impressed the president. Roosevelt gave him a temporary position, a chance to put his ideas into effect. The Hopkins plan became the backbone of Roosevelt's New Deal: optimism in grim times, work when there was none, food when there was none, art, literature, construction, electrification, singing and dancing, laughter in dark times. Unemployment fell and rose again and fell again. Roosevelt's policies worked and failed, and yet he and Hopkins pursued them, sure they would finally succeed; the party sang their motto for grim times: "Happy Days Are Here Again." It was tough-guy irony. Midway through the decade, Hitler came to power, and in 1939 he sent the Luftwaffe to bomb Poland. The war Roosevelt and Hopkins had begun to prepare for was on. Hopkins shifted his interest to foreign affairs, becoming the architect of Lend-Lease, the program to supply arms and matériel to the Allies. The boys from Groton and Grinnell turned to war. Roosevelt, suffering from the aftermath of polio, and Hopkins, weak and painfully thin from an intestinal problem that made it impossible for him to digest fats and proteins, carried on a war of men, matériel, and optimism.

Roosevelt died before the end of the war. Hopkins survived him, but after his son, an eighteen-year-old Marine, was killed in action, the energy that had seen him through sickness, the Depression, and war finally flagged. American optimism also started to flag near the end of the war. And yet, after Hiroshima, Nagasaki, and public knowledge of the Holocaust, in the brief respite before the beginning of the Cold War, the boys came home all dressed in blue or khaki and sounding the carillon of American optimism again. Kennedy gambled the world on the Cuban Missile Crisis and won, but after that the certainty about the future, the optimism of the Social Gospelers, which had lasted through the Depression and the Second World War, was muted. Johnson dared the one thing the Social Gospel had neglected through all its history: he gave up the longtime dominance of his political party on behalf of civil rights; he knowingly spent what he feared was the last measure of American optimism. What remained of optimism lived on in Martin Luther King, and when he was assassinated, that was the end of it. After him, political laughter lost its optimistic timbre, it had the sound of hungry chickens. An advertising agency said, "It's morning in America."

The segue to a new national political movement was complete.

The question an American outside the movement must ask is how this movement can end or be ended before it brings down both church and state. If the movement continues down its current path, if the party of Roosevelt can only succeed by Bill Clinton's political logic, meaning it transforms itself into a second party chosen by the movement, the decision will give birth to an idea beyond pessimism, a politics of despair. Maybe that can only be avoided if some grand or catastrophic event occurs to change the definition of security in America. Events do change the world, but ideas are a better lever. It could be that the beginning of a new movement took place some years ago or it might happen tomorrow. An undercurrent of optimism still exists in America; there is that difference between a history of reaction and one of confluence. To avoid despair Americans will have to abandon the practice of capitulation to the movement. Millions of citizens will have to be as brave as old men or smooth-cheeked children. There is an American sermon to deliver on the unholiness of pessimism.

It will not be the sermon spoken by Rauschenbusch or Gladden or Martin Luther King, but there will be echoes, reflections, unforgotten ethics. The American confluence is like a river, and the river remembers, for it is always made of the same creeks and streams, and although the rain may make the flow of one constituent tributary greater or lesser from time to time, the confluence remains. In the worst of times since the Civil War, the believers in the need for religion to be concerned with the body as well as the soul—pacifists, romantics, unionists, socialists, democrats, men and women out of New England and the Midwest, Congregationalists and Baptists, ecumenists, pursuers of the possibility of the kingdom of God—came forward through Panic and Depression to revitalize the country. The last, best acts of Lyndon Johnson, the death of Dr. King, and the ascent of Reagan, Bush, Clinton, and Bush again appeared to be the finish of it all, the making of a different river. It was not.

EPILOGUE

On a warm afternoon in the late spring in Washington, three generations of my family walked together through the memorial to FDR, which is made of many statues, artificial waterfalls, and a series of low stone walls bearing his best-known words and telling in sculptures and incised stone of the four terms of his presidency. The memorial spreads across some distance beneath the cherry trees, and the grassy places between the statues and the quotations give observers time to ponder one thing before the next, so the effect is not unlike turning the pages in a book of short poems. At the end of the walk, after the section on the fourth term, when Roosevelt has died, the strollers come to the edge of the Tidal Basin, where they can sit and look at the water, which has the appearance of a small lake that is hardly disturbed at all by the boats crossing in the distance.

My older grandson, who was eleven years old, sat beside me on a great flat rock to look out at the water and carry on the conversation we had begun earlier in the day. We were separated from the rest of the family by several yards, which gave us some privacy. He and I talked about justice, which interests him because his father is an attorney. The boy asked how justice had begun in the world, and because it was a long afternoon and he likes stories, I told him about the *Oresteia*, how Athena had stopped the ancient cycle of vengeance in the family of King Agamemnon. It was, I said, the story of the first trial by jury, of the end of the ancient world of Homer and the beginning of modern civilization. It is a long and complex story, but it is not difficult to keep a child interested when Aeschylus is the storyteller.

He listened while Aeschylus told, through my brief précis, how Agamemnon sacrificed his daughter to propitiate the gods before the Greek fleet sailed to make war on Troy, and Agamemnon's wife avenged her daughter by killing the victorious king upon his return, and was then slain by her son Orestes to avenge the murder of his father. But the goddess Athena prevented the killing of Orestes by convincing the Greeks to hold a trial by jury.

By the time Athena had cast her vote to bring the jury to a tie, saving the life of Orestes and ending the cycle of vengeance, evening was coming on and we began the long walk across the grass to the road, where we had begun the day. The boy and I walked slowly, falling behind the others, more and more separated from them. We were quiet, the grass was thick and high, not yet mowed that year.

He said, "I would rather die a good man than live a bad man."

That is exactly what he said. I did not answer, and he did not say anything more.

The boy carries American history in his genes. His father's great-grandparents arrived speaking Spanish and Russian. One of his mother's ancestors, John Howland, was washed overboard in a gale during the voyage of the *Mayflower*, and at the cost of a sailor's life was rescued from the sea. The boy learned something about history from his maternal grandmother, and his mother continues to teach him and his sister, taking them to museums in small New England towns where family artifacts are housed. I do not know how this history and the presidency of FDR and the trial of Orestes mixed in him that day, but I do know that the confluences of which men and nations are composed show more clearly in a child.

The boy is an ocean swimmer; he swims very far out into the sea. His mother watches from the shore. They are confident that the sea will bring him home again.

When concentrating or uncomfortable he appears to be a solemn young fellow, but underlying the slightly husky voice that adults often attribute to sadness, laughter waits. Of all his schoolmates none takes greater delight in telling stories, in laughing and creating laughter in others.

Where does this American laughter begin and how can it be so intricately bound up, in a boy of eleven years, with thoughts of life and death, good and evil? What conflicting streams flow through Americans, what binds us to democracy, permits the confluence of diverse ideas, histories, hopes, feelings, angers? How is it that a boy of eleven, descendant of an early-seventeenth-century Puritan, ponders good and evil in the presence of death, and yet at other times laughs?

The hope of America lives in the gathering and overcoming of history and the moment, as it happens in the boy. This national political movement, like the others that went before, will end; and like the boy, we will come home from the sea.

ACKNOWLEDGMENTS

Once more unto the breach, dear Sylvia, once more. After fifty years, you still facilitate this lack of modest stillness and humility. Thank you.

Starling Lawrence is the author of many fine fictions and furious comments. This is his book as well as mine. I could not ask for a better friend or a more talented editor.

Two of America's best writers of fiction, both gracious Southern women, Nelle Harper Lee and the late Eudora Welty, contributed greatly to this book. Nelle and I talked a lot about the book while I was working on it. She shared her knowledge of English history and the history of the English in America, as well as her wisdom about race, religion, and politics in the American South. I am grateful to her for those gifts and for her friendship of more than twenty-five years.

Tony and James Shorris are clear thinkers and good advisors. Tony asked the difficult questions about the distinction between security in this national political movement and the one that preceded it. James moved the general concept to a more comprehensible place. When writing a book such as this, it is good to have a professor at Princeton's Woodrow Wilson School and a Washington lawyer for advisors.

Morgen Van Vorst is the smartest young editor I know, and she is kind to old writers. Fred Weimer is a gentle and precise copy editor, for which I am grateful.

Ten years ago *Harper's Magazine* and W. W. Norton published work I had written about the Clemente Course in the Humanities. The course started as an experiment to prove a point in the book *New American Blues: A Journey Through Poverty to Democracy*. There was a second book, *Riches for the Poor: The Clemente Course in the Humanities*, which detailed the workings of the course after several years. There are now Clemente Courses, sometimes by other names—notably the Odyssey Course in Illinois and Wisconsin—in many parts of the United States. It has also spread to Canada, Mexico, Argentina, the Dominican Republic, Australia, and Korea. Bard College has been the center of the course since its inception. There are now hundreds of faculty, all of whom are college professors of the first rank. Thousands of students, the majority of them between the ages of seventeen and thirty-five, have graduated from the course. Many have gone on to enter two- or four-year colleges, most have gotten out of poverty; all have better lives. The professors tell me they learn something new from the students every year. I learn from both the professors and the students and the people who fund the course. This book would have been very different if it had not been for the professors and students in the course. They have taught me, among other things, to love democracy and never to be timid. I am honored to have been their student.

Daniel Born, who edits anthologies and the *Common Review* for the Great Books Foundation, suggested books and people. Peter H. Dailey and Peter Hannaford made introductions, one to Richard Wirthlin, the other to a fellow who arranged for me to attend the 2004 Republican National Convention. Many of the people on the religious right with whom I talked during these last several years surprised me. They were not at all what I had been led to expect by books and newspaper and magazine articles. I liked them. When we talked, I followed what I think should be the rule for writers: I told them what I was doing, that I would record our conversation, and I always preceded the conversation by telling them my own politics, which differed from theirs. Many of them appear in this book, and I thank them for their openness. If I have offended them by the conclusions I came to in this book, I beg their forgiveness.

Some people whom I have not quoted by name were very helpful, and I thank them: Juleen Turnage at the headquarters of the Assemblies of God; Michael DeWilde of Grand Valley State University; Steve

Schmidt of the 2004 Republican National Committee and 2006 Schwarzenegger campaign manager; Murray Persky, M.D.; Charles Stewart, M.D.; Richard Gose; Kelly Purcell; my sister Mary Jean Roberts; Mark Pestana; Christopher Butler; Greg DeWilde; David Hart; Robert Asahina; Wendy Willis; Susan Doss; Emily Auerbach, my dear friend and colleague, for her help on constancy in the works of Jane Austen; Dalton Tananaka; Tracey Schmidt; William and Ruth Cleveland; Nancy Brown; Kathy Cook; Cameron Greenhaw (Kristine Greenhaw's husband); U.S. Representative Thomas Cook; Christopher Norfleet; Lewis Lapham; John R. MacArthur; Katrina vanden Heuvel; Roger Hodge; Joy Castro; James C. Yu; John W. McNulty; Rudy Tellez; Thomas Carruthers; many staff people at the Republican National Convention; Jerry Falwell Ministries and Liberty University; Focus on the Family; and many members of Assemblies of God, Nazarene, Evangelical Covenant, Baptist, Jehovah's Witness, Methodist, Presbyterian, Mennonite, Episcopal, and Roman Catholic churches, as well as synagogues.

INDEX

ABC-TV, 64, 69*n*
abolitionism, 9–11, 99, 111, 113, 130, 238, 264, 280, 281
abortion, 27, 28, 72*n,* 91, 101, 191, 245, 271
  crime and, 152–53
  partial-birth, 231
  pro-choice stance on, 229*n,* 231, 233, 237
  pro-life stance on, 72*n,* 88*n,* 134, 155–56, 162, 211, 229–31, 234, 242, 246, 294, 307, 311
Abraham, 49
Abramoff, Jack, 149*n,* 314
Abu Ghraib prison, 67*n*
Abundant Living Faith, 98
Achebe, Chinua, 17
Adams, John, 245
Addams, Jane, 60
Adler, Mortimer, 180
Adorno, Theodor, 170
Aeschylus, 5, 154, 346
Afghanistan, 67*n*
  anti-U.S. forces in, 49, 58
  Russian war with, 227
African Americans, 12, 60, 168*n,* 278–87
  crime and, 152–53, 233
  poverty among, 165, 286
  religious beliefs of, 92, 110
  voting of, 233–34, 279*n,* 281
  see also civil rights movement; racism; slavery
After Virtue (MacIntyre), 153, 154–56, 157–58, 163, 201*n,* 222, 236*n,* 296
Agamemnon (Aeschylus), 5, 313*n,*
Agency for International Development, U.S., 87*n*
Age of Faith, 81
Age of Information, 42
Agincourt, Battle of, 244
agnosticism, 12, 75, 91, 100, 126
AIDS, 28, 148, 181*n,* 211

Air Force, U.S., 36, 132, 136
airlines:
  body searches by, 65*n*
  decontrol of, 208
  watch lists of, 65*n*–66*n*
Alabama–West Florida Methodist Conference, 282*n*
Albom, Mitch, 18
Albright, Madeleine K., 64
alcohol, 121, 147–48, 151, 203
Al-Farabi, 201*n*
Allen, Danielle, 158*n*
Allen, George, 210
Allende Gossens, Salvador, 54, 55
Al Qaeda, 160, 165, 269
Alrayyes, Samah, 87*n*
Alter, Robert, 301
Altmire, Jason, 211
American Conservative Union, 313
American Dilemma (Myrdal), 165
American Enterprise Institute, 65, 194, 267
American Petroleum Institute, 68
American Progress Action Fund, 226
American Religious Identification Survey (ARIS), 95*n*
American Revolution, 112, 207*n,* 216, 226, 335
Americans for Tax Reform (ATR), 86, 160, 163, 236, 331
American Spectator, 241*n,* 302*n*
American Theocracy (Phillips), 263*n*
Amish, 99
Ammerman, Nancy T., 71*n*
Anabaptists, 9, 99
anarchy, 60, 75
Ancient City, The (Fustel de Coulanges), 25
Andrewes, Lancelot, 96
anti-Catholicism, 11, 25